LIBRARY OF NEW TESTAMENT STUDIES

637

Formerly the Journal for the Study of the New Testament Supplement series

Editor
Chris Keith

Editorial board
Dale C. Allison, John M. G. Barclay, Lynn H. Cohick, R. Alan Culpepper,
Craig A. Evans, Robert Fowler, Simon J. Gathercole, Juan Hernández Jr.,
John S. Kloppenborg, Michael Labahn, Matthew V. Novenson, Love L. Sechrest,
Robert Wall, Catrin H. Williams, Brittany E. Wilson

Dating Acts in Its Jewish and Greco-Roman Contexts

Karl L. Armstrong

LONDON • NEW YORK • OXFORD • NEW DELHI • SYDNEY

T&T CLARK
Bloomsbury Publishing Plc
50 Bedford Square, London, WC1B 3DP, UK
1385 Broadway, New York, NY 10018, USA
29 Earlsfort Terrace, Dublin 2, Ireland

BLOOMSBURY, T&T CLARK and the T&T Clark logo are trademarks of
Bloomsbury Publishing Plc

First published in Great Britain 2021
This paperback edition published 2022

Copyright © Karl L. Armstrong, 2021

Karl L. Armstrong has asserted his right under the Copyright, Designs and Patents Act,
1988, to be identified as Author of this work.

For legal purposes the Acknowledgements on p. ix constitute an extension
of this copyright page.

All rights reserved. No part of this publication may be reproduced or
transmitted in any form or by any means, electronic or mechanical,
including photocopying, recording, or any information storage or retrieval
system, without prior permission in writing from the publishers.

Bloomsbury Publishing Plc does not have any control over, or responsibility for, any
third-party websites referred to or in this book. All internet addresses given in this
book were correct at the time of going to press. The author and publisher regret any
inconvenience caused if addresses have changed or sites have ceased to exist, but can
accept no responsibility for any such changes.

A catalogue record for this book is available from the British Library.

A catalog record for this book is available from the Library of Congress.

ISBN: HB: 978-0-5676-9646-5
PB: 978-0-5676-9858-2
ePDF: 978-0-5676-9647-2
ePUB: 978-0-5676-9649-6

Series: Library of New Testament Studies, ISSN 2513–8790, volume 637

Typeset by Newgen KnowledgeWorks Pvt. Ltd., Chennai, India

To find out more about our authors and books visit www.bloomsbury.com
and sign up for our newsletters.

To St. Luke the historian, theologian, and one of the greatest authors of all time—and his God in whom he faithfully served, who ultimately and graciously enabled me to finish writing this book

Contents

Acknowledgements		ix
List of Tables		xi
Abbreviations		xii

1	**A New Plea for an Early Date of Acts**		1
	Introduction		1
	Historiographical Survey of the Date of Acts		4
	The Early Dating Advocates (pre-70 CE)		5
	The Middle Dating Advocates (post-70 CE to ±80)		11
	The Late Dating Advocates (90–130 CE)		15
	Overview of the Present Study		20
2	**A Historiographical Approach to the Date of Acts**		23
	Introduction		23
	Contemporary Approaches to the Date of Acts		26
	Modern Movements and Trends in Historiography		29
	Historiography: Principles, Procedures, and Sources		33
	Conclusion: A Historiographical Approach to the Date of Acts		45
3	**The Date of Acts and Its Sources**		47
	Introduction		47
	The Sources of Acts		48
	The Itinerary/Diary/Travelogue Hypothesis		65
	Luke's Concern with Geography, Travel, and Lodging		69
	Reinterpreting Dupont's Overall Conclusion		70
	Conclusion: The Date and Sources of Acts		72
4	**The Sources of Acts: Paul's Letters and the Works of Josephus**		75
	Introduction		75
	The Sources of Acts and Paul's Letters		76
	Analysis of Selected Texts of Acts and Paul's Letters		78
	The Sources of Acts and the Works of Josephus		84
	Analysis of Selected Texts of Acts and the Works of Josephus		86
	Conclusion: Paul's Letters, the Works of Josephus, and the Sources of Acts		95

5	The Un-Enigmatic End of Acts	97
	Introduction	97
	Acts 28 and the History of Interpretation	99
	Ancient Interpretation of the Enigma	100
	Modern Interpretation of the Enigma	108
	Contemporary Interpretation of the Enigma	110
	Conclusion: The Un-Enigmatic End of Acts	123
6	The End of Acts and the Jewish Response	125
	Introduction	125
	Jewish Condemnation	127
	Jewish Tragedy	129
	Jewish Hope	132
	Isaiah 6:9-10 in Light of the Jewish Portrait of Paul in Acts	134
	Conclusion: The End of Acts and the Jewish Response	137
7	The End of Acts and the Comparable Age of Its Variants	139
	Introduction	139
	The "Western" Front	141
	The New Quest for the "Western" Text	149
	Evaluation of the End of Acts Variants	152
	Conclusion: The End of Acts and the Comparable Age of Its Variants	155
8	Acts in Its Jewish and Greco-Roman Historical Contexts	157
	Introduction	157
	Acts in History	158
	The Fall of Jerusalem: Dividing the Early and Middle Groups	165
	Acts and the City of Rome	171
	The Great Fire of Rome	172
	Post-Fire Persecution under Nero	176
	Conclusion: Acts in Its Jewish and Greco-Roman Historical Contexts	182
9	Conclusion: Dating Acts in Its Jewish and Greco-Roman Contexts	183

Appendix: The Manuscript Record for Acts 28:11-31	187
(A) Manuscripts with an Alexandrian Ending	187
(B) Manuscripts without Acts 28:11-31	189
(C) Manuscripts with a Western Ending	191
Bibliography	195
Index of Subjects	223
Index of Sources	226
Index of Manuscripts	230

Acknowledgements

My interest in this controversial topic began in 2012 during my graduate studies at Acadia Divinity College in Wolfville, Nova Scotia, and came to maturity during my doctoral studies at McMaster Divinity College (MDC) in Hamilton, Ontario. I am still amazed at how such an important aspect of NT studies has flown under the radar and during my time at MDC I fully realized its significance. There are several people I would like to thank for the many ways they have helped bring this topic to life.

First, I would like to express my gratitude to the professors at MDC who helped make this a reality. In particular, I wish to thank Kelvin Mutter who was instrumental in helping me stay the course while giving me my first opportunity at publishing. I am grateful for Stanley Porter and Cynthia Long Westfall's constructive input during the earlier and formative stage of this manuscript. Stan, in particular, has helped me shape my research and bring this to a whole new level. I am further grateful to Eckhard Schnabel for his thoughtful corrections, suggestions, and insights throughout. A special thanks is also due to Rainer Riesner for sending me some of his own research while connecting me with Alexander Mittelstaedt. Thank you, Alexander, for sending me a copy of your insightful book.

Before I go any further, I want to give a tremendous note of appreciation to the staff of Mills Memorial Library at McMaster University in Hamilton, Ontario. Access to such a world-class collection of physical and digital resources has made my life so much easier over the past few years. My sincere thanks to you all for going out of your way in assisting me in my quest to source some hard to find materials in such a timely fashion—thank you!

I also had the privilege of studying with many fine classmates and scholars at MDC who encouraged me to stay the course while listening to my ideas and providing feedback. I would like to mention in particular David Yoon and David Fuller. My thanks are also due to Nathan Nadeau for his friendship and the many conversations we have had on Luke-Acts and historiography. I am grateful to my friends Marc and Cynthia Richard, David Watt, and Jake Chitouras for their friendship and support over the years. My thanks are due to Pastor Shawn Erb and the fine people of Dundas Baptist Church for their support and listening to my ramblings relating to the origins of the earliest Christian communities.

I also want to thank John and Dawn Martens who adopted me as their Nova Scotian son and welcomed me with their hospitality and good cheer (at a time when I needed it most). Special thanks are due to Miriam Martens not only for her love and support throughout this project, but also for her expert editorial oversight. Her background in history at McMaster University has also been a significant asset in helping me bring this manuscript to a place where it may engender further interdisciplinary conversation among historians. I am grateful for the countless hours she has invested in this project and I am sure our readers will be as well!

To my family in Nova Scotia: I am sorry for my absence these past several years and this project would have been impossible without your love and support. To my mother Sally, I am so thankful for your regular enquiries and conversations as to how I am doing and how my work is coming along. To my father Leslie, thank you for being there in ways that words cannot express and instilling in me a great love for history. The countless conversations we have had on this much-neglected subject lies beneath the fibre of all of my research. Furthermore, this project is dedicated to the memory of my grandfather—Carl Bishop Armstrong—and the company in his name that has allowed me to complete my studies and write this book.

Karl L. Armstrong
Hamilton, Ontario, August 30, 2020

Tables

1.1	Key dates relating to Acts in the early Roman imperial period (*c.* 60–150 CE)	6
1.2	The early dating advocates (pre-70 CE)	8
1.3	The middle dating advocates (post-70 CE to ±80)	13
1.4	The late dating advocates (90–130 CE)	16
3.1	Lk. 1:1-4 and Acts 1:1-3	61
4.1	Acts 9:23-25/2 Cor. 11:32-33	79
4.2	Acts 9:21; 22:3/Gal. 1:13-14, 23	81
4.3	Promised Spirit: Acts 2:33/Gal. 3:14/Eph. 1:13	83
4.4	Theudas and Judas: Acts 5:36-37 and Jos. *Ant.* 20.97-102	89
4.5	The Egyptian Liberator: Acts 21:38; Jos. *War* 2.261-63; Jos. *Ant.* 20.169-71	94

Abbreviations

AB	Anchor Bible
ABPRSSS	Association of Baptist Professors of Religion Special Studies Series
AGJU	Arbeiten zur Geschichte des antiken Judentums und des Urchristentums
AHR	*American Historical Review*
AnBib	Analecta biblica
ANTC	Abingdon New Testament Commentary
ASNU	Acta seminarii neotestamentici upsaliensis
BAFCS	The Book of Acts in Its First Century Setting
BBR	*Bulletin for Biblical Research*
BDAG	Bauer, Walter, Frederick W. Danker, William F. Arndt, and F. William Gingrich. *Greek-English Lexicon of the New Testament and Other Early Christian Literature*. 3rd ed. Chicago: University of Chicago Press, 2000.
BECNT	Baker Exegetical Commentary on the New Testament
BENT	Beiträge zur Einleitung in das Neue Testament
BETL	Bibliotheca ephemeridum theologicarum lovaniensium
BG	Biblische Gestalten
Bib	*Biblica*
BibInt	Biblical Interpretation Series
BLG	Biblical Languages: Greek
BR	*Biblical Research*
BSPS	*British Journal for the Philosophy of Science*
BZNW	Beihefte zur ZNW
CahRB	Cahiers de la Revue Biblique
CBQ	*Catholic Biblical Quarterly*
CEH	*Central European History*
CTL	Crown Theological Library
CurBR	*Currents in Biblical Research*
EBC	Expositor's Bible Commentary
ECM	*Novum Testamentum Graecum Editio Critica Maior*
EBib	Études Bibliques
ETL	*Ephemerides theologicae lovanienses*
EvTh	*Evangelische Theologie*
Exp	*Expositor*
ExpTim	*Expository Times*
FN	*Filología neotestamentaria*
HeyJ	*Heythrop Journal*
HNT	Handbuch zum Neuen Testament
HTR	*Harvard Theological Review*

HTS	Harvard Theological Studies
IBRB	Institute for Biblical Research Bibliographies
ICC	International Critical Commentary
Int	*Interpretation*
INTF	Institut für Neutestamentliche Textforschung
IVPNTC	The IVP New Testament Commentary Series
JBL	*Journal of Biblical Literature*
JETS	*Journal of the Evangelical Theological Study*
JGRChJ	*Journal of Greco-Roman Christianity and Judaism*
JRS	*Journal of Roman Studies*
JSNT	*Journal for the Study of the New Testament*
JSNTSup	*Journal for the Study of the New Testament*, Supplement Series
JSOT	*Journal for the Study of the Old Testament*
JSOTSup	*Journal for the Study of the Old Testament*, Supplement Series
JTS	*Journal of Theological Studies*
KEK	H.A.W. Meyer (ed.), Kritisch-exegetischer Kommentar über das Neue Testament
LCL	Loeb Classical Library
LEH	Lust, Johan, Erik Eynikel, and Katrin Hauspie. *A Greek-English Lexicon of the Septuagint*. Rev. ed. Stuttgart: Deutsche Bibelgesellschaft, 2003.
LNTS	Library of New Testament Studies
L&N	Louw, Johannes P., and Eugene A. Nida. *Greek-English Lexicon of the New Testament Based on Semantic Domains*. 2 vols. New York: United Bible Societies, 1988.
MDAI(RA)	*Mitteilungen des Deutschen Archäologischen Instituts (Römische Abteilung)*
MJTM	*McMaster Journal of Theology and Ministry*
Mnemosyne	Mnemosyne: Bibliotheca Classica Batava
MNTC	Moffatt NT Commentary
NA[28]	*Novum Testamentum Graece*, Nestle-Aland, 28th edition
NIBC	New International Biblical Commentary
NICNT	New International Commentary on the New Testament
NIGTC	The New International Greek Testament Commentary
NovTSup	*Novum Testamentum*, Supplements
NovT	*Novum Testamentum*
NTG	New Testament Guides
NTM	New Testament Monographs
NTS	*New Testament Studies*
NTTS	New Testament Tools and Studies
NTTSD	New Testament Tools, Studies and Documents
OTM	Oxford Theological Monographs
PAST	Pauline Studies
PBA	*Proceedings of the British Academy*
PCNT	Paideia Commentaries on the New Testament
PLL	Princeton Legacy Library
PNTC	Pillar New Testament Commentary

PRS	*Perspectives in Religious Studies*
PS	*Population Studies*
PTMS	Princeton Theological Monograph Series
RB	*Revue Biblique*
RBL	*Review of Biblical Literature*
RECM	Routledge Early Church Monographs
RelSRev	*Religious Studies Review*
RGHS	Routledge Guides to Using Historical Sources
RHPR	*Revue d'histoire et de philosophie religieuses*
RNTS	Reading the New Testament Series
SBG	Studies in Biblical Greek
SBL	Society of Biblical Literature
SBLRBS	Society of Biblical Literature Resources for Biblical Study
SBLStBL	Society of Biblical Literature Studies in Biblical Literature
SBLSymS	Society of Biblical Literature Symposium Series
SBLTCS	Society of Biblical Literature Text-Critical Studies
SCM	Student Christian Movement
SD	Studies and Documents
SemeiaSt	Semeia Studies
SH	*Social History*
SHBC	Smyth & Helwys Bible Commentary
SNTSMS	Society for New Testament Studies Monograph Series
SNTW	Studies of the New Testament and its World
SP	Sacra Pagina
SPCK	Society for Promoting Christian Knowledge
StPatr	Studia Patristica
SSNT	Studia Semitica Novi Testamenti
StBibLit	Studies in Biblical Literature (Lang)
SUNT	Studien zur Umwelt des Neuen Testaments
SymS	Symposium Series
TANZ	Texte und Arbeiten zum neutestamentlichen Zeitalter
ThBeitr	*Theologische Beiträge*
THKNT	Theologischer Handkommentar zum Neuen Testament
TLZ	*Theologische Literaturzeitung*
TNTC	Tyndale New Testament Commentaries
TRHS	*Transactions of the Royal Historical Society*
TSK	Theologische Studien und Kritiken
TU	Texte Und Untersuchungen
TynBul	*Tyndale Bulletin*
UBSGNT	United Bible Societies' Greek New Testament
VC	*Vigiliae christianae*
WTJ	*Westminster Theological Journal*
WUNT	Wissenschaftliche Untersuchungen zum Neuen Testament
ZAC	*Zeitschrift für Antikes Christentum*
ZAW	*Zeitschrift für die alttestamentliche Wissenschaft*

ZECNT	Zondervan Exegetical Commentary on the New Testament
ZNW	*Zeitschrift für die neutestamentliche Wissenschaft und die Kunde der älteren Kirche (1920–2005), des Urchristentums (1900–1919)*
ZWT	*Zeitschrift für wissenschaftliche Theologie*

1

A New Plea for an Early Date of Acts

Introduction

Over a century ago, Rackham gave perhaps the best surviving defence for an early date of Acts.[1] Since then, his arguments have been discussed, adapted, challenged, and dismissed. Although this work goes beyond his original arguments, the title of this chapter is an intentional reference in appreciation of his pioneering insights that have not been duly considered amidst this ongoing debate.

Without diminishing the inherent complexities, and the additional evidence that has come into play since 1899, Rackham put the matter thus: "If the later date be correct, St. Luke is guilty of nothing less than a literary crime: he excites all his readers' interest in the fate of St. Paul, and then leaves him without a word as to the conclusion."[2] Given the nature and aims of the narrative (i.e., Lk. 1:3), Rackham's observation remains valid. Nevertheless, the process of arriving at a certain date for any historical document or the (pre-)determination that the said author is guilty of a literary crime requires a comprehensive examination of the evidence.[3] A brief lesson from history should be

---

[1] See Richard B. Rackham, "The Acts of the Apostles II. A Plea for an Early Date," *JTS* 1 (1899): 76. See also Adolf Harnack, *The Date of the Acts and of the Synoptic Gospels* (trans. J. R. Wilkinson; CTL 33; New York: Putnam, 1911), 95.

[2] Rackham, "Plea," 80.

[3] Acts scholars (i.e., Joseph B. Tyson) from the Westar Institute (home of the Jesus seminar that was founded by Robert W. Funk) rightly propose that Acts "must be interpreted in terms of its historical context" (caveat 2). Dennis E. Smith, "Report on the Acts Seminar," *The Fourth R* 20-1 (January-February 2007), para. 2. However, it seems rather circular that on the one hand they place great emphasis on the historical context for Acts (and this is voted to be second century), but consider Acts as "Myth, and should not be confused with history" (para. 1). First, scholars have shown to varying degrees the general reliability of Acts as a historical document: e.g., Martin Hengel, *Acts and the History of the Earliest Christianity* (trans. John Bowden; London: Fortress, 1979); W. Ward Gasque, *A History of the Interpretation of the Acts of the Apostles* (repr., Grand Rapids: Eerdmans, 1975); Colin J. Hemer, *The Book of Acts in the Setting of Hellenistic History* (WUNT 49; Tübingen: Mohr Siebeck, 1989); the large collection of essays in BAFCS; Daniel Marguerat, *The First Christian Historian: Writing the "Acts of the Apostles"* (Cambridge: Cambridge University Press, 2002). Second, since a historical context requires datable historical elements, how can the seminar view Acts as "myth," and not "history" (to some degree at least)? Third, and based on their own criteria, how is it possible to date Acts in the first place? And if so, what has the seminar discovered that has so decidedly found the "mythical" context of Acts to be in the second century? Evidently one's views on the date of Acts are directly related to the book's perceived historical reliability. Cf. Stanley E. Porter,

sufficient to illustrate this point. In December 1770, John Adams—the future second president of the United States—was given the seemingly impossible task of defending the British soldiers and their captain in the famous Boston Massacre trial. They were on trial for firing into a Boston mob that had resulted in five deaths.

When the evidence was presented and cross-examined, Adams soon proved the innocence of the British soldiers, despite the consensus view of their guilt.[4] The evidence revealed how these frightened soldiers were only trying to defend themselves from an assault on their lives—and were certainly not guilty of a "bloody massacre." In the end, the captain was acquitted along with six out of eight soldiers, and two were given a reduced sentence of manslaughter. After weighing the evidence before the court, Adams concluded with these words: "Facts are stubborn things; and whatever may be our wishes, our inclinations, or the dictates of our passion, they cannot alter the state of facts and evidence."[5]

Setting aside the subjective nature of how we approach "facts" and "evidence" for the moment, the lesson should be clear and applicable to the task of dating Acts. Regardless of one's opinion, this debate requires careful interpretation of facts and evidence that rises above, and in the end, may be quite different than our own wishes or inclinations. My concern is that some of the recent views regarding the date of Acts have been presented as conclusive, whereupon examination there are serious problems in how the conclusions are drawn. Failures in methodology aside, there is also a tendency in the debate to ignore the valuable argumentation of scholars over the past century and earlier.

Meanwhile, there are numerous scholars who claim a certain date of Acts with only scant reference to one or two scholars, while others do not present any argumentation at all.[6] Having said that, this proposal will by no means be a panacea to this scholarly issue, but it will be a wake-up call for those that think this issue is settled; it is far from it. The aim of this work is not to convince everyone that the date for Acts presented is "definitive," but is rather a new plea to reconsider an early date for Acts.

When Paul Met Jesus: How an Idea Got Lost in History (Cambridge: Cambridge University Press, 2016), 75, 78.

[4] According to John Tosh, *The Pursuit of History: Aims, Methods and New Directions in the Study of Modern History* (6th edn; London: Routledge, 2015), 108, the "evaluation of historical evidence may seem to be not unlike the cross-examination of witnesses in a court of law: in both cases the point is to test the reliability of the testimony."

[5] William Gordon, *The History of the Rise, Progress, and Establishment, of the Independence of the United States of America* (London: Charles Dilly and James Buckland, 1788), 1:296. Although some events in history are inescapably factual, the empirical emphasis on facts and evidence as arbiters of truth has been greatly challenged by poststructuralist historians. See Anna Green and Kathleen Troup, eds., *The Houses of History: A Critical Reader in Twentieth-Century History and Theory* (2nd edn; Manchester: Manchester University Press, 2016), 13–25, 289–300; Edward Hallett Carr, *What is History?* (2nd edn; repr., London: Penguin, 1990), 9, 23; and "Principles for Selecting Facts" in Chapter 2, this volume.

[6] A few examples: Marguerat, *Historian*, 229; James D. G. Dunn, *The Acts of the Apostles* (Grand Rapids: Eerdmans, 1996), xi; Marianne P. Bonz, *The Past as Legacy: Luke-Acts and Ancient Epic* (Minneapolis: Fortress, 2000), 163; Beverly R. Gaventa, *The Acts of the Apostles* (ANTC; Nashville: 2003), 51; Glenn E. Snyder, *Acts of Paul: The Formation of a Pauline Corpus* (WUNT 352; Tübingen: Mohr Siebeck, 2013), 13–14.

Little has changed since Hemer's instructive 1989 work with respect to the "huge variety of divergent and often contradictory criteria and arguments" regarding the date of Acts.[7] Where Hemer argues for a dating of Acts in 62 CE, others date the book much later.[8] Ever since Pervo—who dates Acts to *c.* 115 (110–120 CE)—turned his attention to this critical subject in 2002, he has lamented how little research has been done in recent decades concerning the date of Acts.[9] He is also correct in his assessment that the 80–85 CE date is really more of a "political compromise" than the result of "scientific analysis."[10]

Fitzmyer, who perhaps represents the vanguard of the middle ground date of 80–85 CE, makes the surprising claim that "there is no good reason to oppose that date, even if there is no real proof for it."[11] Furthermore, although I disagree with Tyson's late date of Acts (120–125 CE), I heartily share his surprise at Fitzmyer's concluding comments that the interpretation of Acts "depends little on its date or place of composition."[12] For better or worse, the historical context of Acts is married to its interpretative significance.[13]

---

[7] Hemer, *Acts*, 366–70 (370). There are some recent and notable exceptions: See Alexander Mittelstaedt, *Lukas als Historiker: Zur Datierung des lukanischen Doppelwerkes* (TANZ 43; Tübingen: Francke, 2006); Porter, *When Paul Met Jesus*, 75–9; idem, "The Early Church and Today's Church: Insights from the Book of Acts," *MJTM* 17 (2015–16): 72–100; idem, "Dating the Composition of New Testament Books and Their Influence upon Reconstructing the Origins of Christianity," in *Mari Via Tua: Philological Studies in Honor of Antonio Piñero* (eds. Israel Muñoz Gallarte and Jesús Peláez; Estudios de Filología Neotestamentaria 11. Córdoba: Ediciones El Almendro, 2016), 553–74; Eckhard J. Schnabel, *Acts* (ZECNT 5; Grand Rapids: Zondervan, 2012), 27–8, 1062–3; Karl L. Armstrong, "A New Plea for an Early Date of Acts," *JGRChJ* 13 (2017): 79–110; and idem, "The End of Acts and the Comparable Age of its Variants," *FN* 31 (2018): 87–110; idem, "A New Plea for an Early Date of Acts" (PhD diss., McMaster Divinity College, Hamilton, ON, 2019).

[8] Hemer, *Acts*, 408.

[9] Richard I. Pervo, "Acts in the Suburbs of the Apologists," in *Contemporary Studies in Acts* (ed. Thomas Phillips; Macon, GA: Mercer University Press, 2009), 29–46 (30); idem, *Acts* (Hermeneia; Minneapolis: Fortress, 2009), xv, 5; and idem, "The Date of Acts," in *Acts and Christian Beginnings: The Acts Seminar Report* (ed. Dennis E. Smith and Joseph B. Tyson; Salem, OR: Polebridge Press, 2013), 6.

[10] Idem, "Suburbs," 31.

[11] Joseph A. Fitzmyer, *The Acts of the Apostles* (AB 31; New York: Doubleday, 1998), 54. Fitzmyer's argument relates to the Temple's destruction and the siege of Jerusalem (see Chapter 8). Gaventa, *Acts*, 51, writing in 2003, also argues for a date somewhere in the 80s or 90s, although she appears indifferent to the issue of dating Acts. Where Fitzmyer at least provides a critical assessment of the existing arguments and opinions, Gaventa offers only a single paragraph to the issue and does so without any serious consideration of the evidence or the identity of "many scholars" who support this middle ground date.

[12] Fitzmyer, *Acts*, 55; Joseph B. Tyson, *Marcion and Luke-Acts: A Defining Struggle* (Columbia: University of South Carolina Press, 2006), 1, also pp. 1–23.

[13] Tyson's, *Marcion*, 1–2, logic here is sound as is Pervo's aim to "undermine the widespread view that the dating of (Luke) and Acts, has little, if any, importance for the understanding of their texts." Richard I. Pervo, *Dating Acts: Between the Evangelists and the Apologists* (Santa Rosa, CA: Polebridge, 2006), viii. Further, Craig Keener, *Acts: An Exegetical Commentary* (4 vols; Grand Rapids: Baker Academic, 2012–15), 1:401, admits that if he is wrong about his post 70 CE date of Acts this will "bring into question" some of his "interpretive judgements at key points." On the historical/historiographical context see Tosh, *Pursuit* (6th edn), 10, 119, 173, 176, 290; Alun Munslow, *Deconstructing History* (2nd edn; Routledge: London, 2006), 45.

Historiographical Survey of the Date of Acts

A survey of the literature shows just how complex this debate is, and decades later, Cadbury's caution is worth repeating:

> Is there any other method by which the date of the gospel and Acts can be fixed? Probably not. At least none has yet been discovered. The extreme limits within which the composition of the two books must fall are c. 60 A.D. or a little earlier, when Paul reached Rome, and c. 150 A.D., when Marcion made use of the gospel. The two extremes are improbable; but just as there is no decisive proof that Luke was not written before the fall of Jerusalem, there is also none that it was used by any writer before Marcion.[14]

If the "extremes are improbable" according to Cadbury, what is the new and compelling evidence suggested by Tyson and Pervo that enables such a late date of Acts to be so compelling?[15] Second, where is the "decisive proof that Luke was not written before the fall of Jerusalem?"[16]

For some NT scholars the pendulum has swung decisively as a result of Tyson's *Marcion and Luke-Acts: A Defining Struggle* and especially Pervo's *Dating Acts: Between the Evangelists and the Apologists*.[17] What is both interesting and alarming is that in the last fourteen years there have not been any dedicated responses to their positions. Is this a case of *qui tacet consentire videtur* (whoever is silent is taken to agree)? Furthermore, there has not been any serious consideration of Mittelstaedt's arguments for an early date (62 CE) in *Lukas als Historiker: Zur Datierung des lukanischen Doppelwerkes*.[18]

---

[14] Henry J. Cadbury, "The Identity of the Editor of Luke and Acts," in *The Beginnings of Christianity Part I: The Acts of the Apostles* (eds. Frederick J. Foakes-Jackson and Kirsopp Lake; 5 vols; London: Macmillan, 1922), 2:358. Elsewhere Cadbury refrains from picking an exact date for Acts when he claims the evidence is "equally indefinite, within certain obvious quite wide limits." Idem, *The Making of Luke-Acts* (New York: Macmillan, 1927), 327, 360. Either way, Cadbury's upper limit (150 CE) should be reduced accordingly since Roth considers the text of Marcion's gospel to be "clearly related to Luke *and* prior to the middle of the second century." Cf. Dieter R. Roth, *The Text of Marcion's Gospel* (NTTSD 49; Leiden: Brill, 2015), 1. Also, the upper limit may become further reduced because of the similarities between Polycarp, *Phil.* 1.5 and "some Western manuscripts of Acts 2.24" that potentially date these Western expansions to c. 112–15 CE (the date of Polycarp). See Barbara Shellard, *New Light on Luke: Its Purpose, Sources and Literary Context* (JSNTSup 215; London: Sheffield Academic, 2002), 30; Mikeal C. Parsons, *Acts* (PCNT; Grand Rapids: Baker Academic, 2008), 17.

[15] Cadbury, "Identity," 2:358.

[16] Ibid.

[17] The 2013 work by Snyder, *Acts of Paul*, edited by Pervo, is a good example.

[18] Cf. Mittelstaedt, *Lukas als Historiker*. See also Keener, *Acts*, 1:385; Snyder, *Acts of Paul*, 14; and Christoph Stenschke, review of *Lukas als Historiker: Zur Datierung des lukanischen Doppelwerkes*, by Alexander Mittelstaedt, *NovT* 48 (2006): 387. Pervo, *Dating Acts* was unaware of Mittelstaedt's 2004 dissertation at the time of his publication of *Dating Acts* in 2006, but mentions this book in his 2009 essay, "Suburbs," 31 (n. 17). Pervo suggests Mittelstaedt's work is a mere "reiteration" of Hemer and Robinson's previous arguments that "basically restated" Harnack's influential work. This seems to be an overgeneralization of Mittelstaedt's important contribution. The fact that Pervo confuses Alexander's first name for Andreas lends to this supposition. Cf. Adolf Harnack, *The Acts of the Apostles* (trans. J. R. Wilkinson; London: Williams & Norgate, 1909), 290–7.

The diversity of past and recent opinions on the date of Acts warrants a systematic response that may prove beneficial for not only NT scholars and theologians, but also for historians since the book of Acts is of immense importance for any study on the religious and social history of the early Roman Imperial period.

When it comes to the date of Acts, there are three main groups to which scholars subscribe (with some overlap): early (pre-70 CE), middle (post-70 CE to ±80 CE), or late dating (90–130 CE)—(see Table 1.1).[19] Some have dated Acts as early as the late 50s (Blass) and as late as the middle of the second century (Townsend). The main criteria in the debate that are repeatedly produced as argument points are the following: (1) the end of Paul's imprisonment (*c*. 62 CE); (2) the fire of Rome and Nero's persecution (64–65 CE); (3) the outbreak of the Jewish War (66 CE); (4) the destruction of Gaza (66 CE);[20] (5) the "traditional" death of Paul (67 CE); (6) the fall of Jerusalem (70 CE); (7) the date of Mark;[21] (8) the date of the third gospel (after 70 CE or a proto-Luke pre-70 CE); (9) the uncertain lifespan of Paul's companion (±80); (10) the insertion of the "curse of the Minim" into the Eighteen Benedictions (*c*. 85–90); (11) the appearance of Josephus's *Antiquities* (*c*. 93 CE) and/or his whole works (*c*. 100); (12) and the circulation of Paul's letters ±90.[22]

The Early Dating Advocates (pre-70 CE)

The "early" group has a long tradition that goes back to ancient times.[23] The main issue is that Acts ends without any clear reference to the outcome of Paul's trial.[24] In the modern period, it was the earlier work of Blass (1895–98), Rackham (1899) and

---

[19] Fitzmyer, *Acts*, 52. Likewise Hemer suggests there are three main camps: (1) early, pre-70; (2) a date ±80; and (3) a date "near the end of the first century or in the second." Hemer, *Acts*, 373. My dates are borrowed from Hemer, supplemented by Fitzmyer and Pervo, and at times clarified by the author. More recently Porter narrows these groups to be around 63 CE (with Paul's imprisonment under Nero), around 85 CE, and "around but no later than" 130 CE. Porter, *When Paul Met Jesus*, 76.

[20] In Acts 8:26 Hemer explains there is no clear editorial allusion to the destruction of Gaza in 66 CE. Hemer, *Acts*, 371 (n. 17).

[21] Ibid., 371. Dating Acts based on Mark alone is too simplistic especially because Acts relates to contemporary events more than "any other New Testament book" (ibid., 376). Peterson asks: "Why must there have been more than a decade between the publication of Mark and the appearance of Luke-Acts?" David G. Peterson, *The Acts of the Apostles* (PNTC; Grand Rapids: Eerdmans, 2009), 5. A mid-date view of Acts (i.e., 85 CE) based on the standard synoptic solution and a relatively late date for Mark is problematic because both are "far from certain." Cf. Porter, *When Paul Met Jesus*, 77. And yet, some Acts scholars continue to date Acts based on the date of Mark. E.g., Gaventa, *Acts*, 51.

[22] The criteria here are reproduced from Hemer, *Acts*, 371; cf. also Shellard, *New Light on Luke*, 31. Hemer, *Acts*, 371, notes that despite uncertainty in many of these cases, most of these events are presented as *termini post quem* along with other kinships with Gnostic writings, the Domitianic persecution, the Pastorals, Plutarch, Justin Martyr, or "with cultural phenomena exclusively characteristic of a chosen date almost anywhere along the spectrum." I agree with Keener who questions the criteria for dating any document "no earlier than its first clear attestation." Keener, *Acts*, 1:399.

[23] The view is implied as early as the late second century when line 36 of the late second-century Muratorian fragment assumes that Luke's compilation happened "in his own presence" (*sub praesentia eius*) while also omitting the martyrdom of Peter and Paul as well as his trip to Spain. See "Ancient Interpretation of the Enigma" and my note 57 in Chapter 5 on the date of the fragment.

[24] Keener, *Acts*, 1:385.

Table 1.1 Key dates relating to Acts in the early Roman imperial period (*c.* 60–150 CE)

41–54 CE	Reign of Claudius
50–60s	Circulation of Paul's letters
54–68	Reign of Nero
60–61	Paul (as a prisoner) goes to Rome
62	End of Paul's imprisonment + death of James (the brother of Jesus)
63–64	Death of Paul (terminus for the circulation of his letters)
July 19, 64	Great Fire of Rome
64	Post-fire persecution of Christians in Rome under Nero
64–67	Death of Peter
66	Outbreak of the Jewish War (66–74 CE) and the destruction of Gaza
68	Death of Nero (r. 54–68)
68–69	Year of the four Emperor's (Galba, Otho, Vitelius ending with Vespasian)
69–79	Reign of Vespasian; Clement of Rome writes *1 Clement* (but a date in the 80s or 90s is possible, see my note 45 in Chapter 5)
Pre-70 CE	**Early dating advocates**
70	Destruction of the Jewish Temple
71	Roman triumph
73–74	Fall of Masada
75–79	Josephus writes *Jewish War*
79	Eruption of Mount Vesuvius and the destruction of Pompeii and Herculaneum
79–81	Reign of Titus
Post-70 CE to ±80	**Middle dating advocates**
81–96	Reign of Domitian
85–95	Persecution of Christians under Domitian
93–94	Josephus writes *Antiquities of the Jews*
94–95	Apostle John dies on the Isle of Patmos
96–98	Reign of Nerva
98–117	Reign of Trajan
90–130 CE	**Late dating advocates**
100	Josephus's *Life* and *Against Apion* circulated shortly before his death
117–38	Reign of Hadrian
132–35	Bar Kokhba rebellion and the Second Jewish War
138–161	Reign of Antoninus Pius
144	Marcion founds his church and writes his gospel sometime before 150 CE.

Harnack (*c.* 1911) who launched the core arguments for the early group.[25] Where Harnack is usually given credit with the earliest and most significant view for an early

---

[25] Richard B. Rackham, *The Acts of the Apostles: An Exposition* (9th edn; London: Methuen, 1922), 50–5; Adolf Harnack, *Zur Apostelgeschichte und zur Abfassungszeit der Synoptischen Evangelien* (BENT IV; Leipzig: Hinrichs, 1911), 86, 113; idem, *Date of the Acts*, 92–3, 114–16; Friedrich

date of Acts (64 CE), it was in fact Rackham's article published in the first issue of *JTS* (1899) that presents the first "classic" defence for an early date of Acts.[26] For Rackham, Acts ends the way it does because the author is unaware of the fate of Peter and Paul, James and the persecution of the Christians in Rome under Nero, the destruction of Jerusalem (and the Temple)—and at the same time, he considers the relations between the church and Rome to be peaceful.[27]

Starting with the earliest date (Blass, 57–59 CE) scholars' arguments offer a wide range of early dates to choose from (see Table 1.2). Many scholars in this group give Acts an early date for the following reasons:[28] (1) Luke's failure to mention Paul's death or his pending trial before Caesar;[29] (2) the Great Fire of Rome in 64 CE;[30] (3) the persecution of Christians under Nero;[31] (4) Luke's apologetic purpose of showing Christianity as a *religio licita* under Nero is problematic; (5) the peaceful tone of Acts that is *inconsistent* with an awareness of Paul's tragic martyrdom and the subsequent persecution of the church; (6) the description of the early Jerusalem church that was still in contact with the Temple, Synagogues, Pharisees and Sadducees is far too idyllic to have been written after the Jewish Rebellion and Jerusalem's destruction in 70 CE;[32] (7) the author *seems* unaware of Paul's letters;[33] (8) the "obvious parallel" between the death of Jesus and the death of Paul is missing;[34] (9) and the Temple-based Jewish Christian prayers in

---

Blass, *Evangelium secundum Lucam* (Leipzig: Teubner, 1897), lxxix; idem, *Philology of the Gospels* (London: Macmillan, 1898), 33–4; and (the earlier) idem, *Acta Apostolorum sive Lucae ad Theophilum liber alter* (Göttingen: Vandenhoeck & Ruprecht, 1895), 1–5. See also Fitzmyer, *Acts*, 52.

[26] See Richard B. Rackham, "Plea," 76–87. Hemer, *Acts*, 367 (n. 3), notes that Harnack's earlier views shifted from a range "between 78 and 93" but by the time he wrote his *Acts* (290) he was "already inclined to the early date." See also, Pervo, *Dating Acts*, 373 (n. 12).

[27] Rackham points to many prior OT parallel passages regarding Jerusalem (and the Temple's) destruction (Cf. Jer. 20:4; Deut. 28:64; 1 Kgs 8:46; Isa. 5:5, 58:18; Dan. 8:13; Zech. 12:3; 1 Macc. 4:60; Isa. 29:3, 37:33; Jer. 6:6, 52:4-5; Ezek. 4:1-3; Ps. 137:9; Hos. 13:16). Luke's language is no surprise because Jerusalem had already been twice "surrounded by armies" in the preceding century and a half. See Rackham, "Plea," 76–87. Dodd most notably carries this argument in a convincing, systematic fashion. Cf. Charles H. Dodd, "The Fall of Jerusalem and the 'Abomination of Desolation,'" *JRS* 37 (1947): 47–54.

[28] See Fitzmyer, *Acts*, 52.

[29] Keener, *Acts*, 1:385.

[30] Cf. Peter Lampe, *From Paul to Valentinus: Christians at Rome in the First Two Centuries* (ed. Marshall D. Johnson; Minneapolis: Fortress, 2003), 47; Tacitus, *Ann.* 15.38-43; and Ray Laurence et al., *The City in the Roman West* (Cambridge: Cambridge University Press, 2011), 117–18.

[31] Lampe, *Paul to Valentinus*, 401; idem, "Roman Christians Under Nero (54–68 CE)," in *The Last Years of Paul: Essays from the Tarragona Conference, June 2013* (eds. Armand Puig i Tàrrech et al.; WUNT 352; Tübingen: Mohr Siebeck, 2015), 111–29; Tacitus, *Ann.* 15:44.2, 4; Keener, *Acts*, 1:387; and Pierson Parker, "The 'Former Treatise' and the Date of Acts," *JBL* 84 (1965): 53.

[32] Given the narrated rejection of (Jesus), and the persecution of the apostles by the Jewish leadership, it seems reasonable to expect the author to capitalize on the Temple's destruction (e.g., Ezra 5:12).

[33] This topic is discussed in Chapter 4. Where some scholars like Pervo are convinced that Acts reflects Paul's letters, others maintain that the author "makes no use of Paul's letters." Cf. Christopher Mount, *Pauline Christianity: Luke-Acts and the Legacy of Paul* (NovTSup 104; Leiden: Brill, 2002), 169 (n. 17).

[34] Fitzmyer, *Acts*, 52. Considering the detailed treatment of Jesus's death in Luke, and Stephen in Acts 7, there is every reason to expect a note on the outcome of Paul's trial. Rackham, while commenting on the missing "obvious parallel to the Passion of the Gospel," explains how we should otherwise

Table 1.2 The early dating advocates (pre-70 CE)

Date argued	Scholars
57–59 CE	Blass[a]
Near the end of Paul's imprisonment (c. 61)	Mattill, Finegan, and Wikenhauser (1921)
61–63 (Alexandrian), Western (c. 67)	Delebecque (du texte premier = Alexandrian)[b]
Before Peter arrives in Rome (c. 62)	Filson
62	Blaiklock, Hemer, Mittelstaedt, Schnabel, Edmundson, Reicke, Harrison, and Robinson[c]
Immediately after 62	Bihel
62–63	Armstrong and Parker[d]
63	Lightfoot, Smith, Fuller, Robertson, and Porter[e]
62–64	Vine, Carson, Moo, Morris, and Peterson[f]
Before 64	R. R. Williams and Guthrie
By 64	Rackham and Harnack[g]
64	Torrey and Longenecker
Early 60s	Goodenough, Munck, and Larkin[h]
64–70 (or immediately following)	Manson
After Paul's death (c. 64–68)	Wikenhauser (1958) and Dupont
66–70	C. S. C. Williams and Schneckenburger[i]
Pre-70	Russell
Just before 70	Bock[j]
Towards 70	Marshall[k]
Around 70	Ellis

[a]Blass, *Evangelium secundum Lucam*, lxxix; idem, *Philology of the Gospels*, 33–4.

[b]Joël Delobel, "The Text of Luke-Acts. A Confrontation of Recent Theories," in *The Unity of Luke-Acts* (ed. J. Verheyden; BETL 142; Leuven: Leuven University Press, 1999), 88, interprets Delebecque's date as "about" 62 CE. Delebecque places Paul's first captivity in Rome to be from 61–63 CE. Édouard Delebecque, *Les Deux Actes des Apôtres* (EBib 6; Paris: J. Gabalda, 1986), 375. He says it is likely that during this time (and before the fire of 64) Luke took advantage "pour rédiger au moins la majeure partie du texte premier des *Actes* [=Alexandrian]" (to write at least most of the first text of the Acts, 376). He claims that "l'incendie de Rome en 54 [sic, meaning 64]" is obviously an editorial oversight (382). The remaining (Western) text (380) was finished "a la fin de l'ete 67" (at the end of the summer of 67). In his conclusion (p. 417), he seems to indicate that "il a retouche, perfectionne, un texte initial" (he retouched, perfected, an initial text) between the years of 63 and 67 CE. Hence by 67 CE, or a little afterwards, the Western text is finished. See Chapter 7.

[c]See Hemer, *Acts*, 408. Schnabel, *Acts*, 28, suggests that Acts was written sometime "after Paul's release in AD 62." Blaiklock says that a "date in the neighbourhood of AD 62 seems reasonable." Edward M. Blaiklock, *The Acts of the Apostles: An Historical Commentary* (London: Tyndale Press, 1959), 17. John A. T. Robinson, *Redating the New Testament* (London: SCM, 1976), 19, 72, 112, settles on 62 CE but implies a range of 57–62 CE (352). Mittelstaedt concludes that Luke was written in late Autumn of 59 in Caesarea, while Acts was written in 62 CE in Caesarea or Philippi. See Mittelstaedt, *Lukas als Historiker*, 251–5.

[d]Armstrong, "A New Plea," (2017): 79–110; Parker, "'Former Treatise,'" 52–8.

[e]Hemer, *Acts*, 369, places Lightfoot's chronology *after* the fall of Jerusalem—"early seventies." However, Hemer's reference is either incorrect or he is quoting from another source. He refers to the 1893 edition of William Smith and John M. Fuller, eds., *A Dictionary of the Bible* (2nd edn; 3rd vol.; London: John Murray, 1893), 40, 27. The dictionary reference on Acts (13–14) clearly argues for a date of 63 CE that reflects Lightfoot's chronology elsewhere (both the earlier 1868 and later 1898 editions argue for this date). See Joseph B. Lightfoot, *Biblical Essays* (New York: Macmillan, 1893), 217–22, and his chapter on "St. Paul's History After the Close of Acts," 419–37. Lightfoot's chronology places Paul in Rome in 61 CE (see Lightfoot, *Biblical Essays*, 217–22) and based upon the two years of his captivity at the end of Acts his release would have been between 63 and the summer of 64 CE because of the Great Fire (429). From 63–66 CE Paul goes east, in 67 CE he revisits Macedonia and then is martyred in the spring of 68 CE before the death of Nero (223). Subsequently, Lightfoot claims, "the Pastoral Epistles will have been written in the year 67 or 68" (429). I find it doubtful that Lightfoot would date the pastorals at this time and then date Acts in the seventies. Furthermore, he states: "Here St. Luke's narrative ends abruptly; so that we are without information as to what occurred afterwards" (429). Lightfoot comes short of dating Acts but it seems reasonable to

Table 1.2 (*Continued*)

conclude he would consider 63 CE based on his chronology. Recently, Porter, *When Paul Met Jesus*, 78, expressed a similar view: "A date of around A.D. 63 has, in my opinion, the most to commend it, even though it is not as widely held as the intermediate view."
[f]Donald A. Carson, Douglas J. Moo, and Leon Morris *An Introduction to the New Testament* (Grand Rapids: Zondervan, 1992), 190–4. The second edition of Donald A. Carson and Douglas J. Moo, *An Introduction to the New Testament* (2nd edn; Grand Rapids: Zondervan, 2005), 330, "suggest a date not long after A.D. 62" and in the "mid-60s." While Peterson thinks a "date in the 70's seems entirely reasonable" he suggests that "a good case can be made for a date as early as 62–64." Peterson, *Acts*, 5. These scholars note the following factors: (1) ignorance of Paul's letters; (2) Judaism "as a legal religion"; (3) the lack of any reference to Nero's persecution; (4) or the outcome of Paul's Roman incarceration.
[g]See Rackham, "Plea," 76–87; Harnack, *Date of Acts*, 92–3, 114–16. Harnack (93) thinks that Luke's "absolute silence concerning everything that happened between the years 64 and 70 A.D. is a strong argument for the hypothesis that his book was written before the year 64 A.D." Cf. also Gasque, *History*, 131–3.
[h]William J. Larkin Jr., *Acts* (IVPNTC; Downers Grove, IL: InterVarsity Press, 1995), 18.
[i]For Schneckenburger, the silence regarding the destruction of Jerusalem and its Temple is key—and thus argues for a date "subsequent to the death of Paul, but prior to the destruction of Jerusalem." See Gasque, *History*, 39, and his synthesis of Matthias Schneckenburger's *Über den Zweck der Apostelgeschichte: Zugleich eine Ergänzung der neueren Commentare* (Bern: Fischer, 1841), 231–5.
[j]Darrell L. Bock, *Acts* (BECNT; Grand Rapids: Baker, 2007), 27.
[k]I. Howard Marshall, *The Acts of the Apostles* (TNTC; repr., Downers Grove, IL: Inter-Varsity Press, 2008), 51.

Acts.[35] In summary, Acts "reflects the situation and concerns of the church in the pre-70 CE period and betrays no clear indication of a later period."[36]

One recent proponent of an early date—and a challenger to middle and late dating advocates—is Mittelstaedt. His book *Lukas als Historiker* came out in Germany (2006) at the same time as Pervo's *Dating Acts* and Tyson's *Marcion and Luke-Acts*, all three of which are the most recent monographs dealing with the date of Acts. At the core of Mittelstaedt's thesis is the destruction of Jerusalem as a criterion for dating.[37] In his analysis of Luke and his sources, Mittelstaedt discusses two basic possibilities with regard to the prophecies of the city's destruction: "Either the events of the Jewish war are reflected here, which must be formulated with reference to the OT, or the citations are independent of contemporary history, of purely theological background, which would barely be imaginable in view of the drama and gravity of the Jewish war after 70."[38] The prophecies in Luke therefore provide us with only two options: they reflect

---

be at a loss to understand chapter 20 to the end. The plan of Acts disappears and the end becomes "unintelligible" afterwards. Rackham, "Plea," 78.

[35] Since the prayer forms in Acts reflect the Temple and not the synagogue, there is "little evidence to suggest that Luke's picture contains elements from post-70 developments in Jewish and Christian worship." Cf. Daniel K. Falk, "Jewish Prayer Literature and the Jerusalem Church," in *The Book of Acts in Its Palestinian Setting* (ed. Richard Bauckham; 5 vols; BAFCS 4; Grand Rapids: Eerdmans, 1995), 4:267–301 (267).

[36] Hemer, *Acts*, 382. Rhee rightly explains that "just like any other literature, Christian literature reflects and is shaped by the historical and cultural context in which it is born." Helen Rhee, *Early Christian Literature: Christ and Culture in the Second and Third Centuries* (RECM; Abingdon: Routledge, 2005), 9.

[37] Mittelstaedt, *Lukas als Historiker*, 49–163. This will be covered in detail in Chapter 8.

[38] Mittelstaedt, *Lukas als Historiker*, 14. "Entweder sind hier Ereignisse des Jüdischen Krieges reflektiert, die durchaus in Anlehnung an das AT formuliert sein können, oder die Zitate haben einen von der

the events of the Jewish war, or they do not.³⁹ There is plenty of textual evidence to suggest they do not in light of what actually happened post-70 CE; the description can hardly be written in retrospect of 70 CE.⁴⁰

Mittelstaedt also considers the destruction of Jerusalem to be clearly eschatological in the third gospel. Not only is the Temple an integral part of the Acts narrative, but he also explains how Acts 6:13 and following are written in the present tense (=imperfective aspect) when mentioning Temple details, and the narration of the Sadducees strongly suggests the Temple is still standing at the time of writing.⁴¹ However, the use of the present tense to indicate present time formulates an insufficient argument given the advances in Greek scholarship. For example, Porter claims that "one cannot start with the individual verb tenses to establish extra-textual temporal reference."⁴² The present-tense usage in Hebrews (or Acts) for example, does not necessarily mean that the "author was writing before the destruction of the Temple."⁴³ Unfortunately, none of the major works on the date of Acts (including Pervo, Tyson, and Mittelstaedt) have duly considered recent linguistic research towards this debate (and verbal aspect theory was well-established by 2006).⁴⁴

The next major section, "Das Schweigen über den Tod des Paulus," examines the oldest church traditions about the time of writing, the last block of Acts and the martyrdom of Stephen, Paul's trial before Caesar, the farewell speech to the Ephesians (Acts 20:17-35), the oldest news about Paul's death, Paul and Peter in John's Revelation, the fire of Rome and the persecution under Nero.⁴⁵ At this juncture, he reasons effectively that Paul "lebt noch" (yet lives) at the time when Acts was written, which occurs prior to the summer of 64 CE.⁴⁶ He states, "It is time to balance the books. Luke describes an epoch or writes in an epoch that still knows nothing about a Christian persecution from the side of the Romans; nothing indicates the death of Paul."⁴⁷

Zeitgeschichte unabhängigen, rein theologischen Hintergrund, was angesichts der Dramatik und der Folgenschwere des Jüdischen Krieges nach 70 kaum noch vorstellbar ware."

³⁹ With regard to the Lukan prophecies (i.e., Lk. 13:35; 19:43-44 and 21:20) see Chapter 8.
⁴⁰ Mittelstaedt, *Lukas als Historiker*, 152; Stenschke, review of *Lukas als Historiker*, 387.
⁴¹ Mittelstaedt, *Lukas als Historiker*, 159-62. It is noteworthy that καταλύω and ἀλλάσσω in verse 14 are both in the future tense with regard to Stephen's reference to Jesus who "will overthrow this place" (καταλύσει τὸν τόπον τοῦτον) and "will change the customs" (ἀλλάξει τὰ ἔθη).
⁴² See Stanley E. Porter, "The Date of the Composition of Hebrews and the Use of the Present Tense-Form," in *Crossing the Boundaries: Essays in Biblical Interpretation in Honour of Michael D. Goulder* (eds. Stanley E. Porter et al.; BibInt 8; Leiden Brill, 1994), 295-314 (312).
⁴³ Ibid., 312.
⁴⁴ For a summary of key developments in Greek verbal structure and verbal aspect theory since the 1970s see Stanley E. Porter and Andrew W. Pitts, "New Testament Greek Language and Linguistics in Recent Research," *CurBR* 6 (2008): 215-22, and also Stanley E. Porter, *Idioms of the Greek New Testament* (2nd edn; BLG 2; Sheffield: Sheffield Academic, 1994), 25-6; idem, *Verbal Aspect in the Greek of the New Testament, with Reference to Tense and Mood* (SBG 1; New York: Peter Land, 1989), 17-65.
⁴⁵ Mittelstaedt, *Lukas als Historiker*, 165-220.
⁴⁶ Ibid., 219-21.
⁴⁷ "Es ist an der Zeit, Bilanz zu ziehen. Lukas beschreibt eine Epoche bzw. schreibt in einer Epoche, die von einer Christenverfolgung von römischer Seite noch nichts weiß. Nichts deutet auf den Tod des Paulus." Ibid., 219.

Mittelstaedt considers "further criteria" such as the non-use of Paul's letters, the death of James and the justification of the pagan mission, the Italic cohort in Caesarea, whether Luke knew the works of Joseph or a common source, and Luke's research in Caesarea and Jerusalem.[48] His final summary affirms his previous tenets while offering a specific chronology and set of circumstances with regard to the writing and date of Acts:

> In conclusion, in agreement with prior representatives of early-dating, it follows that in any case the book of Acts was finished by 64, more likely, 62, and the material for the gospel had been collected in Caesarea by 57–59 at the earliest. The location of Theophilus and the place of completion of the book of Acts was in no case Rome, since Luke already collected his material in Caesarea and knows nothing of the end of Caesar's trial, which is best explained by the fact that [when] he returned to the East before the end of the two years, Paul was there.[49]

In summary of the early dating arguments, as exemplified in Mittelstaedt's work, it seems that the core concern is attention to the historical context (i.e., Rome and Jerusalem) and how that fits with the narrative of Acts. For this group, Luke's silence on several key events in the history of both the church and Rome remains the chief concern, and yet the reasons extend beyond the silence of these notable events.[50] While it is difficult to reconcile the silence with regard to the persecution under Nero, it is incomprehensible that Luke should at the same time paint Rome in such a favourable light.[51] Similarly, to neglect the fire of Rome is perplexing enough (as there is no political or theological motivation to do so), but incredible that the final events in the narrative provide no hint of the city's widespread destruction, which is the very place where the narrative ends with Paul preaching "unhindered" (Acts 28:31).

The Middle Dating Advocates (post-70 CE to ±80)

The middle segment (with some overlap) seems to represent the current majority opinion among scholars.[52] For this group, dating Acts before 70 CE is too early and

---

[48] Ibid., 221–49.
[49] Ibid., 254 (see 251–5 in context). "Abschließend ergibt sich in Übereinstimmung mit früheren Vertretern der Frühdatierung, daß die Apg in jedem Fall vor 64, eher noch 62 vollendet wurde und das Material für das Evangelium am ehesten 57–59 in Caesarea gesammelt worden ist. Standort des Theophilus und Ort der Vollendung der Apg war in keinem Fall Rom, da Lukas sein Material schon in Caesarea sammelte und zudem nichts genaues vom Ende des Kaiserprozesses weiß, was am einfachsten damit zu erklären ist, daß er noch vor dem Ende der zwei Jahre, die Paulus dort war, in den Osten zurückkehrte."
[50] See "Principles for Interpreting Sources" in Chapter 2.
[51] Granted there are some exceptions such as Paul's treatment by the Roman magistrates at Philippi (Acts 16:22-23) or when Felix expected a bribe and refused to free Paul as a favour to the Jews (Acts 24:26, 27). However, this is nothing compared to Nero's treatment of the Christians in 64 CE (see Chapter 8).
[52] Spencer agrees with "most scholars" who date Acts after 70 CE but "before the letters of Paul, which Acts does not allude to" since they were "collected and circulated close to the end of the century."

after 90 CE is too late. A significant number of scholars reason that Acts was probably written in the 70s, after the fall of Jerusalem.[53] With this in mind, we find a range of dates that fall somewhere within 70–80 CE (see Table 1.3).

Troftgruben suggests further reasons for a post-70 CE date that are summarized here.[54] First, the difficulty of the "many" in the early 60s CE who would "have undertaken to compile a narrative" before Luke.[55] Second, only after the destruction of Jerusalem (70 CE) does the phrase in Lk. 13:35 "your house is abandoned" make sense.[56] Third, in Mk 13:2, Jesus pronounces judgement upon the Temple and the "abomination of desolation" in Mk 13:14 is replaced by "Jerusalem surrounded by camps" in Lk. 21:20.[57] Fourth, that Lk. 19:43-44 "alludes to Roman earthworks of the sort described by Josephus" indicates a post-70 dating (cf. *War* 6.150, 156).[58] Hence, many in this middle group prefer a date after 70 CE but before 81–96 CE because of a lack of reference to the Domitian persecution during this time.[59]

Since Keener has offered a more defendable view in recent years, it is worth exploring his reasons for a date "closer to 70" within the broader "centrist" position (70–80s).[60] For a date of Acts in the first century, he offers several reasons: (1) authorship by a "companion of Paul" best explains the "we" sections;[61] (2) the "massive correspondences between Acts and first-century historical events" reflect a high degree of memory or at least a "heavy reliance on early sources"; and (3) the "Pauline apologetic" reflects localities and memories of an earlier period.[62] Although he maintains a "closer to 70" date, it is cautiously couched within a very broad range of possibilities that sound appealing to "most scholars."[63]

Since Keener considers the arguments "compelling" for the author being a travelling companion of Paul, he "would restrict any date estimate … to within the

---

F. Scott Spencer, *Acts* (Sheffield: Sheffield Academic, 1997), 16. Keener, *Acts*, 1:384, also maintains this "centrist" position. Meanwhile, Fitzmyer, *Acts*, 54, adds to this list: Marxsen, Michaelis, Perrot, Pesch, and Vielhauer. Contrary to Fitzmyer's list, Dupont and C. S. C. Williams should be on the "early" list as that seems to be a better fit based on their views. See Hemer, *Acts*, 368.

[53] The destruction of Jerusalem and the Temple is the hinge between early and middle groups. Troy M. Troftgruben, *A Conclusion Unhindered: A Study of the Ending of Acts within Its Literary Environment* (WUNT 2/280; Tübingen: Mohr Siebeck, 2010), 10.

[54] Troftgruben, *Conclusion Unhindered*, 10.

[55] Fitzmyer, *Acts*, 54.

[56] Ibid. However, Jeremiah had previously used even stronger language in Lam. 2:7 or Jer. 22:5, "this house is for desolation."

[57] See "The Fall of Jerusalem: Dividing the Early and Middle Groups" in Chapter 8.

[58] Fitzmyer, *Acts*, 54. This is weak in light of Dodd's, "Jerusalem," 48, arguments, and the manner of Roman siege tactics against a walled city.

[59] Fitzmyer, *Acts*, 54.

[60] See Keener, *Acts*, 1:384 (and his full argument pp. 383–401).

[61] Ibid., 1:384. See also his note on Acts 16:10 (3:2350–2374).

[62] Ibid., 1:384. He reasons that producing such "detailed charges merely for entertainment would have undercut Luke's apologetic for Paul" (384).

[63] Ibid., 1:400. Here he states that "to an extent any suggested date is merely an educated guess." This echoes the language of "political compromise" that is typical of middle dating advocates as previously noted by Pervo, "Suburbs," 31. Keener does a thorough job of working through the arguments, but a date in the 70s, and especially in "the 80's requires a great deal of explaining away." Pervo, "Suburbs," 46.

Table 1.3 The middle dating advocates (post-70 CE to ±80)

Date argued	Scholars
Shortly after 70	Headlam[a]
After 70	Page and Hanson
72–74	Bartlet
75	Zahn
About 75	D. J. Williams
70–80	Keener[b]
Based on the date of Luke	Knowling
Doubts an early date	Neil
80 (earlier is possible)	Clarke
No later than 80	Plummer, and Boismard[c]
80	Meyer, Johnson, Boismard, and Lamouille[d]
Late 70s or early 80s	Bruce and Witherington[e]
75, or possibly 80 and 85	Haenchen[f]
Late-middle advocates	
80s	Marguerat and Dunn[g]
70–90	Kümmel
After 70, but before the circulation of Paul's letters	Spencer
Immediately after 81	Ramsay
75–90	Ehrhardt
c. 85	Macgregor, Fitzmyer[h]
80–90	Schneider, Weiser, Juel, Jervell, Hengel, Tannehill, Puskas, and Troftgruben[i]
80s or early 90s	Maddox
85–90	Goguel
Late 80s or early 90s	Barrett[j]
Before c. 90	Jackson
Last quarter of the first century	Trocmé

[a] Arthur C. Headlam, "Acts of the Apostles," in *A Dictionary of the Bible: Language, Literature, and Contents* (eds. James Hastings et al., 4 vols; Edinburgh: T&T Clark, 1908), 30.
[b] See Keener, *Acts*, 1:384 (and his full argument pp. 383–401). He seems to lean very close to 70 CE because "charges against Paul and his death in Roman custody remain a live apologetic issue." Ibid., 1:384 (on p. 400 he ponders, "early 70's, with dates in the 80s and 60s still plausible.")
[c] Hemer, *Acts*, 369, says "not before 80" in reference to Marie-Emile Boismard in his "Bulletin," *RB* (1954): 275. However, here Boismard explains that Luke wrote his gospel "after the ruin of Jerusalem (but no later than 80)" (après la ruine de Jérusalem [mais pas plus tard que 80]).
[d] Luke T. Johnson, *The Gospel of Luke* (SP 3; Collegeville, MN: Liturgical, 1991), 2 (probably between 80 and 85 but possibly earlier); Marie-Emile Boismard and Arnaud Lamouille, *Les Actes des deux Apôtres* (3 vols; Paris: Gabalda, 1990), 1:43.
[e] Earlier, Bruce shifted his opinion from "a little earlier than the persecution of 64" CE to the "late 70s or early 80s." See Frederick Fyvie Bruce, *The Book of Acts* (NICNT; repr., Grand Rapids: Eerdmans, 1983), 21–3 (here p. 22), 31 (n. 9) and idem, *The Acts of the Apostles: The Greek Text with Introduction and Commentary* (3rd edn; Grand Rapids: Eerdmans, 1990), 9–18 (here p. 18) respectively. See also: Ben Witherington III, *The Acts of the Apostles: A Socio-Rhetorical Commentary* (Grand Rapids: Eerdmans, 1998), 62.
[f] While Ernst Haenchen, *The Acts of the Apostles* (Oxford: Blackwell, 1971), does not commit to a date, his comments (86) imply a date of 75 CE but also a date of 80 CE (164, 244–5) and possibly 85 CE (257). In a note of disappointment, Pervo, *Dating Acts*, 461, admits that Haenchen "does not argue for a 'late date' for Acts . . . he does not depart from the 'consensus.'"
[g] Marguerat suggests a date of "around the 80's" but without reason. Cf. Marguerat, *Historian*, 229. Similarly, Dunn's, *Acts*, xi, single paragraph on the date of Acts is disappointing as he states: "not much hangs on the date of the composition, but a date in . . . the 80s fits best with the evidence."
[h] Fitzmyer, *Acts*, 55.

Table 1.3 (*Continued*)

ⁱJacob Jervell, *Die Apostelgeschichte* (Göttingen: Vandenhoeck & Ruprecht, 1998), 86; Hengel, *Acts*, 63; Robert C. Tannehill, *Luke* (ANTC; Nashville: Abingdon, 1996), 26; Charles B. Puskas, *The Conclusion of Luke-Acts: The Significance of Acts 28:16–31* (Eugene, OR: Pickwick, 2009), 32; Troftgruben, *Conclusion Unhindered*, 10.
ʲCharles K. Barrett, *The Acts of the Apostles* (2 vols; ICC; Edinburgh: T&T Clark, 1998), 2:xlii, thinks this date range is probable while at the same time admits it is "complicated by several factors."

probable lifetime of such a companion."[64] Moreover he states that the "date of Acts is uncertain, but my best guesses . . . are in the early 70s, with dates in the 80s and 60s still plausible, and a date in the 90s not impossible. The arguments limiting the range between 70 and 90 (the majority view) seem to me stronger than the alternatives."[65] He then emphasizes once more his preference for a date in the early 70s CE because of his views of Lukan authorship and the "strong apologetic for Paul engaging a range of concrete accusations about his involvement in specific local riots."[66] Last, he seems to settle on a post-70 date that is "within ... living memory of Paul."[67]

While the early and middle groups do not find the evidence for a late date of Acts to be convincing—most notably due to dependence on Josephus and Paul's letters—the middle group cannot seem to go earlier than 70 CE for the various reasons outlined above. They place remarkable significance on the historical nature of Acts, but most of these scholars do not view Luke as the author and companion of Paul. Furthermore, placing Luke in the 60s presents a major hurdle for them along with the prophecies relating to Jerusalem and the destruction of the Jewish Temple. Although their arguments rest upon Luke's redaction of Mark, Dodd and others have made a

---

[64] Keener, *Acts*, 1:400; Larkin, *Acts*, 18. Although I appreciate Keener's discussion on Luke's estimated age, if Luke was already 20–30 years old in 50 CE (when he first began travelling with Paul), the likelihood of writing Acts later than 70 CE (though possible) diminishes exponentially based on life expectancy in the ancient world. For example, Frier observes that almost "all ancient historians now accept the view, originally propounded by Keith Hopkins in 1966, that for the general population, average Roman life expectancy at birth is likely to have lain in a range from 20 to 30 years." Cf. Bruce W. Frier, "More is Worse: Some Observations on the Roman Empire," in *Debating Roman Demography* (ed. Walter Scheidel; Mnemosyne 211; Leiden: Brill, 2001), 144; Keith Hopkins, "On the Probable Age Structure of the Roman Population," *PS* 20 (1966): 245–64 (263–4). More recent discussion on life expectancy at birth remains at "about 25." Cf. Peter Garnsey and Richard Saller, *The Roman Empire: Economy, Society and Culture* (2nd edn; Oakland, CA: University of California Press, 2015), 233. Karen Cokayne, *Experiencing Old Age in Ancient Rome* (London: Routledge, 2013), 3, qualifies this range by explaining that if a child survived the "early danger years" to age 10, life expectancy was increased by 37.5 years (or a total age of 47.5 years). Hence, following Keener, if Luke was 30 at 50 CE, he would have reached average life expectancy (based on Cokayne's research) around 67 CE. By the 60s CE, Luke would already have started to live beyond average life expectancy. Therefore, any argument that is tied to the age of the author as a companion of Paul requires qualification.

[65] Keener, *Acts*, 1:400.

[66] Ibid. His argument is far more compelling for a pre-70 date: "Luke the apologist would hardly invent a history of local riots surrounding Paul, yet unable to deny them, he must explain them, at a time when the local memories of such riots remained alive and Paul's legacy remained contested."

[67] Ibid., 1:401. While citing Acts 22:3-21 specifically, Keener notes that if he is mistaken this will "bring into question" some of his "interpretive judgements at key points" and "affect only a relatively small portion" of his commentary. However, a post-70 date of Acts significantly alters how we interpret several aspects of Acts. Regardless, a relatively small portion ("even less than 1 percent") of a massive commentary (4,459 pages) like Keener's represents a significant amount of material.

convincing case that the language is anything but decisive and does not on its own necessitate a post-70 date of Acts.[68]

The Late Dating Advocates (90–130 CE)

Promoters of a late date for Acts include those listed in Table 1.4. Scholars in this group place great emphasis on Acts having connections with late first-century and second-century writings (i.e., Josephus, Marcion, Justin Martyr, Polycarp, and Clement), although this is not the majority view.[69] Credit goes to F. C. Baur in 1847 as the trailblazer among the late dating advocates.[70] Since Overbeck's views are "much more dependent" upon Baur and his followers, it is not surprising to see his preference for a very late date of Acts as well.[71] Overbeck was an early, but highly influential Acts scholar who argued in 1870 that Acts could "not have been written during the apostolic age, or even as early as the last two decades of the first century."[72]

Overbeck claims that Acts "either must be an example of a completely meaningless fabrication, or presuppose a length of time between its date and the events it narrates sufficient to allow for the development."[73] For him, Acts is "strongly affected by the influences of legend" and the image of Paul is "strongly distorted," leading to a date beyond the apostolic age.[74] Overbeck finds five items in church history that are comparable to what we read in Acts: (1) the advanced state of church affairs, (2) the apologetic nature of Acts, (3) the *parousia* as part of the "indefinite" future, (4) the start of the "hierarchical constitution of the Church," and (5) the polemic against Gnosticism (as suggested by Acts 20:29).[75]

Over a century later, Pervo, in his monograph *Dating Acts*, argues that the author of Acts is familiar with Paul's ten letters, the later writings of Josephus (*c.* 100 CE), and the Pastoral Epistles and Polycarp (*c.* 125–130).[76] Just like Overbeck, he argues that Acts should carry a date of *c.* 115 (110–120 CE) from Ephesus "or its general environs."[77] Spencer remains unconvinced in his dual review of *Dating Acts* and *Marcion and*

---

[68] See Chapter 8 and "The Fall of Jerusalem: Dividing the Early and Middle Groups."
[69] Fitzmyer, *Acts*, 53. Although a "faithful late-date remnant" remains, most do not subscribe "for good and persuasive reasons." Porter, *When Paul Met Jesus*, 77. Pervo dates Clement (*1 Clem.*) to 100 CE and claims it shares a "good deal" with Acts. Pervo, "Suburbs," 36, and Pervo, *Dating Acts*, 301–5. He says that Acts "*may* be attested by Polycarp, ca. 130 CE." Pervo, "Suburbs," 35, and Pervo, *Dating Acts*, 17–20.
[70] Tyson, *Marcion*, 3–5.
[71] Gasque, *History*, 81.
[72] Cf. Ibid., 85, and Wilhelm, M. L. De Wette, *Kurze Erklärung der Apostelgeschichte* (ed. Franz Overbeck; 4th edn; Leipzig: Hirzel, 1870)—this 4th edition of De Wette's commentary is "edited and greatly expanded" by Overbeck.
[73] Gasque, *History*, 332 (trans. from p. 85); De Wette, *Apostelgeschichte*, lxiv.
[74] Gasque, *History*, 85, 332; De Wette, *Apostelgeschichte*, lxiv.
[75] Gasque, *History*, 85–6; De Wette, *Apostelgeschichte*, lxiv–lxv.
[76] Stanley E. Porter, *Paul in Acts* (repr., Peabody, MA: Hendrickson, 2007), 14–19, in his critique of Pervo's 1987 *Profit with Delight*, relays how his use of anachronistic literary comparisons "verges on parallelomania." (18).
[77] Pervo, *Acts*, xv, 5. Pervo maintains a date of 115 CE in "Suburbs," 36, and his later "The Date of Acts," 6.

Table 1.4 The late dating advocates (90–130 CE)

80s or 90s CE	Gaventa and Windisch (possibly 100–110)[a]
c. 90	McNeile, Dibelius, Goodspeed, and Roloff
c. 90, 85–100	Davies
90–95	Streeter
80–100	Conzelmann[b]
90–100	Lake
Towards the end of the first century (at the earliest)	Bornkamm
90s to 100s	Kee
95–105	Burkitt
98–100	Shellard[c]
c. 100	von Soden, Moffatt, Talbert, Lohse, and Bonz (at the end of the first century CE)[d]
90–110	Schmithalls
100–105	Jülicher and Enslin
100–110	Koester[e]
105–130	Schmiedel
110	Parsons[f]
c. 115 (110–120)	Pervo[g]
c. 115–130	Drury and O'Neill[h]
120–125	Tyson[i]
125	Knox
before 130	Mount[j]
135	Barnikol and Couchoud[k]
Second or third decade of the second century	Overbeck
Deep into the second century	Baur[l]
Middle of the second century	Townsend[m]

[a]Gaventa, *Acts*, 51. Gaventa thinks there is "little evidence" regarding the date of composition of Acts. She considers a date after 70 CE due to the "destruction of Jerusalem (based on Lk. 19:41-44; 21:20-24) and Luke's dependency upon Mark. Since Mark is dated "around 70 CE" and Luke is dependent upon Mark, she assumes a date "after 70" (51). Her upper limit is due to the use of Acts by second-century writers such as Irenaeus (c. 180). Gaventa suggests this second-century usage of Acts implies that "Acts must have been composed and well circulated by then" (51). Hence, she arrives at a date in the 80s or 90s that rests between the two end points suggested by "many scholars" (51). Gaventa does not name any of these scholars, nor does she refer the reader to the considerable array of criteria and evidence available for an earlier or later date.

[b]Hans Conzelmann, *Acts of the Apostles* (Hermeneia; Minneapolis: Fortress, 1987), xxxiii, suggests that "somewhere between 80 and 100 best fits all the evidence."

[c]Shellard, *New Light on Luke*, 30. This is a very specific range that depends largely on Polycarp, *Phil.* 1.5 and "some Western manuscripts of Acts 2.24" that potentially places a cap on the date of the Western text of Acts in line with the early (c. 112–115 CE) date of Polycarp (since they share a common variant). Shellard settles on 98–100 CE but argues based on the Polycarp connection in particular that "Luke-Acts cannot be too much later than 95–100 CE." Shellard, *New Light on Luke*, 25. Cf. also Parsons, *Acts*, 17; Pervo, "Suburbs," 35; and idem, *Dating Acts*, 17–20.

[d]Charles H. Talbert, *Reading Acts: A Literary and Theological Commentary on the Acts of the Apostles* (RNTS; New York: Crossroads, 1997), 237. Bonz, *The Past as Legacy*, 163, without presenting any evidence, states that "Luke is writing at the end of the first century CE." Idem, "Luke's Revision of Paul's Reflection in Romans 9–11," in *Early Christian Voices: In Texts, Traditions, and Symbols—Essays in Honor of François Bovon* (ed. David H. Warren et al.; BibInt 66; Boston: Brill, 2003), 151, claims that Luke is editing Paul's words at the end of Acts. She further estimates that Luke is writing much later from a "more wholly Gentile perspective" (151). This is problematic especially for reasons of a short life expectancy (as stated in my note 64 from this chapter). Perhaps this thinking is recycled from earlier scholars like James C. O'Neill, *The Theology of Acts in its Historical Setting* (London: SPCK, 1961), 93, who considered Acts to reflect the theological developments of the second century. See Tyson, *Marcion*; Pervo, *Dating Acts*; and also Pervo, *Acts*, 685—they all assume a similar projection.

Table 1.4 (*Continued*)

ᵉMore recently, Helmut Koester, *Introduction to the New Testament: History and Literature of Early Christianity* (2nd edn; 2 vols; New York: de Gruyter, 1995–2000), 2:314, scaled back his date from 135 (as noted by Hemer, *Acts*, 370) to 100–110 CE.
ᶠParsons settles for about 110 CE "though a release anytime within the first two decades of the second century (ca. AD 100–120) would have provided sufficient time for Polycarp's knowledge of the book." Cf. Parsons, *Acts*, 17.
ᵍPervo, *Acts*, xv, 5. Later he argues for a date of 115 CE in "Suburbs," 36 and in "The Date of Acts," 6.
ʰO'Neill's, *Theology of Acts*, 21, 25, date is between 115 CE and 130 CE. He considers Edgar J. Goodspeed's, *An Introduction to the New Testament* (Chicago: University of Chicago Press, 1937), view that Paul's letters were "rescued from obscurity and 'published' as a collection" about 90 CE (O'Neill, *Theology of Acts*, 21). "If Goodspeed's thesis is accepted," says O'Neill, then "Luke-Acts cannot be later" than about 90 CE (21). In the end, he argues against this notion via Polycarp as the "first of the Fathers to use a published collection of Paul's letters" (24).
ⁱTyson, *Marcion*, 1–23.
ʲMount says that Luke-Acts was "probably completed sometime before about 130." Mount, *Pauline Christianity*, 168 (n. 17). His reasoning seems to rest on the hypothesis that Luke-Acts belongs after Mark and Matthew, but before Marcion "whom Tertullian places in Rome around 144" (n. 17). He ties this with Papias's comments that also occur prior to 130 CE (169, n. 17).
ᵏPervo, *Dating Acts*, 363.
ˡSince Baur considered the Paul of Acts and the Paul of the epistles as "irreconcilable," he gave a date for Acts as "deep into the second century" (tief in das zweite Jahrhundert). See Gasque, *History*, 40.
ᵐTownsend argues for a much later date "that approaches the middle of the second century." See John T. Townsend, "The Date of Luke-Acts," in *Luke-Acts: New Perspectives from the Society of Biblical Literature Seminar* (ed. Charles H. Talbert; New York: Crossroad, 1984), 47–62. Townsend relies heavily upon comparing Acts with second-century Pseudo-Clementine literature.

Luke-Acts, stating that they "do not quite hit their desired chronological and historical targets."[78] Likewise, Tannehill, while appreciating Pervo's efforts, also remains cautious and states that "P's alternative date of 110–120 should not be taken as the final word."[79]

In Pervo's later short article, "The Date of Acts," he pegs Acts to the world of the Apostolic Fathers (100–150 CE) suggesting that Acts is familiar with post-100 CE "institutions" and "terminology and concepts."[80] Conversely, is this not a chicken and egg anachronistic fallacy? Is it not simpler to argue that the second-century writers are engaging with already established issues and concepts in Acts?[81] It is ironic that one scholar could argue that the early second century is a better theological fit, where

---

[78] F. Scott Spencer, Review of *Dating Acts: Between the Evangelists and the Apologists* by Richard I. Pervo and *Marcion and Luke-Acts: A Defining Struggle*, by Joseph B. Tyson," *Int* 62 (2008): 190–3 (192). He (192) goes on to say that "arguing for direct dependence on particular sources (other than the repeatedly flagged Greek Old Testament [LXX]) or a specific polemical context (Marcionite or otherwise) is a difficult case to make with an anonymous theological narrative like Acts."

[79] Robert C. Tannehill, review of *Dating Acts: Between the Evangelists and the Apologists*, by Richard I. Pervo," *CBQ* 69 (2007): 828.

[80] Pervo, "The Date of Acts," 6; Pervo, "Suburbs," 29–46. It is very doubtful that the kind of Jewish political power narrated in Acts would be present post-70 CE. Cf. Richard N. Longenecker, *The Acts of the Apostles* (12 vols; EBC; Grand Rapids: Zondervan, 1981), 31–4. Likewise, Keener, *Acts*, 1:400, observes Pervo's anachronisms.

[81] Is it really improbable that in the first century the church (or any religious group) held leadership positions (Acts 6:1-7; 20:17-35), helped their widows (Acts 6:1-7; 9:36-41), and dealt with the "misuse of funds" (Acts 5:1-11; 8:14-25) and "deviant teaching?" Contra Pervo, "The Date of Acts," 6. Second, these social structures are already found in the gospels and Paul's earlier letters. Should

others use the exact same argument to argue the exact opposite.[82] The evidence clearly points to Acts as the progenitor.

Pervo's influence continues to be prevalent as seen in Snyder's *Acts of Paul: The Formation of a Pauline Corpus* where he defends Pervo's views while explaining that there is a "*counter-consensus developing* within scholarship on Acts that its 'original text' should be dated as a whole to the second quarter, if not into the third quarter, of the second century."[83] Snyder maintains that Pervo's *Dating Acts* "has provided the most recent thorough argument for late dating," then commences with a summary from Pervo's appendix of late dating scholars who continue to be impacted by Baur and his students.[84] Snyder completely bypasses the contributions "within scholarship" of the early and middle groups, with just a single passing reference to Mittelstaedt's, *Lukas als Historiker*.[85] Although the date of Acts is not central to Snyder's focus, there is still a clear and disappointing dismissal of the arguments put forth by the early and middle groups and an uncritical approval of the "counter-consensus" represented by Pervo and Tyson in particular. It seems that "birds of a feather, flock together" when it comes to the dating issue.

Unfortunately, like Pervo, Tyson opts for a second-century date of Acts rather than critically engaging the arguments of scholars who date Acts in the first century. He dismisses the position of the early group as "flawed" while the middle group is "built on an inadequate foundation."[86] Keener refers to a certain mentality where scholars "dismiss their position rather than considering their arguments seriously"—and it seems that Tyson's dismissal appears to be based on presuppositions on Marcion and the early church as well as those shared by the Westar Institute's sponsored "Acts Seminar."[87] Upon closer examination of Tyson's position, it is arguably "flawed" and his "foundation" is built without solid argumentation.

Tyson argues for a range between 100 and 150 CE because of the church's struggle "with Marcion and Marcionite Christianity."[88] He narrows this to 120–125 CE when Marcion was gathering followers—hence, Luke-Acts is in fact, a reaction to Marcion.[89] This date is problematic for several reasons, first because it fails to account for the combined arguments from the early and middle groups discussed above. Second, it is problematic because it was not until July 144 CE that Marcion left Orthodoxy to found

---

we now date the earliest New Testament letters (e.g., Galatians) into the second century because Galatians addresses (1) deviant teaching all through it (e.g., Gal. 1:6-9), (2) leadership structures (Gal. 2:2, 8, 9), (3) doing good to one's neighbours and one's church family (Gal. 5:6, 13, 14; 6:2, 10), and (4) paying their instructors (Gal. 6:6)?

[82] E.g., Conzelmann, *Acts*, xxxiii, as noted by Bock, *Acts*, 27.

[83] Snyder, *Acts of Paul*, 13–14 (my emphasis). His work stems from his earlier dissertation at Harvard University in 2010 that was given further feedback by Pervo later that fall for his 2013 book.

[84] Ibid., 14 (n. 54). Pervo, *Dating Acts*, 359–63. Tyson, *Marcion*, 5, repeats Baur and the Tübingen school's emphasis on the conflict between the Pauline and Petrine groups that extended into the second century: "Thus, the conciliatory Acts could not have been written until well into the second century."

[85] Cf. Snyder, *Acts of Paul*, 14 (n. 54).

[86] Tyson, *Marcion*, 22.

[87] Keener, *Acts*, 1:383; Tyson, *Marcion*, xii (recall my note 3 above).

[88] Tyson, *Marcion*, 23.

[89] Ibid., 78, and 127 respectively.

his own church.[90] Third, Barton suggests that Marcion was "not a major influence on the formation of the New Testament."[91]

Fourth, Roth considers the text of Marcion's gospel to be "clearly related to Luke *and* prior to the middle of the second century"—together this strains Tyson's late date range of 100–150 CE while his narrowed range of 120–125 CE remains troublesome for the other reasons listed here.[92] Fifth, since Polycarp, *Phil.* 1.5 shares a common variant with some Western manuscripts of Acts 2:24 and can be dated as early as c. 112–115 CE, this presents a further difficulty in Tyson's hypothesis that Luke-Acts is a reaction to Marcion, since the former was circulating at least a decade before the latter.[93] Sixth, Tyson rightly claims that the author of Acts "stresses the community's fidelity to Jewish traditions and practices" and how the "missionary method used by the Paul of Acts and his message to Jews stands in stark contrast to Marcionite theology."[94]

Few, if any, would disagree with Tyson's observations here, but where is the solid evidence that the author of Acts is "reacting against certain fundamental features of Marcionite theology"?[95] The simple and most obvious explanation is that the Jewishness of Acts reflects a time in history when the Temple, its institutions, practices, people, and prayers were central to the early church, and this was clearly not the case in Marcion's day.[96] Additionally, a last point speaks directly to the foundation of Tyson's argument. While second-century manuscripts of Acts are admittedly fragmentary, there remain only references to Marcion's version of Luke by later Christian writers.[97] And for his entire theory, there is not one single available Marcion inspired manuscript of Acts to compare with canonical Acts. Since lower criticism forms the "foundation" for any higher critical study, the foundation of Tyson's position is not only flawed but missing entirely.[98]

---

[90] Lampe, *Valentinus*, 250.
[91] Barton, "Marcion Revisited," 341–54 (354). See Michael J. Kruger, *The Question of Canon: Challenging the Status Quo in the New Testament Debate* (Downers Grove, IL: InterVarsity Press, 2013), 19 (n. 19), who also acknowledges how "Marcion's role in the formation of the canon has been minimized in recent years." Harnack was an early and influential proponent of the idea that "Marcion was responsible for the origins of the New Testament canon." (19 [n. 19]). See Adolf Harnack, *Marcion: Das Evangelium vom fremden Gott* (Leipzig: Hinrichs, 1924) and also John Knox, *Marcion and the New Testament: An Essay in the Early History of the Canon* (Chicago: University of Chicago Press, 1942), *et passim*.
[92] Roth, *Marcion's Gospel*, 1; Tyson, *Marcion*, 23, and 78 respectively.
[93] Shellard, *New Light on Luke*, 30.
[94] See Tyson, *Marcion*, 69, and repeated in: Joseph B. Tyson, "Marcion and the Date of Acts," in *Acts and Christian Beginnings: The Acts Seminar Report* (eds. Dennis E. Smith and Joseph B. Tyson; Salem: Polebridge, 2013), 8–9.
[95] Ibid., 9.
[96] See Falk, "Jewish Prayer," 267.
[97] See Chapter 7 with regard to the textual history of Acts. For an updated comprehensive list of the extant sources for Marcion see Roth, *Marcion's Gospel*, 46–82 (for a reconstruction of Marcion's gospel as it follows canonical Luke see pp. 412–36).
[98] See Stanley E. Porter and Andrew W. Pitts, *Fundamentals of New Testament Textual Criticism* (Grand Rapids: Eerdmans, 2015), 3, on the foundational aspects of textual (or lower) criticism.

Overview of the Present Study

Given the current state of scholarship discussed above, and in light of the issues and arguments presented among the early, middle, and late proponents, the aim of this study is to provide a comprehensive solution to this ongoing research problem. The primary goal of this first chapter is to bring the reader up to date on the exact nature of the debate as well as provide an overview of the common questions and opinions associated with the topic in general.[99] A subsidiary goal is to go beyond a survey of positions and listen carefully to the views of scholars from ancient times to the present day with an ear for the presuppositions and problems that lie beneath them.

Chapter 2 explores the various methodological approaches in concert with the presuppositions of key scholars, including my own.[100] The underlying philosophy of approach for this project is that historical *and* literary concerns need to be addressed to ensure a firm foundation for any conclusions. The approach then is to critically examine the sources as well as the major theories on the date of Acts and apply the principles of historiography, textual criticism, papyrology, and modern linguistics to the debate.

Chapter 3 examines the sources for Acts and considers how various theories impact the way we date Acts. This chapter also re-examines several source-related subjects such as the "we" passages, Luke's prefaces, and his attention to matters of geography, lodging, and politics. Subsequently, in Chapter 4, the issue of Acts being dependent upon Paul's letters or the works of Josephus remains at the centre of the debate and are examined in sequence. As a result, such theories are shown to remain problematic and Acts is decisively placed into a much earlier time frame than espoused by the late group of scholars in particular.

Since the end of Acts has played a key role in the date of Acts debate, Chapter 5 examines the various interpretations that frequently start with the presupposition of a post-70 CE date based on the so-called majority of scholarship without any substantial justification or engagement with the existing research. These theories are examined in detail and found to be highly speculative and methodologically troublesome. Subsequently, Chapter 6 explores the scholarship on the Jewish response to the gospel in Acts (and Acts 28:17-28 specifically) and finds further evidence in support of an early date of Acts.

With the aid and application of modern principles of papyrology and textual criticism, the purpose of Chapter 7 is to understand the significance of the Acts variants in relation to the often debated and yet ever-present "Western" tendencies (see also: "Appendix: The Manuscript Record for Acts 28:11-31"). Here it is shown that the manuscript record for the end of Acts (28:11-31) offers additional evidence for an early date of Acts in light of the unique transmission history of its texts. Chapter 8

---

[99] Cf. Jeannette Kamp, Susan Legêne, Matthias van Rossum, and Sebas Rümke, eds., *Writing History! A Companion for Historians* (Amsterdam: Amsterdam University Press, 2018), 22–3.

[100] Stanley E. Porter and Jason C. Robinson, *Hermeneutics: An Introduction to Interpretive Theory* (Grand Rapids: Eerdmans, 2011), 10.

inculcates the insights from the previous chapters and places the book of Acts in a realistic historical setting and timeline that is supported by, but not dependent on, literary theories and devices alone. In the concluding Chapter 9, I have provided a survey of what I consider to be the most important points from each chapter. My hope is that this chapter will act as a summary guide for further research on dating Acts, the NT, and other ancient documents.

2

A Historiographical Approach to the Date of Acts

Introduction

Until recently, there has been very little response to the three most prolific and conflicting monographs on the date of Acts—Pervo, Tyson, and Mittelstaedt.¹ The first two monographs, as outlined in Chapter 1, argue for an early second-century date while the third argues for an early date of 62 CE. While Pervo in particular has received widespread attention, Mittelstaedt has not.² Meanwhile, a great number of scholars are content to give the issue of dating Acts a passing reference as if it has no bearing on the interpretation of Acts or its place in *history*, which is (or should be) a fundamental concern to NT scholars.³

The date of Acts (and the interpretation of Acts in general) is currently, and historically, a matter of relentless debate. There are countless ways that an ancient text such as the book of Acts has been interpreted and yet, from a position informed by *historiography*, any interpretation that fails to seriously consider its date will suffer a measure of deficiency. Chronology is also vital for the interpretation of texts and yet students and scholars alike "usually accept dates given to them in textbooks without thinking about where the dates are derived from or on what sort of evidence they

---

¹ The methods and conclusions are very conflicting: Mittelstaedt, *Lukas als Historiker*; Pervo, *Dating Acts*; and Tyson, *Marcion*. Since Hemer, *Acts*, 365–414, the most recent and thorough commentary covering this issue is Keener, *Acts*, 1:382–401. Cf. also Snyder, *Acts of Paul*, 13–14; Porter, *When Paul Met Jesus*, 75–9; idem, "Early Church," 72–100; and most recently, Armstrong, "A New Plea," (2017): 79–110, and idem, "Variants," 87–110.
² I am not sure why this detailed work flew under the radar but I am surmising it did for three reasons: (1) it is in German, or (2) it argues for an early date which is not as popular a position against the middle and later dating groups, or (3) the date of Acts has not received the attention it deserves in recent years. Perhaps it is some combination of all three.
³ Recently, Daniel A. Woolf, *A Concise History of History: Global Historiography from Antiquity to the Present* (Cambridge: Cambridge University Press, 2019), 3, suggested that the word history means the "forms in which the past is recovered, thought of, spoken and written down." According to Tosh, *Pursuit* (6th edn), x, the word history carries two meanings in general discussion. It refers both to "what actually happened in the past" as well as the "representation of that past in the work of historians." Roy Harris, *The Linguistics of History* (Edinburgh: Edinburgh University Press, 2004), 31–2, claims that the question "What is History?" is a "bogus question to start with" (see his argument on p. 15 outlining the linguistic difficulties of claiming that history carries two meanings).

are based."[4] As reported in the first chapter, many reputable and well-intentioned NT scholars are guilty of the same thing. There is nothing wrong with accepting a certain date for a document or an event, but it should never be done without some measure of critical enquiry.[5]

For NT scholars, it seems problematic to quickly venture into matters of interpretation without first tackling the core issue of dating. However, this dating process is not as "cut and dried" as the "acceptance of a specific numerical date for a particular object or event might allow us to believe."[6] Regardless of the inherent difficulties with such a task, an approach to the date of Acts that is informed by recent historiographical theory and methods offers a better framework and ability to deal with sources and evidence.[7]

Dating is a complex enterprise. Biers further comments on how the "specifics of the ancient world are seen through a haze, or fog, depending on where one looks, and chronology can be one of the more hazy areas."[8] The date of Acts and the associated chronology of the events it narrates (and excludes) is no exception to this haze as the ongoing debate suggests. The present study embraces the "haze," but also attempts to expand on the "scene" while painting a clearer, alternative version of the story given the available data.[9]

Setting aside the "haze" of the dating issue, I do sympathize with Pervo's argument that the "general consensus by which Acts has been dated *c.* 80–90 is not well founded."[10] My contention is that there are simply too many problems with any date beyond 64

---

[4] William R. Biers, *Art, Artifacts and Chronology in Classical Archaeology* (London: Routledge, 1992), x.

[5] See Marc Bloch, *The Historian's Craft* (trans. Peter Putnam; New York: Vintage, 1953), 20.

[6] Biers, *Chronology*, x.

[7] There have been only a few NT studies to date. Cf. Beth Sheppard, *The Craft of History and the Study of the New Testament* (SBLRBS 60; Atlanta: SBL, 2012); Michael R. Licona, *The Resurrection of Jesus: A New Historiographical Approach* (Downers Grove, IL: InterVarsity Press, 2010), and Stanley E. Porter, "The Witness of Extra-Gospel Literary Sources to the Infancy Narratives of the Synoptic Gospels," in *The Gospels: History and Christology. The Search of Joseph Ratzinger-Benedict XVI/ I Vangeli: Storia e Cristologia. La Ricerca di Joseph Ratzinger-Benedetto XVI* (eds. Bernardo Estrada et al.; 2 vols; Rome: Libreria Editrice Vaticana, 2013), 1:419–65.

[8] Biers, *Chronology*, x. Biers (x) continues to say that often it is "as if antiquity is being viewed through a telescope backwards; the image in the lens is tiny, only shows a portion of the scene, and there is no depth or perspective in the picture."

[9] There are some exceptions in history where the chronology is not hazy. The destruction of Pompeii and Herculaneum by the eruption of Vesuvius in 79 CE provides one of the clearest examples of historical dating. See Biers, *Chronology*, 18; Alison E. Cooley and M. G. L. Cooley, *Pompeii and Herculaneum: A Sourcebook* (2nd edn; London: Routledge, 2014), 43; Pliny the Younger, *Ep.* 6:16 and 20; and Cassius Dio, *Hist. Rom.*, 66.19–20. It was from Puteoli (modern-day Pozzuoli), the strategic port city for Neapolis (Naples), that Pliny the Younger wrote his eyewitness account about the eruption that killed his father (Pliny the Elder). Luke mentions Puteoli as a part of a weeklong stopover before finally arriving in Rome (Acts 28:13-14). Since there does not appear to be any clear motive for omitting the disaster it either did not happen yet, or it happened so long ago there was no need to mention it. See Cadbury, *Luke-Acts*, 48, and Kamp et al., *Writing History!*, 77.

[10] Pervo, *Dating Acts*, vii. The evidence is lacking for this date as Porter similarly explains that an intermediate date of 80 is "not so much argued for as tacitly accepted, because scholars do not want to accept the late date or an early date." Porter, "Early Church," 93. He claims there is "far more substance to arguing for an early date for Acts" (93) that is "somewhere around AD 62–65, with the Gospel finished beforehand" (95).

CE—especially with the destruction of Jerusalem in 70 CE—that grow exponentially with each passing year into the second century. Every scholar is entitled to their own opinion but there are far too many inconsistencies with the consensus and later dating perspectives. Since any rejection of the middle range (post-70 CE to ±80 CE) requires "arguing against the grain," more effort and assimilation of the evidence will be required than a simple "acceptance of the consensus."[11] The extra effort required to evaluate the literary evidence against the historical record is worth it in light of the importance of Acts for the church, academy, and its contribution to first-century Roman history.[12]

Although the methods vary, the critical task before us is to "illuminate" the place of Acts in the "history of early Christianity."[13] A key factor in this placement is to establish the *historical context* of Acts, which is inexorably tied to its date.[14] A different date produces a different context and a different interpretation—this is at the heart of why this study is so important.[15] An accurate estimation should be of immense value for biblical scholars and theologians for our understanding of the early church, its birth, development, mission, and message.[16] If the book of Acts is a better fit for the second century (rather than the first), then the interpretation of the speeches and events it narrates will be necessarily different.

---

[11] Pervo, *Dating Acts*, viii. Consensus is perhaps too generous of a word to use for 2006, but especially in recent years: Porter, "Early Church," 89–96; Armstrong, "A New Plea," (2017): 79–110; and idem, "Variants," 87–110.

[12] "There can be no doubt," says Cadbury, that this "earliest little essay of Church History is *one of the most important narratives ever written*. Its importance is shown by the extraordinary darkness which comes over us as students of history when rather abruptly this guide leaves us with Paul a prisoner in Rome" (my emphasis). Henry J. Cadbury, *The Book of Acts in History* (London: Black, 1955), 3. Cadbury is correct, but with every difficulty, an opportunity presents itself for a new understanding of old problems. Acts offers a significant amount of information concerning the city of Rome (Acts 2:10; 18:2; 19:21; 23:11; 25:25, 27; 28:11-31) and Jerusalem (Acts 1:4, 8, 12, 19; 2:5, 14; 63 references in total).

[13] Pervo, *Dating Acts*, viii.

[14] Munslow, *Deconstructing History*, 45, refers to the British historian John Tosh, *The Pursuit of History: Aims, Methods and New Directions in the Study of Modern History* (2nd edn; London: Longman, 1991), 53, who says that the "interpretation of the evidence cannot *literally* generate a meaning, without 'a command of the historical context' which will reveal that to which the evidence corresponds" (Munslow's emphasis). Historians (and I would include NT scholars as well) "cannot understand the past by only consulting the textual evidence. They must place it within the broader framework of which they are aware, the context, in order to reconstruct the past as it really was" (Munslow, *Deconstructing History*, 45). Just as an archaeological find requires careful attention to its "precise location in the site," Tosh, *Pursuit* (6th edn), 10, claims that we "must place everything we know about the past in its contemporary context." Although it is critical that we understand the historical context of our written sources we can only achieve this by "reading *other* texts" (original emphasis). See Benjamin Ziemann and Miriam Dobson, "Introduction," in *Reading Primary Sources: The Interpretation of Texts from Nineteenth- and Twentieth-Century History* (eds. Miriam Dobson and Benjamin Ziemann; 2nd edn; RGHS; London: Routledge, 2020), 14. Therefore, historians should study the "material circumstances in which a text was produced and disseminated in order to pinpoint as carefully as possible the milieu in which it was written and read" (14). And since we are learning new things about context all the time, we have to be cautious about our conclusions (editing insight by Porter).

[15] The texts should reflect (with a certain degree of confidence) a particular time period. Bloch, *Craft*, 28, explains that "no historian would be satisfied to state that Caesar devoted eight years to the conquest of Gaul … It is of far greater importance to him to assign the conquest of Gaul its *exact chronological place* amid the vicissitudes of European societies" (my emphasis).

[16] See Fitzmyer, *Acts*, 55, and the merited responses by Tyson, *Marcion*, 1, and Pervo, *Dating Acts*, viii.

Nevertheless, scholars should remain abundantly "charitable in their disagreements" with respect to an estimated date, but given the wide range of dates, vague opinions and statements that remain (1) either too general or (2) unsubstantiated should be ruled out based on a better interpretation of the combined evidence.[17] Dubious estimates on the date of Acts, along with the implications and conclusions on the place of Acts *in* history (or upon the history *in* Acts), should be critically challenged and dismissed.[18]

Contemporary Approaches to the Date of Acts

A survey of the debate reveals that the majority of approaches to dating Acts employ some form of literary, narrative (narratological), or source criticism as a methodology.[19] In short, there appears to be no clearly defined methodology in all three of the most recent monographs, and since the date of Acts is an issue clearly related to history it seems rather negligent that the first two approaches especially—and NT scholars in general—are not aware of or engaged with current trends and methods in historiography.[20]

Pervo, for example, relies on a modern revision of source criticism known as "intertextuality" for his methodology.[21] He relies on MacDonald's version of intertextuality, which has set forth criteria for identifying the "hypertext" and

---

[17] Keener, *Acts*, 1:383.
[18] Cadbury, *Acts in History*, 3.
[19] The literary arguments of Tyson and Pervo especially, while focused predominantly on late first-century and early-mid second-century texts, significantly lack historiographical and text-critical concerns. Hemer, *Acts*, 1–29, 365–408, is correct—Acts must be studied in relation to its historical context.
[20] Pervo, *Dating Acts*; Tyson, *Marcion*; Mittelstaedt, *Lukas als Historiker*. One notable exception is Sheppard's overview of historiography for NT scholars in *The Craft of History and the Study of the New Testament* (SBLRBS 60; Atlanta: SBL, 2012). Porter, "Literary Sources," 1:428 [n. 16], considers Sheppard's work "overall a fine introduction to historiography for New Testament scholars" minus some missing criteria related to his own study. Cf. also Christopher Skinner's, review of Sheppard's *The Craft of History and the Study of the New Testament* in *RelSRev* 40 (2014): 155, short but positive remarks. Meanwhile Richard I. Pervo, review of Sheppard's *The Craft of History* in *CBQ* 77 (2015): 186, does not give Sheppard a favourable review but insists that "the guild does need a current, short, balanced primer in critical thinking, with an outline of the development of various methods." See also Ken Olson, review of Sheppard's *The Craft of History* in *RBL* 06 (2014): 1–4, and Joseph E. Sanzo's, review of Sheppard's *The Craft of History* in *RBL* 06 (2014): 1–4 (both are critical). Porter, "Literary Sources," 1:427, in reference to Licona, *Resurrection*, 19 (n. 8), remarks how it is "not only New Testament scholars that are limited in their exposure to the variety of historiographical methods" but also that "courses in historiography are rarely if ever taught in religious studies departments of even supposedly prestigious institutions." See also Porter's, "Literary Sources," 1:427 (n. 14), assessment of Licona's useful but oversimplified argument from historiography.
[21] Pervo, *Dating Acts*, 7–8, 13, 26–7; Robert F. Stoops, "Introduction: Apocryphal Acts of the Apostles in Intertextual Perspectives," in *The Apocryphal Acts of the Apostles in Intertextual Perspectives* (eds. Robert F. Stoops and Dennis R. MacDonald; SemeiaSt 80; Atlanta: Scholars Press, 1977), 1–10; Dennis R. MacDonald, ed., *Mimesis and Intertextuality in Antiquity and Christianity* (London: T&T Clark, 2001). See also Julia Kristeva, *The Kristeva Reader* (ed. Toril Moi; New York: Columbia University Press, 1986), 37, who is the progenitor of this method that sees texts behind texts. Intertextuality goes beyond finding an author's source while recognizing that the "production and reception of texts is always conditioned by a larger web of 'texts,' both written and unwritten." Pervo, *Dating Acts*, 7; Stoops, "Apocryphal Acts," 1.

"hypotext" in determining intertextual relationships.²² Pervo considers the "sheer volume of parallels" between Acts and other texts and admits he does not "apply these criteria to each case, but with two exceptions, they are *implicit throughout*."²³ However, criteria aside, should not a true "parallel" be explicit and obvious?²⁴ Perhaps the parallels are much easier to see if one is already conditioned to find them—as he automatically presumes (without justification) that Josephus's *Antiquities* and the Pauline letter collection "appeared later than the conventional date of (Luke and) Acts."²⁵

Setting aside Pervo's method, Tyson's methodology seems rather ambiguous. He appears passionate about Marcion, his life, theology and practice, influence and relationship to Paul's letters, and Marcion's version of the gospel; however, it seems that this preoccupation feeds his presupposition and ultimately his conclusion.²⁶ Tyson's actual method seems to be finding literary "themes" and "patterns" in Acts while examining the "characterization" of Peter and Paul and then drawing conclusions based on those themes.²⁷

Meanwhile Mittelstaedt's "Vorgehensweise" seems to employ a historical-critical method akin to Hemer that emphasizes the "Datierungskriterium,"²⁸ "Die Zerstörung Jerusalems,"²⁹ and "Die anderen Datierungskriterien."³⁰ For Mittelstaedt this really

---

[22] Pervo, *Dating Acts*, 26; Dennis R. MacDonald, *The Homeric Epics and the Gospel of Mark* (New Haven: Yale University Press, 2000), 8–9. Pervo (26) explains that the "hypertext" indicates the "receptor text" which is "the proposed user of a source" while the "hypotext" points to the "undoubted or hypothetical source." The criteria he (26) adapts are "accessibility, analogy, density, order, distinctiveness, and interpretability."

[23] Pervo, *Dating Acts*, 27 (my emphasis). The two exceptions are "accessibility" and "order." Some of the "parallels" are dubious, such as highlighting "circumcision" in Acts 10:45; Gal. 2:12; Rom. 4:12; Col. 4:11; and Tit. 1:10. Cf. Idem, *Dating Acts*, 91. The "search for parallels is an attractive and often useful undertaking, but it is also fraught with danger." See Hemer, *Acts*, 63, and Samuel Sandmel, "Parallelomania," *JBL* 81 (1962): 1–13.

[24] His selective application of criteria seems to seriously weaken what he constitutes as a "parallel"—since he considers them to be "implicit throughout."

[25] Pervo, *Dating Acts*, 380 (n. 89). Chapter 4 of this volume directly addresses these two areas of historic debate in detail. Pervo's, *Acts*, xv, "delight" in finding parallels with Acts and ancient novels began with his doctoral work.

[26] Cf. Tyson, *Marcion*, his chapter 2 (24–49). Tyson's view stems from his teacher John Knox, who earlier proposed that Acts was "composed as a post-Marcionite and anti-Marcionite text" with one of the author's purposes being to "disassociate Paul from Marcion." See Tyson, *Marcion*, 16 (here), and his chapter 3 (50–78); John Knox, "Acts and the Pauline Letter Corpus," in *Studies in Luke-Acts: Essays Presented in Honor of Paul Schubert* (eds. Leander E. Keck and J. Louis Martyn; Nashville: Abingdon, 1966), 279–87. Tyson (23) hypothesizes that the "struggle of the church with Marcion and Marcionite Christianity provides the most likely context for the writing of Acts." Recall my six arguments in Chapter 1 (pp. 18–19) against Tyson's hypothesis that (Luke-) Acts is a reaction to Marcion.

[27] Tyson, *Marcion*, 50–78 (on the characterization of Peter see pp. 60–2; on Paul see 62–76). Marcion, p. 69, attributes the "stark contrast" (between Marcionite theology and Paul's missionary method) as an attempt by Luke to convince a Jewish audience that Jesus is the fulfilment of the prophets. Could not this contrast be more easily attributed to Marcion's anti-Jewish sentiment towards Luke's writing decades later?

[28] Mittelstaedt, *Lukas als Historiker*, 49–250.

[29] Ibid., 49–163.

[30] Ibid., 165–250 (this section includes a note on "Das Schweigen über den Tod des Paulus" [165–220] and "Weitere Kriterien" [221–50]).

comes down to a balancing of probabilities: "And where proven facts are the exception, the balancing of probabilities is a legitimate, and sometimes the only possible method for obtaining scientific knowledge."[31] The basic premise of his argumentation is sound; however, his methodology is not well developed and he does not seem to understand or value the ways that papyrology and textual criticism contribute to the argument. In the end, he concludes with an early date for Acts being written in 62 CE in either Caesarea or Philippi.[32]

It is unfortunate and ironic that Pervo and Tyson especially neglect both the historical context and the actual manuscripts of Acts.[33] They compare the first-century and second-century literary environment with the book of Acts, find some parallels, and argue for dependency.[34] Oftentimes these "over-imaginative" approaches, which differ little from traditional historical criticism, suggest the author of Acts is endowed with "sophisticated literary skill" enough to intentionally ignore the broader historical context and especially Paul's letters.[35] While addressing the texts is a fundamental aspect of this debate, it is vital to place these texts within a historical framework that values the contributions of previous scholars. Rather than relying on a simple comparison of "vocabulary and style" used between ancient authors (i.e. Luke and Josephus), the scope for this project is much more comprehensive and draws from multiple disciplines.[36]

In essence, there are two major fields of research in this debate centering on (1) comparative texts and (2) the historical context. While later dating advocates rely primarily on a comparative study of the texts (Pervo/Tyson especially), the middle and especially early groups (recall Chapter 1) draw heavily upon historical considerations; the decisive and dividing issue that separates the early and middle groups is the fall of Jerusalem, with Acts and its relationship to the city of Rome a close second. Since the events alluded to in Acts and Josephus can often be dated with relative accuracy, and at times with precision, it seems negligent to ignore elements of historical criteria (i.e., datable matters of history) in favour of speculative literary theories, comparisons, and devices (see Chapter 5).

At the same time, higher literary critical methods applied in this debate are often lacking in a lower critical foundation of modern principles of textual criticism and devoid of any consideration of recent advances in grammar and linguistics. There is also a distinct lack of awareness of the long-standing epistemological debates occurring

---

[31] Ibid., 17. "Und wo bewiesene Fakten die Ausnahme sind, ist das Abwägen von Wahrscheinlichkeiten eine legitime, weil zuweilen die einzig mögliche Methode zur Gewinnung wissenschaftlicher Erkenntnis."
[32] See ibid., 251–5.
[33] Along with other foundational text critical issues (see Chapter 7).
[34] Recall my comments on the "chicken and egg anachronistic fallacy" in Chapter 1 (17).
[35] See Charles K. Barrett, review of *The First Christian Historian: Writing the "Acts of the Apostles,"* by Daniel Marguerat, *JTS* 55 (2004): 255.
[36] E.g., Pervo, *Dating Acts*, 13. Dating *any* historical document requires attention to several factors but especially to the primary and secondary sources. See Kamp et al., *Writing History!*, 33–60; Robert C. Williams, *The Historian's Toolbox: A Student's Guide to the Theory and Craft of History* (2nd edn; Armonk, NY: M. E. Sharpe, 2007), 56–78. The dividing and decisive issue among historians boils down to *how* primary sources and historical texts should be read. See Ziemann and Dobson, "Introduction," 1–2, 5–16.

among philosophers and historians.[37] Therefore, a comprehensive approach to this problem is necessary in order to address the (1) historical and (2) literary (text-critical and linguistic) concerns fairly and adequately.[38] A historiographical approach draws from principles of historiography and will provide a "strong" and "adequate" foundation for addressing the criteria within the two major fields of inquiry.[39]

This historiographical approach (from start to finish) is a consciously subjective reflection of the many ways that each of the ancient, modern, and more recent scholars have contributed to the date of Acts and its place in history.[40] One could say that this historiography is merely *a* written history of *how* the date of Acts has been interpreted—but knowing this history is only the beginning.[41] In doing so, the goal is to discover what "actually [or probably] happened in the past" through the *narrative* of Acts and the interpreters who have contributed to the subject since ancient times.[42]

Modern Movements and Trends in Historiography

This section will provide a brief overview of some of the key figures and major movements in historiography from empiricism to post-structuralism. The purpose of this overview is meant to give a snapshot of the ongoing discussion of what *history* is and how we should approach it from the mid-nineteenth century up to the present day.[43] Since historiography as a discipline is relatively unknown in NT studies, this section is designed to provide some basic knowledge of the trends, methods, and principles.

---

[37] Green and Troup, *Houses*, 289 (2nd edn), explain that since the 1980s and 1990s "controversies raged around history and postmodernism, and history and poststructuralism." Cf. also Ziemann and Dobson, "Introduction," 1–20; Philipp Müller, "Understanding History: Hermeneutics and Source-criticism in Historical Scholarship," in Ziemann and Dobson, *Reading Primary Sources*, 23–40; Christoph Reinfandt, "Reading Texts after the Linguistic Turn: Approaches from Literary Studies and their Implications," in Ziemann and Dobson, *Reading Primary Sources*, 41–58.
[38] The issue of whether Acts should be considered as a historical document is taken up in greater detail in Chapter 8.
[39] Contra Tyson, *Marcion*, 22.
[40] Williams, *Toolbox*, 117; Michael J. Salevouris and Conal Furay, *The Methods and Skills of History: A Practical Guide* (4th edn; Chichester, West Sussex: Wiley-Blackwell, 2015), 255.
[41] Alun Munslow, *A History of History* (London: Routledge, 2012), 7.
[42] See Tosh, *Pursuit* (6th edn), x; Devin O. Pendas, "Testimony," in Ziemann and Dobson, *Reading Primary Sources*, 258. Naturally there is a very important filter in this process as demonstrated by the critical works by Hayden White, *Tropics of Discourse: Essays in Cultural Criticism* (Baltimore: Johns Hopkins University Press, 1978) and idem, *The Content of the Form: Narrative Discourse and Historical Representation* (Baltimore: Johns Hopkins University Press, 1987)—see esp. p. 4 and his comments on the "nature of narration and narrativity."
[43] For further study and links to research on the broader movements see Green and Troup, *Houses* (2nd edn); Roger Spalding and Christopher Parker, *Historiography: An Introduction* (Manchester: Manchester University Press, 2007); Eileen Ka-May Cheng, *Historiography: An Introductory Guide* (London: Continuum, 2012); Norman James Wilson's, *History in Crisis? Recent Directions in Historiography* (2nd edn; Upper Saddle River, NJ: Pearson Prentice Hall, 2005), 70–104, instructive chapter 5 on the "Varieties of Histories" and the essays in Michael Bentley, ed., *Companion to Historiography* (London: Routledge, 1997). See also Woolf, *A Concise History*, and his excellent bibliography at the end of each chapter.

Empiricist Historiography

Without question, empiricism remains the most persuasive epistemological movement, having been popularized by Leopold von Ranke in the mid-nineteenth century.[44] Even today most historians (and arguably the vast majority of NT scholars) are being influenced by some form of empiricism in their methodology.[45] The first principle of empirical history emphasizes careful source evaluation, the second requires "impartial research," and the third principle employs the "inductive method of reasoning."[46] The empirical method, therefore, relies on historians not forcing their questions on the material, but rather allowing the material to raise questions of its own.[47] This caution becomes all the more valuable given the fact that the "premature consignment of unfamiliar evidence to familiar categories" is difficult to avoid as even "apprentice historians know."[48]

In fact such predetermined theorizing is quite common and frequently the by-product of "inferences" that are "impossible to prove."[49] The reason for such incompatibility among the various interpretations is that the same evidence can produce "two quite different stories about the past."[50] This is exactly what is happening with the date of Acts debate—everyone is sifting through the same evidence but arriving at different conclusions (see Selecting and Interpreting Primary and Secondary Sources below). Further complicating matters is the fact that there seems to be widespread disagreement on what constitutes "evidence."

---

[44] Green and Troup, *Houses* (2nd edn), 13–14. On Ranke and his influence see John Warren, "The Rankean Tradition in British Historiography, 1840 to 1950," in *Writing History: Theory and Practice* (eds. Stefen Berger et al.; London: Arnold, 2003), 23–41; Spalding and Parker, *Historiography*, 8–10; Richard J. Evans, *In Defence of History* (London: Granta, 1997), 15–23; Carr, *History?*, 5; Bently, *Companion to Historiography*, 419–23; George G. Iggers, *The German Conception of History: The National Tradition of Historical Thought from Herder to the Present* (rev. edn; Middletown, CT: Wesleyan University Press, 1983); and Leopold von Ranke, *The Theory and Practice of History* (Indianapolis: Bobbs-Merrill, 1973).

[45] Green and Troup, *History* (2nd edn), 13. According to Ian Evans and Nicholas D. Smith, *Knowledge* (Cambridge: Polity Press, 2012), 1–19, there continues to be a great need to focus on theory *and* method in historiography.

[46] Green and Troup, *Houses* (2nd edn), 15.

[47] G. R. Elton, *The Practice of History* (Sydney: Sydney University Press, 1967), 83. Quentin Skinner, "Sir Geoffrey Elton and the Practice of History," *TRHS* 7 (1997): 307, similarly affirms the "salutary warning" that we need to "avoid fitting the evidence" that we examine into "pre-existing patterns of interpretation and explanation."

[48] Skinner, "Sir Geoffrey Elton," 307. See, for example, Philip Abrams's, *Historical Sociology* (Shepton Mallet, UK: Open, 1982), 306–7 critique of G. R. Elton, *Reformation Europe* (London: Fontana, 1963) where everything from Elton's choice for the title of the book to the familiar tale of Luther's 95 theses being nailed to the door of the church in Wittenburg is a case of "sociological theorising on a major scale" (307). Tosh, *Pursuit* (6th edn), 154, rightly explains that "facts are not given, they are selected. Despite appearances, they are never left to speak for themselves."

[49] Green and Troup, *Houses* (2nd edn), 19. See also Tosh (6th edn), and his chapter 7 (148–79) on the limits of historical knowledge. It is no surprise then to hear of the difficulties in finding agreement among historians (or NT scholars for that matter) given the fact that many historical events are "open to a multiplicity of interpretations." Green and Troup, *Houses* (2nd edn), 20. See also White, *Tropics of Discourse*, 55, and his concern for the adequacy/inadequacy of interpreting events. For significant events that have often been neglected entirely by the middle and late group, see Chapter 8 of this volume.

[50] Green and Troup, *Houses* (2nd edn), 20.

All of this subjectivity leads us to the question of relativism, where "absolute truth is unattainable" because "all statements about history are connected or relative to the position of those who make them."[51] If we are ever to regain respect within the broader discipline of history, NT scholars must deal with the relativist critique—that the historians' contemporary situation influences their interpretations of the past. Ultimately, historical writing is the product of the historian "while the historian, before he begins to write history, is the product of history."[52]

This is a useful point concerning our historiographical approach to the date of Acts. Before we begin with the "facts" we need to start first with the mind of the "historian." What are the chief influences and presuppositions behind each of the scholars and how might this affect their selection of sources and ultimately their interpretation? What underlying theories are driving their inferences and conclusions? Regardless, certain epistemological processes are at work in each case long before the assemblage and interpretation of the bits of data that recreate a certain view of history.[53]

Post-structural Historiography

After the Second World War, the landscape of historiography changed dramatically with the advent of postmodernism.[54] Historians began to think about history not as a collection of facts from *the past* but as *a story*—an imperfect interpretation of those events in time.[55] Since the advent of postmodernism, the influence of post-structuralism

---

[51] Ibid., 20. Peter Novick, *That Noble Dream: The 'Objectivity Question' and the American Historical Profession* (Cambridge: Cambridge University Press, 1988), 259 in his watershed study on the question of objectivity points to the earlier work of the revisionist historian Beard who argues that historians should strive towards objective truth even though such truth is illusive. Novick (573) looks at the issue of historical objectivity in historiography from its enthronement in the 1880s to the 1980s and finds it problematic and a "sweeping challenge to the objectivist program of the founding fathers of the historical profession." See Charles A. Beard, "That Noble Dream," *AHR* 41 (1935): 86–7 and more recently Reinfandt, "Reading Texts," 41–58.

[52] Carr, *History?*, 40. Carr (22) contends that the "facts of history never come to us 'pure' ... they are always refracted through the mind of the recorder." Hence our "first concern" should not be with "the facts which it contains but with the historian who wrote it" and the historian who interprets it (22). See also Novick, *Dream*, 259, and earlier Beard, "Dream," 86–7.

[53] Cf. Porter, "Witness," 1:431–2. For a recent discussion on epistemology, knowledge, and understanding see the recent essays in Stephen R. Grimm et al., eds., *Explaining Understanding: New Perspectives from Epistemology and Philosophy of Science* (New York, NY: Routledge, 2017) and especially Christoph Baumberger, "What is Understanding? An Overview of Recent Debates in Epistemology and Philosophy of Science," in *Explaining Understanding*, 1–34; Ernst Sosa, *Epistemology* (Princeton, NJ: Princeton University Press, 2017); James Pryor, "Highlights of Recent Epistemology," *BSPS* 52 (2001): 95–124; Evans and Smith, *Knowledge*, 1–19; and the insightful essay by Antony Easthope, "Romancing the Stone: History-Writing and Rhetoric," *SH* 18 (1993): 235–49 (esp. pp. 236–40 and his section on the "Epistemological Question").

[54] See Williams, *Toolbox*, 117. Munslow, *Deconstructing History*, 18, claims that *deconstructive history* is sometimes equated with postmodern history and the linguistic turn. Stella Tillyard, "All Our Pasts: The Rise of Popular History," *TLS* 5402 (2006): 9, claims that "we did not need postmodernism to tell us that objectivity was always a chimera, that individual historians, their lives, loves and beliefs, are always there, in choice of subject and argument and in the very words they write." Cited by Reinfandt, "Reading Texts," 47.

[55] Cf. White, *Tropics of Discourse*, 55; Idem, *Form*; Frank R. Ankersmit et al., eds., *Re-Figuring Hayden White* (Stanford, CA: Stanford University Press, 2009); Paul Herman, *Hayden White: The Historical Imagination* (Cambridge, UK: Polity Press, 2011), *et passim*. Munslow, *A History*, 7, uses the helpful

on historiography has reinforced the importance of subjectivity in historical accounts.[56] Post-structuralism branched away from empiricists' sole reliance on "facts," noting that facts are of no value without an understanding of the subject's language.[57]

Hence, the issue of using and interpreting language is central to this shift in thinking that has otherwise been referred to as a "linguistic turn."[58] Accordingly, post-structuralist historians argue that "language shapes our reality" but at the same time it does "not necessarily reflect it."[59] Consequently, where post-structural historians

---

description of "the-past-*as*-history" as a "reminder of the practical situation that 'the past' and 'history' belong to different ontological categories. Their 'being' is different. The ontological category of 'the past' can be defined as what once was but is no more, whereas 'history' exists in the category of a narrative that we construct (or write if you prefer) about 'the past.'" In summary, he (7) says that "history is a narrative" written about the past. For further study, see Frank R. Ankersmit, *History and Tropology: The Rise and Fall of Metaphor* (Berkeley: University of California Press, 1994); idem, *Narrative Logic: A Semantic Analysis of the Historian's Language* (The Hague: Matinus Nijhoff, 1983); John D. Caputo, *Deconstruction in a Nutshell* (New York: Fordham University Press, 1997); Jacques Derrida, *Writing and Difference* (trans. Alan Bass; Chicago: University of Chicago Press, 1978); idem, *Of Grammatology* (trans. G. C. Spivak; Baltimore: The Johns Hopkins University Press, 1976); Keith Jenkins, ed., *Postmodern History Reader* (London: Routledge, 1997); idem, *At the Limits of History: Essays on Theory and Practice* (London: Routledge, 2009); Michel Foucault, *The Archaeology of Knowledge* (New York: Harper & Row, 1972); Alun Munslow, *The New History* (Harlow, UK: Pearson-Longman, 2003).

[56] Anna Green and Kathleen Troup eds., *The Houses of History: A Critical Reader in Twentieth-Century History of Theory* (New York: New York University Press, 1999), 7. Postmodern, post-structural and even deconstruction are often used as synonyms by some historians. It is helpful to see postmodernism as a "'historical description . . . of an age,' poststructuralism as 'a . . . bundle of theories and intellectual practices, that derives from a creative engagement with its predecessor, structuralism,' and deconstruction as 'a method of reading.'" See Green and Troup, Houses (2nd edn), 290, citing Jane Caplan, "Postmodernism, Poststructuralism, and Deconstruction: Notes for Historians," *CEH* 22 (1989): 262–8. Cf. also Thomas C. Patterson, "Post-structuralism, Postmodernism: Implications for Historians," *SH* 14 (1989): 83–8. Spalding and Parker, *Historiography*, 26, observe that since postmodernism, "everything could be deconstructed, even the individual person"—even "authorial intent was inaccessible or irrelevant." Meanwhile, Munslow, *Deconstructing History*, 2, argues that postmodernism is not a new thing but a re-evaluation of modernism. On structuralism and post-structuralism, see further Porter and Robinson, *Hermeneutics*, 14–16, 154–213 (their chapters 7 and 8).

[57] Green and Troup, *Houses* (1st edn), 7.

[58] On the so-called linguistic turn, see Christopher Lloyd, "History and the Social Sciences," in *Writing History: Theory and Practice* (eds. Stefan Berger et al.; London: Arnold, 2003), 83–103 (86). See also Reinfandt, "Reading Texts," 41–58; Elizabeth A. Clark, *History, Theory, Text: Historians and the Linguistic Turn* (Cambridge, MA: Harvard University Press, 2004), 1–8; Harris, *Linguistics*, 9–13. In his estimation as a linguist, Harris thinks that most, if not all, historians fail to grasp the turn. He (13) explains the serious problem of how Western historians have "managed to ignore" the fact that their "contribution to human knowledge was itself language-dependent (not just dependent on the adoption of particular narrative forms or rhetorical devices)." His thesis is that a certain philosophy of language "sponsors" a certain philosophy of history (vii). As a result, a postmodern shift in history has occurred and we are left with no choice but to converse with the issues on a theoretical and practical level as there is no going back to the good old days of modernist interpretation. NT scholars in particular seem unaware and unprepared to deal with this post-structural shift. See Kevin Passmore, "Poststructuralism and History," in *Writing History: Theory and Practice* (eds. Stefan Berger et al.; London: Arnold, 2003), 138, and Porter, "Witness," 1:430–1.

[59] Green and Troup, *Houses* (1st edn), 7–8. Hence, a central criticism against empiricism rests in the "rejection of any correspondence between reality or experience, and the language employed to describe it." Ibid., 8. However, the counter-criticism against post-structuralism is that this perspective (in theory) can lead to an unfettered "subjectivism" which in turn paves the way for an unacceptable form of "moral relativism." Green and Troup, *Houses* (2nd edn), 20. They (292) caution

are more cautious with the *facts* of history—and their subsequent interpretation/ deconstruction of those facts—still, some events in history seem to be inescapably factual.[60] For example, although some of the events that occurred in the 60s and 70s CE (i.e., fall of Jerusalem and the fire of Rome) continue to be variously interpreted, we are certain that they occurred (cf. Chapter 8).[61] If we can date those events with relative certainty then it seems reasonable to date Acts in relation to them.

Historiography: Principles, Procedures, and Sources

Where empirical methods and assumptions are inadequate for a comprehensive interpretation of the past, post-structural historiography offers a stronger framework for tackling important NT studies.[62] However, this is not an easy task because at present there are no clear examples to follow for approaching the date of Acts from the vantage point of historiography and post-structuralism.[63] Furthermore, there have been few examples of a historiographical method that have been applied to an issue in NT studies.[64]

However, there have been more dedicated works and selected essays published over the last decade that describe critical historiographical principles and methods that can be applied to biblical studies.[65] Meanwhile, some NT scholars like Porter—who comes short of describing his own "historiographical method"—offer helpful guidelines for dealing with "ancient historiography."[66] Porter advises that we must recognize

---

that post-structuralist theory, which can result in "plural, mutable readings and interpretations," enables a "relativist position and destroys any claim to historical objectivity."
[60] A classic case is the Jewish Holocaust in World War II. See Green and Troup, *Houses* (2nd edn), 20; Passmore, "Poststructuralism," 134–6.
[61] While keeping these principles in mind there is no room for dogmatism with respect to *how* these factual events relate to the book of Acts. The goal is to offer the best plausible explanation given the great divide between the first-century sources and the intellectual framework of the scholars who have weighed in on this issue. See Passmore, "Poststructuralism," 135.
[62] Porter, "Witness," 1:432. Historians and NT scholars alike must avoid the extremes of a naïve positivism on the one hand and an unbounded subjectivism on the other.
[63] Further complicating matters is the fact that among historians there are only recognizable clusters of perspectives to draw from (i.e., constructionist, reconstructionist, deconstructionist). Moreover, Ziemann and Dobson, "Introduction," 2, point to a lack of examples that show the "actual practice of textual interpretation." See, for example, Callum G. Brown, *Postmodernism for Historians* (Harlow: Longman, 2004), 48, 72; Evans, *Defence*, 103–28; Mary Fullbrook, *Historical Theory* (London: Routledge, 2002), 98–121; Martha C. Howell and Walter Prevenier, *From Reliable Sources: An Introduction to Historical Methods* (Ithaca, NY: Cornell University Press, 2001), *et passim* and Tosh, *Pursuit* (6th edn), 98–121. However, rather than trying to map out a "poststructuralist history," Green and Troup instead refer to a "poststructuralist approach to history," *Houses* (2nd edn), 296. Meanwhile, Passmore, "Poststructuralism," 138, suggests that post-structuralism is productive in the sense of provoking "new questions" rather than "methodological innovation."
[64] See Licona, *Resurrection* and especially Sheppard's *Craft* (application section: chapters 8–10, pp. 183–234) for some examples of historiography applied to NT studies.
[65] Some recent examples on the praxis of history are Kamp et al., *Writing History!*; Tosh, *Pursuit* (6th edn); Williams, *Toolbox*; Salevouris and Furay, *Methods and Skills*, and the essays in Ziemann and Dobson, *Reading Primary Sources*, and also Laura Sangha and Jonathan Willis, eds., *Understanding Early Modern Primary Sources* (London: Routledge, 2016).
[66] Porter, "Witness," 1:431.

that "residual raw data of the past" is frequently the "product of uncontrollable or unpredictable factors, including natural and human intervention."[67]

This data forms the "basis of facts" that formulates the "sayings and actions" that are "selected for explanation and/or interpretation."[68] Therefore, it is the "interpretation and explanation of those facts" that lead to the "writing of and production of history."[69] Before we attempt to describe something that happened in the past we must realize that what we are trying to read has already gone through a complex (and subjective) process of interpretation. As a consequence of this heightened awareness of subjectivism, many post-structural historians are convinced that the "ground of reality" has been shaken.[70]

Selecting and Interpreting Primary and Secondary Sources

Only a hardened empirical-analytical historian could maintain that the "ground of reality" has not been shaken. However, even as theoretical controversies continue to dominate the broader conversation, there is an urgent need for historians (and even theory-friendly post-structuralists) to translate their theory into a recognizable framework that can be used to deal with an actual issue of historical significance. Accordingly, the first part of this section offers a framework for dating Acts while suggesting some practical guidelines and principles for the selection, analysis, and interpretation of sources.[71] The second part of this section describes the principles of modern textual criticism and papyrology that are used as a method for engaging the source documents.

According to Ziemann and Dobson, the heated debates that have occurred since the 1980s about the "nature of historical knowledge" among postmodernists (and their critics) have unsettled historians.[72] The postmodernists want to liberate the old "empiricist" notions of finding truth via the "facts" without any further conceptual framework.[73] This is, and has been, not only a systemic problem with the modernist interpretation of history, but remains a largely undiagnosed (and unaddressed) problem in recent biblical interpretation.[74] Although the ongoing epistemological

---

[67] Ibid.
[68] Ibid., 1:431–2.
[69] Ibid., 1:432.
[70] Ibid.
[71] According to Müller, "Understanding History," 23, it was Droysen who had a "hard time convincing his fellow historians that the decisive part in studying history was not the *verification* but the *interpretation* of sources" (my emphasis). Furthermore, Müller (29) explains that Droysen did not think that the sources themselves could "yield historical knowledge"—he saw them as the "indispensable basis of history; but in his eyes they only revealed their significance if they were interpreted by the historian." Droysen's principles are key to this volume. See Ziemann and Dobson, "Introduction," 3; Johann Gustav Droysen, *Outline of the Principles of History* (Boston: Ginn, 1897), et passim.
[72] Ziemann and Dobson, "Introduction," 1. The issue as noted earlier in this chapter rests on epistemology whereby language is "at the core of the controversy" between the post-structuralists and their critics (1). Ziemann and Dobson (1) essentially argue that this "epistemological conflict" relates to the "nature and the possibilities of knowledge about the meaning of language and of written texts in particular."
[73] See, ibid.; Keith Jenkins, *Re-thinking History* (repr., London: Routledge, 2003), 30, 45; Evans, *Defence*, 127, 106, 109.
[74] Porter, "Witness," 1:427–31.

debate among historians is not going to be solved here, the solution rests in the way we handle sources.

Essentially, the debate between the "realists" and poststructuralists is "largely focused on the way primary sources or historical texts should be *handled, read* and *interpreted* in order to make true assertions about the past."[75] Since the "nature of textual interpretation" is at the core of these controversies, offering further "abstract deliberations" will not solve anything.[76] Instead, the solution requires a sincere attempt to "reflect theoretical differences" in view of the "actual empirical work of the historian."[77] In spite of those theoretical differences, the "heart of an historian's work" is the purposeful "reading and interpretation of texts."[78]

Principles for Selecting Sources

Before we discuss the ways we can interpret sources and texts, an integral part of this discussion involves the actual *selection* of sources. This is absolutely essential for dating any document simply because of the fact that its date is to a large degree dependent on the dates of other documents (cf. Chapter 4). Moreover, there is a great deal of subjectivism when it comes to choosing primary and secondary sources.[79]

In the mind of the historian, the interpretive process begins long before the actual interpretation of the sources. A case in point is seen in Tyson's obsession with Marcion's second-century version of Luke's gospel and Pervo's exclusive focus on comparing the writings of Josephus and Paul's letters with Luke and Acts. No scholar, including myself, is exempt from the bias that occurs in selecting some sources while neglecting others.

One of my own presuppositions is that many of the events in Acts can be compared chronologically with the Roman writers, and not just the events described by Josephus. Examining Josephus and Paul's letters for clues are important (see Chapter 4) but we should also be open to other sources of information (Chapter 8). For example, Tosh

---

[75] Ziemann and Dobson, "Introduction," 1 (my emphasis). Sources are "the" focal point of praxis for any historian regardless of their specific label that is sometimes difficult to define. See Munslow, *Deconstructing History*, 20–8. Many recent books that belong to the realist camp offer their views on epistemology and postmodernism while arguing that history is ultimately "based on the proper reading and weighing of sources" (Ziemann and Dobson, 1–2 [2]). According to them many of these works do not provide a clear example of the "actual practice of textual interpretation for the purposes of the historian" (2). In reference to Tosh, *Pursuit* (6th edn), 119, they regard such realist methodologies as "little more than the obvious lessons of common sense" (2). On this point, I think they are bending Tosh a little far—since he makes it clear that such an approach is far more systematic and supported by a "secure grasp of historical context and, in many instances, a high degree of technical knowledge." See Tosh, *Pursuit* (6th edn), 119.

[76] Ziemann and Dobson, "Introduction," 2.

[77] Ibid., 2. Alun Munslow, *The Routledge Companion to Historical Studies* (2nd edn; London: Routledge, 2006), 89, admits that "most historians today accept a middle position that rejects extreme empiricism." While discussing the aesthetic turn he (21) says that most historians conceive of history as "empirical-analytical" rather than seeing history as a "literary construction of the author-historian."

[78] Ziemann and Dobson, "Introduction," 2. See also the other instructive volumes in the *Routledge Guides to Using Historical Sources*. It would be beneficial for historians, biblical scholars, and textual critics to work together on a similar volume that deals specifically with ancient texts.

[79] On the classification and distinction between primary and secondary sources, see Tosh, *Pursuit* (6th edn), 73; Kamp et al., *Writing History!*, 36–7 and Williams, *Toolbox*, 15.

advocates for the "constant reassessment of the original sources" rather than resting on "what has been handed down by earlier historians."[80] Therefore, it seems reasonable to expect a careful (albeit subjective) examination of all the available documents from the period in question.[81] As this book will hopefully demonstrate, many of the documents that are contemporary with Acts are either largely ignored or neglected outright, and this points to *a priori* assumptions at work.

This dismissal of sources seems to be a limiting factor in historical research—unless of course an explanation for such dismissal is provided, but in many cases no explanation is put forth. Going one step further, it also seems crucial for any historical enquiry to read and carefully evaluate the interpretations of other historians who have weighed into the matter. This requires a full study of the "whole gamut of academic publications" available on the subject in order to acquire the (1) "necessary background information" and the (2) "theoretical and historiographical context."[82] Our selective engagement (or lack thereof) with primary and secondary sources raises further interpretative issues.

One of the major drawbacks arising from using written materials as primary historical sources is that historians convey their discoveries through the "same medium."[83] This is evident not only in their "choice of research topic" but also in the final project—since historians are "influenced"

> ... to a greater or lesser extent by what their predecessors have written, accepting much of the evidence they uncovered and, rather more selectively, the interpretations they put on it. But when we read the work of a historian we stand at one remove from the original sources of the period in question—and further away still if that historian has been content to rely on the writings of other historians.[84]

Accordingly, the first step in assessing the quality of any historical work is to consider its level of consistency with "all the available evidence"—including new sources or old ones that are "read in a new light."[85]

This selection process can also be seen in the relationship between *sources* and what constitutes *evidence*.[86] The historian ultimately (and subjectively) chooses what *they* consider to be evidence,[87] and this selection process occurs regardless of whether

---

[80] Tosh, *Pursuit* (6th edn), 73.
[81] Kamp et al., *Writing History!*, 36. Ziemann and Dobson, "Introduction," 15, highlight the fact that sources "rarely come alone" and therefore the "collation of different texts remains an important business for the historian."
[82] Kamp et al., *Writing History!*, 37. However, it remains impossible for any historian to examine "all existing" source material that bears on a research question. Green and Troup, *Houses* (1st edn), 5. For most scholars there simply is not enough time to examine everything. Cf. Tosh, *Pursuit* (6th edn), 98.
[83] Ibid., 73.
[84] Ibid.
[85] Ibid.
[86] Green and Troup, *Houses*, vi (2nd edn), observe how "every piece of historical writing has a theoretical basis on which *evidence is selected*, filtered and understood" (my emphasis).
[87] Although every historian selects their own sources and how to interpret the evidence, some unconscious choices are not easily identified or explained. For example, Fritz Stern, "Introduction," in *Varieties of History: From Voltaire to Present* (ed. Fritz Stern; 2nd edn; London: Macmillan, 1970),

the approach stems from a form of unbiased "scientific empiricism" or from theory-friendly post-structuralism.[88] And although the selection of *sources* and *evidence* is influenced by a particular theoretical basis or *a priori* knowledge, ultimately this process of choosing is up to the individual historian.[89] Therefore, a new theoretical framework, paired with a new combination of data and access to new sources, allows the historian to write *a* new story of the past.[90]

Principles for Selecting Facts

As incredulous as the title suggests, not only do historians select their sources and evidence, they choose which "facts" are worthy to emphasize and which ones to leave out.[91] It is argued here that what we consider to be historical "facts" are actually the direct result of the interpretative choices of historians who have been influenced by their own present mindset.[92]

For example, Carr famously compares the plight of modern historians to that of the "ancient or medieval" historian who has the advantage of acquiring and whittling down a "manageable corpus" of historical "facts" over many years.[93] The modern historian therefore has the "dual task of discovering the few significant facts and turning them into facts of history" and working to weed out what is considered insignificant.[94] He considers this compilation of "irrefutable and objective facts" to be the locus of the nineteenth-century historical "heresy."[95]

Carr subsequently outlines the effects of this heresy on the modern "would-be" historians and their specialized works over the last hundred years as a case of "knowing more and more" about "less and less."[96] The problem, he argues, is the modern historian's "unending accumulation of hard facts as the foundation of history."[97] This commonly

---

24 explains how the "writing of history inflicts on every historian choices for which neither his method nor his material provides a ready answer." He (24) goes on to say that in some cases only the historian can offer such an answer but "this has kept history a live, changing pursuit." Cf. also Wilson, *History in Crisis?*, 2–3. It is also possible that the historian may not fully understand—or even be aware of—their choices because of the influence of prior knowledge. Munslow, *Companion*, 89.

[88] Green and Troup, *Houses* (2nd edn), vi.

[89] Peter Loewenberg, *Decoding the Past: The Psychohistorical Approach* (2nd edn; New Brunswick, NJ: Transaction Publishers, 2002), 15, explains how "each historian and each age redefines categories of evidence in the light of its needs, sensibilities, and perceptions. The value of any conceptual framework is what new combinations of data or inferences from the data it may contribute to the historian's ability to interpret documents and the other raw material of history."

[90] Munslow, *A History*, 7, makes an important ontological distinction between "reproducing *the* story" and "producing *a* story" (emphasis original). Empiricists would have us believe that their version of history is "the" most likely history rather than offering "a" certain point of view.

[91] Beard, "Dream," 87, points to the well-neglected task of "exploring the assumptions upon which the selection and organization of historical facts proceed."

[92] Ibid., Beard explains how we "do not acquire the colorless, neutral mind by declaring our intention to do so. Rather do we clarify the mind by admitting its cultural interests and patterns—interests and patterns that will control, or intrude upon, the selection and organization of historical materials."

[93] Carr, *History?*, 14.

[94] Ibid., 15.

[95] Ibid.

[96] Ibid.

[97] Ibid., 15–16.

held empirical fallacy is that *facts* "speak for themselves" and that we "cannot have too many facts" without asking the (still) fundamental question of "What is History?"[98]

Carr's key observation is that the empirical—and by extension, today's practical realist's—reliance on facts and documents is insufficient to determine what actually happened in the past.[99] In order to determine what actually happened in the past, the historian needs to work through and decipher the documents in what he refers to as the "processing process."[100] As Carr states, "The facts, whether found in documents or not, have still to be processed by the historian before he can make use of them."[101] This issue is far more pressing once we realize that we only have access to a collection of contemporary documents that are separated by both "word and world"—and these facts and documents alone do not "constitute history," but rather the historian's interpretation of the material.[102]

Principles for Selecting Events

Every historian not only has a process for selecting sources, facts, and evidence, but also controls the selection of events—and their level of significance—that are described in a narrative (such as Acts). For example, Spalding and Parker discuss this event selection process describing how "factors that are seen as relatively unimportant may be downplayed or even ignored completely by the author of a monograph."[103] In my view, this process reflects the date of Acts debate precisely—every scholar (including myself) who is weighing in on the debate is choosing certain events that contribute to their argument while ignoring others. As a result, there needs to be a clear justification in the selection (or omission) of every event in question.

When it comes to the interpretation of an event and weighing its significance, Collingwood advises that the historian "investigating any event in the past, makes a distinction between what may be called the *outside* and the *inside* of the event"

---

[98] Ibid., 16. Cf. also Michael Cox, "Introduction: E. H. Carr—a Critical Appraisal," in *E. H. Carr: A Critical Appraisal* (ed. Michael Cox; Hampshire, UK: Palgrave, 2004), 1–18; Anders Stephanson, "The Lessons of *What is History?*," in *Carr: A Critical Appraisal*, 283–303; Keith Jenkins, "An English Myth? Rethinking the Contemporary Value of E. H. Carr's *What is History?*," in *Carr: A Critical Appraisal*, 304–21.

[99] Carr, *History?*, 16.

[100] Ibid.

[101] Ibid., 16. For Carr (16), such documents can only tell us what the "author of the document thought" and "none of this means anything until the historian has got to work on it and deciphered it." He (16–19) illustrates the "processing process" with the example of statesmen Gustav Stresemann who left behind an enormous amount of documents pertaining to his years as the Foreign Minister of the Weimar republic in 1929 (over 300 boxes) and Bernhard, his dedicated secretary, who wrote three volumes at over 600 pages each; and Bernhard's text would have been all that remains had it not been for the British and American governments who photographed all of the documents. A later abridgement and translation of Bernhard's work continued to emphasize Western policy achievements while it significantly minimized Stresemann's foreign policy work to the Soviet Union. Carr (19) makes the point that it was not Bernhard or the translator who "started the process of selection" but Stresemann himself. Additionally, Stresemann's original history leaves out the accounts of the Soviet Ambassador in Berlin.

[102] See Munslow, *A History*, 8, and Carr's, *History?*, 19, respectively.

[103] Spalding and Parker, *Historiography*, 57.

(my emphasis).[104] He uses the examples of Julius Caesar's crossing of the Rubicon and his death at the senate house in Rome—both are datable events in time, but are representative of something much larger.[105] Collingwood considers the *outside* of an event to mean "everything belonging to it which can be described in terms of bodies and their movements."[106] The *inside* of the event is described in "terms of thought" where Caesar's crossing is seen as the "defiance of Republican law" and his death as the "clash of constitutional policy between himself and his assassins."[107]

Accordingly, the historian must give due consideration for both the *inside* and the *outside* of the event since these episodes are "not mere events" but "actions, and an action is the unity of the outside and inside of the event."[108] Although the interpretative work starts by "discovering the outside of an event" the historian should reflect upon the event as "an action" with the primary goal of thinking oneself "into this action" in order to "discern the thought of its agent."[109]

Consequent reasoning suggests that within the book of Acts, there exists an *outside*, as well as the *inside* aspect of the events with the *action* forming a link. As an extension of this concept, Collingwood describes historical knowledge as relating to "what mind has done in the past" while concurrently it is the "redoing of this, the perpetuation of past acts in the present."[110] The past then comes alive as we "plunge" ourselves into the "evidence and experience the past" as best as we can—"by rethinking it."[111] By rethinking the thoughts of the past, we relive the past. This is not a simple subjective imposition of our ideas onto past events; it is a conscious and critical reflection upon the difficult questions of the activities of people in the past.[112]

All of this discussion on the subjective process of selection permeates the historian's thought from start to finish.[113] In the end, every historian chooses what sources to study, how to study them, what to emphasize, what to include and what to leave out. Given the striking emphasis and influence of post-structural theory on the study of primary sources, it seems obligatory for any historian to not only justify their choices along

---

[104] Robin G. Collingwood, *The Idea of History* (Oxford: Oxford University Press, 1946), 213.
[105] Ibid.
[106] Ibid.
[107] Ibid.
[108] Ibid. The historian is concerned with the crossing of the Rubicon "only in its relation to Republican law, and in the spilling of Caesar's blood only in its relation to a constitutional conflict" (213).
[109] Ibid.
[110] Ibid., 218.
[111] Munslow, *Deconstructing History*, 68. Collingwood, *Idea*, 218–19, uses the example of the so-called dark ages of history where historians can find "nothing intelligible" but "such phrases tell us nothing about those ages themselves, though they tell us a great deal about the persons who use them, namely they are unable to re-think the thoughts which were fundamental to their life."
[112] Carr, *History?*, 23, builds on this concept stating that the "reader in his turn must re-enact what goes on in the mind of the historian. Study the historian before you begin to study the facts."
[113] The contention that history is "inescapably value judgemental" frequently "turns on the consideration that, in elaborating their accounts, *historians have to select*. Their obligation with regard to a *chosen subject matter* is presumably to tell us what is important about it. And importance seems to be a category of value, although a very general one" (my emphasis). Cf. William Dray, "Philosophy and Historiography," in *Companion of Historiography* (ed. Michael Bentley; London: Routledge, 1997), 770.

the way but to explain them so that others may test and see if their interpretations not only cohere with other narratives, but also correspond with the "available evidence."[114]

Principles for Interpreting Sources

The selection of sources, events, facts, and evidence leads us to another aspect of the research process: how to interpret sources. Heidegger reasoned that all of human understanding is interpretative and explains that "all acts of interpretation, are inseparable from our situatedness."[115] No matter how objective a historian intends to be in their interpretation, there will always be "presuppositions and prejudgments" that colour their interpretation of a source.[116]

This is a fundamental principle in historiography because interpretation is what historians do.[117] History was "originally an attempt to tell a true story" and essentially get the facts straight but since the postmodern debates the lines have blurred between "story and explanation, literature and history."[118] Some postmodernist thinkers consider "all the past a text and historians merely tellers of a relatively meaningful (or meaningless) story that they construct from textual fragments found."[119] As a consequence it becomes much harder to separate fact from fiction in the texts we read, but at the same time the stories do contain varying amounts of truth that we can work with and interpret.

Reinfandt claims that in light of the postmodern shift, it is no longer possible to determine meaning simply by referring to "facts or objects in reality" and accordingly, the question of what historians are supposed to do indeed becomes pressing.[120] In saying that we cannot grasp "reality as such in its totality and ultimate meaningfulness" does not mean that "reality does not exist."[121] Reinfandt further remarks that our belief in historical truth "can survive the onslaught of deconstruction if one acknowledges that interpretations are all we have."[122] As a result, this essentially boils down to a *subjective* process of distinguishing between "acceptable ('true') and unacceptable ('false') interpretations."[123] Therefore, our interpretations hinge not so much on our correct gathering of sources and evidence (as crucial as that process is) but on our *subjective* framework for determining a better interpretation of that evidence.[124]

---

[114] Tosh, *Pursuit* (6th edn), 73.
[115] Porter and Robinson, *Hermeneutics*, 10, see also 8–10, 57–69.
[116] Ibid., 10 (and also 9, 57–71).
[117] Sheppard, *Craft*, 15, argues that the historian's "primary task may be boiled down to one word: 'interpretation.'"
[118] Williams, *Toolbox*, 9.
[119] Ibid.
[120] Reinfandt, "Reading Texts," 51.
[121] Ibid.
[122] Ibid. Passmore, "Poststructuralism, 136, says that "just because truth claims cannot be established absolutely, does not mean that they cannot be established at all." Williams, *Toolbox*, 9, insists that historians remain "doggedly concerned with approximating the truth about the past on the basis of available evidence" while at the same time being acutely aware of our own "present situation and inclinations."
[123] Reinfandt, "Reading Texts," 51.
[124] This will vary depending on the theoretical framework of the historian as a reconstructionist, constructionist, deconstructionist (or some blend in between). Reinfandt, "Reading Texts," 51.

This leads to the question of how we read texts. A broadly post-structuralist view sees texts as "not so much 'carrying' meaning from a source to a recipient but rather bearing traces of meanings intentionally 'inscribed' as well as medially, socially and institutionally 'framed.'"[125] This perspective requires us to evaluate both our texts critically as well as the "act of reading itself" as essentials parts of the ongoing interpretative process.[126] This does not require us to subscribe to a "fixed body of work or to this or that school or approach"—rather, it necessitates an "awareness of the contingency of one's own and other people's practice of ascribing meaning to texts."[127] From this perspective, theory then can be seen primarily as a "mode of persistent questioning," as a safeguard from letting our own "*provisional* answers 'harden' into dogma" (original emphasis).[128] Being aware of *how* scholars interpret Acts is critical to this debate because in many ways the meaning of a text is determined without a clear explanation.

This persistent questioning of other readings and meanings allows space for other valid (and perhaps more appropriate) interpretations, some of which have been uncritically set aside.[129] My suspicion is that some of the literary attempts suggesting what the author of Acts *really meant* are nothing more than politically (or theologically) infused opinions that are missing significant elements relating to the narrative (see Chapter 5).[130] How else can one explain the continued popularity of theories that see Jerusalem's destruction in the synoptic gospels as a prophecy (after the event) despite the simpler explanation that allows it to be written before?[131]

Another key aspect of source interpretation is to consider what is *absent* in the text. There can be a myriad of reasons as to why and how much or how little an author decides to write about a certain person or event in the past, but it is equally valid to also consider "what is not in the text."[132] During the process of interpreting sources it is imperative to realize that they not only contain "'demonstrable' information" but that they may also exhibit "various kinds of 'silence'" and for many different reasons.[133] The book of Acts is certainly not exempt to the reality of silence in the narrative. However, as Chapters 5 and 8 will attempt to demonstrate, a number of the explanations concerning the profound silences in Acts do not consider some valid alternatives.

---

[125] Ibid., 53.
[126] Ibid., 54.
[127] Ibid.
[128] Ibid., 54; Beard, "Dream," 87.
[129] Ziemann and Dobson, *Introduction*, 6–16, offer a helpful checklist for interpreting texts from the past in light of the "plurality of possible readings" (6). Here they wisely caution against any "fixed set of rules" for this interpretative process such as those proposed by Arthur Marwick, *The New Nature of History: Knowledge, Evidence, Language* (London: Palgrave, 2001), 179–85.
[130] Haenchen, *Acts*, championed the idea that Luke was not simply a *historian* and *theologian*, but a skilled *writer* and storyteller. Some scholars—notably Pervo—have followed Haenchen's tendency to see Luke as predominantly a creative writer. See Pervo, *Acts*, xv. However, the process of interpreting Luke requires a delicate balance since we must not become too preoccupied with one aspect to the neglect of the other two. See Karl L. Armstrong, "The Impact of Ernst Haenchen on the Interpretation of Acts," in *Luke-Acts in Modern Interpretation* (eds. Stanley E. Porter and Ron C. Fray; Grand Rapids: Kregel, forthcoming).
[131] See Hemer, *Acts*, 375; Bock, *Acts*, 27; Porter, *When Paul Met Jesus*, 78 and Chapter 8 of this volume.
[132] Kamp et al., *Writing History!*, 77.
[133] Ibid.

Recently, Kamp, Legêne, Rossum, and Rümke explained three types of silences that offer a useful guideline for interpreting the silences found in the narrative of Acts.[134] The first type of silence is because the information was "completely self-evident so no-one even thought to explain it."[135] The second type of silence is because "something was consciously omitted because it had to be withheld."[136] The third type of silence is because there was a "taboo on the subject so that the author could not find the words to describe something that was cloaked in shame or that even literally had no name."[137]

The interpretation of the silences in Acts has and will continue to play a key role in determining its date. Certain events that are missing from Acts such as the fire of Rome in 64 CE can be assessed with these and other criteria in mind (Chapter 8). However, the search for silences should only be undertaken after the historian has an "explicitly formulated research question and good knowledge of the secondary literature."[138] Furthermore, silences in the text are "rarely evident" and are usually not the first question to be asked during the interpretation of sources.[139] Nonetheless, silences can be found in the "context of research" and the "example of searching for silences" reflects the important relationship between archival research and methodology.[140]

Principles for Sources and Textual Criticism

An important part of this historiographical approach to the date of Acts addresses the literary environment by applying principles of modern textual criticism, papyrology, and linguistics in concert with the guiding source principles above.[141] This venture is

---

[134] Ibid. They draw from Ann Stoler who introduces these forms of silence where they assist her in the process of reading the archives in the remainder of her work. See Ann Laura Stoler, *Along the Archival Grain: Epistemic Anxieties and Colonial Common Sense* (Princeton: Princeton University Press, 2009). She states that while "attending to that which is 'not written,' there is something of Lévi-Strauss's vision of anthropology in what follows" (3). She does not mean to say that this process is about finding the "'hidden message' or those subliminal texts that couch 'the real' below the surface and between the written lines. Rather it seeks to identify the pliable coordinates of what constituted colonial common sense in a changing imperial order." She then distinguishes between (1) "what was 'unwritten' because it could go without saying and 'everyone knew it,'" and (2) "what was unwritten because it could not yet be articulated," and (3) "what was unwritten because it could not be said" (3). Many thanks to Sebas Rümke and Susan Legêne for clarifying this section of their book for me, and for Inge van der Bijl at Amsterdam University Press for facilitating this exchange in time for publication.

[135] Kamp et al., *Writing History!*, 77.
[136] Ibid.
[137] Ibid.
[138] Ibid., 77–8; Tosh, *Pursuit* (6th edn), 111.
[139] Kamp et al., *Writing History!*, 77.
[140] Ibid., 78. Kamp et al. cite specific research contexts such as slavery, or persecution or with respect to "one's belief, political convictions, or ideology."
[141] The following works (and this is by no means exhaustive) undergird my approach to textual criticism: Kurt Aland and Barbara Aland, *The Text of the New Testament* (trans. Erroll F. Rhodes; 2nd edn; Grand Rapids: Eerdmans, 1989); Ernst C. Colwell, *Studies in Methodology in Textual Criticism of the New Testament* (ed. Bruce M. Metzger; NTTSD 9; Leiden: Brill, 1969); Bruce M. Metzger, *The Text of the New Testament: Its Transmission, Corruption, and Restoration* (3rd edn; New York: Oxford University Press, 1992); Bruce M. Metzger and Bart D. Ehrman, *The Text of the New Testament: Its Transmission, Corruption, and Restoration* (4th edn; Oxford: Oxford University Press, 2005); Philip W. Comfort, *Encountering the Manuscripts: An Introduction to New Testament*

appropriate for two very important reasons. The first is that the application of textual criticism is a necessary practice within the field of history.

While discussing the process of historical dating, Greene and Moore explain how historical writing normally has a "clear purpose" to either "represent an event, an individual or a regime in a good or bad light (depending on the writer's attitude), or to use history to make a particular point."[142] They go on to explain that before we begin to evaluate information from the past, it is necessary to consider the following criteria:

> ... *the date and quality of surviving manuscripts*; the *distance* (in time and place) *of the author* from the events described; the author's *record of accuracy* if items can be checked independently; the *quality of the sources* available to the writer; and any *personal biases or motives* that might have led the writer to present a particular version of events (my emphasis).[143]

These documentary concerns and criteria are valuable for historical inquiry and used as a guide throughout the remaining chapters.

The second reason is that the textual record of Acts is complex, and yet all three of the most recent and major monographs on the date of Acts have either *missed* or *dismissed* this critical field of documentary evidence.[144] Since the book of Acts has been subjected to significant revision(s) throughout the early development of its text, this generates a valuable collection of source material. Failure to adequately address the textual record and the so-called Western expansions overlook an important piece of the puzzle (cf. Chapters 3 and 7). Scholars who solely rely on the "text" of Acts found in the NA[28] or *UBSGNT* are limiting themselves to one set of manuscripts and the exclusion of the Western textual variations found in others.[145] These variants are not

---

Paleography and Textual Criticism (Nashville: Broadman & Holman, 2005); Eldon J. Epp and Gordon D. Fee, *Studies in the Theory and Method of New Testament Textual Criticism* (Grand Rapids: Eerdmans, 1993); James K. Elliott, *New Testament Textual Criticism: The Application of Thoroughgoing Principles, Essays on Manuscripts and Textual Variation* (NovTSup 137; Leiden: Brill, 2010); Scot McKendrick and Orlaith O'Sullivan, eds., *The Bible as Book: The Transmission of the Greek Text* (London: Oak Knoll, 2003); Charles E. Hill and Michael J. Kruger, eds., *The Early Text of the New Testament* (Oxford: Oxford University Press, 2012); David C. Parker, *An Introduction to the New Testament Manuscripts and their Texts* (Cambridge: Cambridge University Press, 2008); idem, *Textual Scholarship and the Making of the New Testament* (Oxford: Oxford University Press, 2012). Porter and Pitts, *Fundamentals*, 129-36 (chapter 10) further provides a framework that incorporates traditional text critical methods with advanced linguistic insights.

[142] Kevin Greene and Tom Moore, *Archaeology: An Introduction* (New York: Routledge, 2010), 155.

[143] Ibid. See also Roger S. Bagnall, *Reading Papyri, Writing Ancient History* (2nd edn; London: Routledge, 2019); Biers, *Chronology*; and Robert Jones Shafer, *A Guide to Historical Method* (The Dorsey Series in History; 2nd rev. edn; Homewood, Illinois: The Dorsey Press, 1974), 119-22. According to Peter Kosso, *Knowing the Past: Philosophical Issues of History and Archaeology* (Amherst, NY: Humanity Books, 2001), 51, there are a few key criteria for assessing the "credibility of a textual report" such as the degree of (1) the "ancient author's access to the event" and (2) the "preparation of the text," and (3) its "treatment through time."

[144] Cf. Kamp et al., *Writing History!*, 23.

[145] See James H. Ropes, "The Text of Acts," in *The Beginnings of Christianity*, 3:i–cccxx, 1–371 and more recently: Christopher M. Tuckett, "How Early is the 'Western' Text of Acts?," in *The Book of Acts as Church History: Textual Traditions and Ancient Interpretations* (eds. Tobias Nicklas and Michael Tilly; BZNW 120; Berlin: de Gruyter, 2003), 69-86 (70), and idem, "The Early Text of Acts," in

simply "scraps on the cutting room floor" as they have much to tell us about the early history of the church while providing clues to its date.[146]

This is a widespread problem in Acts studies in general, but an acute problem for the scholarship relating to its date. For example, Keener (along with the majority of Acts commentaries) does not engage the manuscript record of Acts in relation to the debate.[147] Furthermore, all three of the major monographs that address the date of Acts are, in varying degrees, lacking in attention to these important text-critical concerns. Starting with Tyson, it is clear that he does not seriously engage matters of textual criticism, which is especially risky considering his precarious reliance upon Marcion's recreated version of Luke's gospel.[148]

While Mittelstaedt and his view for an early date of Acts (62 CE) contains many valuable insights that have been ignored by English scholarship there is very little space given to the manuscripts and texts of Acts. He suggests that where "Archaologie und Papyrologie" do not present "empirischen Fakten" and the researcher has to rely on studying "tradierter Texte," we are often left with a balancing of probabilities.[149] While this is true, and he does present several pieces of historical and archaeological evidence in his analysis, he does not engage the textual record of Acts to consider how that may further tip the scales in this debate.

Although Pervo is familiar with the textual record, and while on occasion he makes a note in his comparisons with Acts and other literature that a certain reading is uncertain, he does not clearly factor the variants or the book's textual history in his study. In his chapter 2, he briefly addresses and then dismisses the value of the manuscript evidence:

> Paleographical evidence is not relevant to this inquiry, as no one proposes to date Acts later than 175 CE, and there are no manuscripts of Acts that are indisputably earlier than 200–250. The criterion of manuscript evidence, which is not very

---

The Early Text of the New Testament (eds. Charles E. Hill and Michael J. Kruger; Oxford: Oxford University Press, 2012), 157–74.

[146] Cf. Hill and Kruger, "Introduction," 1–19 (5) in reference to Bart D. Ehrman's principle in "The Text as Window: New Testament Manuscripts and the Social History of Early Christianity," in *The Text of the New Testament in Contemporary Research: Essays on the Status Quaestionis* (eds. Bart D. Ehrman and Michael W. Holmes; SD 42; Grand Rapids: Eerdmans, 1995), 361–79.

[147] Keener, *Acts*, 1:383–401. Keener certainly refers to many key early texts and on occasion refers to P^{52} in his footnotes; see, for example, 1:398–9 notes 102 and 108 (though no mss. of Acts here that I am aware of). To be fair he does include "text criticism" as part of his limitations section (see 1:7–11) and claims that he does "not neglect textual questions at necessary points" (1:7). He does not, however, factor the manuscript record with regard to the date of Acts (and this is not surprising given the scope of his work) but he is well aware of the issues in this helpful section as he remarks how the book of Acts "provides the thorniest text-critical situation in the NT" (1:7–8).

[148] Recall my note 26 in this Chapter and the substantial problems with his view. Even Pervo, *Dating Acts*, 25, questions whether Marcion knew Acts, and if he did, did he reject it? Pervo (25) further wonders at what point Marcion encountered Luke's gospel "and the form in which he found it." He thinks that Marcion "as the first certain witness to the gospel of Luke" may have seen a copy in Sinope as early as 110–120 CE (25). This point alone pushes back Tyson's date of Acts earlier from 120–125 CE. Tyson, *Marcion*, 78.

[149] Mittelstaedt, *Lukas als Historiker*, 17 (see section 1.1.2 [17–20]: "Zur Problematik von argumenta e silentio"). My thanks to Keener, *Acts*, 1:385, for helping me discover this important work.

precise, does not provide certain evidence for the existence of Acts in the second century. Other criteria will have to be invoked.[150]

On the contrary, paleographical evidence is very relevant to this inquiry because there have been significant text-critical studies that attest that even the Western text of Acts is an early second-century text (and possibly earlier).[151]

Furthermore, Pervo also fails to understand that external criteria (or evidence) in textual criticism is not only concerned with the date of the *document* but also the date of the *text*.[152] He seems to recognize this principle but dismisses it in the next breath: "Nor is the date of the ms. a sure indicator of the antiquity of its text; late mss. may be quite valuable. For the present purpose, however, the date of the ms. is fundamental."[153] Since we are not dating actual manuscripts earlier than the second century, the date of the *text* and its development becomes an even greater arbiter of the evidence (see Chapter 7).

Conclusion: A Historiographical Approach to the Date of Acts

This chapter has explored the critical issue of theory and method with regard to dating Acts. What was found is that (among the three monographs especially) there is no clearly defined method of approach to this historic issue. On the one hand, datable matters of history have often been ignored while on the other, the textual record has not been given the treatment it deserves. So far Pervo's application of intertextuality and Tyson's largely undefined literary and thematic obsession with Marcion's gospel are incapable of grappling the greater matters of historiography and textual criticism. While Mittelstaedt's historical-critical method effectively addresses the broader historical arguments, he does not (along with Pervo and Tyson) address the substantial textual record of Acts.

---

[150] Pervo, *Dating Acts*, 15. His "criterion of manuscript evidence" remains undefined (15). The other criterion he refers to as the "criterion of external citation" (15).

[151] Tuckett, "How Early," 69–86 (85–86); idem, "Early Text," 157–74; Stanley E. Porter, "Developments in the Text of Acts before the Major Codices," in *The Book of Acts as Church History: Textual Traditions and Ancient Interpretations* (eds. Tobias Nicklas and Michael Tilly; BZNW 120; Berlin: de Gruyter, 2003), 31–67; David D. Parker, "Codex Bezae: The Manuscript as Past, Present and Future," in *The Bible as Book: The Transmission of the Greek Text* (eds. Scot McKendrick and Orlaith O'Sullivan; London: Oak Knoll Press, 2003), 43–50 (48–9); Eldon J. Epp, "Issues in New Testament Textual Criticism: Moving from the Nineteenth Century to the Twenty-First Century," in *Rethinking New Testament Textual Criticism* (ed. David A. Black; Grand Rapids: Baker Academic, 2002), 17–76 (38, 41); and Ropes, "Text of Acts," x, ccxliv.

[152] See Léon Vaganay, *An Introduction to New Testament Textual Criticism* (ed. C. B. Amphoux; trans. H. Heimerdinger; Cambridge: Cambridge University Press, 1991), 74; Metzger, *Text*, 209; Porter and Pitts, *Fundamentals*, 104. Similarly, historians have long recognized the need for evaluating a document via external criticism. See Tosh, *Pursuit* (6th edn), 102–4 (and 95–147 where he offers some useful guidelines for the authenticity and reliability of a document). Cf. also Shafer's, *Guide*, 117–62, on external and internal criticism.

[153] Pervo, *Dating Acts*, 376 (n. 1).

Where other methods are arguably deficient, a historiographical approach is capable of addressing the textual and historical issues related to the date of Acts. This approach is conceptually rooted in the concepts and principles of historiography that are outlined in this chapter while the practical work with the texts draws from modern methods of textual criticism.

3

The Date of Acts and Its Sources

Introduction

Smith calls the "spate of literature" on the sources of Acts simply "astounding."[1] He is right in this assessment but the great volume of source work on Acts from the early twentieth century has withered in recent decades.[2] Perhaps the greatest reason for this lack of focus on the sources of Acts in recent years is the inherent difficulties of such a pursuit.[3] For instance, Dupont's often quoted "negative" conclusion on the sources of Acts on its own can leave the most rigorous scholars discouraged.[4] The state of the research on the sources of Acts is certainly not without significant difficulties, but a fresh examination of the existing research reveals a more favourable prognosis.

Although a *complete* study of the sources of Acts is far beyond the scope of this chapter—should such an enterprise even be possible—the emphasis needs to be upon what we know (and do not know) about the sources, and especially the way this data

---

[1] Taylor C. Smith, "The Sources of Acts," in *With Steadfast Purpose: Essays on Acts in Honor of Henry Jackson Flanders, Jr.* (ed. Naymond H. Keathley; Waco, TX: Baylor University Press, 1990), 55–75 (55).

[2] See Hans H. Wendt, *Die Apostelgeschichte* (8th edn; KEK 3; Göttingen: Vandenhoeck & Ruprecht, 1899); Harnack, *The Acts*, 162–202; Frederick J. Foakes-Jackson and Kirsopp Lake, "Prolegomena II: Criticism," in *The Beginnings of Christianity*, 2:122–208; Haenchen, *Acts*, 14–50; and Jacques Dupont, *The Sources of Acts: The Present Position* (London: Darton, Longmann & Todd, 1964), 9–14, for an extensive review of sources. See also his earlier version: *Les sources du livre des Actes: État de la question* (Bruges: Desclée de Brouwer, 1960). Pervo, *Dating Acts*, 1, laments the lack of source work on Acts in recent times. Refer to his helpful list of scholarship on the sources of Acts (347–58).

[3] "After nearly two hundred years of intensive research on Luke-Acts the mystery of Luke's sources still remains." Smith, "Sources," 75. Calling Luke's sources a mystery is perhaps going too far since the Septuagint (LXX) is an obvious source in Acts—although its form varies considerably. Pervo, *Dating Acts*, 9 and 374 (n. 38).

[4] See Dupont, *Sources*, 166 (especially his often quoted first point). See also Lewis R. Donelson, "Cult Histories and the Sources of Acts," *Bib* 68 (1987): 1; Marshall, *Acts*, 39–40 and Porter, *Paul in Acts*, 10 (n. 1), who states that he is "not as pessimistic" as Dupont. Porter's chapter 2 (pp. 10–46) is an updated version of his earlier essay: Stanley E. Porter, "The 'We' Passages," in *The Book of Acts in Its Graeco-Roman Setting* (eds. David W. Gill and Conrad Gempf; BAFCS 2; Grand Rapids: Eerdmans, 1995), 2:545–74.

can impact our view of the date of Acts.[5] Therefore, the goal is to reflect upon and provide some answers to this guiding question: "How does our knowledge of source theories impact the way we date Acts?"[6]

It is true that the question of sources that Luke uses in writing Acts is "more easily raised than answered," and yet we must raise them because one's *interpretation* of sources directly relates to the issue of dating.[7] For instance, if Acts is dependent on some passages in Paul's letters (and not simply reflecting a common oral tradition), then obviously the date of Acts must take into account the letters of Paul.[8] Additionally, if Acts is dependent upon Josephus's *Antiquities*, this establishes a *terminus a quo* of 93–94 CE for the date of Acts with a range somewhere in the vicinity of 100 and 130 CE.[9] If Pervo is correct, then everyone who dates Acts before 93–94 CE is unambiguously wrong. Therefore, the issue of sources is obviously paramount to this proposal for an early date of Acts.

The Sources of Acts

Dupont's classic study is worth a fresh re-examination given the quality of his work and the influence his conclusions have had on Acts scholarship ever since.[10] And although his final assessment seems notoriously discouraging, many of his other reflections provide valuable insights that may have been missed, misunderstood or misapplied.[11] At the same time there are other studies on the sources of Acts that need to be examined before addressing the major dependency theories (see Chapter 4).

Much of the pioneering research up to the time of Dupont employed a combination of purpose, source, and form-criticism to the "we" and "they" source issues in Acts along with the various forms of the itinerary/diary hypothesis.[12] However, one critical method that appears to be missing in Dupont's work—and in more recent studies—is

---

[5] Recall "Principles for Selecting Sources" from Chapter 2. According to Greene and Moore, *Archaeology*, 155, a fourth criterion for the process of historical dating requires attention to the "quality of the sources available to the writer." See also Tosh, *Pursuit* (6th edn), 73; Bagnall, *Reading Papyri*; and Biers, *Chronology, et passim*.

[6] See "Principles for Interpreting Sources" in Chapter 2.

[7] Longenecker, *Acts*, 221. Nock says that the "relation of Acts to its sources is a thorny topic … For Acts we have only internal evidence and the author's stylistic skill and singleness of purpose make it very hard to probe beneath the surface." Arthur D. Nock, review of *Aufsätze zur Apostelgeschichte*, by Martin Dibelius, *Gnomon* 25 (1953): 497–506 (499).

[8] See Chapter 4. See also the instructive essay by Adam Z. Wright, "A Challenge to Literary Dependency: Deficiencies in Memory to Explain Differences in Oral Tradition," *JGRChJ* 15 (2019): 9–30.

[9] See Pervo, *Dating Acts*, 149–99 (198).

[10] Hemer, *Acts*, 335, refers to this "classic work" that "shows the difficulty clearly"—since it was undertaken "so meticulously and comprehensively." Gasque, *History*, 3, states that "because Dupont has done his job so very well, it has been unnecessary to stress the source criticism of Acts."

[11] See Dupont's, *Sources*, 157–65, and his second, third and fourth points (166–8).

[12] Ibid., 75. For those who are unfamiliar, the "we" passages are sections in Acts where the author employs the first-person pronoun in the text. Traditionally, scholars consider Acts 16:10-17 to contain the first "we" passage where 20:5-15 and 21:1-18 contain the second. The third case is found in Acts 27:1–28:16.

textual criticism.¹³ Given the significant textual variation in Acts, a study of the sources from a text-critical perspective merits further research and may help to answer some of the unsolved "source" mysteries.¹⁴ New approaches to the text are also required since the previous approaches seem to have reached their zenith.

Single Source Theories

If we consider all of the source theories, the "simplest explanation" (though laden with difficulties) is one that "confines itself to a single source."¹⁵ Beyond any general single source theory, there are also some theories (notably by Weiss) that are concerned with finding a single source in the first part of Acts.¹⁶ After Weiss concluded the existence of a single source for the first part of Acts, he considered the possibility of a single source for the second part of Acts.¹⁷ Instead, Dupont supposes that the "unevenness" of this composition is due to a combination of the author's "personal memories" and notes along with other "traditions" that were later incorporated into his work.¹⁸ He suggests that this "process" is not only the reason behind the bumps in the narrative but also an explanation for those passages whose "adventitious character is undeniable."¹⁹

---

[13] For example, Dupont, *Sources*, 76 (n. 1), prefers to "ignore" the "we" in the Western text of Acts 11:28. Meanwhile Porter, *Paul in Acts*, 29 (n. 58), highlights the serious implications of this potential "we."

[14] Smith, "Sources," 75. Stevens rightly claims that "neglecting textual variation means ignoring important features of history." Chris S. Stevens, review of *The Synoptic Problem: Four Views*, by Stanley E. Porter and Bryan R. Dyer, eds., *JGRChJ* 13 (2017): 12–16 (15). The textual variation in Acts is a serious and long-standing issue. In fact, Kenyon calculated that the D text is about 8.5 per cent longer than the (neutral) β-text (18,401 words vs 19,983). Cf. Frederic G. Kenyon, "The Western Text in the Gospels and Acts," *PBA* 24 (1939): 310; Barrett, *Acts*, 1:26, and Tuckett, "How Early," 85.

[15] Dupont, *Sources*, 17. If this single source is extended to "Acts as a whole" then the net result is a book that has been edited and "transformed" from an "earlier text to a greater or lesser degree" (17). There are many "weaknesses" with the various single source theories such as Loisy's "extreme position" that has been often criticized (17–24 [20]). Cf. Alfred Loisy, *Les Actes des Apôtres* (Paris: Emile Nourry, 1920). According to Loisy, the author "completely disfigured the work of Luke." Dupont, *Sources*, 21; Loisy, *Actes*, 89 and 104. According to Kümmel, it seems that the theory of Acts being a "much-altered edition of an earlier work" was abandoned by 1942. Dupont, *Sources*, 24, and Werner G. Kümmel, "Das Urchristentum," *ThR* 14 (1942): 81–93; idem, "Das Urchristentum. II. Die Quellen für die Geschichte des Urchristentums," *ThR* 14 (1942): 155–73 (167).

[16] Dupont, *Sources*, 25–32. This research was championed by Weiss in his grand survey on the sources of Acts (25); Bernhard Weiss, *Lehrbuch der Einleitung in das Neue Testament* (Berlin: Wilhelm Hertz, 1886), 569–84. Weiss noted the "strong Hebrew character" of the first half of Acts, while the language of the second part was "more Greek" and comes closer to that found in the prologue addressed to Theophilus (25–6). Weiss accepted the fact that the author was a companion of Paul and wrote the second part from "oral information" and "personal memories" (26). For Weiss this "Judaeo-Christian" source (for the first part) had undergone many "editorial changes" that resulted in "difficulties of interpretation" with the use of an underlying "basic document" (26). Nigel A. Turner, *A Grammar of New Testament Greek. IV. Style* (Edinburgh: T&T Clark, 1976), 45–63, also discusses the Hebraic character in the early part of Acts (cf. my note 19 below).

[17] Dupont, *Sources*, 26. However, the major problem for Dupont (that remains to this day) is that "all attempts" to discover the "content and character" of this source remain unsuccessful (26).

[18] Ibid., 27.

[19] Ibid., 27. Here he lists the following examples of "discourses and fragments of least importance": Acts 13:6-12; 14:8-18; 16:1-8, 25-34; 17:19; 20:7-12, 16-38; 21:8-14; 23:26-30; 25:14-21, 24-27; 28:17-23. Other attempts such as Charles C. Torrey's, *The Composition and Date of Acts* (HTS 1; Cambridge, MA: Harvard University Press, 1916), Aramaic source hypothesis behind the first fifteen chapters of Acts may be useful in some specific cases but not as an "explanation" for the origin of Acts (Dupont, *Sources*, 31). See also Harald A. Sahlin, *Der Messias und das Gottesvolk: Studien zur protolukanischen*

Parallel Source Theories

The Parallel source theory—also referred to as two-source theory—is the view that the "composition of the text" is the result of a combination of two earlier accounts; a theory first proposed by Spitta.[20] Spitta's hypothesis was subsequently modified by others until Harnack considered the question of sources with his landmark study.[21] Harnack reasoned that it was "not possible to take either vocabulary or style as a basis: they were everywhere the same; if Luke used sources, he merely reproduced them in his own language and imposed his personal stamp on them."[22] Harnack also discounted the "criterion of discrepancies" because these inaccuracies and contradictions can be found throughout the book and "clearly indicate a certain negligence on the part of the writer."[23] Harnack, along with later writers, variously built upon Spitta's original (Source A and B) parallel source theory in the first part of Acts.[24] Such explanations for the "composition of Acts" remain questionable.[25]

Complementary Source Theories

The third group is in many ways an extension of the previous parallel source theories since they often reflect "complementary sources."[26] For example, De Zwaan found at least three sources in the first half of Acts: (1) the "we" passage material that "must go back to the years 56–62" CE, (2) an outline that was composed during 75–80 CE, and (3) the final composition of sources that were written under Trajan (c. 110 CE).[27] A few

---

Theologie (ASNU 12; Uppsala: Almqvist & Wiksells, 1945), who proposed that "Proto-Luke" was behind Lk. 1:5–Acts 15:33 (Lk. 1:5–3:7 was written in Hebrew and the rest in Aramaic). Cf. also Aubrey W. Argyle, "The Theory of an Aramaic Source in Acts 2:14–40," *JTS* 4 (1953): 213–14, and Raymond A. Martin, "Syntactical Evidence of Aramaic Sources in Acts 1–15," *NTS* 11 (1964): 38–59. More recently, Turner, *Style*, 45–63, thinks the Aramaic influence to be minimal (45–46) while the Hebrew influence is "far more extensive" and goes beyond the infancy narrative (46). He claims "there is no doubt that some of the Aramaisms, Hebraisms, and Semitisms must be attributed to the use of sources" along with Greek sources "which had been translated therefrom" (55).

[20] Dupont, *Sources*, 33–50 (33). It was Friedrich Spitta, *Die Apostelgeschichte: Ihre Quellen und deren geschichtlicher Wert* (Halle: Waisenhauses, 1891), 34, who initially saw a "Source A" that provided the material for up to chapter 24 of the third gospel and Acts 1:15 to the end. Spitta considered the "we" sections to be of "great historical value" since Luke was an eyewitness (Dupont, *Sources*, 34; Spitta, *Die Apostelgeschichte*). Source B that "scarcely deserves credence" was added (after 70 CE) and was described as a "popular account" with a "weakness for legends" (34). Spitta (34) estimated that the "fusion of the two documents" probably occurred near the "end of the first century" by an "impartial editor."

[21] Dupont, *Sources*, 35; Adolf Harnack, *Die Apostelgeschichte* (BENT III; Leipzig: Hinrichs, 1908), 131–88; idem, *Acts of the Apostles*, 162–200.

[22] Dupont, *Sources*, 35; Harnack, *Die Apostelgeschichte*, 131, and Turner, *Style*, 55–7.

[23] Dupont, *Sources*, 35. After these criteria were dealt with, Harnack surmised that it was "impossible to prove" that Acts 15:36 onwards was "based on sources" (35). He claimed that "at most" what we can say is that "Luke made use of personal notes, or a travel journal, to narrate the events in which he took part in Paul's company"—along with the "information he gleaned from the lips of other witnesses of this period" (35). See also Harnack, *Die Apostelgeschichte*, 13, 159–77 and 177–82.

[24] Dupont, *Sources*, 37–8.

[25] Ibid., 50.

[26] Ibid., 51–61 (51).

[27] Ibid., 55. The first (55) is a document "written in Aramaic" underlying 1:3–5:16 and 9:31–11:18 that was "composed shortly before the Jewish revolt." The second is a tradition received while Luke was

decades later Trocmé found extra layers in the first part of Acts—especially those that hail from specific sources such as a Hellenistic source in Acts 6:1-7.[28] He also thinks that from Acts 13:4 onwards Luke uses a "diary" which "supplies at least the outlines of the narrative to the end of the book."[29] In the end, the "varied sets of documents" that Trocmé seeks for his reconstruction did not "meet with much favour."[30]

Antioch Source Theories

Harnack's work sparked further studies on the Antioch source by Wendt and Jeremias, which in turn led to two key essays by Bultmann and Benoit.[31] Subsequently, Jeremias examines Harnack's hypothesis and challenges the two parallel source view in Acts 2–5 claiming the increase in details, paired with a change in tone, is an indication of a "new source."[32] After Jeremias, Bultmann addresses Haenchen's scepticism on the sources for Acts and claims that it is easier to understand certain passages (such as Acts 15:1-35) if there is a written source behind it.[33] For Benoit, Luke was not interested in simply

---

in Caesarea (about 57–59 CE) based on Acts 8:4-40 and 12:1-24. The third source is a "tradition associated with Antioch and Jerusalem" that supplies Acts 5:17–8:3; 11:19-30 and 12:25–15:35. Acts (55) further "makes use of material coming from Luke: 9:1-30 and from 15:36 to the end." See Johannes De Zwaan, *De Handelingen der Apostelen* (Groningen [The Hague]: Wolters, 1920), 10–15.

[28] Dupont, *Sources*, 60. Etienne Trocmé, *Le 'Livre des Actes' et l'histoire* (Paris: Presses Universitaires de France, 1957), 154–214 (on the sources for chapters 1–15).

[29] Dupont, *Sources*, 60. See "The Itinerary/Diary/Travelogue Hypothesis" below.

[30] Ibid., 60. See also, Frederick C. Grant, *The Gospels: Their Origin and Their Growth* (London: Faber and Faber, 1957), 126. Grant outlines five groups of sources: (1) an ancient tradition (Jerusalem or Judaea related to Peter); (2) a tradition related to Stephen and Acts 6:1–8:1a; (3) a Caesarean tradition concerning Philip: Acts 8:1b-40; (4) an "Antioch tradition" stemming from Barnabas and Saul (Acts 4:36ff; 11:19-30; 12:24–14:28 and 15:1–16:5); and (5) various "Pauline" source material (from 9:1-30; part of 12:24–14:48; 15:1–16:5 plus the remaining 16:6–28:31). Dupont (61) thinks that it is "no longer possible to distinguish or identify" this material because Luke has rewritten them.

[31] See Harnack, *Die Apostelgeschichte*; Hans H. Wendt, "Die Hauptquelle der Apostelgeschichte," *ZAW* 24 (1925): 293–305; Joachim Jeremias, "Untersuchungen zum Quellenproblem der Apostelgeschichte," *ZNW* 36 (1937): 205–21; Rudolf Bultmann, "Zur Frage nach den Quellen der Apostelgeschichte," in *New Testament Essays: Studies in Memory of Thomas Walter Manson* (ed. Angus J. Brockhurst Higgins; Manchester: Manchester University Press, 1959), 68–80, and Pierre Benoit, "La deuxième visite de Saint Paul à Jérusalem," *Bib* 40 (1959): 778–92 (vs. Dupont, *Sources*, 69 [n. 28]: 778–96). A few years before Harnack, Wendt, *Die Apostelgeschichte* (8th edn), 63, (in relation to an Antioch theory of sorts) hypothesized that the "rewriting" of the "we" sections demonstrates how the author of these sections should *not* "be identified with the writer of Acts." Wendt, "Die Hauptquelle der Apostelgeschichte," 293–305, and also Porter, *Paul in Acts*, 39.

[32] Jeremias, "Quellenproblem der Apostelgeschichte," 205–21; Dupont, *Sources*, 64. Jeremias sought to remove the interpolations in order to demarcate this source (i.e., Acts 8:5-40; 9:31–11:18; 12:1-24 and 15:1-33). As a result, we are left with a written Antioch source of "great value" (64). Jeremias attributes Acts 6:1–8:4; 9:1-30; 11:19-30; 12:25–14:28 and 15:35 to the end of the book as the Antioch source. Subsequently, Dupont, *Sources*, 65, challenges Jeremias's methodology based on Kümmel's argument in "Das Urchristentum. II," 155–73.

[33] Bultmann, "Quellen der Apostelgeschichte," 68–80 (68), and Haenchen, *Acts*. This leads to the consideration of a greater source at Luke's disposal which would "account for the linking of the periscopes" for large parts of the book. See Dupont, *Sources*, 67. This "account of Paul's missions" depends in part on an "itinerary" that was "written in the first-person plural" as discussed by Dibelius and subsequently borrowed by Haenchen; Dupont, *Sources*, 67, 94 and Martin Dibelius, *Studies in the Acts of the Apostles* (ed. Heinrich Greeven; London: SCM, 1956), 73–4. Bultmann claims the presence of the itinerary is "unmistakable" from Acts 16 onwards (Dupont, *Sources*, 67).

"reproducing the sources" he received since he places his "personal stamp" on them as indicated by the substantial editing throughout his entire book.[34] While this helps us to understand the process of composition, the challenge of identifying specific sources remains.

The "We" Source Theories

One "fairly obvious" source for Acts relates to the long-standing conversation concerning the internal "we" sections.[35] If the author's intention was to give the impression that he was included in the passages (even when he was not) then other literary and linguistic factors are at work.[36] Conversely, the "simplest" and "most obvious" solution is that the "we" passages imply that the author was personally present during those times.[37] However, the simplest solution may not be the best interpretation of the available data since the other side to this equation begs the question: "Why would an author who is writing the entire work retain the "we" sections if it, like the rest of the work, is his own?" The arguably "simple" and "obvious" alternative is that this represents some other person that was present in the narrative, or why else retain "we"?[38]

And yet, Bultmann considers the Antioch source and the itinerary to be separate—at least to the extent that it is "unlikely" they "ever formed a literary unity" (69).

[34] Dupont, *Sources*, 70; Benoit, "La Deuxième Visite," 778–92. Hence the difficulty in identifying sources since we are dealing with edited fragments. Benoit, "La Deuxième Visite," 780; Dupont, *Sources*, 70. Benoit's real contribution lies in his understanding of "Luke's processes of composition" (72). The sections which "Luke dovetails" are not simply documents that he received as they are "rewritings by his own hand" that are later "joined" together with "omissions and link passages" (Benoit, 790; Dupont, 72). Weiss, *Einleitung*, 569–84 seems to have influenced Dupont's thinking here as well.

[35] Bruce, *Acts* (3rd edn), 40. See also, Henry J. Cadbury, "'We' and 'I' Passages in Luke-Acts," *NTS* 3 (1957): 128–32; Porter, *Paul in Acts*, 10–46; Susan M. Praeder, "The Problem of First Person Narration in Acts," *NovT* 29 (1987): 193–218; Sean A. Adams, "The Relationships of Paul and Luke: Luke, Paul's Letters, and the 'We' Passages of Acts," in *Paul and His Social Relations* (eds. Stanley E. Porter and Christopher D. Land; Pauline Studies 7; Leiden: Brill, 2013), 125–42; Hemer, *Acts*, 308–34; Colin J. Hemer, "First Person Narrative in Acts 27–28," *TynBul* 36 (1985): 79–86; William S. Campbell, "The Narrator as 'He,' 'Me,' and 'We': Grammatical Person in Ancient Histories and in the Acts of the Apostles," *JBL* 129 (2010): 385–407; idem, *The 'We' Passages in the Acts of the Apostles: The Narrator as Narrative Character* (SBLStBL 14; Atlanta: SBL, 2007), *et passim*; Vernon K. Robbins, "By Land and By Sea: The We-Passages and Ancient Sea Voyages," in *Perspectives on Luke-Acts* (ed. Charles H. Talbert; ABPRSSS 5; Edinburgh: T&T Clark, 1978), 215–42 and his earlier essay: idem, "The We-Passages in Acts and Ancient Sea Voyages," *BR* 20 (1975): 5–18. The "we" passages, as a source in Acts, are for many scholars a rose with many thorns. See Dupont, *Sources*, 75–112 (esp. pp. 75–93). The issue is attractive as it bears greatly on matters of its "historical reliability" according to Porter, *Paul in Acts*, 10, and the "questions of source and authorship" but the debate is contentious and prickly at the same time. For an annotated bibliography see Joel B. Green and Michael C. McKeever, *Luke-Acts and New Testament Historiography* (IBRB 8; Grand Rapids: Baker, 1994), 140–3 and also "Acts in History" in Chapter 8 of this volume.

[36] E.g., Porter, *Paul in Acts*, 38–42, and Dupont, *Sources*, 77, who notes the "many writers" who reject the simple solution for "various reasons."

[37] Dupont, *Sources*, 77. Today, this conclusion still finds favour. See Keener, *Acts*, 3:2373; 1:413.

[38] Porter, in addition to this editorial insight, argues that the "we" sections point to a "previously written 'we' source" that "probably" originated elsewhere. Porter, *Paul in Acts*, 41. He questions the connection between the prologue (Lk. 1:1-4) as indicative of the author's eyewitness testimony (41). He considers it to be "more likely" the author of Acts used a "continuous, independent source, probably discovered in the course of his investigation of the events of early Christianity" (41).

Definition of the "We" Passages

At this juncture, it seems appropriate to define the "we" passages before engaging the various proposals.[39] Where many traditionally speak of three "we" passages (Acts 16:10-17 = the first; 20:5-15 and 21:1-18 = the second; and 27:1-28:16 = the third), Porter has made a convincing case that there are at least five "we" sections.[40] The first extends from Acts 16:10-17, the second from 20:5-15, the third from 21:1-18, the fourth from 27:1-29, and the fifth being Acts 28:1-16.[41] One minor contention is that the fifth "we" passage should be extended beyond verse 16 all the way to verse 29 (and possibly 31).[42]

A far greater contention arises from the possibility of a sixth passage—or better to call it, the first of six—if we consider the "we" found in the "Western" text of Acts 11:28.[43] Rather than ignore this rogue "we" to the textual scrap-pile, it is worth serious consideration.[44] Since this "we" is early, it offers a clue to the source debate and the date of Acts.[45] For example, Wendt considered the reading of the "we" in Bezae at 11:28 to be authentic while offering a clue to the origins of the Antioch source.[46] Wendt

---

[39] Porter, *Paul in Acts*, 10, 28–33, and Foakes-Jackson and Lake's four hypotheses in: Dupont, *Sources*, 89.

[40] Dupont, *Sources*, 76; Campbell, *The 'We' Passages*, 1; and Porter, *Paul in Acts*, 28–33.

[41] See Porter, *Paul in Acts*, 28–33.

[42] Cadbury, "'We' and 'I' Passages," 128, says that if the guard is still there, it is very doubtful that the "we" group left Paul in Rome by himself—since only three days have passed (Ἐγένετο δὲ μετὰ ἡμέρας τρεῖς). Furthermore, the nature of the exchange between Paul and the Jews in the remaining verses implies an eyewitness from among the "we" that just landed in Rome. The alternative is that "they" left Rome within two days of arriving there, leaving the apostle alone. Similarly, Keener, *Acts*, 3:2350 (n. 501), explains that Paul's travelling companion "must have been in the same geographic vicinity with Paul" for the entire section. We can only speculate when Paul's company (including Luke) left the city (or if they did at all) during Paul's two-year house arrest in Rome (c. 60–62; 2 Tim. 4:11).

[43] Dupont, *Sources*, 76 (n. 1), refers to "several" unnamed writers that think this "we" at Acts 11:28 should be added, but for him it "seems preferable to ignore." However, his focus was not upon textual criticism, nor was he privy to the resurgence in the broader textual studies on the Western variants of Acts that began in the 1980s—see Delobel, "Luke-Acts," 83. See Peter Head, "Acts and the Problem of Its Texts," in *The Book of Acts in Its Ancient Literary Setting* (eds. Bruce W. Winter and Andrew D. Clarke; 5 vols; BAFCS 1; Grand Rapids: Eerdmans, 1993), 415–44 (420 [n. 30]), for a list of the Western passages that are different from the Alexandrian. For the details of those differences see also Hemer, *Acts*, 193–201. Hemer (200) remarks how the Western readings have an "early pedigree as a revision" and "may preserve correct traditions or inferences."

[44] Cf. Hill and Kruger, "Introduction," 1–19 (5), in reference to Ehrman, "Text as Window," 361–79. The Western "we" of Acts 11:28 is a microcosm of a much larger problem. For example, Eldon J. Epp, "Anti-Judaic Tendencies in the D-Text of Acts: Forty Years of Conversation," in *The Book of Acts as Church History: Text, Textual Traditions and Ancient Interpretations* (eds. Tobias Nicklas and Michael Tilly; BZNW 120; Berlin: de Gruyter, 2003), 11, remarks how the "text of Acts" is "legendary for its problems." Charles K. Barrett, *Luke the Historian in Recent Study* (London: Epworth, 1961), 22, similarly complains that in "no other New Testament book is the problem so vexed." And yet, the "Old Uncial text" *and* the Western text (taken together) "give us an excellent idea of what Luke had to say" (22). Even if we conclude the Western "we" was *not* in the "initial" text of Acts, it formed a very early and significant branch of the textual tradition. See Chapter 7 of this volume.

[45] Bruce, *Acts* (3rd edn), 275, remarks on the importance of this "we" passage primarily because it appears "earlier than any in the β text" (β = the Alexandrian text with Codex Vaticanus (B) as the primary witness, see p. 70).

[46] Dupont, *Sources*, 63 (n. 6), hints at Wendt's support of this but without a specific reference. See Hans H. Wendt, *Die Apostelgeschichte* (6th and 7th edn; KEK 3; Göttingen: Vandenhoeck & Ruprecht, 1888), 21–2 (and his footnote at the bottom of both pages).

may be correct, especially given the renaissance of recent theories on the text(s) of Acts.[47]

More recently, the reading of the text of Acts 11:28 without the "we" variant indicates a "certainty of 'A'" as it stands in the UBSGNT.[48] The implication is that if this "we" was original, the "entire argument" in Porter's chapter and in "many other treatments of the 'we' passages would have to be re-assessed."[49] This is reason enough to warrant a further investigation—but also because of the early date of the Western text. At the very least this should be investigated because of the renewed emphasis in textual criticism on the value of all variants (especially the early ones) as important for the study of early Christianity.

Instead of the established text of Acts 11:28 (ἀναστὰς δὲ εἷς ἐξ αὐτῶν ὀνόματι Ἄγαβος ἐσήμανεν) accepted by the NA/UBSGNT there is a Western variant: (ἦν δὲ πολλὴ ἀγαλλίασις· συνεστραμμένων δὲ ἡμῶν ἔφη <u>εἷς ἐξ αὐτῶν ὀνόματι Ἄγαβος σημαινων</u>) "There was great joy, and when we were gathered together <u>one of them named Agabus</u> said signifying."[50] The reading text of Bezae is reproduced here (folio 461v, col. 1, line 31 of Acts 11:27):

---

[47] This view is dependent upon my hypothesis (in Chapter 7) that both textual families developed before 70 CE. This relates to Epp's theory that the Western and Alexandrian texts are comparable in age. See Eldon J. Epp, "Traditional 'Canons' of New Testament Textual Criticism: Their Value, Validity, and Viability—or Lack Thereof," in *The Textual History of the Greek New Testament: Changing Views in Contemporary Research* (eds. Klaus Wachtel and Michael Holmes; SBLTCS 8; Leiden: Brill, 2012), 100, and Armstrong, "Variants," 87–110. Furthermore, Bruce, *Acts* (3rd edn), 9, says that if the Western text of Acts 11:28 "reflects the tradition (which is likely), then the tradition must not be later than the middle of the second century." In light of an early Western text, it is more probable that the variant generates the tradition because the former likely arose before the latter. The later tradition comes from Eusebius (*Hist. Eccl.* 3.4.6) who writes: "And Luke, whose family was from Antioch, and a physician by profession, a close associate of Paul" (Λουκᾶς δὲ τὸ μὲν γένος ὢν τῶν ἀπ Ἀντιοχείας, τὴν ἐπιστήμην δὲ ἰατρός, τὰ πλεῖστα συγγεγονὼς τῷ Παύλῳ). And also Jerome (*De vir. ill.* 3.7:1): "Lucus medicus Antiochensis" and the *Anti-Marcionite Prologue* to Luke: "Luke, the doctor from Antioch, disciple of the apostles, remained unmarried and died in Boeotia at age eighty-four." See Keener, *Acts*, 1:410. Keener, 1:411 (n. 58), says that some use the variant in 11:28 (which "places the author in Antioch" as "secondary evidence") to support Lukan authorship. Last, Keener, *Acts*, 1:411, via Bruce, *Acts* (3rd edn), 427, and earlier Frederick C. Conybeare, "The Commentary of Ephrem on Acts." In *The Beginnings of Christianity*, 3:442, point to a unique reading in Acts 20:13 following Ἡμεῖς δὲ from an old Syriac text (syr[vet?]) of an uncertain date that ties Luke to this we passage.

[48] Porter, *Paul in Acts*, 28 (n. 58). Porter (n. 58) questions the "validity of including A readings" in the GNT.

[49] Porter, *Paul in Acts*, 29 (n. 58). Porter (n. 58) says the "textual traditions of Acts" fall outside his "purview." My purpose here is not to "prove" this text but simply that it is, at the very least, an early and notable variant.

[50] Note that φημί [imperfect, active, indicative, third-person, singular] is not found in the established text while σημαίνω [present, active participle] is unique to D. The underlined text represents the same text found in the critical edition and the variants. The NA[28] shows only the following supporting manuscripts for this reading: D, p, w, and mae (G[67]) where the NA[26] did not list (w) but included the old Latin of Bezae and Augustine (c. 430 CE) as well. William A. Strange, *The Problem of the Text of Acts* (SNTSMS 71; Cambridge: Cambridge University Press, 1992), 43, includes the following additional manuscripts: it[62] (ro), vg[1259*.1260. 1277.1282]. See also Marie-Emile Boismard and Arnaud Lamouille, *Le texte occidental des Actes des Apôtres: Reconstitution et rehabilitation* (rev. edn; 2 vols; Paris: Gabalda, 2000), 195–6. Bezae Codex (D) (05) is usually dated to the fourth or fifth century CE. See Barrett, *Acts*, 1:5; Tuckett, "How Early," 70–1. The old Latin version p (54) is from the twelfth century CE and w (58) is fourteenth or fifteenth century.

(31) προφῆται εἰς ἀντιόχειαν
(32) ἦν δὲ πολλὴ ἀγαλλίασις (v. 28)
(33) συνεστραμμένων δὲ ἡμῶν

Folio 462v, col. 1:
(1) ἔφη[51] εἷς ἐξ αὐτῶν ὀνόματι ἄγαβος
(2) σημένων[52] διὰ τοῦ $\overline{πνς}$[53]
(3) λειμὸν μέγαν[54] μέλλειν ἔσεσθαι.

Additionally, manuscript G[67] represents an early fourth or fifth century witness to the Western text of Acts 11:28.[55] The text of G[67] must be earlier than the "date of the MS itself" because it is not the "working copy of the translator of this Coptic version, but is the work of a professional copyist working from an older MS."[56] Petersen compares D with G[67] and transcribes 11:27-28 as: "down to Antioch, *and there was great joy about our returning*."[57] Until more early and comparable manuscripts are discovered, G[67] "must be accorded the very great importance which it properly deserves."[58]

There is another reason why the Western "we" should be given serious consideration—the early papyri. Although P[45] contains Acts 11:24-30 and follows the Alexandrian tradition at verse 28, it is the *only* early Acts manuscript with 11:28. P[45] is interesting because despite its affinity with the Alexandrian uncials (ℵ, A, B, C), when

---

[51] Boismard and Lamouille, *Le Texte Occidental*, 196, do not think ἔφη is possible here: "Dans D, la séquence εφ η (=εφη) . . . σημενων est impossible." However unlikely ἔφη is the more difficult reading (and what we find in Bezae). See Metzger, *Text*, 120. Boismard and Lamouille's conjecture does not seem palpable as they argue the scribe was distracted by ἀνέστη and the Latin *ait*. This they think is verified by G[67] since it has ἀνέστη in place of ἔφη. They could be right, but there is nothing in D to imply that ἔφη should be split. Bruce, *Acts* (3rd edn), 275, the INTF and the NA[28] all assume ἔφη.
[52] The Nestle-Aland and also Boismard and Lamouille, *Le Texte Occidental*, 196, should be corrected as Bezae has σημένων here and not σημαίνων.
[53] This is the *nomen sacrum* for πνεύματος and has the line above the letters to signify it as such.
[54] Corrector 1 added λη just above and between the α and the ν = μέγαλην (μέγαν is the original hand). You can see μεγάλην in P[45] (folio 25r, col. 1, line 7).
[55] Eldon J. Epp, "Coptic Manuscript G67 and the Rôle of Codex Bezae as a Western Witness in Acts," *JBL* 85 (1966): 197-212 (207); Hans-Martin Schenke, ed., *Apostelgeschichte 1, 1-15, 3 im mittelägyptischen Dialekt des Koptischen (Codex Glazier)* (TU 137; Berlin: Akademie Verlag, 1991), 1; and Pierpont's curatorial note. G[67] has not yet been digitized.
[56] Epp, "Coptic Manuscript," 199. This may explain some of the differences between D and G[67] (i.e., ἀνέστη in G[67] vs. ἔφη in D). Theodore C. Petersen, "An Early Coptic Manuscript of Acts: An Unrevised Version of the Ancient So-Called Western Text," *CBQ* 26 (1964): 229 (n. 12), says they "were ordered from a professional copyist, perhaps for the purpose of having them replace older papyrus manuscripts." Roberts thought it should be dated to the "very late fourth or the fifth century" while Skeat suggested the fifth century. Petersen, "Coptic Manuscript," 225 (n. 3). Pierpont library says it is fifth century and Bruce M. Metzger, *The Early Versions of the New Testament: Their Origin, Transmission, and Limitations* (Oxford: Clarendon, 1977), 119, thinks it is fourth or fifth century.
[57] Petersen, "Coptic Manuscript," 239 (original emphasis). See also Epp, "Coptic Manuscript," 207. Epp (207) notes the "additional συνεστραμμενων δε ημων of D (and the other witnesses above, plus Ado) is perhaps attested also by the 'about *our* returning'" of G[67]. Metzger claims that in Acts Bezae is "fond of the verb συστρέφειν, which it introduces in 10:41; 11:28; 16:39; 17:5." Bruce M. Metzger, *A Textual Commentary on the Greek New Testament* (1st edn; London: United Bible Societies, 1971), 381.
[58] Epp, "Coptic Manuscript," 199.

it comes to the gospels (Matthew, Luke, and John) they are known to exhibit a mix of Alexandrian *and* Western traditions.[59] Of greater importance is the fact that *none* of the remaining five early Acts papyri contain Acts 11:28 (along with the early third-century parchment 0189).[60] This is significant because it is possible that the Western "we" may have originally been a part of those early manuscripts.

To be clear, none of this discussion is a bid to redefine the source debate and insist that the first "we" passage begins at Acts 11:28.[61] At the very least this "we" represents a very early variant and a correspondingly earlier tradition than previously thought in light of my proposal for an early date of the Western text of Acts (cf. Chapter 7). Where the traditional connections between Antioch and Luke as the author of Acts merit a level of caution, an early source for the Western text at Antioch may increase the strength of this connection in light of Cadbury's earlier assessment:

> Large sections of the book represent Antioch as the center of the story, the starting point for Gentile Christianity and for the name Christian, and the "home base" of Paul's work for foreign missions. A proselyte of Antioch is mentioned by name among the Seven at Jerusalem, and later five teachers resident at Antioch are listed. One of these, Lucius of Cyrene, was apparently at an early time identified with the author Lucas.[62]

Further to the point is Cadbury's observation that the "first appearance of the pronoun 'we' is at Antioch" and it is found in a "very early form of the text (commonly called 'Western')."[63] What is proposed here is that the origin of the Western variant (or

---

[59] See Comfort, *Manuscripts*, 66.

[60] To date there are only six early papyri for Acts (P29, P38, P45, P48, P53, and P91) and one third-century parchment (0189). See Tuckett, "Early Text," 157, and his note 1. We cannot know for certain if they contained the Western "we" but it is very possible since three of the earliest six papyri of Acts show Western readings (P29, P38, and P48), and the proto-Alexandrian P91 is too fragmentary to tell. Tuckett, "How Early," 74; Comfort, *Manuscripts*, 64 and 69 and Barrett, *Acts*, 1:2.

[61] Porter, *Paul in Acts*, 29 (n. 58).

[62] Cf. Cadbury, *Luke-Acts*, 245. Although Bruce, *Acts* (3rd edn), 9, struggles with the equivalence of "Lucius of Cyrene" (Acts 13:1) with Luke (as the author of Acts) he says that Luke "certainly shows a special interest in Antioch" and goes on to list examples (9). It does not seem coincidental that the account of the church's founding in Antioch is much "fuller" than any other Gentile church (9 [note his reference should be to Acts 11:19-26 instead of 1:19-26]). The emphasis on Nicolas, a proselyte of Antioch (Acts 6:5), along with the special and early role of Barnabas stands out so much from the surrounding narrative that the same charge with regard to the extra "we" in 11:28 (that the scribe(s) is are/following the Antioch tradition) could be laid against these passages as well: Acts 4:36-37 (and possibly Ananias and Sapphira 5:1-11 and further); 9:27; 11:19-30; from 12:25 all the way to 15:4; 15:12, 22, 25, 36-39 where Barnabas "leaves Antioch with Mark to prosecute his mission in Cyprus" (9). Acts 15:39 is the last we hear of this key leader from Antioch while the rest of the book (to Acts 28:31) rests unequivocally on Paul. It is entirely plausible that Barnabas (and/or Luke) could very well be the primary "Antioch" source for the middle half of Acts (c. 11:19–15:39) where Paul (and/or Luke, Silas and Timothy) make up the second Rome source from Acts 15:40 onwards to 28:31. See also Richard Glover, "'Luke the Antiochene' and Acts," *NTS* 11 (1964): 97–106, and Markus Öhler's chapter on "Der historische Barnabas–ein Rekonstructionsversuch," in *Barnabas: Die historische Person und ihre Rezeption in der Apostelgeschichte* (WUNT 156; Tübingen: Mohr Siebeck, 2003), 478–86 and also Markus Öhler, *Barnabas: Der Mann in der Mitte* (BG 12; Leipzig: Evangelische Verlagsanstalt, 2005), *et passim*.

[63] Cadbury, *Luke-Acts*, 245. Bruce thinks that ἡμῶν in Acts 11:28 is "probably due to the reviser's acquaintance with the tradition that Luke was a native of Antioch." Bruce, *Acts* (3rd edn), 275;

however we define it) began here at Antioch first, which in due course launched the known traditions connecting Antioch with the author of Luke-Acts.[64] This hypothesis is compatible with an early date of the Alexandrian and Western families.

It is further proposed that Luke, along with his own notes and memories, relied on Barnabas as a source from Antioch as well for the middle half of Acts (*c*. 11:19–15:39), while Paul (along with Luke, Silas or Timothy) provided the Rome source for the last section of Acts (*c*. 15:40–28:31).[65] There is also the possibility that the addition of the "we" passage in Acts 11:28 was an intentional deletion by other scribes in an attempt to minimize this Antioch tradition for ecclesiastical reasons.[66] These interpretations should be given fair consideration rather than simply ignoring the textual record and the historiographical context behind them.[67]

"We" Proposals

Although a concrete solution to the problem of the "we" passages is beyond the purview of this inquiry, this aspect of the source issue impacts one's view of dating.[68]

Longenecker, *Acts*, 405; Barrett, *Acts*, 1:564. Pervo, *Acts*, 296, also maintains that the use of the first-person plural "either reflects or helps to create the association of the author of Acts with Antioch." Pervo (n. 63) via Haenchen, *Acts*, 374 (n. 7), argues that it is likely that the "author was identified with Lucius of Cyrene" from Acts 13:1. In addition to the Antioch association, Pervo, *Acts*, 296, supposes that the insertion of the "we" (here in 11:28) reflects a second-century preference for eyewitness accounts. In his footnote (62) he cites the following as his reasoning: "'We' does not otherwise occur after the arrival of new characters in Acts." This seems to be pure speculation that grew out of his second-century view of Acts in the first place. While discussing the tradition that links Luke with Antioch, Hemer, *Acts*, 345 states that the "we" in the Western reading of Acts 11:28 "may reflect the early currency of this tradition" and also the "occasional identification in Acts of an Antioch-source." See also Eusebius, *Hist. Ecc.* 3.4.6 and Dupont, *Sources*, 36, 62–72.

[64] Here I am appealing to transcriptional probabilities in light of the historical conditions and the possibility of the author's (or better reviser's) purpose in writing. See Gordon D. Fee, "Textual Criticism of the New Testament," in *Studies in the Theory and Method of New Testament Textual Criticism* (eds. Eldon J. Epp and Gordon D. Fee; SD 45; Grand Rapids: Eerdmans, 1993), 14; Metzger, *Text*, 209; Comfort, *Manuscripts*, 292, and Porter and Pitts, *Fundamentals*, 110–28. If this "we" passage is early, perhaps this variant sparked the Antioch tradition instead of the other way around. Although it may simply be a scribe's (or editor's) attempt to reinforce the tradition that Luke is from (or connected with) Antioch, it seems that ἦν δὲ πολλὴ ἀγαλλίασις fits the earlier context of χαίρω in verse 23 and the growth of the church in verse 24. It is also worth noting how ἀγαλλίασις in the Western version of Acts 11:28 is also found in Lk. 1:14, 44; Acts 2:46 (and Hebrews 1:9; Jude 24). Additionally, one of the words from the variant is found in the same form in Lk. 1:14 ἀγαλλίασις (nominative, feminine, singular) while in Acts 2:46 ἀγαλλίασις appears in the dative (feminine, singular). The variant from Antioch reflects the earlier picture of a happy (11:28[D]/2:46), growing (11:21, 24/2:47), sharing (2:45/11:29) church that gathered (11:28[D]/2:44, 46) in Jerusalem in Acts 2:42-47.

[65] Recall my note 62 above and Hengel, *Acts*, 39 (pointing to the significance of Antioch and Barnabas), 65; Haenchen, *Acts*, 86–87, 369 and the previous section on the "Antioch Source Theories."

[66] Cf. Kirsopp Lake, *The Influence of Textual Criticism on the Exegesis of the New Testament* (Oxford: Parker and Son, 1904), 10; Epp, "Traditional 'Canons,'" 127; Vaganay, *Introduction*, 60. These changes could be motivated by political or doctrinal motivations.

[67] See "Principles for Interpreting Sources" in Chapter 2 and Reinfandt, "Reading Texts," 41–58.

[68] The "we" (and they) passages point to a source (or sources). If the sources are connected with the author then the writing of Acts must fall within the life of the author and (to some degree) the lives of the persons he narrates, and especially the datable events that they have participated in. Even if it can be proven—and it has not—that the "we" passages did not originate with the author and instead

Setting aside the first of five (or six "we" passages if we allow for the Western variant of Acts 11:28), what is to be made of the major proposals?[69] The traditional explanation still carries a great number of adherents who follow the "simplest" and "most obvious solution."[70] This traditional explanation of the "we" passages goes back at least as far as Holtzmann, who thought the "narrator who says 'we' in certain parts of Acts is to be identified with the writer of the work."[71] Subsequently, Harnack became the "great champion" for those who identified the author of the "we" passages as the author of Acts.[72] Afterwards, Cadbury agreed with Harnack concerning the "unity of the language" that exists between the "we-passages and the rest of the book."[73]

However, this only demonstrates that Luke has reworked his sources so much that the "criterion of vocabulary or style" of a passage becomes useless when it comes to assessing whether or not its composition makes use of a document.[74] Accordingly,

point to other sources, this only reinforces the multiple attestation of the events in Acts that can be dated. See also Kosso's, *Knowing the Past*, 51, criteria for assessing textual credibility.

[69] Porter, *Paul in Acts*, 10, offers a summary of the four respective positions: (1) traditional—the author was a personally present eyewitness, (2) source-critical—a literary source (diary/itinerary) from the author or "more likely from another writer," (3) redaction-critical—a document that reflects the "author's imaginative editorial manipulation," or (4) literary-critical—the "we" passages are literary creations. See also Dupont, *Sources*, 89.

[70] Keener, *Acts*, 3:2373; Dupont, *Sources*, 77. One of the major reasons why Keener supports a date of Acts close to 70 CE (see *Acts*, 1:384) rests on his view that a "companion of Paul" best explains the "we" passages. See Keener, *Acts*, 3:2373 and his note on Acts 16:10 (*Acts*, 3:2350–74). Since Keener considers the arguments "compelling" for the author being a travelling companion of Paul, he "would restrict any date estimate . . . to within the probable lifetime of such a companion." Keener, *Acts*, 1:400. See my note 64 in Chapter 1. If we follow Keener's estimation that Luke was about 30 years old at 50 CE, he would have reached average life expectancy around 67 CE—thus restricting the time frame accordingly. Hengel similarly claims that the "we" passages "do not go back to an earlier independent source, nor are they a mere literary convention, giving the impression that the author was an eyewitness." Hengel, *Acts*, 66. As far as the author conveying the "impression of personal integrity and trustworthiness by a literary device" Marshall, like Hengel, remains unconvinced. See I. Howard Marshall, review of *The "We" Passages in the Acts of the Apostles: The Narrator as Narrative Character*, by William Sanger Campbell, *JTS* 59 (2008): 755–7 (756).

[71] Dupont, *Sources*, 82; Heinrich J. Holtzmann, *Lehrbuch der historisch-kritischen Einleitung in das Neue Testament* (2nd rev. edn; Freiberg: J. C. B. Mohr [Paul Siebeck], 1886), 406–9. Holtzmann focused on three common areas of justification for the now traditional position: (1) the "ecclesiastical tradition," (2) the "unity of style and language" of Luke-Acts, (3) that Lk. 1:3 implies the "manner of using the first person plural in the latter part of his work." Dupont, *Sources*, 82.

[72] Dupont, *Sources*, 83. Dupont, 83 (n. 21), notes that Cadbury and Dibelius (n. 20) followed a similar line of reasoning as Adolf Harnack, *Luke the Physician: The Author of the Third Gospel and the Acts of the Apostles* (trans. J. R. Wilkinson; London: Williams & Norgate, 1909), 8–11. Harnack reasoned that Luke must have been the author of the "we" passages based on language and style (Dupont, *Sources*, 85). Harnack's views were preceded by William M. Ramsay, *The Church in the Roman Empire before A.D. 70* (4th edn; London: Hodder and Stoughton, 1895), 6–8 and Rackham, *Acts*, xli–xlii.

[73] Dupont, *Sources*, 87; Porter, *Paul in Acts*, 35. However, Cadbury challenged Harnack's belief that the author of the "we" passages is the same as the "writer of the whole work." Dupont, *Sources*, 87. Cadbury's views are discussed by V. H. Stanton, "Style and Authorship in the Acts of the Apostles," *JTS* 24 (1923): 361–81 (esp. pp. 374–81)—however, Stanton (unsuccessfully) tried to maintain the linguistic argument that there was "no source underlying the we-sections" and that they are wholly Luke's creations in the "manner" of his writing (Dupont, *Sources*, 88 [n. 34]). In a later response to Stanton, Cadbury did "not hesitate to adhere to [his] former conclusion." Cadbury, *Luke-Acts*, 67 (n. 2).

[74] Dupont, *Sources*, 87–8. Closer to his conclusion, Dupont states that "the way in which Luke rewrites his sources removes all possibility of discovering in his narrative the traces of a style and of interests

Cadbury further observes that unlike the Semitic fashion of preserving the "distinctive language of the originals" Luke's method was to paraphrase and refashion his material into "his own style."⁷⁵ So it appears reasonable to conclude with Cadbury (and Dupont) that we simply cannot rely on Luke's style as an arbiter of sources because of the simple fact that he smoothed them over to the point of obscurity.⁷⁶

Furthermore, since the "we" sources have been modified in some fashion from the "original narrative" we cannot prove a source based on the presence of a "we" passage nor can we separate them from the surrounding context written in the third person.⁷⁷ One solution produced the Antioch source theory while the other began with Norden who thought it was "memoirs" underlying the narrative of Acts; subsequently, Dibelius developed the itinerary/travel diary hypothesis.⁷⁸ In the end, we are left with a narrator who "counts himself among the companions of Paul" by the use of the first person in the context of a third person narrative where Luke is not mentioned.⁷⁹

The "We" Passages and the Prologue

Another facet of the "we" source debate is the prologue found at the start of the two-volume work (Lk. 1:1-4). Cadbury claims that in the study of the "earliest Christian history no passage of scripture has had more emphasis laid upon it than the brief preface

---

which would not be his" (147). Beyond this he cites the "calming of the storm" of Mk 4:35-39 that has been "so much rewritten" by Luke (8:22-24) that it "contains a proportion of Lucan characteristics at least equal to that of the account of the storm in Acts 27" (88). Similarly, Cadbury, in *Luke-Acts* thinks the style of Luke rules out any clear detection of an independent source.

⁷⁵ Cadbury, *Luke-Acts*, 68. This practice—that Luke shares with other Greek and Latin writers—impedes the "determination of his sources by the criterion of vocabulary" (68). See also Turner, *Style*, 45–63.

⁷⁶ However, the way Luke handled his sources cannot rule out the use of a source either. Dupont, *Sources*, 88–9. For a conclusive explanation of the "we" passages we must look elsewhere. Unfortunately, the fact that Luke's source is no "mere fiction" does "not necessarily mean that the writer was an eyewitness." Dupont, *Sources*, 93. It does imply that he had "some sort of access to some sort of eyewitness material for this part of his narrative." Barrett, *Luke the Historian*, 22. Another option is to consider the "we" narratives as a "literary fiction." Richard I. Pervo, *Profit with Delight: The Literary Genre of the Acts of the Apostles* (Philadelphia: Fortress, 1987), 57. Pervo represents perhaps the vanguard of this approach that has been variously and successfully discounted by Campbell, "Narrator," 387–8; Porter, *Paul in Acts*, 13–19 (esp. p. 25), and Keener, *Acts*, 3:2351–6. Keener (2353) states that a "majority of scholars reject the literary-fiction approach" (2353).

⁷⁷ Dupont, *Sources*, 94. In other words, both the "we" and the "they" suggest a common origin since they are so closely linked.

⁷⁸ Eduard Norden, *Agnostos Theos: Untersuchungen zur Formengeschichte religiöser Rede* (4th edn; Stuttgart: B. G. Teubner, 1956), 34, 313–31; Dupont, *Sources*, 94 and Dibelius, *Studies*, 73–4. The idea of memoirs underlying the narrative goes back to the nineteenth century, but it was Norden who developed the idea. He drew attention to the fact that the "we" and "they" existed side by side in many travel accounts—especially in sea voyages. He hypothesized that a document underlying Acts included the "we" and "they" passages which he considered to be a "clearly defined literary type." Dupont, *Sources*, 94–6 (96). This "memoranda" consists of the author's "personal memories" that are conveyed in the first person while "additional information" relating to the events he did not take part were recorded in the third person (96–7). The good thing about Norden's solution is that it accounts for the "we" and "they" source while also reflecting the practice of other ancient writers as well (98). Unfortunately, he tried to show that the "we" (via the problematic example of Esdras and Nehemias) is not meant to "present himself as a companion of the Apostle" (98).

⁷⁹ Dupont, *Sources*, 99.

of Luke."[80] Subsequently, Dupont states that the "explicit claim to have been present at a part of the events should come into the interpretation of the passages written in the first person."[81] Since this weighs on our interpretation of sources, the two prologues require a closer look (see Table 3.1). Starting with Lk. 1:1, there is the question of the πολλοί "many" compilers to which the writer seems to indicate that he has been privy to some of the events relating to his composition.[82] In verse 2 he signifies that he is among those who have "*received* the tradition" but not among those who were "*behind* the tradition"—"those who from the beginning became eyewitnesses and servants of the word" (my emphasis, Lk. 1:2).[83]

At the outset, Lk. 1:3 does not give the *impression* that he was carelessly throwing together some edifying stories. In verse 4, the expressed goal for Luke is that Theophilus and his readers "know the truth about the things that [they] have been taught." It is no stretch of interpretation that some level of understanding is already implied in this verse with περὶ ὧν κατηχήθης λόγων.

It is remarkable given the sizable differences among the Acts manuscripts that there are *no* significant variants in Lk. 1:1-4 (as per the NA[28]).[84] If there was a place that variants would naturally occur, here is a prime location. Instead we have a very early and stable text that agrees among often competing text-types (or families).[85] Where Western and Alexandrian traditions agree, there is every reason to assume we have the best and earliest text.[86] This does not rule out the possibility that the preface may only give the *impression* of participation and scrutiny of sources, but the integrity of the text does imply that the author's *intention* has been preserved without political or doctrinal altercation.

---

[80] Henry J. Cadbury, "Appendix C—Commentary on the Preface of Luke," in *The Beginnings of Christianity*, 2:489–510 (489).

[81] Dupont, *Sources*, 101 (see also 52 and 102). Dupont is adamant that the preface implies the author's personal participation. A casual reading of the preface does imply that the author is "presenting himself" as a "contemporary and eyewitness" for at least part of the story he is telling (102). However, Luke may be *presenting* himself as a participant in order to support the eyewitness nature of the first-person plural (even if he was not actually present during some or all of the events).

[82] Ibid., 103.

[83] Ibid., 103. Dupont contends that this does not preclude him from being an "eyewitness or minister of the word," just that he was not one from the beginning.

[84] My aim here is to value and evaluate every variant and any perceived "motives" and changes in the tradition that may impact our interpretation of the "we" sections (via the prologues). Cf. Elliot, *Textual Criticism*, 49.

[85] Given the well-established Western tendency of expansion this is a likely place for scribes to enhance the eyewitness nature of the events narrated. See Brooke F. Westcott and Fenton J. A. Hort, *The New Testament in the Original Greek II* (2nd edn; New York: Harper, 1896), 122–6, 174 and William M. Ramsay, *St. Paul the Traveller and the Roman Citizen* (London: Hodder and Stoughton, 1905), 24–7. See more recently: Head, "Problem," 415–44 (415); Strange, *Problem*, 38–56; Armstrong, "Variants," 106–7, and Chapter 7, this volume. The reason why the prefaces must be so early (perhaps the closest we can come to the initial text) is because of the lack of interpolations, deletions, and additions. Therefore (in theory), a lack of revision should point to the earliest text. See Porter, "Developments," 34, further on the "revision" or "interpolation" theory.

[86] This usually implies a superior witness. Metzger, *Text*, 218; Porter and Pitts, *Fundamentals*, 105.

Table 3.1 Lk. 1:1-4 and Acts 1:1-3

Lk. 1:1-4[a]	NA[28]	Variants
(1) Inasmuch as many have undertaken to compile a narrative about the events that took place among us,[b]	(1) Ἐπειδήπερ πολλοὶ ἐπεχείρησαν ἀνατάξασθαι διήγησιν περὶ τῶν πεπληροφορημένων ἐν ἡμῖν[c] πραγμάτων,	
(2) just as they were handed down to us by those who from the beginning became eyewitnesses and servants of the word,	(2) καθὼς παρέδοσαν ἡμῖν οἱ ἀπ' ἀρχῆς αὐτόπται καὶ ὑπηρέται γενόμενοι τοῦ λόγου,	
(3) it seemed good to me also, having investigated everything carefully from the beginning, to write to you in an orderly manner, most excellent Theophilus,[d]	(3) ἔδοξεν κἀμοὶ παρηκολουθηκότι ἄνωθεν πᾶσιν ἀκριβῶς καθεξῆς σοι γράψαι, κράτιστε Θεόφιλε,	
(4) so that you may know the truth about the things that you have been taught.	(4) ἵνα ἐπιγνῷς περὶ ὧν κατηχήθης λόγων τὴν ἀσφάλειαν.	The original scribe of D had: περὶ τῶν, the first corrector erased the τ leaving, περὶ ὧν.[e]
Acts 1:1-3[f] (1) (So) I wrote the first book, Theophilus, about everything that Jesus began to do and teach,	(1) Τὸν μὲν πρῶτον λόγον ἐποιησάμην περὶ πάντων, ὦ Θεόφιλε, ὧν ἤρξατο ὁ Ἰησοῦς ποιεῖν τε καὶ διδάσκειν,	*ὁ is missing before Ἰησοῦς in B (03)/Vaticanus and D (05)
(2) until the day when, having given commands to the apostles through the Holy Spirit he had chosen, he was taken up;	(2) ἄχρι ἧς ἡμέρας ἐντειλάμενος τοῖς ἀποστόλοις διὰ πνεύματος ἁγίου οὓς ἐξελέξατο ἀνελήμφθη.	*ανελήφθη is added before ἐντειλάμενος in D sy[hmg] (sa mae) *ἀνελήμφθη is replaced by καὶ ἐκέλευσε κηρύσσειν τὸ εὐαγγέλιον in D sy[hmg] (sa mae)
(3) to whom also he presented himself alive after his suffering by many convincing proofs, appearing to them over a period of forty days and speaking (the things) about the kingdom of God.	(3) οἷς καὶ παρέστησεν ἑαυτὸν ζῶντα μετὰ τὸ παθεῖν αὐτὸν ἐν πολλοῖς τεκμηρίοις, δι' ἡμερῶν τεσσεράκοντα ὀπτανόμενος αὐτοῖς καὶ λέγων τὰ περὶ τῆς βασιλείας τοῦ θεοῦ·	Starting with Folio 415v/col.1/line (11) D adds after τεσσεράκοντα: … ἡμερῶν[g] (12)… ὀπτανόμενοις[h] …(13) τὰς[i] …

[a]Folio 182v of Bezae (D/05). The first corrector adds at the top of the folio: εὐαγγέλιον κατὰ λουκᾶν. Col. (1) ἐπειδήπερ πολλοὶ ἐπεχείρησαν ἀνα (2) τάξασθαι διήγησιν περὶ τῶν (3) πεπληροφορημένων ἐν ἡμῖν (4) πραγμάτων καθὰ παρέδοσαν ἡμῖν (5) οἱ ἀπ' ἀρχῆς αὐτόπται καὶ ὑπηρέται (6) γενόμενοι τοῦ λόγου (3) ἔδοξε κἀμοὶ (7) παρηκολουθηκότι ἄνωθεν πᾶσιν (8) ἀκριβῶς καθεξῆς σοι γράψαι (9) κράτιστε θεόφιλε ἵνα ἐπιγνῷς (10) περὶ τῶν κατηχήθης λόγων τὴν ἀσφάλειαν. Bezae places the gospels in this Western order: Matthew, John, Luke, Mark and then Acts. See Matthew Crawford, "A New Witness to the 'Western' Ordering of the Gospels: GA 073 + 084," *JTS* 69 (2018): 1–7. He recently discovered via the concordance table of a sixth-century mss (GA 073+74) that it also held to the Western order.
[b]My translation here in verse 1 draws upon L&N's, 13.106, understanding of πληροφορέω.
[c]The original scribe of Bezae used a special red ink right up to ἡμῖν in verse 1. See Vaganay, *Introduction*, 7–8, on the various types of ink scribes used.
[d]Cf. L&N 61.1. They define καθεξῆς as "a sequence of one after another in time, space, or logic—in order, in sequence, one after another." They translate καθεξῆς σοι γράψαι as such: "to write to you in sequence or . . . in an orderly manner."

Table 3.1 (*Continued*)

ᵉThe twenty-sixth to twenty-eighth editions of the Nestle-Aland do not mention this.
ᶠFolio 415v (D/05) begins with: Col. 1, line (1) πρᾶξις αποστόλων then line (2) τὸν μὲν πρῶτον λόγον ἐποιησάμην (3) περὶ πάντων ὦ θεόφιλε (4) ὧν ἤρξατο ιης ποιεῖν τε (5) καὶ διδάσκειν ἄχρι ἧς ἡμέρας (6) ανελήφθη ἐντειλάμενος τοῖς ἀποστόλοις (7) διὰ πνς ἁγίου οὓς ἐξελέξατο καὶ ἐκέλευσε (8) κηρύσσειν τὸ εὐαγγέλιον (9) οἷς καὶ παρέστησεν ἑαυτὸν ζωντα (10) μετὰ τὸ παθεῖν αὐτὸν ἐν πολλοῖς τεκμηρίοις (11) τεσσεράκοντα ἡμερῶν (12) ὀπτανόμενοις αὐτοῖς καὶ λέγων (13) τὰς περὶ τῆς βασιλείας τοῦ θυ. There are a few common *nomina sacra* here including: ιης = Ἰησοῦς (line 4), πνς = πνεύματος (line 7), and θυ = θεοῦ (line 13). See Comfort, *Manuscripts*, 199–253. Up until column 4 (ending with τε) the scribe used red ink here as well.
ᵍThe original scribe wrote: τεσσεράκοντα ἡμερῶν while the first corrector adds δι᾽ between τεσσεράκοντα ἡμερῶν = τεσσεράκοντα δι᾽ ἡμερῶν. The second corrector indicates it should be: δι᾽ ἡμερῶν τεσσεράκοντα reflecting the majority reading/critical edition.
ʰIt looks like the first corrector may have erased the iota from ὀπτανόνομενοις to ὀπτανόμενος.
ⁱInstead of τά.

Although the transmission history of Acts 1:1 is stable and relatively colourless with regard to variation (see Table 3.1), verse 2 is more problematic syntactically.[87] The critical text reads: "Until the day when, having given commands to the apostles through the Holy Spirit he had chosen, he was taken up" (ἄχρι ἧς ἡμέρας ἐντειλάμενος τοῖς ἀποστόλοις διὰ πνεύματος ἁγίου οὓς ἐξελέξατο ἀνελήμφθη.). Although some perceive some awkwardness when separating ἀνελήμφθη at the end from ἄχρι ἧς ἡμέρας at the start, there is nothing impossibly irregular about it.[88] Perhaps this is awkward for us due to our bias in English translation, but perhaps not so much for a reader in first-century Hellenistic Greek. There is also the tedious business of correcting a sentence on parchment if in fact ἀνελήμφθη (Acts 1:2) was an afterthought (which the Western reviser appears to be attempting to fix).

Luke could have begun with the idea of the ascension but wrote about the time first, and then the commands of Jesus, that were given to the apostles (he had chosen) through the Holy Spirit, then . . . ἀνελήμφθη "he was taken up." The difficulty diminishes further as we consider the phrase in Acts 1:2 based on its clausal structure ([ἄχρι ἧς ἡμέρας] + [ἐντειλάμενος τοῖς ἀποστόλοις διὰ πνεύματος ἁγίου] + [οὓς ἐξελέξατο] + ἀνελήμφθη). In this light, ἄχρι ἧς ἡμέρας is less disjointed from ἀνελήμφθη since they function together as part of the same larger clause. The problem of οὓς ἐξελέξατο separated from τοῖς ἀποστόλοις is also less of an issue from this perspective.

Acts 1:2 of Codex Bezae (D) reads: ἄχρι ἧς ἡμέρας ἀνελήφθη ἐντειλάμενος τοῖς ἀποστόλοις διὰ πνς ἁγίου οὓς ἐξελέξατο καὶ ἐκέλευσε κηρύσσειν τὸ εὐαγγέλιον "Until the day when he was taken up having given commands through the Holy Spirit to the apostles he had chosen, and instructed them to proclaim the gospel."[89] There seems to be an

---

[87] Although not as problematic as Pervo, *Acts*, 36–7, suggests. See Keener's, *Acts*, 1:660–6, "unproblematic" explanation on Acts 1:2.
[88] Longenecker, *Acts*, 253. Bruce, *Acts* (3rd edn), 99, similarly reasons that although the Alexandrian text is "awkward" with regard to the separation from οὓς ἐξελέξατο and τοῖς ἀποστόλοις it "gives good sense." Porter (via personal communication on February 6, 2019) suggests that having an "adjunctive participle is not a problem in periodic style." See Armstrong, "A New Plea," (2019): 98 further on the clausal structure of Acts 1:1-2.
[89] Others have attempted to reconstruct the Western text as such: "on the day when he chose the apostles through the Holy Spirit and instructed them to proclaim the gospel." Boismard and

interpolation here and a possible attempt to smooth the grammar by placing ἀνελήφθη earlier in the sentence while adding: καὶ ἐκέλευσε κηρύσσειν τὸ εὐαγγέλιον. The main thing to observe here is that there are no major issues in the variants among the major families that would weaken the link between the author's intention in the prefaces and the "we" source.[90]

Parallels to the Prefaces

If we compare the prefaces of the third Gospel and Acts with other contemporaneous literature of the time, the parallels are evident.[91] However, these parallels need to be made with care as Cadbury "repeatedly expressed the warning that such likeness in form between Luke's material and the popular parallels is not to be misconstrued."[92] For example, Alexander suggests that the "preface of Luke-Acts does not fit the genre of Greek historiography" but *Fachprosa* (trade prose) which is found in technical/scientific literature.[93] Contrary to her "evidence" is the fact that the Greek NT reflects *Zwischenprosa* (between prose).[94] Perhaps more decisive is that Acts should be

---

Lamouille, *Le Texte Occidental*, 48–9. I agree with Pervo, *Acts*, 37, that this is "unlikely to be original" as it deletes the ascension (ἀνελήμφθη).

[90] The way we interpret the prefaces impacts our assessment of the sources of Acts which in turn impacts one's view of dating. As argued above, Luke's preface (Lk. 1:1-4) should be a factor in how we interpret those passages written in the first-person plural. Additionally, Acts 1:1-3 demonstrates continuity with the "former book" (Acts 1:1) that is addressed once more to Theophilus, otherwise there would be no point in factoring the link between the author's intention in Luke and the "we" passages in Acts.

[91] Kamp et al., *Writing History!*, 36. E. Earle Ellis, *The Gospel of Luke* (London: Nelson, 1966), 62; Joseph A. Fitzmyer, *The Gospel According to Luke I–IX* (AB 28; New York: Doubleday, 1981) 288–9. Walter L. Liefeld, *Luke* (12 vols; EBC; Grand Rapids: Zondervan, 1981), 821, asserts that ἐπειδήπερ "inasmuch" is common to Thucydides, Philo, and Josephus and also the biography of Diogenes Laertius.

[92] Cadbury, *Luke-Acts*, 146. See Porter's, *Paul in Acts*, 18, criticism of Pervo's "paralellomania" and Chapter 4, this volume.

[93] Loveday C. A. Alexander, *Acts in Its Ancient Literary Context: A Classicist Looks at the Acts of the Apostles* (LNTS 289; London: T&T Clark, 2005), 16. Alexander states that this conclusion "was forced on me by the evidence" (16). See also her earlier essay: idem, "Luke's Preface in the Context of Greek Preface Writing," *NovT* 28 (1986): 48–74, and her revised Oxford thesis: idem, *The Preface to Luke's Gospel: Literary Convention and Social Context in Luke 1.1-4 and Acts 1.1* (SNTSMS 78; Cambridge: Cambridge University Press, 1993). For a recent discussion on the genre of Acts see Stanley E. Porter, "The Genre of Acts and the Ethics of Discourse" in *Acts and Ethics* (ed. Thomas E. Phillips, NTM 9. Sheffield: Sheffield Phoenix, 2005), 1–15; Thomas E. Phillips, "The Genre of Acts: Moving Toward a Consensus?" *CurBR* 4 (2006): 365–96; Richard A. Burridge, "The Genre of Acts Revisited," in *Reading Acts Today: Essays in Honour of Loveday C. A. Alexander* (eds. Steve Walton et al.; LNTS 427; London: T&T Clark, 2011); Daniel Lynwood Smith and Zachary Lundin Kostopoulos, "Biography, History and the Genre of Luke-Acts," *NTS* 63 (2017): 390–410; and Andrew W. Pitts, *History, Biography, and the Genre of Luke-Acts: An Exploration of Literary Divergence in Greek Narrative Discourse* (BibInt 177; Leiden: Brill, 2019).

[94] See Stanley E. Porter, "The Greek of the New Testament as a Disputed Area of Research," in *The Language of the New Testament: Classic Essays* (ed. Stanley E. Porter; JSNTSup 60; Sheffield: JSOT Press, 1991), 11–38 (32); Porter, *Paul in Acts*, 16 (n. 16), 21–2 (n. 43) and Palmer's critique of Alexander's earlier position: Darryl W. Palmer, "Acts and the Ancient Historical Monograph," in *The Book of Acts in Its Ancient Literary Setting* (ed. Bruce W. Winter and Andrew D. Clarke; 5 vols; BAFCS 1; Grand Rapids: Eerdmans, 1993), 1–29 (here 21–6: "IX. The Genre of Acts in Light of its Preface"). Meanwhile, Alexander, *Ancient*, 1, graciously acknowledges a "number of recent commentators"

considered a "short historical monograph," which is much more palatable than the other options.[95]

More appropriate parallels are found with the start of Josephus's *Against Apion* who writes: "In my history of our *Antiquities*, most excellent (κράτιστε) Epaphroditus, I have, I think, made sufficiently clear to any who may peruse that work the extreme antiquity of our Jewish race."[96] From his second book he writes: "In the first volume of this work, my most esteemed Epaphroditus, I demonstrated the antiquity of our race."[97]

Of greater importance than finding parallels is Fitzmyer's observation that sees Luke's incipits as examples of free composition that are not only "independent of any source-material" but that they also demonstrate his talent as one who writes in a contemporary literary form.[98] Accordingly, it *seems* likely then that the author's prologues are reinforcing the *impression* of participation in the events associated with the "we" passages.[99] However, Luke's claim is to have followed the events for a "considerable time" only and not "from the beginning" (Lk. 1:3).[100] Taken at face value, a claim to have "direct knowledge of the events" may simply be some sort of literary device.[101]

It is possible that an author who claims to have "carefully investigated everything for a long time" (Lk. 1:3) intends to show himself a witness of the events narrated by his

---

who took issue with her 1993 monograph. See David E. Aune, "Luke 1:1–4: Historical or Scientific Prooimion?," in *Paul, Luke, and the Graeco-Roman World: Essays in Honour of Alexander J. M. Wedderburn* (eds. Alf Christopherson et al.; JSNTSup 217; Sheffield: Sheffield Academic, 2003), 138–48, for a summary of criticism. Although Palmer, "Monograph," 1:26, grants that the "formal parallel" should remain between the "mention of tradition in Lukan and scientific prefaces" the greater parallel "between the *content* of scientific treatises and Luke-Acts is not so compelling" (my emphasis).

[95] Palmer, "Monograph," 1:29 (here) and 3. See also his earlier essay, "Acts and the Historical Monograph," *TynBul* 43 (1992): 373–88. Phillips, "Consensus?," 365–96, explains that the "emerging consensus of scholarship" agrees with Balch that Luke-Acts "belongs to 'historical literature' concerned with changing institutions, literature that includes not only histories but also political biographies of founders" (384). Cf. also David L. Balch, "Μεταβολὴ Πολιτειῶν: Jesus as Founder of the Church in Luke-Acts: Form and Function," in *Contextualizing Acts: Lukan Narrative and Greco-Roman Discourse* (eds. Todd C. Penner and Caroline V. Stichele; SBLSymS 20; Atlanta: Society of Biblical Literature, 2003), 139–88 (186). Phillips (384–85) suggests that "Acts is ancient history of various kinds and the mixture of genres within Acts makes further narrowing of the categories unwarranted."

[96] Jos. *Apion* 1.1 and H. St. J. Thackeray et al., trans., *Josephus* (LCL; 13 vols; Cambridge, MA: Harvard University Press, 1926–65), 1:163. Note the address in Acts 1:3: κράτιστε Θεόφιλε.

[97] Jos. *Apion* 2.1 and Thackeray et al., *Josephus*, 1:293. Compare the start of Jos. *Apion* 2.1: Διὰ μὲν οὖν τοῦ προτέρου βιβλίου, τιμιώτατέ μοι Ἐπαφρόδιτε with that of Acts 1:1 Τὸν μὲν πρῶτον λόγον ἐποιησάμην περὶ πάντων, ὦ Θεόφιλε, ὧν ἤρξατο ὁ Ἰησοῦς ποιεῖν τε καὶ διδάσκειν. Another interesting parallel is found in the *Letter of Aristeas to Philocrates*, 1:1-12: "Inasmuch as the account of our deputation to Eleazar, the High Priest of the Jews, is worth narrating, Philocrates." Taken from Moses Hadas, ed., *The Letter of Aristeas to Philocrates* (New York: Harper, 1951), 93.

[98] Fitzmyer, *Luke I–IX*, 288.

[99] Dupont, *Sources*, 102. There is a real sense that Luke (like any "writer of an historical work") is emphasizing in the prologues his indebtedness to others for their information, but also his participation and presence, which may or may not be factual (106).

[100] Dupont, *Sources*, 107.

[101] Ibid., 108. Nock knows of only "one possible parallel for the emphatic use of a questionable 'we' in consecutive narrative outside literature which is palpably fictional." See Nock, review of *Aufsätze zur Apostelgeschichte*, 503 (see also n. 2); Dupont, *Sources*, 129 (n. 61).

use of the first person.¹⁰² Furthermore, the impression of participation in the preface is possible given the fact that the fictional use of a "we" in "consecutive narrative" is rare.¹⁰³ On the contrary, it is equally possible that this theory is the "fake news" of the ancient world as some maintain.¹⁰⁴ Another factor is that even if the "we" passages do not represent some form of "personal participation" by the author, we also need to consider how the first-century readers of Acts would interpret this.¹⁰⁵ Consequently, there is no decisive proof either way that the author's intention in the prologue implies his later presence during the "we" sections (to some degree).¹⁰⁶ Regardless of one's view, the theory of a "we" source has left "deep roots in the field of research on the sources of Acts."¹⁰⁷

The Itinerary/Diary/Travelogue Hypothesis

As noted earlier, Dibelius developed the itinerary/travel diary hypothesis while Norden focused on the "memoirs" behind the narrative of Acts.¹⁰⁸ Although there has been a tendency to label this source in a specific manner, the theory has been variously and extensively defined. Dibelius initially envisioned this *itinerary* "or whatever we like to call the account which the author had at his disposal" to be much wider in scope than is often described.¹⁰⁹ In light of the criticisms marshalled against this theory, the

---

¹⁰² Ibid., 108.
¹⁰³ The idea that the "we" sections are "meant to create the impression of an eyewitness account" comes in many forms. See Nock, review of *Aufsätze zur Apostelgeschichte*, 503 (esp. n. 2) and Dupont, *Sources*, 129. Keener, *Acts*, 1:413, "against many NT scholars" continues to "maintain that 'we' in Acts as in other ancient historical narratives nearly always constituted a claim that the narrator was present." Contrary examples would negate this point.
¹⁰⁴ Cf. Hans Conzelmann and Andrea Lindemann, *Interpreting the New Testament: An Introduction to the Principles and Methods of NT Exegesis* (trans. S. S. Schatzmann; Peabody, MA: Hendrickson, 1988), 241, cited from Porter, *Paul in Acts*, 25. Porter (25, n. 50) says that this view "probably" stems from Dibelius, *Studies*, 204–6, and is repeated more recently by Campbell (recall my note 70 above).
¹⁰⁵ Dupont, *Sources*, 131. Praeder, "Problem," 217, thinks that it was either the author or "one or more of his source authorities had some role in Paul's sea and land travels"—although some of the "we" passages could be the product of "Lukan redaction and composition" (217). Meanwhile, Hemer, "Narrative," 108, remarks how "personal participation" in the "we" passages "take us nearer to the historical Paul."
¹⁰⁶ On the contrary, Porter, *Paul in Acts*, 37, considers the use of the first-person plural in Acts to be different from other historical works. It is "surprising" that beyond Luke's intention "to provide an orderly account" (between Lk. 1:1-4 and Acts 1:1) the "use of the first person" is found "only in the latter chapters of Acts" and only at "specific points." However, the gap is reduced if the first "we" occurs at Antioch (11:28)—and the material up to 11:18 represents older sources that Luke gathered (likely from the church in Jerusalem/Judea), and after Acts 11:19 until 15:39 to be some combination of an Antioch/Barnabas source that was later revised by Luke—and from Acts 15:40 onward this formulates the Rome (Luke/Paul/Silas/Timothy) source until the end of Acts. Even at the Jerusalem council we get a clear picture of how (in Acts 15:2) Paul, Barnabas, and "some others among them" (καί τινας ἄλλους ἐξ αὐτῶν) were the "they" who "reported everything [or lit. how much]" (ἀνήγγειλάν τε ὅσα) in verse 4. That the author is a companion of Paul seems very likely, although naming this companion is beyond certainty according to Cadbury, *Luke-Acts*, 356. See also, Dupont, *Sources*, 108 (n. 47).
¹⁰⁷ Dupont, *Sources*, 93; Keener, *Acts*, 3:2350-74.
¹⁰⁸ Norden, *Untersuchungen*, 34, 313-31; Dibelius, *Studies*, 73-4.
¹⁰⁹ Dibelius, *Studies*, 73-4.

purpose here is not to define a specific itinerary (as some would define) but to revisit it as a broadly defined "account" of personal notes used by the author.[110]

"Everywhere it seems," says Dibelius, "that there underlies the account of the journeys an itinerary of stations where Paul stopped, an itinerary which we may suppose to have been provided with notes of his journeys, of the founding of communities and of the result of evangelising."[111] He finds examples of this itinerary where aspects of Paul's missionary journeys (i.e., Acts 13:4–14:28 and 15:36–21:16) were "based on a written document" that "supplied the framework and served as a guiding thread."[112]

Dibelius refers to this itinerary as Luke's earliest source that is comprised of a series of notes and he thought it was especially discoverable in those places where the purpose was clearly not "to entertain" (i.e., Derbe, Thessalonica, or Berea [Acts 14:21; 17:1-9, 10-12]).[113] He goes on to describe his theory further: "For this central part of his work there had been supplied to him a series of notes. To this itinerary he now made his own additions, as well as inserting other traditions. Among the former we may include the speeches particularly, but also many editorial observations (i.e. Acts 14:22 ff., and Acts 19:20)."[114]

Accordingly, Dibelius saw "only one way of accounting for the procedure—the writer uses the first person plural to indicate his presence at the side of Paul."[115] Cadbury had also discussed the idea of an "itinerary" relating to Paul's travels independently from Dibelius.[116] In addition to the "speeches in Acts," Cadbury refers to the "series

---

[110] Gottfried Schille, *Die Apostelgeschichte des Lukas* (THKNT 5; Berlin: Evangelische Verlags-Anstalt, 1983), 337-8; Haenchen, *Acts*, 84-6; Hans Conzelmann, *Die Apostelgeschichte* (HNT 7; Tübingen: Mohr Siebeck, 1963), 5-6. The way we interpret the itinerary hypothesis impacts our assessment of the sources of Acts, which in turn informs the way we date Acts. It seems entirely plausible that Luke (in addition to personal memories and other sources from his church contacts) made use of a broadly defined itinerary (as per Dibelius's suggestion). This observation reinforces the datable elements in Acts while at the same time mitigates the notion of Acts as a later literary creation.

[111] Dibelius, *Studies*, 5.

[112] Dupont, *Sources*, 114.

[113] Dibelius, *Studies*, 6. Dupont, *Sources*, 115, also thinks these passages are out of place unless they are to some degree "imposed on the writer by the source he was using." Doubtless, a source is involved at these points (as per Dibelius's suggestion), but the content of this source is edited for Luke's purposes. Barrett, *Luke the Historian*, 12, remarks how Luke was a "historical writer" but also a "religious writer." For an expanded treatment of this duality see I. Howard Marshall, *Luke: Historian and Theologian* (Exeter: Paternoster, 1979).

[114] Dibelius, *Studies*, 6.

[115] Dupont, *Sources*, 118 (and 120). Dibelius further subscribed to the traditional view that the author was Luke the physician, a companion of Paul, and who was possibly from Antioch (Dupont, 118-19). There are several ancient sources that support the identification of Luke the physician as the author of Acts: Col. 4:14; *Muratorian Fragment*, 2-8 (the gospel), 34-39 (of Acts); Irenaeus, *Her.* 3.1.1; 3.13.3; 3.14.1; Tertullian, *Marc.* 4.2; Clement of Alexandria, *Strom.* 5.12 and Origen (cited by Eusebius, *Hist. Eccl.* 6.25) and the *Anti-Marcionite Prologue* to Luke. Luke as a companion of Paul is less certain though see Col. 4:14; Phlm. 23-24 and 2 Tim. 4:11; Mark A. Powell, *What Are They Saying about Acts?* (New York: Paulist, 1991), 33, and Keener, *Acts*, 1:410–11. Most importantly, P^{75} that is dated to the early third century (c. 200-225 INTF) contains the "oldest sure evidence of a contemporary name." See Parker, *Introduction*, 313. We can see this on Folio 44r, Col. 1 (lines 7–9): (7) εὐαγγέλιον (8) κατά (9) λουκᾶν. The John inscription follows on lines 11–12: (11) εὐαγγέλιον (12) κατά ἰωάνην.

[116] Dupont, *Sources*, 120 (n. 32). Cadbury, like Dibelius, seems to rely on Norden's earlier work. See Cadbury, *Luke-Acts*, 6, 8, 125, 145, and 196.

of detailed itineraries given for part of Paul's journey."[117] While he considers some of the factors leading to the development of these itineraries, he asks whether "the longer episodes included in the narrative" (i.e., Philippi and Ephesus) were (1) once a part of the "original" outline *or* if they were (2) "episodes derived from [a] separate transmission but inserted into it" (i.e., the outline) along with the "presence of the 'we' in parts (but by no means all) of the itinerary."[118]

Cadbury muses about other possibilities such as the itinerary being a "continuous geographical outline" that crystallizes earlier (auto?) biographical information.[119] Further to this, he contends that such a form has some "parallels in contemporary literature."[120] Cadbury considers the *Reisebericht* or "travel tale" found among popular literature as an especially relevant parallel for Acts.[121] This *travel tale* included both land and sea travels where the "story of storm and shipwreck on a desert island" was ever popular:

> Characteristic of their style is the brief seriatim itinerary with the names of places, companions and duration of stay such as found in Acts. But the most impressive characteristic of all is the *frequent use of the first person*. The testimony of eyewitnesses is a desideratum in all narrative, but especially in travel narrative, and nowhere is the use of the first person more abundant.[122]

The issue of whether or not Luke's notes (Acts 27:44) *could* have survived the shipwreck is a contentious one and far from settled.[123] Porter may be right in saying the notes were destroyed; however, Keener makes several "stronger arguments" that go beyond Nock's reference to Caesar preserving his papers while swimming (i.e., Suet. *Jul.* 64).[124] If Keener is correct, it does to some degree "undermine Porter's own thesis of

---

[117] Cadbury, *Luke-Acts*, 60.
[118] Ibid., 60. He is a bit unclear at this point but this is my interpretation of what he said.
[119] Ibid., 60. He advises that the "itinerary in Acts" is a different genre and to some degree "discontinuous," 61. Dibelius and Dupont also discounted the possibility of a "continuous narrative prior to that of Acts," Dupont, *Sources*, 114 and 136. Porter, *Paul in Acts*, 35, affirms this as well.
[120] Cadbury, *Luke-Acts*, 60. See also p. 140 on the difference between the popular and literary forms.
[121] Ibid., 144.
[122] Ibid., 144 (my emphasis).
[123] See Porter, *Paul in Acts*, 38 (n. 95) countering Brian M. Rapske, "Acts, Travel and Shipwreck," in *The Book of Acts in Its Graeco-Roman Setting* (eds. David W. J. Gill and Conrad Gempf; 5 vols; BAFCS 2; Grand Rapids: Eerdmans, 1995), 2:1–47 (34 [n. 151]) and his reliance on Nock, review of *Aufsätze zur Apostelgeschichte*, 499 (n. 3). See also James Smith, *The Voyage and Shipwreck of St. Paul: With Dissertations on the Life and Writings of St. Luke, and the Ships and Navigation of the Ancients* (London: Longmans, Green, 1880); Bruce, *Acts* (3rd edn), 508–29; J. M. Gilchrist, "The Historicity of Paul's Shipwreck," *JSNT* 18 (1996): 29–51; Ayse D. Atauz, *Eight Thousand Years of Maltese Maritime History: Trade, Piracy, and Naval Warfare in the Central Mediterranean* (Gainesville: University Press of Florida, 2008), 29–31, and Keener, *Acts*, 4:3555–660.
[124] Keener, *Acts*, 4:3658. To be fair, Nock left the matter open: "Any companion keeping a travel diary *might well have lost it* in the shipwreck; to be sure, Julius Caesar preserved his papers while swimming 200 paces" (my emphasis). Nock, review of *Aufsätze zur Apostelgeschichte*, 499 (n. 3). For Caesar to swim for approximately three hundred metres with his papers in his left hand seems highly unlikely even for the best of swimmers. Regardless, Keener, *Acts*, 4:3658–59, argues first that Luke could have relied upon his memory of the occasion. Second, he could easily have prepared ahead of time to preserve his notes beforehand in watertight containers

the source."¹²⁵ It does not seem necessary to argue for the survival of notes when Luke (or his source) could rely on memory—and a scary one they would not soon forget— or from conversations with Paul and others in the shipwreck.¹²⁶

There are some further qualifications and criticisms concerning the itinerary hypothesis.¹²⁷ For example, although Nock agrees with Dibelius (via Cadbury) that Luke wrote Acts as a companion of Paul, he rightly questions the itinerary as a single source.¹²⁸ Instead of speaking of a single "Itinerar" he rightly asks: "May there not rather have been several distinct travel-diaries covering separate periods, e.g. that of the collection for the saints in Jerusalem (cf. [Acts] 20, 3–5)?"¹²⁹ Based on the personal records and diaries of travellers Nock suggests that "whether this travel material comes from one or from more documents is not very important, save for the fact that if there was only one, it is perhaps harder to account for some of the many omissions in this part of the story."¹³⁰

In perhaps the greatest criticism of Dibelius's itinerary, Schille raises some important weaknesses.¹³¹ It is true that Luke's literary prowess makes it difficult in assessing whether we are dealing with one or more sources, or if something like a travelogue or itinerary is behind it (or them).¹³² However, Dibelius's (and Cadbury's) theory has not been eradicated completely, and one has only to take a closer look at Schille's theories for they reveal "much imagination and little critical sense."¹³³ The value in Schille's criticisms is

---

(not that he needed them to remember the trauma of what just happened). Keener's third and fourth point relate to his second where the notes could have survived the shipwreck either in whole or in part. Last, he (4:3659) suggests that Luke would have had a backup copy somewhere of his "most important notes" that he "probably left with Christians in Caesarea" or back in Syro-Palestine.

¹²⁵ Keener, *Acts*, 4:3657 (n. 1020). The other issue of the "consistent syntax" of these sections "in comparison with the rest of the material" requires a future linguistic analysis. Porter, *Paul in Acts*, 39.

¹²⁶ See Wright, "Challenge," 9–30 (esp. p. 9 [n. 1] and the extensive list of current research on memory and biblical studies).

¹²⁷ See Dupont, *Sources*, 137–65.

¹²⁸ Nock, review of *Aufsätze zur Apostelgeschichte*, 502. Amidst his "formidable" objections, Nock gives credit to Henry J. Cadbury, "The Knowledge Claimed in Luke's Preface," *Exp* 24 (1922): 401–20, for changing his mind. In his response to Cadbury, Robertson validates Cadbury's argument "at almost every point" in the former essay. Cf. A. T. Robertson, "The Implications in Luke's Preface," *ExpTim* 35 (1924): 319–21, esp. p. 321. His only contention is his "denial of research by the author" as he insists the "use of ἄνωθεν with παρηκολουθηκότι falls in also with the idea of careful preparation before writing" (321; Lk. 1:3). See also, Henry J. Cadbury, "The Purpose Expressed in Luke's Preface," *Exp* 21 (1921): 431–41. Alexander, *The Preface*, 128, also indicates that παρηκολουθηκότι does not connote research specifically but in the end a "thorough acquaintance" is the net result (cited by Keener, *Acts*, 1:185). See also L&N 36.32.

¹²⁹ Nock, review of *Aufsätze zur Apostelgeschichte*, 500.

¹³⁰ Ibid.

¹³¹ "Bei einer genaueren Prüfung verliert die Itinerar-Hypothese ihre Schlagkraft. Vielleicht ist sie nichts anderes als ein letzter Rest jener Quellentheorien, die M. Dibelius so scharf gerügt hat. Der Hinweis auf die schriftstellerische Fähigkeit des Lukas vermag mehr zu erklären, als selbst M. Dibelius annahm." See Gottfried Schille, "Die Fragwürdigkeit eines Itinerars der Paulusreisen," *TLZ* 84 (1959): 174, 165–74. "In a closer examination, the Itinerar hypothesis loses its clout. Maybe it is nothing but a last remnant of those source theories that M. Dibelius has criticized so sharply. The reference to the literary capacity of Luke can explain more than even M. Dibelius assumed."

¹³² See Dupont, *Sources*, 147–56.

¹³³ Ibid., 156 and also 145 (n. 15). Based on Haenchen's assessment of Schille's theories, Dupont (156) explains that if the itinerary "is not inevitable" then there is "no reason to fall back on a

that the itinerary theory is "only an hypothesis" and that in some respects it is delicate.[134] Setting aside the itinerary, there are other source options worth investigating.

Luke's Concern with Geography, Travel, and Lodging

Perhaps the most prevalent frustration relating to the source debate is how Dupont points to the problems and lack of agreement and then "refuse[s] to proffer a comprehensive thesis."[135] Dupont may not have offered a "comprehensive" thesis, but the section *before* his conclusion is very close to one and has not received the attention it deserves.[136] The importance that Luke places upon geographical considerations offers a path forward, both in the patterns of his gospel as well as in the "very extensive information" that goes beyond "editorial additions."[137] First, we can see Luke's geographical interest in the "general arrangement of his work" that "governs the general plan" of both the gospel and Acts.[138] The second consideration relates to the expanded details of geography found in Luke-Acts.[139]

What Cadbury observes is that the explanation of these places in the text are "not really distributed along geographical lines" which opens up the possibility of a source.[140]

---

hypothesis which claims to explain everything by speaking of the facility with which Luke could compose a narrative and give it the appearance of history." See also Bultmann's, "Quellen der Apostelgeschichte," 68–80, defence of Dibelius's itinerary hypothesis.

[134] Dupont, *Sources*, 156 (see page 151 for his critique of Schille's criticisms). Dupont, *Sources*, 151, appears to have kept the door open to the itinerary hypothesis; not only because of his criticism of Schille's critique, and his criticism of Haenchen's *acceptance* of Schille's critique, but especially his claim that "Criticism of the hypothesis of the itinerary is not yet very far advanced" (157).

[135] Examples include Donelson, "Cult Histories," 1; Marshall, *Acts*, 39. This is partially true, but in fairness to Dupont he has provided a vast array of insights throughout this chapter.

[136] "The Characteristics of Luke" (Dupont, *Sources*, 157–65). For this he relies on Jacques Dupont, "Le salut des gentils et la signification théologique du livre des Actes." NTS 6 (1960) : 132–55; Philippe H. Menoud, "Le plan des Actes des Apôtres," NTS 1 (1954): 44–51; and Cadbury, *Luke-Acts*; Henry J. Cadbury, "Lexical Notes on Luke-Acts III. Luke's Interest in Lodging," JBL 45 (1926): 305–22.

[137] Dupont, *Sources*, 159. On the geography in Acts see Martin Hengel, "The Geography of Palestine in Acts," in *The Book of Acts in Its Palestinian Setting* (ed. Richard Bauckham; 5 vols; BAFCS 4; Eerdmans: Grand Rapids, 1995), 27–78.

[138] Dupont, *Sources*, 158. The author is clearly interested in the geographical details of the terrain in Luke-Acts as Cadbury and others have long established. Cadbury, *Luke-Acts*, 241. See further reading regarding the general plan of Luke and Acts in Dupont, *Sources*, 158 (n. 57); idem, "Salut, 132–55, and Menoud, "Plan," 44–51.

[139] Luke is very much interested in "punctuating his whole narrative from the beginning with geographical observations." Dupont, *Sources*, 160. Some of these passages Cadbury lists as examples: "Nazareth, a town in Galilee" (Lk. 1:26), "Capernaum, a town in Galilee" (Lk. 4:31), "the region of the Gerasenes, which is across the lake from Galilee" (Lk. 8:26), "a village called Emmaus, about seven miles from Jerusalem" (Lk. 24:13), and many other such examples in Luke-Acts.

[140] Cadbury, *Luke-Acts*, 242. He wonders whether or not the author is speaking with familiarity. For example, the Latin place names closer to Rome (i.e., Syracuse, Rhegium, Puteoli, the Forum of Appius and Three Taverns) are not given any expansive details (as compared to those in Palestine). Either Luke is from the area and did not see any need to expand on the Italian places (that would be relatively unknown in Judea or Galilee), or second, Rome (or environs) is his current address at the time of writing, or third, his intended audience (i.e., Theophilus) is in Rome and a lack of expansion here as compared to the earlier narrative in Acts (i.e., 1:12) suggests familiarity and perhaps an

Another aspect of Luke's geographical interest is something Harnack originally drew attention to and Cadbury later explored.[141] Luke is supremely concerned with the details of where the people in his narrative live, the places they travel, and their lodging.[142] In response to Harnack's "ironical rejection of a source"—because some of the lodging passages occur in the "we" section and others do not—Cadbury suggests instead that they "may be sometimes derived from a source" or they "may be introduced by the evangelist in rewriting a source."[143] For example, in Acts 9:11 there is given a full address: "Saul of Tarsus, Care of Judas, Straight St., Damascus."[144] In Acts 10:5-6 we hear of "Simon who is called Peter. He is lodging with Simon the Tanner, whose house is by the sea" (in Joppa).[145] Either way such lodging references point to a source(s).[146]

Reinterpreting Dupont's Overall Conclusion

Beyond Dupont's overall "stated" conclusion that is notoriously bleak, his full conclusion and cumulative research throughout his book deserves our attention.[147]

---

unfamiliarity of places outside of Rome. See Cadbury, *Luke-Acts*, 241–2; Dupont, *Sources*, 160 (n. 64), 161.

[141] Harnack, *Die Apostelgeschichte*, 95 (n. 1); Cadbury, "Lodging," 305–22; idem, *Luke-Acts*, 249–54.

[142] Dupont, *Sources*, 161. This is especially observable in the second half of Acts. Cadbury, "Lodging," 306–7. Blass, *Acta Apostolorum*, 227, thought the purpose here was really to let his readers know who the host was (as noted by Cadbury, "Lodging," 306). Among such examples Cadbury considers the possibility that Philip the evangelist and his four unmarried daughters (Acts 21:8-9) are a possible source (306). He also thinks the example of "Mnason of Cyprus" in Acts 21:16 is "altogether enigmatic" (305). Bezae once had a variant (before it was mutilated) that places Mnason's hospitality at a "certain village" between "Caesarea and Jerusalem" (305–6 [n. 2]). At present, all that can be seen (from the end of verse 15) in line 23 is: ἀναβαίνομεν εἰς ἰερ[οσόλυμα]... (24) εκ κεσα[ρείας] (25)... (Note the use of the diaeresis above the iota in line 23 and how the first corrector removed απο and wrote εκ in its place). Ropes called this mutilation an "irregular tear, or cut" where the Latin side is partially destroyed and correspondingly "on the Greek side a part of verse 16, the whole of verse 17, and a part of verse 18 have been destroyed." Cf. James H. Ropes, "Three Papers on the Text of Acts," *HTR* 16 (1923): 163–86 (163). Ropes's reconstruction uses the Latin parallel as a "trustworthy guide": line 23: ἀναβαίνομεν εἰς ἰερ[οσόλυμα (24) εκ κεσα[ρείας σὺν ἡμεῖν (25) οὗτοι δὲ ἤγαγον ἡμᾶς (26) πρὸς οὓς ξενιςθῶμεν (27) καὶ παραγενόμενοι εἰς τινα κώ[μην (28) ἐγενόμεθα παρὰ νάσωνί [τινα κυπρίῳ (29) μαθητῇ ἀρχαίῳ κἀκεῖθεν[ἐξερχόμενοι (30) ἤλθομεν εἰς ιεροσ[όλυμα. The NA²⁸ assumes a difference in word order with ἐξιόντες instead of ἐξερχόμενοι that is contrary to Ropes (166) and Cadbury, "Lodging," 306 (n. 2): (29) ἀρχαίῳ μαθητῇ κἀκεῖθεν ἐξιόντες ἤλθομεν. See also Robert P. Casey, "Bently's Collation of Codex Bezae," *HTR* 19 (1926): 213–14.

[143] Cadbury, "Lodging," 306; Harnack, *Die Apostelgeschichte*, 95 (n. 1).

[144] Cadbury, "Lodging," 306.

[145] Ibid.

[146] Ibid., 308, cites many examples from the third gospel where "Jesus lodged at least to various forms of hospitality" that are "not in the other gospels" (309). At other times the evidence points towards a common source such as the centurion's lament that he did not feel worthy to entertain Jesus at his house (cf. 309; Lk. 7:6 = Mt. 8:8). See also Dupont's, *Sources*, 161–2, list of lodging sources. It is "obvious" says Cadbury, "Lodging," 308 (n. 6) that "the same habit of mind has led the author to give some names of places as well as of persons simply because they marked the overnight stops of journeys." Dupont, *Sources*, 162, claims that this either points to a source or the personal experience of the author. Either way, this reveals more detailed information as compared with Matthew and Mark.

[147] Dupont, *Sources*, 166, thinks the "predominant impression is certainly very negative... it has not been possible to define any of the sources used by the author of Acts in a way which will

Second, while his research affirms the complex nature of discovering sources, this further reveals the author's "individual turn of mind."[148] Third, along with the prologue and in comparison with other ancient texts the author "wishes it to be understood that he has personally taken part in the events he is recounting."[149] Fourth, the problem of the "we" passages directly relates to the question of sources and the potential to see Luke as a "travelling companion of the apostle Paul."[150]

[148] meet with widespread agreement among the critics." Marshall, *Acts*, 39, while stating the obvious "difficulty of discovering any sources" echoes Dupont's lament and then states that "nothing has happened subsequently to alter this estimate in any significant way." He further echoes the "general view" that Luke has "successfully managed to conceal whatever sources he used beneath a uniform editorial style" (39). Granted Marshall is hopeful despite Dupont's "pessimistic conclusion" that some theories may be "more plausible than others" (40). See also Conzelmann, *Acts*, xxxvi-vii.

[148] Dupont, *Sources*, 166-7. Dupont (via Cadbury) uses the argument of the "author's psychology" and "characteristic personality" that matches "the writer to Theophilus" (164). This in turn leads Dupont to say this "information" did not originate with a "written source which someone else supplied him with" (164). Accordingly, he (166) finds favour with Benoit's theory of Acts being composed in stages "based not on sources coming from another author, but on Luke's own notes." Benoit, "La Deuxième Visite," 778-92. For Dupont, the secondary matter is compositional in nature—in other words—did Luke use notes, an itinerary, or a travel diary (165)? The solution is not so simple. We can only speculate as to how much or how little these sources are Luke's. Porter's, *Paul in Acts*, 39, hypothesis is that the author of Luke-Acts uses a (redacted) "previously written 'we' source" that was "probably (although not certainly) not originating with the author himself" (41). Cf. also Barrett, *Luke the Historian*, 22, and Werner G. Kümmel, *Introduction to the New Testament* (Nashville: Abingdon Press, 1975), 177. However, Porter, *Paul in Acts*, 39 (n. 97), recognizes the strong tradition that claims the author of Luke-Acts has "included his own eyewitness" to the narrative. See Ramsay, *The Church*, 6-8; Rackham, *Acts*, xli-xlii; Bruce, *Acts* (3rd edn), 4; Johannes Munck, *The Acts of the Apostles* (AB 31; Garden City, NY: Doubleday, 1967), xiii; Hengel, *Acts*, 66; Fitzmyer, *Luke I-IX*, 1.35-53; Joseph A. Fitzmyer, *Luke the Theologian: Aspects of his Teaching* (New York: Paulist, 1989), 1-26 (esp. pp. 3-7, 11-16); Hemer, *Acts*, 321; Gilchrist, "Shipwreck," 36-50; Witherington, *Acts*, 485.

[149] Dupont, *Sources*, 167. According to Porter, *Paul in Acts*, 40, the fact that the "we" source originates with the author himself is a "possibility that cannot be entirely dismissed" (41). I disagree with Alexander's, *The Preface*, 120-3, rendering of αὐτόπται (Lk. 1:2) as a "first-hand witness" (as noted by Porter, *Paul in Acts*, 40 [n. 100]). This may be possible in some contexts, however, there are a few reasons against this rendering here. First, even if we allow for Alexander's sense of the word that might exclude Luke as an "eyewitness" there is nothing in the context to indicate he was *only* and always a first-hand witness to someone else's personal experience (which is a second-hand witness). Second, the BDAG says that αὐτόπτης from (αὐτός, ὀπτεύω = ὁράω) implies "seeing with one's own eyes" and cites several passages to justify this sense of meaning. Similarly, the L&N includes ἐπόπτης with their definition of αὐτόπτης (under domain 24: "Sensory Events and States" [24] and the subdomain "See" [24.1-24.51]) stating it means "one who has personally seen an event and thus has personal knowledge and can be expected to attest to the occurrence of such an event-eyewitness, personal witness." Cf. L&N 24.46. Third, if we consider ἐπόπτης it is difficult to see how ἐπόπται γενηθέντες (2 Pet. 1:16) could be taken to mean anything else except that they were "[personal] eyewitnesses" (τῆς ἐκείνου μεγαλειότητος) "of his majesty." Last, lines 34-9 of the *Muratorian Fragment* give a similar interpretation.

[150] Dupont, *Sources*, 168. Where some follow the ancient tradition that ascribes Acts to Luke the physician and companion of Paul, others do not because they think the picture of Paul in Acts is irreconcilably different from the Paul of his epistles (168). See Haenchen, *Acts*, 112-16 and Philipp Vielhauer, "On the 'Paulinism' of Acts," in *Studies in Luke-Acts* (eds. Leander E. Keck and James L. Martyn; Philadelphia: Fortress Press, 1966), 33-50 (originally published as "Zum 'Paulinismus' der Apostelgeschichte," *EvTh* 10 [1950-51]: 1-15). Where Vielhauer focuses on the alleged theological differences between Paul in Acts and Paul in his letters, Haenchen, *Acts*, 116, instead emphasizes the differences with respect to the "representation" of Paul. See further my discussion on Luke and Paul in Armstrong, "Ernst Haenchen," (forthcoming).

In light of the evidence, it seems likely that Luke is the author of Acts and a companion of the Apostle Paul.[151] What is also likely, though with less certainty, is that Luke has participated in the "we" passages to some degree while corroborating his details along the way through a mix of his own memories, notes, and other oral or written sources from others (i.e., Paul, Barnabas, Silas and/or Timothy).[152] This also does not preclude the possibility that Luke participated in other passages going back to Acts 16:10–17 (or even earlier at Antioch in the Western text of Acts 11:28). Last, the expansive geographical details (along with the mention of specific persons), further reveals an underlying source(s). All of these points support the feasibility of an early date of Acts.

Conclusion: The Date and Sources of Acts

Once again we ask, "How does our knowledge of source theories impact the way we date Acts?" We can respond to this question after distilling the findings of this chapter and being careful to separate what we know from what we do not know and the grey area of possibility in between.[153] The following points are entirely plausible and, in many ways, support an early date of Acts.

First, the majority of scholars view Acts (in varying degrees) as a historical document (cf. "Acts in History" in Chapter 8). Accordingly, Acts is better classed as a short historical monograph and not a work of fiction as some have maintained. The net result is that we can date Acts with relative certainty according to the people, places, and events that it describes as well as those that it does not. A historical document can be placed in a historical context whereas a literary creation is far more difficult to date.

Second, although it continues to be debated, there are good reasons to affirm the traditional association that Luke is the author of Luke (and Acts) and was in some capacity a companion of the Apostle Paul. Accordingly, we can date Acts in relation to the events that are found within the narrative.[154]

Third, instead of a single source Luke clearly used some combination of personal, oral, and written sources that can be subjected to verification and collaboration with other dates and events in time.

Fourth, the "we" (and they) passages indicate that Luke has (to some degree) been a participant in the narrative going back to Acts 16:10–17 (and possibly as early as Acts 11:28) while corroborating his details along the way with other oral (and possibly written) sources. This in effect increases the historical value of Acts since it does not

---

[151] Dupont, *Sources*, 168. Although this continues to be debated I agree with Keener's (*Acts*, 1:402–22) argument.

[152] Recall my note 23 with Harnack's view above. Luke's memory, like ours, is selective and not perfect. See Wright, "Challenge," 9–30.

[153] Reinfandt's, "Reading Texts," 51, highlights the subjective nature of choosing between true and false interpretations that to a large extent depend upon the historian's framework.

[154] The author's access and chronological proximity to the events are key criteria for dating a document. See "Principles for Sources and Textual Criticism" in Chapter 2.

represent a "one perspective" view on the people, places, and events. Luke's handprint is throughout, but underneath there are a variety of collaborating sources.

Fifth, and related to the fourth point, is that an analysis of the prologues indicate that Luke is, more likely than not, presenting himself as a participant beyond giving a simple literary impression. To some degree, this adds an extra layer to the reliability of the narrative which in turn supports an early date.

Sixth, in addition to Luke's own memories and use of oral traditions, his use of written sources must have included some measure of a broadly defined itinerary or at the very least some personal notes that were kept by the author and likely supplemented by others connected with the churches in Acts. This minimizes the likelihood of Acts being a literary creation (or novel) that could not be dated in relation to key events in history.

Seventh, Luke incorporated many points in his narrative related to matters of geography, lodging, and politics that likely point to the form of sources mentioned in the sixth point above.

Eighth, Luke blended his sources with the narrative to such a degree that his personal style (and mind) is visible throughout Acts. Instead of seeing this as a negative source realization, this strengthens the view of Lukan authorship instead of some unknown author that is far removed from tradition and the datable elements in the narrative.

4

The Sources of Acts: Paul's Letters and the Works of Josephus

Introduction

Beyond a general discussion of sources, two critical issues remain that require discussion and analysis: (1) Acts and Paul's letters and (2) Acts and the works of Flavius Josephus. These two areas need to be addressed as they directly impact the views on that date of Acts, perhaps more than any other. Where many scholars do not find clear evidence that Acts is dependent on Paul's letters, Pervo has recently argued against the grain.[1] He boldly states that the "case for coincidences" has been "exploded by the

---

[1] Pervo, *Dating Acts*, 51–147; Armstrong, "A New Plea," (2017): 87–90. Pervo is by no means alone as Shellard, *New Light on Luke*, 31, claims that "Luke did indeed know some, if not all of Paul's letters, as indicated by many items in his narrative." She argues that he does not refer to them "explicitly" but treats them "creatively as he had done his other sources" (31). Her "evidence" (56–8) is based largely upon Mitton's commentary on Ephesians who seems rather interested in the connection between the two books. C. Leslie Mitton, *The Epistle to the Ephesians: Its Authority, Origin and Purpose* (Oxford: Clarendon, 1951), 198–220, esp. p. 205. Hence, if Ephesians is dated in the 90s (Mitton, 260) then for Shellard (58) if Luke-Acts were "completed soon afterwards, perhaps by the same person, this again would support a dating for Luke-Acts close to the turn of the century." Elsewhere, Steve Walton, *Leadership and Lifestyle: The Portrait of Paul in the Miletus Speech and 1 Thessalonians* (SNTSMS 108; Cambridge: Cambridge University Press, 2000), 12, examines Paul's speech at Miletus (Acts 20:18b-35) and finds a "number of parallels of vocabulary with the Pauline epistles." These "parallels" have long been recognized and discussed. See Rackham, *Acts*, 389–96; Conzelmann, *Acts*, 173–6; Bruce, *Acts* (3rd edn), 429–37. Walton (12) refers to Charles H. Dodd, *The Apostolic Preaching and its Development* (London: Hodder & Stoughton, 1936), 32, who thought this "implies either that Luke used the epistles (which he regards as unlikely) or that he used reminiscences of a genuine Pauline speech" (quotation is from Walton). Contrary to Dodd's viewpoint, Walton compares the Miletus speech with (1) segments of Luke's Gospel (99–137), (2) 1 Thessalonians (140–85), as well as (3) Ephesians and 2 Timothy (186–98). Walton's conclusions have met with little success. See Jeffrey A. D. Weima, review of *Leadership and Lifestyle: The Portrait of Paul in the Miletus Speech and 1 Thessalonians*, by Steve Walton, *NovT* 43 (2001): 300–2 (301), and Karl P. Donfried, review of *Leadership and Lifestyle*, by Steve Walton, *JTS* 54 (2003): 253–6 (255). See also Michael D. Goulder, "Did Luke Know Any of the Pauline Letters?," *PRS* 13 (1986): 97–112, and his dubious findings (that Pervo employs) in my note 49 below.

near certainty that Luke used Paul's letters, and the very strong probability that he was familiar with some of Josephus' works."[2]

The Sources of Acts and Paul's Letters

Like the question of Luke's use of Josephus, this issue is an old one. While Cadbury's decided opinion is that Acts is not dependent on Josephus, "the same may be said for the letters of Paul."[3] Cadbury identifies the heart of the methodological problem—to make a valid dependency argument, it is not enough to draw upon similar vocabulary as it may only prove that Paul and the author of Acts spoke the same language.[4] More recently, Keener relays how the majority of scholars (including himself) reject Luke's dependence on Paul's letters.[5]

Despite these views, Pervo concludes that the "cumulative evidence that Luke made use of Pauline letters is rather persuasive."[6] In chapter 4 of his book, Pervo demonstrates many detailed comparisons between Acts and Paul's letters.[7] In his review, Tannehill addresses some of Pervo's risky methodological assumptions.[8] First, that the author had access to Paul's letters (or was familiar with Paul's thinking and theology) is not a new supposition.[9] The relationship is an ongoing debate and certainly requires more

---

[2] Richard I. Pervo, *The Mystery of Acts: Unravelling Its Story* (Santa Rosa, CA: Polebridge, 2006), 4. Pervo's interest in ancient parallels with Acts goes back to his doctoral studies and—along with his interest in Haenchen's commentary on Acts—may be behind his choice of sources and what he constitutes as evidence. See Pervo, *Acts*, xv, and "Principles for Selecting Sources" in Chapter 2.

[3] Cadbury, *Luke-Acts*, 327. Parker, "'Former Treatise,'" 54, claims that the later we date Acts the "more inexplicable becomes its ignorance of Paul's own letters"—and the list of examples of this ignorance "could be extended almost indefinitely."

[4] Cadbury claims the "agreements in vocabulary are not striking but commonplace" (118). See further, Cadbury, *Luke-Acts*, 219 (see also 118–22, 219, 273, 338, and 358); Dupont, *Sources*, 86. Max Krenkel, *Josephus und Lukas: Der schriftstellerische Einfluss des jüdischen Geschichtschreibers auf den Christlichen* (Leipzig: H. A. Haessel, 1894) and William K. Hobart, *The Medical Language of St Luke* (London: Longmans, Green, 1882) share the same fundamental error. Krenkel refers to words and phrases used by both writers "but fails to show that the same words and phrases were *not* used by other writers." Gasque, *History*, 104.

[5] Keener, *Acts*, 1:399 and 1:234. See also Johnson, *Luke*, 2; Joseph A. Fitzmyer, *Luke the Theologian: Aspects of his Teaching* (New York: Paulist, 1989), 16; Spencer, *Acts*, 16; Mount, *Pauline Christianity*, 169 (n. 17); Porter, *Paul in Acts*, 206, and Longenecker, *Acts*, 237. Barrett considers the apparent failure of Luke to use Paul's letters as a "serious matter" for a date of 90 CE—especially where *1 Clement* (c. 96 CE) refers to some. Barrett, *Acts*, 2:xliii. This question is certainly a popular one. See also William O. Walker Jr., "Acts and the Pauline Letters. A Select Bibliography with Introduction," *Forum* 5 (2002): 105-15.

[6] Pervo, *Dating Acts*, 145. Earlier, Conzelmann, *Acts*, p. xxxiii, remarked that it is "almost inconceivable ... that the author of Acts knew nothing at all about the letters."

[7] Pervo claims that Acts "exhibits knowledge of 2 Corinthians (or at least a fragment thereof), Romans (8 references), 1 Corinthians (14 references), Galatians (25 references), Ephesians (19 references), and 1 Thessalonians (13 references)." Pervo, "Suburbs," 33-4 and idem, *Dating Acts*, 139-43 and 320-1.

[8] Tannehill, review of *Dating Acts*, 827–8. Keener, *Acts*, 1:233 (n. 86), is also not persuaded: "Pervo's detailed comparisons are commendable, but they admit of other possible explanations"—they "simply press too much into common use of widespread vocabulary to be plausible."

[9] Fitzmyer, *Theologian*, 16.

attention.[10] Second, what is the evidence for dating the circulation of Paul's letters so late (100 CE)?[11] Porter, building on the earlier work of Trobisch, claims this late date is "arguably wrong" based on his study on the gathering of Paul's letters.[12]

Third, despite a lack of agreement with how the Pauline canon formed, "virtually all are agreed that the gathering of the Pauline corpus required personal involvement at some level."[13] Since Paul died no later than 68 CE, it seems reasonable to conclude that Paul's letters were already in circulation by this time or shortly afterwards.[14] A circulation date of ±68 CE is entirely compatible with an early date of Acts as it also explains why there is no specific reliance upon Paul's letters in Acts.[15] Regardless, Tannehill rightly concludes that the "supposed date of a Pauline letter collection cannot determine the date of Acts."[16]

Consequently, even if Acts is influenced by Paul's letters, as Pervo alleges, this cannot *a priori* peg the date of Acts to a late first- or early second-century date for two major reasons. First, it is entirely possible and reasonable that the author of Acts was influenced by Paul, his thought, vocabulary, and theology, and second, even if it could be proven that Luke relied upon Paul's letters, this could have happened long before 100 CE and perhaps as early as the 60s CE.[17] Therefore, a dependency on Paul's letters in Luke-Acts is entirely compatible with an early date.

---

[10] Porter, *Paul in Acts*, 206; Stanley E. Porter, "When and How Was the Pauline Canon Compiled? An Assessment of Theories," in *The Pauline Canon* (ed. Stanley E. Porter; PAST 1; Leiden: Brill, 2004), 95–127; Barrett, *Acts*, 2:xliii; Keener, *Acts*, 1:399.

[11] Pervo, "The Date of Acts," 5; Armstrong, "A New Plea," (2017): 89 (n. 43). O'Neill, *Theology of Acts*, 21, based on Goodspeed, *Introduction*, considers how Paul's letters were "rescued from obscurity and 'Published' as a collection" about 90 CE. "If Goodspeed's thesis is accepted," says O'Neill, then "Luke-Acts cannot be later" than about 90 CE (21). However, he ultimately discounted this theory based on Polycarp's use of a "published collection of Paul's letters" (24).

[12] Porter, *When Paul Met Jesus*, 77; idem, "Paul and the Process of Canonization," in *Exploring the Origins of the Bible: Canon Formation in Historical, Literary, and Theological Perspective* (eds. Craig A. Evans and Emanuel Tov; Grand Rapids: Baker, 2008), 173–202; idem, "Assessment of Theories," 95–127 (and especially his section on Trobisch's theory on pp. 113–21); David Trobisch, *The First Edition of the New Testament* (Oxford: Oxford University Press, 2000); David Trobisch, *Paul's Letter Collection: Tracing the Origins* (Minneapolis: Fortress, 1994).

[13] Porter, "Pauline Canon," 122. We cannot be certain who it was that began this collection (Timothy and Luke are top contenders), but it seems reasonable that after an examination of the manuscripts it occurred near the end of his life or shortly after by a "close follower if not by Paul himself" (126–7).

[14] See Harry W. Tajra, *The Martyrdom of St. Paul* (WUNT 67; Tübingen: Mohr Siebeck, 1994), 199 (on Paul's death in Rome). Based on the writing practices of Paul's time, there is every reason to believe that he was personally active in his own letter gathering. R. L. Archer, "The Epistolary Form in the New Testament," *ExpTim* 63 (1952): 298, is perhaps the first to argue that Paul's letters were "first published as a series" based on "Seneca's philosophic collection." He dates this collection (along with Mark's gospel) "probably a little before the Fall of Jerusalem, and Luke's a little after that event" (298).

[15] See also Porter, "Pauline Canon," 126. If Acts was written post-80 CE then why does the book "not make any overt or explicit reference to the Pauline letters" which unfortunately is an "assumption of much contemporary scholarship." See Porter, "Pauline Canon," 102.

[16] Tannehill, review of *Dating Acts*, 828. Pervo claims that the author of Acts had access to a Pauline collection that was not available until 100 CE. On the contrary, Keener, *Acts*, 1:234, states that it is "likely that Acts was composed before Paul's letters were collected."

[17] See Pervo's section on Acts and Galatians in *Dating Acts*, 73–96. If Paul's undisputed letters were written in the 40s and 50s CE, and no later than his death (somewhere between 64 and 68), how realistic is it to expect a letter like Galatians to sit on the shelf for 40–50 years before the author of Acts became aware of it and used it? Gamble affirms the often "rapid and wide circulation" of Christian texts. See Harry Y. Gamble, "The Book Trade in the Roman Empire," in *The Early Text of the New Testament* (eds. Charles E. Hill and Michael J. Kruger; Oxford: Oxford University Press,

Analysis of Selected Texts of Acts and Paul's Letters

There is no question that the book of Acts shares a considerable degree of lexical content with Paul's letters, but this is not enough to prove that one is borrowing from the other. Just because a passage of Acts contains a handful of similar words that Paul uses in his letters may only prove they were referring to the same or similar event or theological concept at best, and worst this may only demonstrate they are using a similar vocabulary. From among Pervo's extensive list of parallel passages, the following have been identified as showing the greatest potential for dependency: Acts 9:23-25/2 Cor. 11:32-33 (p. 60); Acts 9:21, 22:3/Gal. 1:13-14, 23 (p. 74); and Acts 2:33/Gal. 3:14/Eph. 1:13 (p. 77).[18] Each is examined in turn with a corresponding table that provides an overview of the texts in question.

Acts 9:23-25/2 Cor. 11:32-33: A Definitive Example?[19]

At the outset, there are some lexical similarities between these two texts that are worth further investigation (see Table 4.1).[20] The key question is one of sources: Is Luke using (1) another written source, (2) oral tradition, (3) his own personal diary/memories, or (4) is he using 2 Cor. 11:32-33 as a specific source? Meanwhile, we must bear in mind the obvious hazards of trying to discover the source of Acts 9:23-25 in the first place.[21] Since there are no clear references in any of the Acts variants, nor any marginal notation indicating a possible source for this text, our relegation of a source to this passage should, at best, remain a possibility.[22]

According to Pervo's train of thought, "Luke made use of canonical 2 Corinthians, which is not attested before *c.* 120–130 (Marcion, possibly Polycarp) and was not available before 100."[23] As a result, this naturally pushes Pervo's date of Acts much later. His date for the first use of 2 Corinthians seems reasonable, but this only provides a *terminus ad quem* for 2 Corinthians. Accordingly, his view on such a late availability for 2 Corinthians is unreasonable and highly assumptive, especially since we can date the "opening of the window" in 2 Cor. 11:32-33 with "reasonable precision to the year 36 CE."[24] As argued above, there are strong reasons to conclude that Paul's letters were in circulation during the 50s–60s CE and that the date of collection (which is speculative to begin with) "cannot determine the date of Acts."[25]

2012), 23–36 (33), and also Porter's, "Dating," 568, time frame for the four gospels written between 40 (or 50) and 65 CE.

[18] See Pervo, *Dating Acts*, 60, 74, and 77, respectively and Tannehill, review of *Dating Acts*, 827–8 (esp. p. 827).

[19] Pervo, *Dating Acts*, 60. He entitles this section: "A Definitive Example: 2 Corinthians" (60–4).

[20] Recall Chapter 2: "Principles for Selecting Sources."

[21] Bruce, *Acts* (3rd edn), 40.

[22] Recalling Frederick J. Foakes-Jackson's, *The Acts of the Apostles* (MNTC; London: Hodder and Stoughton, 1931), vi, caution that NT source-criticism is "largely guess-work."

[23] Pervo, *Dating Acts*, 62.

[24] Douglas A. Campbell, *Framing Paul: An Epistolary Biography* (Grand Rapids: Eerdmans, 2014), 184.

[25] Tannehill, review of *Dating Acts*, 828. Recall my Table 1.1 in Chapter 1.

Table 4.1 Acts 9:23-25/2 Cor. 11:32-33

Acts 9:23-25	NA[28]	2 Cor. 11:32-33	NA[28]
(23) And after some days passed, the Jews plotted together to kill him, (24) but their plot became known to Saul. They were also watching the gates day and night so that they might put him to death; (25) and the disciples took him by night [and] let him down by/through the wall, lowering [him] in a basket.	(23) Ὡς δὲ ἐπληροῦντο ἡμέραι ἱκαναί, συνεβουλεύσαντο οἱ Ἰουδαῖοι ἀνελεῖν αὐτόν· (24) ἐγνώσθη δὲ τῷ Σαύλῳ ἡ ἐπιβουλὴ αὐτῶν. παρετηροῦντο δὲ καὶ τὰς πύλας ἡμέρας τε καὶ νυκτὸς ὅπως αὐτὸν ἀνέλωσιν[c] (25) λαβόντες δὲ οἱ μαθηταὶ αὐτοῦ[d] νυκτὸς διὰ τοῦ τείχους καθῆκαν αὐτὸν[e] χαλάσαντες ἐν σπυρίδι.	(32) In Damascus the ethnarch under Aretas the king was guarding the city of the Damascenes [in order] to capture me, (33) and through an opening I was let down in a basket by/through the wall and escaped his hands.	(32) ἐν Δαμασκῷ ὁ ἐθνάρχης Ἀρέτα τοῦ βασιλέως ἐφρούρει τὴν πόλιν Δαμασκηνῶν πιάσαι με,[a] (33) καὶ διὰ θυρίδος[b] ἐν σαργάνῃ ἐχαλάσθην διὰ τοῦ τείχους καὶ ἐξέφυγον τὰς χεῖρας αὐτοῦ.

[a]Θέλων is added for emphasis in: ℵ, D2, H, K, L, P, Ψ, 0121, 0243, 0278 (vid.), 33, 81, 104, 365, 630, 1175, 1241, 1505, 1881, 2464, (F G 1739), 𝔐, sy^h and bo. The text chosen by the committee is based on: B, D*, sa, and Eus.
[b]Here θυρίς (as a genitive, feminine singular) is "an opening in a wall for the entrance of light and air and for the purpose of seeing in or out – window." Cf. L&N 7.47. Whether this opening contains "glass or shutters" is anyone's guess but the kind in Acts 20:29 is "probably" a simple opening. L&N 7.47.
[c]Codex Alexandrinus has this variant: ὅπως πιάσωσιν αὐτὸν ἡμέρας καὶ νυκτὸς.
[d]There are some minor changes in αὐτός from the genitive to the accusative in some mss (αὐτὸν οἱ μαθηταί).
[e]There are some changes in word order for some mss: διὰ τοῦ τείχους καθῆκαν αὐτόν.

Pervo translates Acts 9:25 as the following: "but his disciples took him by night and *let him down through an opening in the wall, lowering him in a basket.*"[26] The prepositional phrase διὰ τοῦ τείχους has been variously understood. Does it mean "by" the wall or "through" the wall, or even "by means" of the wall?[27] At any rate διὰ τοῦ τείχους plus the verb χαλάω (that are common to both accounts) raises the issue of source. Beyond the lexical parallels, Pervo makes much of the thematic differences between the two accounts that do not seem clear: "Of the two, Luke's account is clearly secondary, for it is difficult to believe that no sooner than Paul was converted and preaching his new faith that a murder plot boiled up in the synagogues of Damascus."[28] How is Acts clearly secondary based on this line of reasoning?

---

[26] Pervo, *Dating Acts*, 60 (italics original).
[27] Διά with the genitive is a "marker of intermediate agent, with implicit or explicit causative agent— through, by." See L&N 90.4; Porter, *Idioms*, 148–9.
[28] Pervo, *Dating Acts*, 60–1.

The danger Paul faced was not something unique to Acts or something Luke is obviously expanding upon (in 2 Cor. 11:32-33). The plots against Paul and threats on his life are regularly narrated in his letters as well as in the Corinthian correspondence (1 Cor. 15:30).[29] In the very same context, and just a few verses before 2 Cor. 11:32-33, Paul recounts his very blunt list of apostolic troubles and trials (2 Cor. 11:23-27). The threats to his person as an ex-persecutor are apparent very early on in the closing of his letter to the Galatians where he boasts of having the "marks of Jesus" (τὰ στίγματα τοῦ Ἰησοῦ).[30]

In both cases there is a story of a plot to capture Paul but he escaped through the city's wall.[31] In Acts it is the Jews who plotted against Paul, in 2 Corinthians it was King Aretas, and it is not too hard to imagine both groups behind the scene in each story.[32] Bruce thinks it is "conceivable that they alerted the ethnarch to his presence in the city."[33] Either way, the fact that they wanted to kill him in Damascus is not unique as Paul faced the same threat in Jerusalem (Acts 9:29).

We can only speculate as to why Luke added some extra details with regard to the Jews (verses 23-24), but did not mention the ethnarch or Aretas.[34] It seems reasonable to suppose that *if* he was working with a copy of Paul's second letter to the Corinthians he would have mentioned something about the ethnarch or Aretas, especially given Luke's interest in political details.[35] At any rate, perhaps his overall "purpose" was not to describe the "political and historical circumstances of the day" but to demonstrate the "genuineness of Saul's encounter with Christ on the Damascus road."[36]

Although it seems clear that both texts are pointing to the same tradition, there are enough differences and reasons to suggest another solution instead of dependency. Since this story is in the earlier part of Acts (and before Antioch), it is conceivable that it came from another oral source that may have been Paul or someone else who passed on the essence of the story.[37]

---

[29] "Why indeed, are we in danger every hour?" (Τί καὶ ἡμεῖς κινδυνεύομεν πᾶσαν ὥραν;).
[30] Τοῦ λοιποῦ κόπους μοι μηδεὶς παρεχέτω· ἐγὼ γὰρ τὰ στίγματα τοῦ Ἰησοῦ ἐν τῷ σώματί μου βαστάζω.
[31] Keener, *Acts*, 3:1683-6.
[32] Longenecker, *Acts*, 376-7, says that "Luke credits the Jews of Damascus as being the perpetrators to kill Saul, whereas in 2 Corinthians 11:32 that honour is given to 'the governor . . . under King Aretas.'"
[33] Bruce, *Acts* (3rd edn), 242.
[34] Shellard, *New Light on Luke*, 49, highlights the prophetic tradition that Luke is following in his "denunciation of the Jewish Cult." I.e., Amos 5:21-23; Isa. 1:11. She figures his attitude towards them is "particularly bitter" (49).
[35] Recall my note 66 in Chapter 3 on doctrinal or political modifications. The differences in the details, and the lack of reference to the ethnarch and King is significant—especially given Luke's interest in rulers, governors, and officials (Acts 8:27; 11:28; 12:1; 16:20-22; 35-38; 17:7; 18:2; 23:24-26, 33-34; 24:1-10; 25:8, 13-14, 21, 24-26; 28:7).
[36] Longenecker, *Acts*, 377. This makes sense given the narrative progression from Acts 9:1 to his escape via a "basket" (σπυρίς) in 9:25.
[37] See Wright, "Challenge," 29.

Table 4.2 Acts 9:21; 22:3/Gal. 1:13-14, 23

Acts 9:21	NA[28]	Gal. 1:13-14, 23	NA[28]
(21) And all those hearing were astonished and said, "Is this not the man who in Jerusalem was destroying[a] those who call on this name, and has he [not] come here to take them as prisoners for the chief priests?"	(21) ἐξίσταντο δὲ πάντες οἱ ἀκούοντες καὶ ἔλεγον· οὐχ οὗτός ἐστιν ὁ **πορθήσας** εἰς Ἰερουσαλὴμ τοὺς ἐπικαλουμένους τὸ ὄνομα τοῦτο, καὶ ὧδε εἰς τοῦτο ἐληλύθει ἵνα δεδεμένους αὐτοὺς ἀγάγῃ ἐπὶ τοὺς ἀρχιερεῖς;	(13) For you have heard of my former way of life in Judaism, how intensely I persecuted the church of God and tried to destroy it.	(13) Ἠκούσατε γὰρ τὴν ἐμὴν ἀναστροφήν ποτε ἐν τῷ Ἰουδαϊσμῷ, ὅτι καθ' ὑπερβολὴν ἐδίωκον τὴν ἐκκλησίαν τοῦ θεοῦ καὶ **ἐπόρθουν** αὐτήν,
(22:3) I am a Jew, born in Tarsus of Cilicia, but brought up in this city, at the feet of Gamaliel, educated in strict conformance[b] to the Law of our forefathers, being zealous for God just as all of you are today.	(22:3) ἐγώ εἰμι ἀνὴρ Ἰουδαῖος, γεγεννημένος ἐν Ταρσῷ τῆς Κιλικίας, ἀνατεθραμμένος δὲ ἐν τῇ πόλει ταύτῃ, παρὰ τοὺς πόδας Γαμαλιὴλ πεπαιδευμένος κατὰ ἀκρίβειαν τοῦ πατρῴου νόμου, **ζηλωτὴς οὑπάρχων** τοῦ θεοῦ καθὼς πάντες ὑμεῖς ἐστε σήμερον·	(14) And I was advancing in Judaism beyond many of my own age in my own race and being extremely zealous for the traditions of my fathers.	(14) καὶ προέκοπτον ἐν τῷ Ἰουδαϊσμῷ ὑπὲρ πολλοὺς συνηλικιώτας ἐν τῷ γένει μου, περισσοτέρως **ζηλωτὴς ὑπάρχων** τῶν πατρικῶν μου παραδόσεων.
		(23) and they only kept hearing that, "The man who formerly persecuted us is now preaching the faith he once tried to destroy."	(23) μόνον δὲ ἀκούοντες ἦσαν ὅτι ὁ διώκων ἡμᾶς ποτε νῦν εὐαγγελίζεται τὴν πίστιν ἥν ποτε ἐπόρθει,

[a]See the entry on πορθέω and the translation of the first half of this verse in L&N 20.37.
[b]Cf. L&N 72.20 on ἀκρίβεια.

Paul the Persecuting Zealot: Acts 9:21, 22:3/Gal. 1:13-14, 23[38]

A further example that may seem at first glance to carry some level of dependency on Paul's letter to the Galatians does not stand up to reason (see Table 4.2).[39] First, there is evidence that some level of oral tradition lies behind the source(s) of Acts.[40]

---

[38] Pervo, *Dating Acts*, 74.
[39] Ibid., 76, says the "data strongly support the hypothesis that Luke has made use of Galatians 1."
[40] Keener, *Acts*, 1:178, claims that Luke's sources were "most often . . . oral reports." Oral tradition in the synoptic gospels has also been long observed but underdeveloped. See Stanley E. Porter and Bryan R. Dyer, "What Have We Learned regarding the Synoptic Problem, and What Do We Still Need to Learn?," in *The Synoptic Problem: Four Views* (eds. Stanley E. Porter and Bryan R. Dyer; Grand Rapids: Baker Academic, 2016), 165–78; Stanley E. Porter, "The Synoptic Problem: The State of the Question," *JGRChJ* 12 (2016): 73–98 and Rainer Riesner, "The Orality and Memory Hypothesis," in *The Synoptic Problem: Four Views* (eds. Stanley E. Porter and Bryan R. Dyer; Grand Rapids: Baker

Long before Acts was written, Paul wrote: "you have *heard* about my former way of life" (Gal. 1:13) and also that "they only kept *hearing*" about this persecutor turned preacher (Gal. 1:23). It is easy to imagine a decade or so after Galatians was written that this information about Paul's life would have become common knowledge by the time Luke wrote Acts.

Second, that Paul as a Jew had a zealous past in terms of the Law is so basic to his earlier letters, and descriptive of most teachers in Judaism (i.e., Acts 22:3), that Luke's mentioning of this in Acts 9:21, 22:3 could have easily come from his own memory, another Christian, or just about *anyone* across the Roman Empire that was familiar with Paul's life and conversion to Christianity (Acts 9:19-21; 26-27; 11:25-26; 15:35; 28:30-31). Surely somebody at Antioch after a "whole year" of Saul/Paul teaching (with the help of Barnabas) "great numbers of people" (Acts 11:26) picked up on the fact of Paul's former, persecuting way of life and his conversion to Christ.

Third, Pervo's interest in the statistical rarity of "being zealous" or "being a zealot" (ζηλωτὴς ὑπάρχων) that is *only* found together here in Gal. 1:14 and Acts 22:3 (but see Acts 21:20) does not offer the kind of evidence required in order to establish a lexical relationship, especially when you consider how very common ὑπάρχω is in the NT and the LXX and how often Paul and Luke use this supposedly "rare" word ζηλωτής.[41] We encounter the verb ὑπάρχω a hundred and fifty-six times in the LXX and sixty times in the NT. Luke uses ὑπάρχω fifteen times in his gospel and twenty-five times in Acts.

This point alone should diminish the value of Pervo's ironclad parallel, and yet Pervo seems to have missed another "rare" example in Acts 21:20: "they are all [being] zealous for the Law" (πάντες ζηλωταὶ τοῦ νόμου ὑπάρχουσιν). So in Acts 21:20 Luke recounts the "thousands" of Jewish believers who are all "zealous for the Law" while a little later he uses this supposedly "rare" combination of lexemes for the apostle Paul as well in Acts 22:3. Hence, if the Jews (21:20) are all zealous for the Law just like Paul is how does this demonstrate anything that the average Greek, Roman, or Jew in the first century would not automatically assume? So far there is nothing to indicate that Luke copied from Galatians, and why would he need to?

Last, in addition to the three uses of ζηλωτής from the eight in the NT used by Paul (Gal. 1:14; 1 Cor. 14:12; Tit. 2:14), ὑπάρχω is used by Paul some twelve times in his letters (out of sixty in the NT). Although we have no other direct examples of ζηλωτής and ὑπάρχω being found in close proximity by Paul (beyond Gal. 1:14), another close example is found with his description of Titus "being very eager" (σπουδαιότερος δὲ ὑπάρχων) in 2 Cor. 8:17.[42] Therefore, it seems best to view some of these lexical parallels

---

Academic, 2016), 89–111. Riesner recognizes how "all three other Synoptic theories acknowledge the existence of an oral tradition" (161). See more recently, Wright, "Challenge," 9–30.

[41] Pervo, *Dating Acts*, 76. Granted (ζηλωτής) is far less common, with only six occurrences in the LXX and eight in the NT (Lk. 6:13; Acts 1:13; 21:20; 22:30; Gal. 1:14; 1 Cor. 14:12; Tit. 2:14; 1 Pet. 3:13). However, employing a fairly common word with a less common word does not make for an exceptional phrase; just a less common one in Hellenistic Greek. Meanwhile Luke's relatively high usage of ζηλωτής (based on the OT and NT alone), paired with the very common ὑπάρχω mitigates an already useless argument that Acts is dependent upon Galatians.

[42] The adjective σπουδαῖος (subdomain 25.75) is grouped with ζηλόω (25.76) and ζηλωτής (25.77/Gal. 1:14 and Acts 22:3) as part of the domain: "Be Eager, Be Earnest, In a Devoted Manner" (cf. L&N 25.68-25.79).

Table 4.3 Promised Spirit: Acts 2:33/Gal. 3:14/Eph. 1:13

Acts 2:33	Gal. 3:14	Eph. 1:13
(33) Therefore, exalted to the right hand of God, and having received from the Father the promised Holy Spirit, he has poured out this that you both see and hear.	(14) in order that in Christ Jesus the blessing of Abraham might come to the Gentiles, so that we might receive the promise of the Spirit through faith.	(13) in whom you also, having heard the word of the truth, the good news of your salvation, in whom also having believed, you were sealed with the promised Holy Spirit,
NA²⁸	NA²⁸	NA²⁸
(33) τῇ δεξιᾷ οὖν τοῦ θεοῦ ὑψωθείς, **τήν** τε **ἐπαγγελίαν τοῦ πνεύματος τοῦ ἁγίου λαβὼν** παρὰ τοῦ πατρός, ἐξέχεεν τοῦτο ὃ ὑμεῖς [καὶ] βλέπετε καὶ ἀκούετε.	(14) ἵνα εἰς τὰ ἔθνη ἡ εὐλογία τοῦ Ἀβραὰμ γένηται ἐν Χριστῷ Ἰησοῦ, ἵνα **τὴν ἐπαγγελίαν τοῦ πνεύματος λάβωμεν** διὰ τῆς πίστεως.	(13) Ἐν ᾧ καὶ ὑμεῖς ἀκούσαντες τὸν λόγον τῆς ἀληθείας, τὸ εὐαγγέλιον τῆς σωτηρίας ὑμῶν, ἐν ᾧ καὶ πιστεύσαντες ἐσφραγίσθητε **τῷ πνεύματι τῆς ἐπαγγελίας τῷ ἁγίῳ**,

as merely indicative of a common oral tradition circulating about Paul's persecuting zeal before his conversion. They could have originated with his letter to the Galatians, but other simpler explanations are more likely.

Promised Spirit: Acts 2:33/Gal. 3:14/Eph. 1:13

Pervo alleges that Luke's source for this connection is Romans and Galatians, although his example includes the later and variously debated letter to the Ephesians (see Table 4.3).[43] He is concerned that all three texts mention the promise of the Spirit (and Gal. 3:14/Acts 2:33 receive it). This apparently provides a "strong case" for an "intertextual connection."[44] The activity and reception of the Holy Spirit is a subject that is paramount to Luke-Acts to the point that much of Luke's theology would disappear without this emphasis.[45]

How then can we reasonably substantiate that Acts 2:33 is somehow dependent upon Gal. 3:14 because of three very common and central Greek words to the theology of the New Testament: ἐπαγγελία, πνεῦμα, λαμβάνω?[46] Obviously the reception of the Spirit is of central importance to Luke in Acts (i.e., 1:8; 2:33, 2:38; 5:3; 8:15, 17, 19; 10:47; 19:2) but this does not provide evidence of dependence.[47] What we find in the immediate context of Acts 2 is an emphasis on David (2:25, 29, 34) and the Psalms 16:8-11 (LXX) and 110:1, but not a single reference to Abraham in the entire chapter.[48]

---

[43] Pervo, *Dating Acts*, 77.
[44] Ibid., 76 (see also his ideas on intertextuality as a method: 7–8, 13, 26–7, 146).
[45] There are approximately thirteen direct references to the Holy Spirit in Luke's gospel and forty-two in Acts.
[46] These words occur multiple times in the NT: ἐπαγγελία (52), πνεῦμα (379), λαμβάνω (258).
[47] Where Paul talks about the reception of the promised Holy Spirit (Gal. 3:14) this is tied to the blessing of Abraham. Wherever Luke mentions Abraham in his gospel and in Acts, this is not discussed.
[48] Additionally, in Acts 2:33 the context is on the resurrection where Jesus "received from the Father the promised Holy Spirit." In Gal. 3:14 it is the Gentiles who (in Christ) "might receive the promise of the Spirit through faith"—on account of the "blessing of Abraham."

It seems rather far-fetched that Luke would draw three words from Paul in Galatians here to develop his apologetic argument that rests on proving that Jesus is Lord and Messiah (Acts 2:36).

In the end, Pervo weighs the two options: (1) "Luke used the letters of Paul" or (2) "Luke had direct contact with Paul and/or his [sic] some of his associates."[49] Those following option 1 see the Paul of Acts as a "Lucan construction designed to deal with issues of a later period."[50] Those who follow option 2 somehow make "Luke a thorn in Paul's flesh, better, a viper in his bosom."[51] Rather than following the majority of scholarship on this second point, Pervo decides in favour of dependency.[52] However, after taking a closer look at the parallels there does not appear to be any merit to his argument.

The Sources of Acts and the Works of Josephus

Another central issue for the date of Acts and its sources rests upon the recurring nineteenth-century claim that Luke depends upon Josephus.[53] Josephus lived

---

[49] Pervo, *Dating Acts*, 100. Many of the remaining "parallels" seem baseless such as highlighting "circumcision" in Acts 10:45 with Gal. 2:12; Rom. 4:12; Col. 4:11 and Tit. 1:10. Cf. Pervo, *Dating Acts*, 91. Pervo, *Dating Acts*, 67, finds another questionable connection between 1 Cor. 7:32-35 and Lk. 10:40-42 via ἀμέριμνος and ἀπερισπάστως/περισπάω. How could Luke invent the story of Mary and Martha based on a "transformation and application of a Pauline principle"? (68). With regard to 1 Cor. 11:16 and Lk. 22:24 Pervo (65) draws the "connection" between δοκέω and φιλόνεικος from Goulder, "Letters," 106. Goulder's earlier study is concerned with the presupposition held by some that Luke knew "all of the major Pauline letters." Cf. Goulder, "Letters," 98. His limited hypothesis that "Luke knew 1 Corinthians and 1 Thessalonians" focuses on the "evidence" via "clusters or collocations of words that occur in common between these epistles and Luke" (98). His method does not appear to be significantly different than Pervo's. Keener, *Acts*, 1:233 (n. 86), righty questions both Goulder's method and his hypothesis while stating that "his evidence is not impressive" (1:234). The stronger connections can easily reflect Luke's contact with Paul. Keener, *Acts*, 1:234–5. One of Pervo's "stronger" examples is from Lk. 18:11 and 1 Cor. 6:9-10. Rather than seeing Luke as drawing from a common list of vices Pervo (65) would argue instead that it is "more difficult to explain the overlap as coincidence than dependence." Where Paul (1 Cor. 6:9-10) mentions a long list of sinners, Luke (18:11) employs three of these for his parable of the Pharisees: ἅρπαγες (thieves), ἄδικοι (rogues), μοιχοί (adulterers) next to this ὁ τελώνης (tax collector—that Paul does not employ). First, the three words are not even found in the same order in both texts, and second, by themselves they are not uncommon in the NT (ἅρπαγες [five times], ἄδικοι [twelve times], μοιχοί [three times]). Third, the irony of this "example" is that where Paul is calling out the sinners, Luke's parable is calling out the hypocrisy of those who do not think they are sinners. Last, since Luke and Paul write about religious themes is it really that suspect they both talk about various types of sinners?

[50] Pervo, *Dating Acts*, 100.

[51] Ibid., 100. He goes on to say that "all of the efforts to transform this viper into a harmless garden snake gliding along in the apostle's path end up slighting both Luke and Paul, neither of whom is allowed to speak his own piece."

[52] Ibid., 51–2, here and elsewhere uses rhetorical language that seems to denigrate anyone with an opposite opinion. In my view, effort is better spent on evaluating the sources and arguments of other scholars.

[53] Porter, "Dating," 557; Hemer, *Acts*, 372, 94–9; Barrett, *Luke the Historian*, 75–6; Gasque, *History*, 103; Pervo, *Dating Acts*, 149–99. Pervo (197) considers this idea "deeply compelling and inherently attractive" while challenging those against this view to come up with a better argument (198). While Shellard, *New Light on Luke*, 31, claims that Luke's use of Josephus is a "contested issue," she finds "numerous verbal connections" between Josephus's *Against Apion* and Luke's prologue

approximately c. 37–100 CE. His *Jewish War* was published in c. 75–79 CE while his *Antiquities of the Jews* was published in c. 93–94 CE.⁵⁴ His last two works *Life* and *Against Apion* were published shortly before his death. This is a critical matter because 93 CE would be the earliest possible date for Acts "if it could be shown that Luke made use of Josephus's *Antiquities*."⁵⁵

Nearly a century ago, Cadbury indicated that the origins of the Lucan dependency hypothesis stem from the writings of Ottius in 1741 and Krebs in 1755 CE.⁵⁶ This flourished based on three main passages in Acts: the first one deals with a certain Theudas (Acts 5:36) who led a rebellion of four hundred men;⁵⁷ the second concerns Lysanias the "tetrarch of Abilene" (Lk. 3:1);⁵⁸ and third, the Egyptian who led a revolt of some 4000 terrorists (Acts 21:38).⁵⁹ Although Krenkel's position has repeatedly been discounted by several scholars, Pervo has recently placed them on the table once more.⁶⁰ Pervo does make a point saying that just because Krenkel's method was insufficient it "does not automatically disprove its hypothesis."⁶¹ Granted a new method may prove a hypothesis, but a hypothesis that has been repeatedly discounted (e.g., the world is flat) does not need a new method, it needs a new hypothesis.

Furthermore, despite Pervo's improved methodology, he has failed to adequately engage the arguments of key scholars (e.g., Cadbury, Foakes-Jackson, and Hemer) who do not subscribe to Josephus dependency theories.⁶² Perhaps even more alarming is that Pervo grants only two pages for "objections to the proposal that

---

(33, see also my "Parallels to the Prefaces" in Chapter 3). She claims that it is "more than likely that Luke used *Jewish War*, quite likely that he used *Jewish Antiquities*, and possibly that he used *Against Apion*" (34). In her estimation, this supports (without justification) a date for Luke-Acts around 100 CE (34). She (32) also fails to interact with the "many critics" who have "dismissed the evidence" Krenkel offered (cf. also 31–4).

⁵⁴ Cf. Peter Schäfer's, *The History of the Jews in the Greco-Roman World* (rev. edn; London: Routledge, 2003), 123–33, concerning the first Jewish War.

⁵⁵ Conzelmann, *Acts*, xxxii.

⁵⁶ Cadbury, "Identity," 2:355–6; Joannes Baptista Ottius, *Spicilegium sive excerpta ex Flavio Josepho ad Novi Testamenti illustrationem* (Leiden: Joannes Hasebroek, 1741), and Johann T. Krebs, *Observationes in Novum Testamentum e Flavio Josepho* (Lipsiae: Wendlerus Joannes, 1755). During the nineteenth century the theory continued to evolve that "Luke was dependent on Josephus." Cadbury, "Identity," 2:356. According to Cadbury (356), it was Keim (and others) by 1878 who "adopted this view" peaking with Krenkel's classic defence in 1894. Cf. Krenkel, *Josephus und Lukas*. Krenkel finds ninety-two passages that are common to Luke and Josephus but not found in the LXX. This "huge overkill of the significant" includes a "13-page list of mostly common words which the two writers share with the Septuagint." Hemer, *Acts*, 372.

⁵⁷ Marshall, *Acts*, 128–9. Barrett, *Acts*, 2:xliii, considers the alleged misreading of Josephus's account of Theudas and Judas to have "little weight."

⁵⁸ The Abilene inscription (c. 15–30 CE) is no longer a serious issue. See Ellis, *Luke*, 87; A. R. C. Leaney, *The Gospel According to Luke* (London: Adam & Charles Black, 1966), 48–50; and William M. Ramsay, *The Bearing of Recent Discovery on the Trustworthiness of the New Testament* (London: Hodder and Stoughton, 1915), 297–300.

⁵⁹ Luke and Josephus are merely writing about the same event (with differing details). Bruce, *Acts* (3rd edn), 453; Morton Smith, "Zealots and Sicarii: Their Origins and Relation," *HTR* 64 (1971): 1–19.

⁶⁰ Pervo attempts to find "additional wheat" from Krenkel's "putative chaff." Pervo, *Dating Acts*, 198.

⁶¹ Ibid., 150.

⁶² Pervo, *Dating Acts*, 149–99. Both Hemer and Cadbury receive only a single passing reference despite their opposing views. Hemer, *Acts*, 372; Cadbury, "Identity," 2:357. Although Cadbury (357) considers these so-called examples of "Lucan errors explained by Josephus" as "very persuasive," they "fall short of demonstration."

Luke used Josephus" and for this he relies only on Witherington's commentary and a 1980 essay by Schreckenberg.[63] The irony is that in the very places where Luke and Josephus intersect, they often contradict each other.[64] Therefore, it seems wise to remain critical of any claim that Acts is dependent upon the late first-century works of Josephus.[65]

Analysis of Selected Texts of Acts and the Works of Josephus

Pervo's argument rests primarily on two passages where he claims the "inaccuracies" in Acts are due to a misreading of Josephus's account: (1) the rebels Theudas and Judas in Acts 5:36-37 and (2) the Egyptian in Acts 21:37-38.[66] Each will be examined in sequence.

Theudas and Judas: Acts 5:36-37; Jos. *Ant*. 20.97-102

The problem with Acts 5:36-37 is that Theudas's revolt "occurred later" than Gamaliel I's speech "should have taken place" (rather than before him), and "long after Judas the Galilean's revolt" in 6 CE.[67] Consequently, scholars have offered various solutions to the dilemma. For example, Pervo claims that "Luke's use of Josephus is extremely

---

[63] Pervo, *Dating Acts*, 194–6; Witherington, *Acts*, 235–9; and Heinz Schreckenberg, "Flavius Josephus und die lukanischen Schriften," in *Neutestamentliche Studien, Festgabe für K. H. Rengstorf zum 75* (eds. W. Haubeck and H. Bachmann; Leiden: Brill, 1980), 179–209.

[64] Hemer, *Acts*, 372. E.g., Theudas in Acts 5:36, the Egyptian messianic pretender (4000 followers in Acts while 30,000 in Josephus), and the Quirinius census—regardless, Josephus is known for inflating numbers. Emil Schürer, "Lucas und Josephus," *ZWT* 19 (1876): 582–3, suggested that "either Luke had not read Josephus, or he had forgotten what he read." See also Hemer, *Acts*, 372–3; Schreckenberg, "Flavius Josephus," 179–209; Kümmel, *Introduction*, 132; Gasque, *History*, 179–80; Foakes-Jackson, *Acts*, xiii–xv; Arnold Ehrhardt, *The Framework of the New Testament Stories* (Manchester: Manchester University Press, 1964), 85–6; Fitzmyer; *Acts*, 53; Longenecker, *Acts*, 32; Bruce, *Acts* (3rd edn), 10, 43–4. More recently, Keener, *Acts*, 1:394, also finds it "highly unlikely" that Luke made use of Josephus while noting Pervo's concession that a mistaken reference to Theudas might be as old as the 60s CE. Pervo, *Dating Acts*, 310.

[65] Pervo admits that proof of dependency is impossible. Pervo, *Dating Acts*, 198.

[66] Ibid., 152–60, "Theudas and Judas" and 161–6, "The Egyptian and Friends."

[67] Keener, *Acts*, 2:1231. Theudas's revolt likely occurred during the governorship of Fadus (44–46 CE) or his successor Alexander (46–48 CE) but certainly before Gamaliel's death (somewhere near 52–54 CE). Thomas S. Caulley, "Notable Galilean Persons," in *Galilee in the Late Second Temple Period and Mishnaic Periods* (eds. David A. Fiensy and James R. Strange; *Life, Culture, and Society*, Volume 1; Minneapolis: Fortress, 2014), 151–66 (esp. pp. 152–3), has recently explored the issue of whether Judas the Galilean from Josephus and Acts 5:37 (who died 6 CE) is the same as Judas the son of Hezekiah. They could very well be the same. See also Acts 22:3 and the essay by Bruce D. Chilton and Jacob Neusner, "Paul and Gamaliel," *BBR* 14 (2004): 1–43 (see esp. n. 1 on the problem of identifying the historical Gamaliel). Which Gamaliel is Luke referring to that taught Paul (Acts 5:34-40 and 22:3)? Chilton and Neusner state that Gamaliel I is "represented as Hillel's successor in the chain of tradition" (1[n. 1]). They (38) place Gamaliel in "Jerusalem in the period between 20 and 50 CE" which "makes his overlap with Paul possible, and his influence in the Diaspora enhances any such overlap." They also claim that the "Temple-oriented material in several of the stories attributed to Gamaliel makes Acts 5:34 seem more plausible than might otherwise be the case" (38).

probable and alternative explanations quite tenuous" (cf. Acts 5:36-37 with Jos. *Ant.* 20.97-102).⁶⁸ On the contrary, alternative explanations are actually quite viable in comparison to such speculative and anachronistic historical inferences between Luke and Josephus.⁶⁹

Pervo's focus is on countering the "most common recourse" that this is a case of two different people named Theudas, despite other valid explanations.⁷⁰ Pervo attempts to counter Bruce's three reasons reproduced here: (1) Luke is a reliable historian, (2) Theudas is a "common name," and (3) the prevalence of "such risings under similar leaders."⁷¹ Evidently, one plausible solution is that the esteemed Jewish leader Gamaliel was "referring to another Theudas" who flourished before 6 CE,⁷² and there does not appear to be any logical reason to rule out of hand these conclusions by Bruce.

Next to Bruce, Marshall's arguments concerning Jos. *Ant.* 20.97 remain convincing—such as the difficulties of Gamaliel describing the rise of Judas *after* Theudas despite this event taking place in 6 CE.⁷³ Marshall (via Knowling) explains that

> no plausible explanation of Luke's alleged error has been offered. There is, therefore, much to be said for the suggestions either that Josephus got his dating wrong or (more probably) that Gamaliel is referring to another, otherwise unknown Theudas. Since there were *innumerable uprisings* when Herod the Great died, and since Josephus describes four men bearing the name of Simon within forty years and three that of Judas within ten years, all of whom were instigators of rebellion.⁷⁴

So it seems that the arguments put forth by Knowling, Bruce, and Marshall must remain at the forefront of any discussion of Theudas's revolt.

And yet, Pervo's bias seems decidedly in favour of dependency on Josephus and his accuracy against the author of Acts, despite the widespread difficulties with Josephus's literary agenda and inflation of historical facts for his own purposes.⁷⁵ As argued below, it matters little *if* Josephus is accurate here and Luke is not—this is not the decisive issue. The decisive issue is whether or not Luke clearly used Josephus's account, and the evidence suggests he did not, especially since zealotry and revolutionary thinking from 46 CE to the revolt in 66 CE was commonplace.

Even a casual reading of the two accounts shows the vast differences in detail while the only similarities are the shared names of the two leaders that had some kind of a following with revolutionary intent. Part of Pervo's bias relates to a supposed

---

⁶⁸ Pervo, *Dating Acts*, 152 (152–60). See his "Table 5.1: Rebels in Order" (154).
⁶⁹ Ibid., 152–60.
⁷⁰ Ibid., 156 and Bruce, *Acts* (3rd edn), 176.
⁷¹ Bruce, *Acts* (3rd edn), 176.
⁷² Ibid., 176; Keener, *Acts*, 2:1232. The phrase in Acts 5:36 "for some time ago" (πρὸ γὰρ τούτων τῶν ἡμερῶν) does not give a clear time frame but it does grant the possibility of an earlier Theudas.
⁷³ Marshall, *Acts*, 128–9.
⁷⁴ Cf. Marshall, *Acts*, 129, in reference to Richard J. Knowling, "The Acts of the Apostles," in *The Expositor's Greek Testament* (ed. W. Robertson Nicoll; 5 vols; London: Hodder & Stoughton, 1897–1910), 2:158 (my emphasis).
⁷⁵ Luke is "marked by carefulness but that of Josephus by carelessness." Hemer, *Acts*, 219. Luke may well be in error here, in which case that only reinforces that he could not have used Josephus.

"methodological flaw" that is "far more wearisome than all of Krenkel's wearisome lists"—the long held view that "if Luke had access to Josephus, he would have made more substantial and careful use of his work."[76] I see his point but this long held view is still a legitimate concern.

As far as ancient standards go, Luke is a fairly accurate user of sources as compared to Josephus (see Chapter 8). Although Keener thinks it is possible that Josephus has his details mixed up, he also thinks that (in this case) Josephus is more likely to be correct given his explicit mention of governors and his interest in revolutionaries (that remain "wholly peripheral" to Luke).[77] Nevertheless, it should be obvious that Luke is *not* drawing on Josephus at this point because the two accounts are so different that Luke Johnson rightly contends it is "impossible either to harmonize or to utterly dismiss either version."[78]

Even the number of Theudas's followers is strikingly different in both accounts. Where Acts 5:36 claims "about four hundred" (ὡς τετρακοσίων), Josephus boasts that Theudas persuaded "the majority of the masses" (πλεῖστον ὄχλον). Few scholars would accept Luke-Acts to be error-free, but the reasons in favour of the Theudas account in Acts being an earlier account (or referring to another Theudas) are just as substantial as Pervo's attempt to insist that Acts is borrowing from *Antiquities*.

As we compare the texts (see Table 4.4), there does not appear to be a strong connection between the two texts. This is true not only because of the extra details found in Josephus's expanded version, but there is also a critical point of chronology between Gamaliel's Theudas/Judas and that of Josephus's with regard to Fadus when he was "procurator of Judaea" (*Ant.* 20.97). Keener argues that it is "chronologically implausible" that Luke follows Josephus.[79] The events that Gamaliel refers to in Acts (Theudas in 5:36 and Judas in 5:37) provide a *terminus ante quem* where the events happened no later than the reign of the governors Cuspius Fadus (44–46 CE) and his successor Tiberius Alexander (46–48 CE).[80] In other words, this is compatible with an early date of Acts.

Stated more plainly, if Luke got his details mixed up, then he is talking about an event that still happened approximately some ten to twenty years earlier than the date of his composition.[81] His words on Gamaliel's lips ("for some time ago") are telling and reflect Luke's reliance on his own memory—he probably does not recall the exact time nor does it matter for his purpose in writing.[82] Luke may also have conflated the additional references to the "sons of Judas the Galilean" (Jos. *Ant.* 20.102), but

---

[76] Pervo, *Dating Acts*, 150.
[77] Keener, *Acts*, 2:1231–2 (1232).
[78] Luke T. Johnson, *The Acts of the Apostles* (SP 5; Collegeville, MN: Liturgical, 1992), 99.
[79] Fitzmyer, *Acts*, 340.
[80] Keener, *Acts*, 2:1231 (n. 218). Under Fadus was the "first instance of an uprising with messianic-apocalyptic overtones, whose political implications the procurator recognized and feared." Schäfer, *History of the Jews*, 117.
[81] That Luke "made a mistake" is due to either being "unaware of the true date of Theudas" or that he confused him with "some other rebel." Barrett, *Acts*, 242. Luke's other "historical assertions can be tested most securely." Cf. Keener, *Acts*, 2:1235 and Rainer Riesner, *Paul's Early Period: Chronology, Mission Strategy, Theology* (trans. Doug Stott; Grand Rapids: Eerdmans, 1998), 333.
[82] Luke's memory, like ours, is selective and not perfect. See Wright, "Challenge," 14–15.

Table 4.4 Theudas and Judas: Acts 5:36-37 and Jos. *Ant.* 20.97-102

Acts 5:36-37	NA[28]	Jos. Ant. 20.97-102[a]	Greek text
(36) for some time ago there rose up Theudas, saying that he himself was someone, and a number of men, about four hundred, joined him. He was killed, and as many as were persuaded [by] him, were dispersed, and came to nothing.	(36) πρὸ γὰρ τούτων τῶν ἡμερῶν ἀνέστη Θευδᾶς λέγων εἶναί τινα ἑαυτόν, ᾧ προσεκλίθη ἀνδρῶν ἀριθμὸς ὡς τετρακοσίων· ὃς ἀνῃρέθη, καὶ πάντες ὅσοι ἐπείθοντο αὐτῷ διελύθησαν καὶ ἐγένοντο εἰς οὐδέν.	(97 [v. 1]) During the period when Fadus was procurator of Judaea, a certain imposter named Theudas persuaded the majority of the masses to take up their possessions and to follow him to the Jordan River. He stated that he was a prophet and that at his command the river would be parted and would provide them an easy passage. (98) With this talk he deceived many. Fadus, however, did not permit them to reap the fruit of their folly, but sent against them a squadron of cavalry. These fell upon them unexpectedly, slew many of them and took many prisoners. Theudas himself was captured, whereupon they cut off his head and brought it to Jerusalem. (99) These, then, are the events that befell the Jews during the time that Cuspius Fadus was procurator.	(97 [v. 1]) Φάδου δὲ τῆς Ἰουδαίας ἐπιτροπεύοντος γόης τις ἀνὴρ Θευδᾶς ὀνόματι πείθει τὸν πλεῖστον ὄχλον ἀναλαβόντα τὰς κτήσεις ἕπεσθαι πρὸς τὸν Ἰορδάνην ποταμὸν αὐτῷ· προφήτης γὰρ ἔλεγεν εἶναι, καὶ προστάγματι τὸν ποταμὸν σχίσας δίοδον ἔχειν ἔφη παρέξειν αὐτοῖς ῥᾳδίαν. (98) καὶ ταῦτα λέγων πολλοὺς ἠπάτησεν. οὐ μὴν εἴασεν αὐτοὺς τῆς ἀφροσύνης ὄνασθαι Φᾶδος, ἀλλ᾽ ἐξέπεμψεν ἴλην ἱππέων ἐπ᾽ αὐτούς, ἥτις ἀπροσδόκητος ἐπιπεσοῦσα πολλοὺς μὲν ἀνεῖλεν, πολλοὺς δὲ ζῶντας ἔλαβεν, αὐτὸν δὲ τὸν Θευδᾶν ζωγρήσαντες ἀποτέμνουσι τὴν κεφαλὴν καὶ κομίζουσιν εἰς Ἱεροσόλυμα. (99) τὰ μὲν οὖν συμβάντα τοῖς Ἰουδαίοις κατὰ τοὺς Κουσπίου Φάδου τῆς ἐπιτροπῆς χρόνους ταῦτ᾽ ἐγένετο.

(continued)

Table 4.4 (*Continued*)

Acts 5:36-37	NA²⁸	Jos. Ant. 20.97-102ᵃ	Greek text
(37) After him, Judas of Galilee rose up in the days of the census and drew away people after him; and that one perished, and as many as were persuaded [by] him were scattered.	(37) μετὰ τοῦτον ἀνέστη Ἰούδας ὁ Γαλιλαῖος ἐν ταῖς ἡμέραις τῆς ἀπογραφῆς καὶ ἀπέστησεν λαὸν ὀπίσω αὐτοῦ· κἀκεῖνος ἀπώλετο καὶ πάντες ὅσοι ἐπείθοντο αὐτῷ διεσκορπίσθησαν.ᵇ	(100 [v. 2]) The successor of Fadus was Tiberius Alexander, the son of that Alexander who had been alabarch in Alexandria and who surpassed all his fellow citizens both in ancestry and in wealth. He was also superior to his son Alexander in his religious devotion, for the (101) latter did not stand by the practices of his people. It was in the administration of Tiberius Alexander that the great famine occurred in Judaea, during which Queen Helena bought grain from Egypt (102) for large sums and distributed it to the needy, as I have stated above. Besides this James and Simon, the sons of Judas the Galilean, were brought up for trial and, at the order of Alexander, were crucified. This was the Judas who, as I have explained above, had aroused the people to revolt against the Romans while Quirinius was taking the census in Judaea.	(100 [v. 2])ῚΗλθε δὲ Φάδῳ διάδοχος Τιβέριος Ἀλέξανδρος Ἀλεξάνδρου παῖς τοῦ καὶ ἀλαβαρχήσαντος ἐν Ἀλεξανδρείᾳ γένει τε καὶ πλούτῳ πρωτεύσαντος τῶν ἐκεῖ καθ᾽ αὑτόν. διήνεγκε καὶ τῇ πρὸς τὸν θεὸν εὐσεβείᾳ τοῦ παιδὸς Ἀλεξάνδρου· τοῖς γὰρ (101) πατρίοις οὐκ ἐνέμεινεν οὗτος ἔθεσιν. ἐπὶ τούτου δὲ καὶ τὸν μέγαν λιμὸν κατὰ τὴν Ἰουδαίαν συνέβη γενέσθαι, καθ᾽ ὃν καὶ ἡ βασίλισσα Ἑλένη πολλῶν χρημάτων ὠνησαμένη σῖτον ἀπὸ τῆς Αἰγύπτου (102) διένειμεν τοῖς ἀπορουμένοις, ὡς προεῖπον. πρὸς τούτοις δὲ καὶ οἱ παῖδες Ἰούδα τοῦ Γαλιλαίου ἀνήχθησαν τοῦ τὸν λαὸν ἀπὸ Ῥωμαίων ἀποστήσαντος Κυρινίου τῆς Ἰουδαίας τιμητεύοντος, ὡς ἐν τοῖς πρὸ τούτων δεδηλώκαμεν, Ἰάκωβος καὶ Σίμων, οὓς ἀνασταυρῶσαι προσέταξεν Ἀλέξανδρος.

ᵃSee Thackeray et al., *Josephus*, 9:441–5. Volume 9 is translated by L. H. Feldman. The divisions in the English translation (beyond Feldman's verse 1 and 2) are my own.
ᵇPervo, *Dating Acts*, 154, did not highlight anything in this example and so the text remains unbolded.

we should keep in mind that "their activity was later than Gamaliel's speech in the narrative world."[83]

The mention of Fadus and Alexander by Josephus allows us to estimate that Luke's source—either by memory, word of mouth, or diary—had been in existence well over

---

[83] Keener, *Acts*, 2:1231 (n. 218).

a decade before he incorporated *his version* of Theudas and Judas into the narrative of Acts by the early 60s CE.[84] Whether Luke is right or wrong, or whether he refers to the same or other revolutionary figures than Josephus is entirely compatible with an early pre-70 date of Acts.

The crux of the debate is whether Luke is specifically relying on Josephus's *Antiquities* as a source, and there are several reasons why that is unlikely (especially if Luke is conflating the stories from another source).[85] First, we cannot assume that Josephus is the only available source for Luke to draw from. After all, the events relating to Acts 5:36-37 were very likely common knowledge for Luke's readers. Second, we are completely in the dark as to what Josephus's source was, assuming that he used a source.[86] Third, it seems incredible to assume that the "clearest trace" of his reliance upon Josephus is found in a place where "Luke contradicts him."[87]

Fourth, reliance upon *Antiquities*—that would date the writing of Acts after 93 CE—is already supremely difficult for many reasons already discussed.[88] Fifth, Keener highlights Luke's attempt to preserve the "thrust of the speech" as "certainly well within the range of ancient historiographic practice."[89] Sixth, there is a clear apologetic purpose in the application of Gamaliel's speech (Acts 5:38-39).[90] Furthermore, the narrative purpose in the shorter passages in Acts is very different than Josephus's.[91] Still other reasons remain.

Seventh, it seems rather negligent of Luke to avoid the tantalizing detail of Theudas as a "certain imposter" by Josephus (*Ant.* 20.97) given his proclivity to denounce sorcery throughout Acts (i.e., Acts 8:9-25; 13:6-12; 19:17-20). Surely, Luke would not have missed this aspect of Josephus's account of Theudas. Eighth, if we follow the transcriptional canon that the *more difficult reading* is to be preferred, the Acts account

---

[84] He may have had this already compiled as a part of the pre-Antioch source(s) of Acts that came from someone connected to the church in Jerusalem or Palestine in general. This also fits in line with Gamaliel's (I) death somewhere near 52–54 CE.

[85] See also, Fitzmyer, *Acts*, 52; Barrett, *Acts*, 1:xliii, and Witherington, *Acts*, 237–8.

[86] Keener, *Acts*, 2:1235; Barrett, *Acts*, 1:296.

[87] Keener, *Acts*, 2:1235.

[88] Recall Chapter 1, this volume; Armstrong, "A New Plea," (2017): 79–110 (esp. pp. 109–10), and Keener, *Acts*, 1:383–401. Luke's "friendlier" perspective towards Pharisaism and Rome as part of his earlier apologetic for Paul does not fit with such a late date (post 93 CE). Keener, *Acts*, 2:1235 (n. 260).

[89] Keener, *Acts*, 2:1236. I.e., Tac. *Ann.* 11.24; Sall. *Catil.* 51.5-6; Jos. *War* 5.376-98 and Jer. 26:17-23. See also Eckhard Plümacher, *Lukas als hellenistischer Schriftsteller* (SUNT 9; Göttingen: Vandenhoeck & Ruprecht, 1972), 38–72 (esp. pp. 41–50); Conzelmann, *Acts*, 42, as cited by Keener, *Acts*, 2:1236 (n. 262, see also his section on speeches: 1:258–319).

[90] Keener, *Acts*, 2:1236-7. The speech contrasts the failed movements of revolutionaries versus the continuing nature of Jesus's movement that would be known by Luke's readers. Keener, *Acts*, 2:1237 and Osvaldo Padilla, *The Speeches of Outsiders in Acts: Poetics, Theology and Historiography* (SNTSMS 144. Cambridge: Cambridge University Press, 2008), 128–30.

[91] If we compare the second half of the two verses in Acts 5:36/37 this apologetic purpose becomes clear (5:36): "and as many as were persuaded [by] him, were dispersed, and came to nothing" (καὶ πάντες ὅσοι ἐπείθοντο αὐτῷ διεσκορπίσθησαν καὶ ἐγένοντο εἰς οὐδέν) and (5:37): "and as many as were persuaded [by] him were scattered" (καὶ πάντες ὅσοι ἐπείθοντο αὐτῷ διεσκορπίσθησαν).

is more likely to be earlier given the possible anachronism of Theudas and Judas.⁹² Ninth, since the Acts account is unquestionably brief as compared to Josephus's, the *shorter reading* is to be preferred.⁹³ Tenth, given Luke's interest in rulers and political details in Acts, it seems rather negligent that he would skip over the note "when Fadus was procurator of Judaea" (Jos. *Ant.* 20.97).⁹⁴

Altogether, these arguments should be enough to cast serious doubt on the hypothesis of Luke's reliance on Josephus in this example. The reasons against dependency are strong enough that any chance of Luke's reliance upon Josephus must remain a hypothetical possibility at best, but logically untenable at worst.⁹⁵

The Egyptian Liberator: Acts 21:38; Jos. *War* 2.261-63; Jos. *Ant.* 20.169-71

The only other example worth examining in detail is the account of the Egyptian in Acts 21:38.⁹⁶ It is very likely that Luke and Josephus refer to the same Egyptian rebel; however, the Acts account represents a tiny footnote in history as compared to Josephus's expanded accounts. If Luke was copying Josephus, surely he would have added more details and done so accurately, which he does not.

The following differences, both small and large, are easily noted. For example, if we compare εἰς τὴν ἔρημον (Acts 21:38) with ἐκ τῆς ἐρημίας (Jos. *War* 2.262) there are interesting differences in syntax. They may very well be the same Egyptian (ὁ Αἰγύπτιος) but Luke employs the preposition εἰς (into) while Josephus uses ἐκ (from). Are the rebels heading out into the wilderness (Acts) or coming from the wilderness to attack Jerusalem (Josephus)? Furthermore, it seems strange that Luke mentions the Sicarii (σικάριος) and Josephus does not mention them in connection with the Egyptian, which may reflect a substantial difference in time.⁹⁷ It seems further unlikely that Luke would fail to mention Felix in his account if he were relying on Josephus.

Accordingly, Luke seems to be writing about an event that happened during the age of the Sicarii and Zealots that is several years prior to the first Jewish Revolt in

---

⁹² Fee, "Textual Criticism," 14. Sometimes a scribe would inadvertently make it more difficult because of a faulty quotation or because he did not understand the grammar, meaning, or context. See Vaganay, *Introduction*, 81.

⁹³ Naturally, Griesbach's canon cannot be followed here in every case. Vaganay, *Introduction*, 80, and also James R. Royse, *Scribal Habits in Early Greek New Testament Papyri* (NTTS 36; Leiden: Brill, 2008), 593-608, prefer longer readings under certain conditions.

⁹⁴ E.g., Acts 8:27; 11:28. Recall my note 35.

⁹⁵ It is simply untenable that Luke has "plainly made use" of Josephus. Pervo, *Dating Acts*, 160.

⁹⁶ Pervo, *Dating Acts*, 161-6 (166), stops just short of calling the evidence for dependence upon Josephus as "'irrefutable.'" This is an "overstatement" given the most casual glance at the comparative texts (see Table 4.5).

⁹⁷ Recall the earlier discussion on the Zealots and Sicarii 44-66 CE in Judea. Pervo, *Dating Acts*, 164-6, thinks that Luke (via the tribune) incorrectly associates the Egyptian and his rebels with Sicarii and hence is conflating Josephus's accounts (166). However, Josephus already mentions the Sicarii just a few verses beforehand in fairly close proximity (cf. *War* 2.254 and 261 where he mentions ὁ Αἰγύπτιος). Additionally, there would be other reasons for the tribune to conflate "two different enemies" as they existed side by side during Felix's time—as both were "undoubtedly on Roman's minds." Keener, *Acts*, 3:3176; Hemer, *Acts*, 180. Last, even Josephus (*War*. 7.253-54) referred to an "earlier resistance movement" (Judas the Galilean) as Sicarii "though the title elsewhere begins in the 50s" CE (Keener, 3:3176 [n. 487]). The Sikarioi (Latin Sicarii) used a "sica" (a short, curved

66 CE, while Josephus is writing long afterwards. Where some have proposed a date of 56 or 57 CE for this revolt, it does not seem to have happened earlier than 55 CE given what "precedes it in Josephus" (see Table 4.5).[98] This event corresponds to the procuratorship of Marcus Antonius Felix (52–60 CE), which is compatible with a date of Acts in the early to mid-sixties CE (cf. Jos. *War* 2.263; Jos. *Ant.* 20.171; Acts 23:24).[99]

Furthermore, how do we explain the enormous difference in numbers between Luke and Josephus (Acts 21:38 = 4,000; *War* 2.261 = 30,000)?[100] And how do we account for the marked difference in numbers between Josephus's two accounts (cf. Jos. *War* 2.261; Jos. *Ant.* 20.171)?[101] While his earlier account (Jos. *War* 2.261) mentions thirty thousand followers, some fifteen years later he writes: "slaying *four hundred* of them and taking *two hundred* prisoners" (*Ant.* 20.171, my emphasis). Now this may be due to transcriptional errors, or a difference in oral or written sources, but Josephus's tendency to "exaggerate numbers" may explain this difference.[102]

Assuredly, it remains the more "improbable" scenario that Luke would "blatantly contradict Josephus at the very point where one was supposed to be dependent on him."[103] It seems rather disappointing that Pervo would find Luke's "confusion" here as evidence of his dependence on Josephus.[104] However, there does not seem to be any wheat in the leftover chaff except a few historical references shared between Luke and Josephus.[105] In the end, it seems that the historian will "get the kind of facts he wants."[106]

---

dagger) and "mingled with the crowds" stabbing their victims with these small daggers often in broad daylight undetected. Schäfer, *History of the Jews*, 118. At the "instigation of Felix" the high priest Jonathan became a notable victim (118; Jos. *War* 2.254-70).

[98] See Hemer, *Acts*, 170; Riesner, *Early Period*, 219; Witherington, *Acts*, 662, and Keener, *Acts*, 3:3174.

[99] As proposed in Chapter 1, Acts was likely written sometime close to 62–63 CE—this allows for five or six years for Luke's source on this event (if he needed one) to reach his pen. Since Acts 21:38 is so brief compared to Josephus's accounts, his source is most likely based on word of mouth. See Schäfer, *History of the Jews*, 118, concerning Felix and the increase in "Zealot influence."

[100] This seems to be an even greater reason why Luke did not rely on Josephus's reports. According to Keener, *Acts*, 3:3174 (n. 476), the proposed solutions to this go back as far as Nathaniel Lardner (1684–1768) and possibly earlier. Two major options are worth considering: (1) either Luke, his tribune (or some other source) are misinformed, or (2) Josephus is misinformed. Keener, *Acts*, 3:3175. Either way this discrepancy increases the gulf between the two accounts substantially.

[101] Keener, *Acts*, 3:3176.

[102] David J. Williams, *Acts* (NIBC; repr., Peabody, MA: Hendrickson, 2002), 372; Hemer, *Acts*, 126-7. For this reason, many scholars accept the lower range of numbers between Luke and Josephus. It seems hard to believe that such a sizable force (of thirty thousand rebels) was repelled by Felix so easily (Jos. *War* 2.263). This scenario may reflect Josephus's pro-Roman bias. At any rate, such numbers (even those of eyewitnesses) were likely estimates that grew in transmission. Keener, *Acts*, 3:3176.

[103] Keener, *Acts*, 3:3173.

[104] Pervo, *Dating Acts*, 166. His cumulative evidence for dependence based on the three rebels (Judas the Galilean, Theudas, and the Egyptian) in Acts seems rather unconvincing.

[105] Pervo, *Dating Acts*, 198 (and 197 for his list of parallels).

[106] Carr, *History?*, 23.

Table 4.5 The Egyptian Liberator: Acts 21:38; Jos. *War* 2.261-63; Jos. *Ant.* 20.169-71

Acts 21:38	Jos. *War* 2.261-63[a]	Jos. *Ant.* 20.169-71[b]
(38) So are you not the Egyptian who some time ago stirred up a revolt and led into the wilderness the four thousand men of the Assassins?	(261) A still worse blow was dealt at the Jews by the Egyptian false prophet. A charlatan, who had gained for himself the reputation of a prophet, this man appeared in the country, collected a following of about thirty thousand dupes, (262) and led them by a circuitous route from the desert to the mount called the mount of Olives. From there he proposed to force an entrance into Jerusalem and, after overpowering the Roman garrison, to set himself up as tyrant of the people, employing those (263) who poured in with him as his bodyguard. His attack was anticipated by Felix, who went to meet him with the Roman heavy infantry, the whole population joining him in the defence. The outcome of the ensuing engagement was that the Egyptian escaped with a few of his followers; most of his force were killed or taken prisoners; the remainder dispersed and stealthily escaped to their several homes.	(169) At this time there came to Jerusalem from Egypt a man who declared that he was a prophet and advised the masses of the common people to go out with him to the mountain called the Mount of Olives, (170) which lies opposite the city at a distance of five furlongs. For he asserted that he wished to demonstrate from there that at his command Jerusalem's walls would fall down, through which he promised to provide them an entrance into the city. (171) When Felix heard of this he ordered his soldiers to take up their arms. Setting out from Jerusalem with a large force of cavalry and infantry, he fell upon the Egyptian and his followers, slaying four hundred of them and taking two hundred prisoners.
NA[28] (38) οὐκ ἄρα σὺ εἶ **ὁ Αἰγύπτιος** ὁ πρὸ τούτων τῶν ἡμερῶν ἀναστατώσας καὶ ἐξαγαγὼν **εἰς τὴν ἔρημον** τοὺς τετρακισχιλίους ἄνδρας τῶν σικαρίων;[c]	**Greek Text** (261 [v. 5]) Μείζονι δὲ τούτου πληγῇ Ἰουδαίους ἐκάκωσεν **ὁ Αἰγύπτιος** ψευδοπροφήτης. παραγενόμενος γὰρ εἰς τὴν χώραν ἄνθρωπος γόης καὶ προφήτου πίστιν ἐπιθεὶς ἑαυτῷ περὶ τρισμυρίους (262) μὲν ἀθροίζει τῶν ἠπατημένων, περιαγαγὼν δὲ αὐτοὺς **ἐκ τῆς ἐρημίας** εἰς τὸ ἐλαιῶν καλούμενον ὄρος ἐκεῖθεν οἷός τε ἦν εἰς Ἱεροσόλυμα παρελθεῖν βιάζεσθαι καὶ κρατήσας τῆς τε Ῥωμαϊκῆς φρουρᾶς καὶ τοῦ δήμου τυραννεῖν χρώμενος (263) τοῖς συνεισπεσοῦσιν δορυφόροις. φθάνει δ᾿ αὐτοῦ τὴν ὁρμὴν Φῆλιξ ὑπαντήσας μετὰ τῶν Ῥωμαϊκῶν ὁπλιτῶν, καὶ πᾶς ὁ δῆμος συνεφήψατο τῆς ἀμύνης, ὥστε συμβολῆς γενομένης τὸν μὲν Αἰγύπτιον φυγεῖν μετ᾿ ὀλίγων, διαφθαρῆναι δὲ καὶ ζωγρηθῆναι πλείστους τῶν σὺν αὐτῷ, τὸ δὲ λοιπὸν πλῆθος σκεδασθὲν ἐπὶ τὴν ἑαυτῶν ἕκαστον διαλαθεῖν.	(169) ἀφικνεῖται δέ **τις ἐξ Αἰγύπτου** κατὰ τοῦτον τὸν καιρὸν εἰς Ἱεροσόλυμα προφήτης εἶναι λέγων καὶ συμβουλεύων τῷ δημοτικῷ πλήθει σὺν αὐτῷ πρὸς ὄρος τὸ προσαγορευόμενον ἐλαιῶν, ὃ τῆς πόλεως (170) ἄντικρυς κείμενον ἀπέχει στάδια πέντε· θέλειν γὰρ ἔφασκεν αὐτοῖς ἐκεῖθεν ἐπιδεῖξαι, ὡς κελεύσαντος αὐτοῦ πίπτοι τὰ τῶν Ἱεροσολυμιτῶν τείχη, δι᾿ ὧν καὶ τὴν εἴσοδον αὐτοῖς παρέξειν ἐπηγγέλλετο. (171) Φῆλιξ δ᾿ ὡς ἐπύθετο ταῦτα, κελεύει τοὺς στρατιώτας ἀναλαβεῖν τὰ ὅπλα καὶ μετὰ πολλῶν ἱππέων τε καὶ πεζῶν ὁρμήσας ἀπὸ τῶν Ἱεροσολύμων προσβάλλει τοῖς περὶ τὸν Αἰγύπτιον, καὶ τετρακοσίους μὲν αὐτῶν ἀνεῖλε, διακοσίους δὲ ζῶντας ἔλαβεν.

[a] See Thackeray et al., *Josephus*, 2:424–5. The corresponding notations in the English for lines 262 and 263 are mine.
[b] See Thackeray et al., *Josephus*, 9:481. The corresponding notations in the English for lines 169, 170, and 171 are mine.
[c] The lexemes in bold text are Pervo's. Notice the difference in prepositions (εἰς vs. ἐκ).

Conclusion: Paul's Letters, the Works of Josephus, and the Sources of Acts

Much ink has been spilled upon these two source issues, and rightly so since they play such a crucial role for the date of Acts. Where some scholars believe that the parallels between Luke and Paul's letters are so impressive that they border on near certainty, my analysis of the texts—along with previous studies—has hopefully demonstrated that Luke did not use Paul's letters. Even if he did this does not preclude an early date of Acts.

The long-standing matter of Luke and Josephus is perhaps a far more critical issue since an early date would be difficult if not impossible to maintain *if* it can be shown that Luke has made use of the works of Josephus. However, since my analysis has shown that Luke did not rely on the works of Josephus for Acts, any later dates based on this hypothesis should be discounted accordingly. Taken together, these points increase our ability to accurately place Acts into an early chronological framework (*c.* 62–63 CE).

5

The Un-Enigmatic End of Acts

Introduction

The end of Acts has been the subject of an enormous debate spanning the last twenty centuries. Fitzmyer claims that "no one knows why the Lucan story ends where it does, despite many attempts to explain it."[1] Barrett explains that the "questions raised by Acts 28 are no new discovery; every student of Acts has encountered them and made some contribution—in some cases a negative one—to their solution. But they constantly call for re-examination."[2] Alexander, commenting in "literary-critical terms," calls the ending of Acts "a notorious puzzle."[3] Likewise Marguerat says, "the way the book of Acts ends is surprising" while its *"enigmatic conclusion* has resisted centuries of enquiry."[4] Although the conclusion of Acts has been debated vociferously since modern times and has certainly become something of an "old chestnut," does it warrant the title *enigmatic*?[5]

Eastman considers the fates of Peter and Paul to be one of the "great mysteries of early Christian history."[6] His summary of the issue is well made and strikes at the heart of the matter:

---

[1] Fitzmyer, *Acts*, 52. Paul A. Holloway, "Inconvenient Truths: Ancient Jewish and Christian History Writing and the Ending of Luke-Acts," in *Die Apostelgeschichte im Kontext antiker und frühchristlicher Historiographie*," (eds. Jörg Frey et al.; BZNW 162; Berlin: de Gruyter, 2009), 419, states that "none of these early proposals have stood the test of time."

[2] Charles K. Barrett, "The End of Acts," in *Geschichte—Tradition—Reflexion: Festschrift Für Martin Hengel* (eds. Hubert Cancik and P. Schäfer; Frühes Christentum; 3 vols; Tübingen: Mohr Siebeck, 1996), 545–55 (555).

[3] Alexander, *Ancient*, 207.

[4] Marguerat, *Historian*, 205 (my emphasis). He (205) asks, like many of us: "Why does Luke remain silent about the appeal to Caesar, which represents the avowed motive for Paul's transfer to Rome (28:19)?" Earlier Cadbury, *Acts in History*, 3, claimed that the importance of Acts for the historian is seen in the "extraordinary darkness" when "rather abruptly this guide leaves us with Paul a prisoner in Rome."

[5] See Lindsey P. Pherigo's, "Paul's Life after the Close of Acts," *JBL* 70 (1951): 277, "*apologia* for dragging this old chestnut out of the fire" (his emphasis).

[6] David L. Eastman, "Jealousy, Internal Strife, and the Deaths of Peter and Paul: A Reassessment of *1 Clement*," *ZAC* 18 (2013): 34–53, here p. 34.

Although Luke has much to say in Acts about the lives and missions of these two apostles [Peter and Paul], he remains strangely silent when it comes to describing the locations and circumstances of their deaths. In the case of Paul the situation is particularly vexing, for Luke takes the reader all the way to Rome with Paul but then ends with the positive but abrupt outcome that Paul was able to preach unhindered.[7]

Given the lack of consensus and often conflicting interpretations on the end of Acts, the goal of this chapter is to ask new questions of the data[8] and present a solution that endorses the ancient interpretations[9] against the variety of modern literary explanations upon "the final stage of the text."[10] A better way forward is one that interprets the textual, literary, and historical environment of Acts instead of relying upon the unsubstantiated claims that developed in the nineteenth century that continue to be parroted and repackaged.

Regardless of one's explanation for the end of Acts, this matter weighs greatly on its date and vice versa. For better or worse, a scholar's interpretation of the end of Acts is usually married to their position on the date of Acts.[11] For example, it is difficult (if not impossible) to maintain a post-70 CE date of Acts if it can be reasonably demonstrated that the end of Acts exhibits no clear evidence of fabrication or that earlier parts in the narrative show no clear sign of foreshadowing.[12] The reverse is also true.

Those who subscribe to the middle ground (post-70 CE to ±80) are in a similar position as the late dating advocates, and they can no longer sit on the fence.[13] For example, Porter maintains that a compromise date of 85 CE "raises as many questions

---

[7] Eastman, "Jealousy," 34. Blaiklock, *Acts*, 195, claims that it is "inconceivable" that Luke would describe the scene with Agrippa on the one hand and fail to narrate the "scene in Caesar's court" on the other "if indeed such a trial took place." Recently, Armand Puig i Tàrrech, "Paul's Missionary Activity during His Roman Trial: The Case of Paul's Journey to Hispania," in *The Last Years of Paul: Essays from the Tarragona Conference, June 2013* (eds. Armand Puig i Tàrrech et al.; WUNT 352; Tübingen: Mohr Siebeck, 2015), 471, affirms the "numerous historical questions" with regard to the "last years of Paul's life."

[8] One of the key principles of post-structural historiography is to continually ask questions of the data, theory, and method of approach behind a given interpretation. See Beard, "Dream," 87; Reinfandt, "Reading Texts," 41–58; Passmore, "Poststructuralism," 138; Ziemann and Dobson, "Introduction," 6–16; and Porter, "Witness," 1:431–2.

[9] Troftgruben, *Conclusion Unhindered*, 8–11.

[10] Ibid., 35 (n. 103). Unfortunately, assumptions about the "text" of Acts is symptomatic of the failure to address matters of textual criticism.

[11] Ibid., 10, is a recent example of how an interpretation on the end of Acts directly relates to an assumed "majority" position that dates Acts to 80–90 CE. The logic flows from an *a priori* view that Luke is well aware of Paul's death since the date of Acts is many years (or decades) later—hence the need for a complicated literary explanation (see "Linkage" below). However, my sincere thanks are due to Troftgruben for sending me a copy of his book many years ago when I began my research on the end of Acts. Although I disagree with him on some key points, his book continues to be indispensable.

[12] Cf. Pervo, *Acts*, 688; Gerd Lüdemann, *The Acts of the Apostles: What Really Happened in the Earliest Days of the Church* (Amherst, NY: Prometheus, 2005), 347–9.

[13] The most recent and in-depth literary explanations leave many significant historical questions unanswered. See Troftgruben, *Conclusion Unhindered*, 35; Puskas, *Conclusion*, 32; Marguerat, *Historian*, 229–30 and Daniel Marguerat, "On Why Luke Remains Silent about Paul's End," in Puig i Tàrrech et al., *The Last Years of Paul*, 305–32.

as it answers, because it leaves unexplained why the book ends where it does with Paul in prison, which would tend to implicate either a third volume . . . or that the author was writing up to the extent of his knowledge."[14] Subsequently, he argues that Acts is "written right after Luke's gospel, reflecting the knowledge of the author up to the moment of writing, that is, with Paul still in prison (and hence no later than AD 65)."[15] This explanation fits well with the ancient accounts and effectively nullifies the so-called *enigma* regarding the end of Acts that a post-70 CE date only creates and perpetuates.

The solution is to place the end of Acts within its *historical context*.[16] In order to accomplish this, this chapter examines the various ancient, modern, and contemporary interpretations regarding the end of Acts with the purpose of understanding the development of the core issues up to the present day. Subsequently, Chapter 6 further demonstrates how recent developments concerning Paul's engagement with the Jews in Acts 28:17-28 further substantiates an early date of Acts. Altogether it is proposed that the simple solution observed by the ancient writers—that Luke wrote only what he was aware of—is far more likely than the elaborate literary explanations that began in the modern period. If the ancient view is correct, then the end of Acts is far less complicated and "enigmatic" than the popular alternatives.

Acts 28 and the History of Interpretation

What happened to Paul at (and after) the end of Acts is at the heart of the interpretative debate. In the middle of the last century, Pherigo expressed concern over the "variety of conclusions," especially those "which end Paul's life with the Roman imprisonment of Acts."[17] My concern is that the majority of scholars today are going through all kinds of complex interpretive hurdles in order to bypass the consistently simple and ancient interpretation that Luke wrote only what he was aware of at the time of writing.[18]

In the last verse of Acts (28:31) we are left with Paul (Luke's associate and protagonist) in Rome under house arrest for two whole years, preaching "with all boldness and without hindrance" (μετὰ πάσης παρρησίας ἀκωλύτως).[19] This verse raises many unanswered questions: What happened after those two years? What happened to his trial and defence that Luke so carefully narrated throughout the last several chapters

---

[14] Porter, "Dating," 553-74, esp. p. 568.
[15] Ibid., 568.
[16] Recall my note 14 from Chapter 2. Whether investigating Paul, Jesus, or Julius Caesar, historical figures require the "construction of a coherent picture or narrative from the literary and archaeological remains from the past." See Craig A. Evans, "The Christ of Faith Is the Jesus of History," in *Debating Christian Theism* (eds. James P. Moreland et al.; Oxford: Oxford University Press, 2013), 458, and also Jonathan L. Reed, *Archaeology and the Galilean Jesus: A Re-examination of the Evidence* (Harrisburg, PA: Trinity Press International, 2002), xi, 1, 212.
[17] Pherigo, "Close of Acts," 277.
[18] See Troftgruben's, *Conclusion Unhindered*, 7-36, survey (esp. 8-11) and also the collection of essays in Puig i Tàrrech et al., *The Last Years of Paul*.
[19] See David L. Mealand, "The Close of Acts and its Hellenistic Greek Vocabulary," *NTS* 36 (1990): 583-97.

of Acts?[20] If the trial was successful, did Paul resume a ministry of teaching in the east or did he venture to Spain as he indicated in his own letter to the Romans (15:24, 28)?[21] Or perhaps his trial was a failure and his readers would have (somehow) already understood his demise under Nero?[22]

Since the end of Acts leaves the reader on a victorious note, how do we explain the silence of his trial, the outcome, his martyrdom, the terrible fate of the citizens of Rome in the Great Fire of 64 CE along with the subsequent and systematic destruction of Christians under Nero?[23] Many of the ancient, modern, and contemporary interpretations tackle the above questions in various ways, but all of them require an explanation of Luke's *perceived* silence on these matters. The various literary explanations that Luke is *not* silent about Paul's fate (i.e., foreshadowing to the elders at Ephesus), or that his silence is motivated by some grand literary purpose is a fairly recent phenomenon in the history of interpretation.[24]

Ancient Interpretation of the Enigma

The way that the ancients first understood the end of Acts and the fate of Paul in the first few centuries CE is rather telling. Not only did the early church struggle to find clarity as to what actually happened, but also none of the explanations assume that Luke was withholding knowledge of Paul's trial, the outcome, or the circumstances in Rome after 64 CE. Next to the prison and pastoral epistles, and the post-canonical literature, the oldest texts worth considering are the variants found at the end (see Chapter 7). At the very least, the early Western text is considered to be the earliest commentary on the primitive text available.[25]

An examination of the manuscript record of Acts 28:16-31 offers no clues or commentary on the fate of Paul, the church in Rome, or the destruction of Rome and Jerusalem.[26] If anything could be said on "what happened next" surely the first scribes and redactors would have commented, but there is only silence across the entire manuscript record. Hence, not only can we say that "Luke knew no more" at the end of Acts, but also that the earliest scribes and correctors did not either.[27]

Beyond the variants, the Prison Epistles offer some clues to Paul's life at the end of Acts. Since it is relatively certain that Paul was a prisoner in Rome (*c.* 60–62), we can try to reconstruct some of the historical context for the end of Acts (28:16, 30) from his "prison" letters.[28] We must do so with caution and be able to discern what we know

---

[20] I.e., Acts 21:27–26:32.
[21] See my note 48 below on the question of a Spanish mission.
[22] The idea that Luke's readers already understood Paul's death is nothing new. See Vernon J. Bartlet, "Two New Testament Problems. I. St. Paul's Fate at Rome," *Exp* 5 (1913): 464-7.
[23] See Chapter 8.
[24] See Troftgruben, *Conclusion Unhindered*, 7–36.
[25] Head, "Problem," 444; Armstrong, "Variants," 95, 98.
[26] Armstrong, "Variants," 106–10.
[27] Cf. Rackham, "Plea," 80; Armstrong, "Variants," 107–8.
[28] On the tradition of Paul's Roman imprisonment see *1 Clem.* 5:6-7; Henry Chadwick, "St. Peter and St. Paul in Rome: The Problem of the Memoria Apostolorum ad Catacumbas," *JTS* 8 (1957): 31–52, and Keener, *Acts*, 4:3722. Where Philemon is generally regarded as authentically Pauline, Colossians

versus what is speculation.[29] For example, on the one hand, caution is necessary because not all of the prison epistles speak to Rome as the location.[30] On the other hand, a Roman imprisonment for Philippians has a large number of supporters and makes the best sense of the data.[31] Therefore this letter offers an important and contemporaneous window into Paul's experience in Rome at the end of Acts.[32]

Paul states "that it has become known throughout the entire palace guard (or the whole praetorium [ἐν ὅλῳ τῷ πραιτωρίῳ]), and by everyone else, that my imprisonment is for Christ" (Phil. 1:13). Reicke explains that in Philippians the *praetorium* as a "group of persons can only mean the imperial bodyguard."[33] Tiberius had placed this "elite guard near the Porta Nomentana in Rome."[34] Additionally, Paul closes this letter (Phil.

and Ephesians are debated; but in any case, they clearly speak about Paul's imprisonment. See Bo Reicke, "Caesarea, Rome, and the Captivity Epistles," in *Apostolic History and the Gospel. Biblical and Historical Essays Presented to F. F. Bruce* (eds. W. Ward Gasque and Ralph P. Martin; Exeter: The Paternoster Press, 1970), 277. One of Paul's travelling companions, a certain Macedonian named Aristarchus (Acts 20:4; 21:29; 27:2) was likely the same person mentioned in the prison epistles (cf. Col. 4:10-18 and Phlm. 23-24). See Keener, *Acts*, 4:3723; Bock, *Acts*, 731–2; J. Bradley Chance, *Acts* (SHBC; Macon, GA: Smith & Helwys, 2007), 495, and also Eusebius, *Eccl. Hist.* 2.22:1. Keener, *Acts*, 4:3723, claims that the Pauline corpus "supplies personal details missing in Acts—namely, that Mark (Col. 4:10; Phlm. 24), Epaphras (Phlm. 23, as a fellow prisoner; Col. 4:12), and Demas (Col. 4:14; Phlm. 24) were with him and later Demas left him (2 Tim. 4:10), that Luke remained (4:11), and that Mark needed to join him (4:11)."

[29] I am more optimistic than Daniel Gerber, "Paul's Literary Activity during His Roman Trial: A Response to Udo Schnelle," in Puig i Tàrrech et al., *The Last Years of Paul*, 453, but his caution with regard to the evidence of Paul's literary activity in Rome is prudent.

[30] Reicke, "Caesarea," 278, where he argues that only Caesarea matches the background of Philemon, Colossians, and Ephesians while Rome fits the background of Philippians (282–6).

[31] See Keener, *Acts*, 4:3723; Markus Barth, *Ephesians* (2 vols; AB 34A; Garden City, NY: Doubleday, 1974), 1:3; Charles H. Dodd, *New Testament Studies* (Manchester: Manchester University Press, 1967), 99; Arthur D. Nock, *St. Paul* (repr., New York: Harper & Row, 1963), 22; Reicke, "Caesarea," 277–86; and Gordon D. Fee, *Paul's Letter to the Philippians* (NICNT; Grand Rapids: Eerdmans, 1995), 34–7. Reicke insists that "Only Rome ... [is] entirely suitable as the location for the writing of Philippians" (283). Udo Schnelle, "Paul's Literary Activity during his Roman Trial," in Puig i Tàrrech et al., *The Last Years of Paul*, 441, says that "all in all, it is still most likely that Philippians was written in Rome about 60 CE." Gerber, "Response," 462, finds Schnelle's conclusion "too specific" for his taste. Meanwhile, Stanley E. Porter, *The Apostle Paul: His Life, Thought, and Letters* (Grand Rapids: Eerdmans, 2016), 67, claims that (for Paul) the Roman imprisonment (rather than Ephesus, Caesarea, Corinth) "still has the most to commend itself, even if one cannot be dogmatic about this conclusion." See his discussion on the various imprisonment scenarios (60–8).

[32] See "Principles for Sources and Textual Criticism" in Chapter 2. Kosso, *Knowing the Past*, 51, explains that one of the key criteria for assessing the "credibility of a textual report" is the "ancient author's access to the event." Paul's letter to the Philippians provides a valuable and credible firsthand account of his incarceration experience.

[33] Reicke, "Caesarea," 283, claims this cannot refer to the "residence of the governor" as in the gospels rather Paul is referring to a "body of people and other individuals." This Latin loan word is the common expression to use when referring to the guard. See Pliny, *Hist.* 25.6.17; Suetonius, *Net.* 9:2; Tacitus, *Hist.* 1.20. Reicke (283) remarks how it is found in several Greek inscriptions: Léon Heuzey and Honoré Daumet, *Mission Archéologique de Macédoine: Texte/Planches* (Paris: Firmin-Didot, 1876), nr.130–31 (pp. 325–6); George Kaibel, ed., *Inscriptiones Graecae. XIV. Inscriptiones Siciliae et Italiae, additis Galliae, Hispaniae, Britanniae, Germaniae Inscriptionibus* (Berlin: Reimer, 1890), nr. 911 (p. 238), (editor's name is missing here and elsewhere); Wilhelm Dittenberger, *Orientis Graeci Inscriptiones Selectae. Supplementum Sylloges Inscriptionum Graecarum* (2 vols; Leipzig: S. Hirzel, 1903–05), nr. 707 (pp. 2:444–5). Cf. also Keener, *Acts*, 4:3722–6.

[34] Reicke, "Caesarea," 283. Evidently, in the first few centuries CE these "praetorian cohorts" would remain in Rome while "at times sections of the guard accompanied the emperor into the field of action" (283). He (283) explains how proponents of the Ephesus theory are misreading inscriptions

4:22) with a specific reference to "Caesar's house" (τῆς Καίσαρος οἰκίας), which could not have been confused with any other city than Rome.[35] Although this data does not provide the solid evidence required to answer the question of "what happened next" after Acts 28:31, the picture of Paul's custody written to the Philippians collaborates well with Luke's picture of Paul's custody in Rome at the end of Acts.

Paul's letter to Philemon is another possible witness to Paul's Roman custody at the end of Acts.[36] Paul is writing to Philemon requesting that he welcome back his runaway slave Onesimus (Phlm. 1, 10-13).[37] Paul indicates that he was a prisoner three times (Phlm. 1, 9, and 13) and lists several of his co-workers: Epaphras, Markus, Aristarchus, Demas, and Luke (Phlm. 23-24).[38] The letter also reflects a measure of *Custodia Liberia* that Paul had with Onesimus that we see in Acts (cf. Phlm. 13 and Acts 28:23).[39] Unfortunately, there is not much beyond this that we can add to our picture of Paul in Acts 28.

A further witness to Paul's incarceration, trial, and fate comes from 2 Timothy.[40] Although the purpose here is not to evaluate the authorship issues concerning this letter, it

that only mention the retired praetorians living there who were acting as "gendarme" (*stationarius*) or policemen (283). Reicke describes the "active praetorians" as having the "responsibility of protecting the emperor and the capital city; the deployment of the group throughout the provinces during Paul's time would have been impossible militarily" (283). Furthermore, since Asia was a "senatorial province . . . no troops were stationed there" (283).

[35] The servants of the emperor lived "primarily in Rome." Reicke, "Caesarea," 285. In the first century CE, Caesar's house (or *palace*) was located on the Palatine hill and could not be confused with any other location. See Bo Reicke, *The New Testament Era: The World of the Bible from 500 B.C. to 100 A.D.* (Philadelphia: Fortress, 1968), 227, and Keener, *Acts*, 3725–6.

[36] Eckhard J. Schnabel, "The Roman Trial before Pontius Pilatus," in *The Trial and Crucifixion of Jesus: Texts and Commentary* (eds. David W. Chapman and Eckhard J. Schnabel; WUNT 344; Tübingen: Mohr Siebeck, 2015), 448–50 (451), thinks that Philemon was written from Rome along with Philippians although the place of composition is debated between Rome and Ephesus (see his note 54 on p. 448). In line with Schnelle (and many scholars), Rainer Riesner, "Paul's Trial and End according to Second Timothy, 1 Clement, the Canon Muratori, and the Apocryphal Acts," in Puig i Tàrrech et al., *The Last Years of Paul*, 408, thinks that "between 57 and 63/64" CE Paul wrote Philippians and Philemon during his "Roman captivity described by Acts 28." Although Riesner acknowledges the possibility that Philippians and Philemon were written from Ephesus this would imply several years "without any Pauline letter, except if one sets, very improbably, some of the captivity epistles in Caesarea" (408). With regard to an Ephesian origin of Philippians and Philemon see Raymond E. Brown, *An Introduction to the New Testament* (New York: Doubleday, 1997), 493–6; Heike Omerzu, *Der Prozess des Paulus: Eine exegetische und rechtshistorische Untersuchung der Apostelgeschichte* (BZNW 115; Berlin: de Gruyter, 2002), 320–31; Jerome Murphy-O'Connor, *Paul: A Critical Life* (Oxford: Oxford University Press, 1996), 175–84; and Wilfried Eckey, *Die Briefe des Paulus an die Philipper und an Philemon: Ein Kommentar* (Neukirchen-Vluyn: Neukirchener, 2006), 20–31.

[37] Schnelle, "Roman Trial," 449, contends that Onesimus, as a runaway slave, would have the status of *fugitivus*. Some have argued that he was not a runaway slave and "sought out Paul as his advocate in a domestic conflict" (449); Peter Lampe, *Der Brief an Philemon* (Göttingen: Vandenhoeck & Ruprecht, 1998), 206. It seems strange that Onesimus would make the journey to Rome and stay with Paul for so long only to serve as an advocate (Schnelle, 450). See F. F. Church, "Rhetorical Structure and Design in Paul's Letter to Philemon," *HTR* 71 (1978): 17–33, on the purpose and rhetorical elements in the letter (i.e., Phlm. 17, 21).

[38] Recall my note 28 above on the persons mentioned in relation to Acts.

[39] Chance, *Acts*, 449.

[40] In particular, 2 Tim. 1:16-17; 2:9-10; 4:6-8, 16. For example, in 2 Tim. 4:16 Paul writes "In my first defence" (Ἐν τῇ πρώτῃ μου ἀπολογίᾳ). Where many see πρώτη ἀπολογία as the "*prima actio* of a present trial" some combine it with an "earlier trial that had ended with some kind of a release." See Riesner, "Paul's Trial," 399; Eusebius, *Hist. Eccl.* 2.22:4–5. Where the legal term ἀπολογία

may be authentically Pauline due to the number of personal names and collaborative details relating to Paul's life.⁴¹ Here Paul (or his follower) gives many personal details surrounding his imprisonment such as his mention of Onesiphorus (2 Tim. 1:16) who "was not ashamed of [his] chain but being in Rome,"⁴² his personal suffering (2 Tim. 2:9-10), his painful note of resignation (2 Tim. 4:6-8), and his comment that "Luke alone is with me" (2 Tim. 4:11).⁴³ The relationship between Second Timothy and what happened to Paul at the end of Acts is a matter of ongoing debate and to some degree a matter of speculation.⁴⁴

Perhaps the oldest post-canonical witness to Paul's life post-Acts comes from the writings of Clement, the Bishop of Rome who (some suggest) wrote his letter to the Corinthians close to 95 CE, while others have made convincing arguments for a much earlier date to the "time of Vespasian" (69–79 CE).⁴⁵ If an early date can be

(defence) occurs eight times as a noun in the NT (and twice in Acts) the verb ἀπολογέομαι occurs six times in Acts (out of the ten times in the NT). Jens Herzer, "Fiktion oder Täuschung? Zur Diskussion über die Pseudepigraphie der Pastoralbriefe," in *Pseudepigraphie und Verfasserfiktion in frühchristlichen Briefen* (eds. J. Frey et al.; WUNT 246; Tübingen: Mohr Siebeck, 2009), 489–536, claims that Second Timothy was written during Paul's first incarceration in Rome. See also Jens Herzer, "Die Pastoralbriefe," in *Paulus Handbuch* (ed. F. W. Horn; Tübingen: Mohr Siebeck, 2013), 538–42, and Riesner, "Paul's Trial," 396. Meanwhile, Christos Karakolis, "Paul's Mission to Hispania: Some Critical Observations," in Puig i Tàrrech et al., *The Last Years of Paul*, 515, thinks that 2 Tim. 4:16-18 is a reference to the "first session" of Paul's trial in Rome. Herzer and Karakolis may be right but it seems more likely that Second Timothy represents a later, darker state of affairs than pictured in Acts 28:16-31. Where Second Timothy does speak "more clearly" (or alludes to) Paul's impending martyrdom I disagree with Riesner, "Paul's Trial," 398, that Luke in Acts "alluded to the martydom [sic] of Paul" (i.e., Acts 20:23-25, 37). See "Foreshadowing and Silence" and my note 118 below.

⁴¹ This letter is still a witness, even if it is not authentically Pauline (editorial insight by Westfall). Riesner, "Paul's Trial," 396, explains how the "contacts in terminology and content between the Pastoral Epistles and Luke-Acts are that striking," so much so that he thinks Luke's role in its composition is likely. See Michaela Engelmann, *Unzertrennliche Drillinge? Motivsemantische Untersuchungen zum literarischen Verhältnis der Pastoralbriefe* (Berlin: de Gruyter, 2012), 44–8; August Strobel, "Schreiben des Lukas? Zum sprachlichen Problem der Pastoralbriefe," *NTS* 15 (1968–69): 191–210; Stanislas D. Lestapis, *L'énigme des pastorales de Saint Paul* (Paris: J. Gabalda, 1976), 129–48; Rainer Riesner, "Once More: Luke-Acts and the Pastoral Epistles," in *History and Exegesis: New Testament Essays in Honor of Dr. E. Earle Ellis* (ed. S. W. Son; London: T&T Clark, 2006), 239–58; Ben Witherington III, *Letters and Homilies for Hellenized Christians: A Socio-Rhetorical Commentary on Titus, 1–2 Timothy and 1–3 John* (Downers Grove, IL: InterVarsity Press, 2006), 54–62. If the letter was not written by Paul but Luke or someone in his circle, it still provides a valuable window into Paul's last days after Acts.

⁴² Here ἅλυσις is singular in 2 Tim. 1:16.

⁴³ This opens the possibility that Paul may have dictated this letter to Luke but it is strange that there is no clear inclination that he did (i.e., Tertius/Rom 16:22). See also Phlm. 24, Col. 4:14, and the later reflection of Irenaeus the Bishop of Lyons (c. 125–202) concerning Luke's relationship with Paul in: *Against Heresies*, 3.1:7; 3.14:1.

⁴⁴ It seems reasonable to interpret Paul as foreseeing his "certain martyrdom 'in Rome' (2 Tim. 4:6-8) during a second and heavier imprisonment 'in chains' (2 Tim. 1:16-17)." Riesner, "Paul's Trial," 400. That 2 Tim. 4:7 reflects Acts 20:24 is plausible; that Luke wrote both seems speculative. Although Longenecker, *Acts*, 572, considers Paul's "tone of resignation" in 2 Tim. 4:6-18 as a clue to the outcome of his second trial we are "forced to look elsewhere for information about Paul's imprisonment and its aftermath."

⁴⁵ Tajra, *Martyrdom*, 167. Pervo, "Suburbs," 36, aims for *c.* 100 CE (see also idem, *Dating Acts*, 301–5). Riesner, "Paul's Trial," 401, makes a convincing argument for the composition of *1 Clement* in the "time of Vespasian" 69–79 CE. For an overview on the authorship, date, literary, rhetorical aspects, and text see Joseph B. Lightfoot and John R. Harmer, *The Apostolic Fathers: Greek Texts and English Translations* (3rd rev. edn by Michael J. Holmes; Grand Rapids: Baker Academic, 2007), 33–43. Based on internal considerations they think the document "probably was penned sometime during

substantiated then this places it much closer to the composition of Acts and worth mining for any information relating to the end of Acts. Clement (*1 Clem.* 5:6) briefly describes the following facts concerning Paul's life: that he was (1) incarcerated seven times, (2) exiled, (3) stoned, (4) and "had preached in the east and in the west" (κῆρυξ γενόμενος ἔν τε τῇ ἀνατολῇ καὶ ἐν τῇ δύσει).[46]

Subsequently, the interpretation of the first part of the next verse (*1 Clem.* 5:7) is a matter of debate where it says Paul, "having taught righteousness to the whole world and having reached the farthest limits of the west" (δικαιοσύνην διδάξας ὅλον τὸν κόσμον καὶ ἐπὶ τὸ τέρμα τῆς δύσεως ἐλθών·).[47] Some (but many do not) see this passage as evidence that Paul reached Spain after his Roman imprisonment in Acts, and whether "west" means Rome, Spain, or simply west goes beyond the "limits" of what can be known since there is no decisive proof either way.[48]

---

the last two decades of the first century" (35). The fact that chapters 5 and 6 probably refer to Nero's persecution and the death of Peter and Paul would certainly make the earliest date to be 64–68 CE. They argue that this point, along with a note on the leaders in 1 *Clem.* 63:3 living from youth to old age "require a date subsequent to the late 60s or early 70s" (35). That "some of the leaders appointed by the apostles are still living" (*1 Clem.* 44:3-5) rules out "any date beyond the turn of the century" (35). The traditional date of 95–97 CE largely based on the "persecution" in 1:1 and 7:1 is attributed to either Domitian (81–96 CE) or Nerva's (96–98 CE) reign rather uncritically (36). The texts simply do not indicate anything that could be concretely connected with either Emperor's reign. A. E. Wilhelm-Hooijberg, "A Different View of Clemens Romanus," *HeyJ* 16 (1975): 266–88, dates it to 69 CE and Thomas J. Herron, "The Most Probable Date of the First Epistle of Clement to the Corinthians," in StPatr 21 (ed. E. A. Livingstone; Leuven: Peeters, 1989), 106–21, suggests 70 CE. Meanwhile, Laurence L. Welborn, "On the Date of First Clement," *BR* 29 (1984): 35–54, considers a late date of 140 CE. Somewhere in the late 60s CE into Vespasian's reign seems reasonable (as per Riesner's suggestion) although some like Jens Herzer, "The Mission and the End of Paul Between Strategy and Reality: A Response to Rainer Riesner," in Puig i Tàrrech et al., *The Last Years of Paul*, 424, think the end of the first century is still possible.

[46] Lightfoot and Harmer, *Apostolic Fathers*, 52–3 (*1 Clem.* 5:6).
[47] Lightfoot and Harmer, *Apostolic Fathers*, 52–3 (*1 Clem.* 5:7).
[48] Ben Witherington III, *New Testament History: A Narrative Account* (Grand Rapids: Baker Academic, 2001), 323–4; Eckhard J. Schnabel, *Early Christian Mission* (Downers Grove, IL: InterVarsity, 2004), 1271–83; idem, *Paul the Missionary: Realities, Strategies and Methods* (Downers Grove, IL: InterVarsity Press, 2008), 115–21; and esp. Tajra, *Martyrdom*, 31, 102–17 and 122, consider this a possibility. Rainer Riesner, "The Pastoral Epistles and Paul in Spain (2 Timothy 4:16–18)," in *Rastreando los orígenes: Lengua y exégesis en el Nuevo Testamento. En memoria del Profesor Mons. Mariano Herranz Marco* (ed. J. M. García Perez; SSNT 17; Madrid: CEU Ediziones, 2011), 316–35, and idem, "Paul's Trial," 400–3, thinks that Paul made it to Spain. Riesner, "Paul's Trial," 409, refers to Harnack who claims that the trip from Rome to Tarraco was not a big deal—as it only took between four and eight days. Cf. Adolf Harnack, *Die Mission und Ausbreitung des Christentums in den ersten drei Jahrhunderten* (4th edn; Leipzig: Hinrichs, 1924), 920 (his note 2). For the speculative witness of the Spanish trip in *Actus Vercellenses* see Riesner, "Paul in Spain," 405. While Tàrrech, "Hispania," 469–506, claims that Paul's visit to Roman Tarraco is "historically plausible" (470) he admits that there is "limited evidence" (505). Just over a century ago Ernst Dubowy, *Klemens von Rom über die Reise Pauli nach Spanien: Historisch-kritische Untersuchung zu Klemens von Rom: 1 Kor. 5, 7* (Freiburg: Herder, 1914), dedicated an entire book to this issue of Paul in Spain and *1 Clem.* 5:5-7. Wolfgang Grünstäudl, "Hidden in Praise: Some Notes on 1 Clement 5.7," in Puig i Tàrrech et al., *The Last Years of Paul*, 376–9, revisits Dubowy's thesis and finds "several weaknesses and inconsistencies" (379) while concluding that Clement "presupposes" Paul's perseverance rather than providing "historical information" (389). Meanwhile, Pherigo, "Close of Acts," 284, and later Herzer, "End of Paul," 423–5, doubt the Spanish mission hypothesis.

Where others entertain Paul's release from prison and a "return of the apostle to his churches in the east" others "combine a short stay in Spain with a last visit to the east."[49] Based upon Acts 20:25 Riesner "argues strongly against another voyage to the east" since Paul tells the Ephesian elders that none of them "will ever see my face again."[50] It seems that we cannot be certain what happened to Paul beyond Acts 28:31 except that he either stayed in prison or was released to a further ministry in the east or the west (Spain).[51] The only thing we can be relatively certain about is his death in Rome somewhere between 64 CE and the end of Nero's reign in 68 CE.[52]

Additionally, *1 Clem.* 5:5 accounts for the martyrdom of Paul (after Peter in v. 4) suggesting that it was "Because of jealousy and strife Paul showed the way to the prize for patient endurance" (διὰ ζῆλον καὶ ἔριν Παῦλος ὑπομονῆς βραβεῖον ὑπέδειξεν).[53] It may be coincidental but it seems striking that Clement's consistent theme of "jealousy and strife" in his letter is found in Paul's letters as well (Rom. 13:13; 1 Cor. 3:3; and 2 Cor. 12:20).[54] Paul's letters in general, and especially 1 Corinthians (1 Cor. 1:10-13; 3:3-7) provide sufficient background for Clement to draw from given the strife and division the Corinthian church had faced and was continuing to deal with.[55] Lightfoot and Harmer also recognize the "same kind of factiousness that Paul

---

[49] Riesner, "Paul's Trial," 397 and Troftgruben, *Conclusion Unhindered*, 19. Raymond E. Brown and John P. Meier, *Antioch and Rome: New Testament Cradles of Catholic Christianity* (New York: Paulist, 1983), 98 (n. 202), remark how it is "generally assumed that he [Paul] was freed from imprisonment, left Rome for further missionary travels, and ultimately returned for a second imprisonment that led to his death. That the travels were to Spain (Rom. 15:24; *1 Clem.* 5:7) is more likely than the visit to Asia Minor and Greece that scholars have constructed on the basis of the post-Pauline Pastorals, a visit unknown to the author of Acts" (20:25, 38). On the contrary, Karakolis, "Critical Observations," 519, questions the evidence of a Spanish trip and thinks it is "more probable that Paul never left Rome" and was "sentenced to death" after a long Roman captivity.
[50] Riesner, "Paul's Trial," 397; Eusebius, *Hist. Eccl.* 2.22:2 and Chrysostom, *Hom. Acts.* 10.3. This is possible but Paul may have returned to the east (but perhaps not Ephesus/Miletus; Acts 20:17).
[51] Schnabel, *Early Christian Mission*, 1271-83.
[52] Tajra, *Martyrdom*, 199.
[53] Lightfoot and Harmer, *Apostolic Fathers*, 51 (Greek on p. 50). Troftgruben, *Conclusion Unhindered*, 20, raises the issue that Clement seemed unclear about the details of "Paul in Rome three decades earlier." This is a good point but also equally valid for an early date of Clement. Clement may be ambiguous on Paul's fate to some degree, but a few verses later he recalls the "vast multitude" that were tortured and killed by Nero, *1 Clem.* 6:1. Tacitus, *Ann.* 15.44.4, also refers to "an immense multitude" that were persecuted during this time. James S. Jeffers, *The Greco-Roman World of the New Testament Era: Exploring the Background of Early Christianity* (Downers Grove, IL: InterVarsity Press, 1999), 319, says it was "perhaps several thousand" Roman Christians who "lost their lives in this persecution." Lampe, *Valentinus*, 82, calls the combined witness of Tacitus and Clement a "coincidence that can hardly be explained by imputing rhetorical exaggeration to both authors."
[54] Clement is either reading Paul's letters or more likely he is dealing with jealousy and strife in the church at Corinth in the 60s or 70s CE. Oscar Cullmann, "Les causes de la mort de Pierre et de Paul d'après le témoignage de Clément Romain," *RHPR* 10 (1930): 294-300, expanded the interpretation that Clement's use of jealousy and strife offers more information regarding the date of the apostles Peter and Paul. See idem, *Peter: Disciple, Apostle, Martyr: A Historical and Theological Study* (2nd edn; trans. Floyd V. Filson; London: SCM, 1962), 91-110, and Eastman, "Jealousy," 34-53 (53), who builds on Cullmann's reasoning in his analysis and similarly claims that "internal jealousy could have been at play in the deaths of Peter and Paul."
[55] *1 Clem.* 3:2, 4; 4:7-13; 5:5; 6:1-3; 9:1; 14:1; 43:2; 45:4; 63:2.

had earlier encountered in Corinth" that "apparently flared up once again in that congregation near the end of the first century."[56]

The next ancient witness comes from the *Muratorian fragment* (or canon) which contains a vital late second- or early third-century reference to the gospels, other early Christian writings, and especially Paul's life in relation to Acts.[57] Lines 34–9 of this text provide a window into Paul's fate: "Moreover, the acts of all the apostles were written in one book. For 'most excellent Theophilus' Luke compiled the individual events that took place in his presence, as he plainly shows by omitting the martyrdom of Peter as well as the departure of Paul from the city [of Rome] when he journeyed to Spain."[58]

As introduced in Chapter 1 (note 23), it is important to note that according to line 36, Luke recorded the events that took place "in his presence" (*sub praesentia eius*). The author's reasoning for this rests on Luke's omission of Peter's martyrdom and Paul's trip to Spain. This may simply be a reflection of Paul's expressed intention to visit Spain on his way to Rome (cf. Rom. 15:24, 28) and the author's knowledge of the deaths of the apostles.[59] Either way, this early account betrays no other known explanation as to why Luke omits this data.

Subsequent to the above discussion, another early interpreter of the end of Acts is the church historian Eusebius of Caesarea (*c.* 265–340). Eusebius states (in reference

---

[56] Lightfoot and Harmer, *Apostolic Fathers*, 33–4. Such continued factiousness in Corinth equally supports an early date of 1 Clement in the 70s CE.

[57] See Bruce M. Metzger, *The Canon of the NT: Its Origin, Development, and Significance* (Oxford: Clarendon, 1987), 305, and Charles E. Hill, "The Debate Over the Muratorian Fragment and the Development of the Canon," *WTJ* 57 (1995): (437) 437–52. The fragment has been traditionally dated to the "end of the second century or the beginning of the third" (437). This "canon" list represents and reflects the writings that were "later agreed upon by the whole church" (437). Earlier Geoffrey M. Hahneman, *The Muratorian Fragment and the Development of the Canon* (OTM. Oxford: Clarendon, 1992), 131, wrote against the traditional date claiming it is an "anomaly" in the development of the canon while giving the fragment an eastern fourth-century origin. Robert M. Grant, *Heresy and Criticism: The Search for Authenticity in Early Christian Literature* (Louisville: Westminster/John Knox, 1993), 110, seems to accept this conclusion. Refer also to the earlier essay by Albert C. Sundberg, "Canon Muratori: A Fourth Century List," *HTR* 66 (1973): 1–41. Koester, *Introduction*, 12, also thinks the fourth century is "more likely." Although Hill (452) thinks Hahneman has "beefed up" Sundberg's hypothesis for a later date of the fragment he finds it "unconvincing and that the traditional dating does far better justice to the evidence." See Charles E. Hill, *The Johannine Corpus in the Early Church* (Oxford: Oxford University Press, 2004), 128–34. Joseph Verheyden, "The Canon of Muratori: A Matter of Dispute," in *The Biblical Canons* (eds. J. M. Auwers and H. J. de Jonge; BETL 163; Leuven: Leuven University Press, 2003), (556) 487–556, emphatically concludes that a "fourth-century, eastern origin for the Fragment should be put to rest not for a thousand years, but for eternity." Cited by Riesner, "Paul's Trial," 403. Riesner (403) states that "a majority of scholars favour an early date." He personally dates the canon to the "turn of the 2nd to the 3rd century" (404) or "around 200" (409). Eckhard J. Schnabel, "The Muratorian Fragment: The State of Research," *JETS* 57 (2014): 239–53, similarly dates it to "around AD 200" (239). Therefore, a late second- (to early third-) century date for this fragment seems reasonable.

[58] Metzger, *Canon*, 305–7 (Appendix 4.1, "The Muratorian Canon"). According to Schnabel, "Fragment," 232 (n. 11), Metzger's translation is "based on the amended text" edited by Hans Lietzmann, *Das Muratorische Fragment und die monarchianischen Prologe zu den Evangelien* (Kleine Texte für theologische Vorlesungen und Übungen 1; Bonn: Marcus and Weber, 1902) and is in turn reproduced by Lee M. McDonald, *The Biblical Canon: Its Origin, Transmission, and Authority* (Peabody, MA: Hendrickson, 2007), 369–71. For the Latin, see Schnabel, "Fragment," 234–6 (that is taken from Lietzmann, *Das Muratorisches Fragment*).

[59] According to Herzer, "End of Paul," 426, the Spanish reference can "easily be explained if we suppose that the *canonicus* knew Rom. 15, which for a Roman author is very likely."

to Luke), "in this way he closed the history" (ἐν τούτοις κατέλυσε τὴν ἱστορίαν).⁶⁰ Some commentators emphasize the abruptness (i.e., cut his history short at this point) where the sense is simply to bring something (i.e., the history) to a close.⁶¹ Eusebius then specifically mentions the "two whole years" (διετίαν ὅλην) from Acts 28:30 and also how "he [Paul] preached without hindrance" (ἀκωλύτως κηρῦξαι) while he also indirectly refers to Paul's imprisonment in verse 16.⁶²

Eusebius is basing his view (in some measure) on the text of Acts 28:30-31 and does not seem aware of additional historical information beyond the biblical texts with regard to events surrounding the end of Acts. He further describes how Paul was initially released and then re-incarcerated where he suffered martyrdom: "Thus after he had made his defense it is said that the apostle was sent again upon the ministry of preaching, and that upon coming to the same city a second time he suffered martyrdom. In this imprisonment he wrote his second epistle to Timothy, in which he mentions his first defense and his impending death."⁶³ Eusebius subsequently mentions Paul's second letter to Timothy and quotes it extensively (vv. 2-6). In verse 7 he states: "But these things have been adduced by us to show that Paul's martyrdom did not take place at the time of that Roman sojourn which Luke records."⁶⁴ Last, in verse 8 he accurately comments upon the changes in Nero's earlier and more peaceful reign in connection with Paul's defence.⁶⁵

Furthermore, the lack of ancient commentaries on Acts greatly increases their historical value—in addition to the previous witnesses.⁶⁶ A notable example is found in the writings of John Chrysostom, writing about 400 (347–407) CE. In his commentary he states in his opening verse: "To many persons this Book is so little known, both it and its author, that they are not even aware that there is such a book in existence."⁶⁷ Chrysostom was by no means on the fringe of Acts scholarship at the time as Quasten refers to Chrysostom's homilies on Acts as the "only complete commentary on Acts that has survived from the first ten centuries."⁶⁸

Further in his first homily on Acts Chrysostom asks: "And why then did he [Luke] not relate every thing, seeing he was with Paul to the end?"⁶⁹ His response to that question seems to indicate that Luke—in the tradition of sacred writers—wrote only

---

⁶⁰ Eusebius, *Hist. Eccl.* 2.22:1.
⁶¹ Contra Troftgruben, *Conclusion Unhindered*, 23.
⁶² Eusebius could be reflecting a tradition here, but it is also equally possible that he was simply following the Acts account.
⁶³ Eusebius, *Ecc. His.* 2:22:2 (*NPNF2-*1:124). Herzer, "End of Paul," 427, notes that Eusebius "explicitly combines" Acts 28 and 2 Tim. 4:16-17. Similarly, Troftgruben, *Conclusion Unhindered*, 8, observes how Eusebius's suggestion is "purely to harmonize the account of Acts with the Pastoral Epistles" (e.g., 2 Tim. 4:16-18).
⁶⁴ Eusebius, *Ecc. His.* 2:22:7 (*NPNF2-*1:125).
⁶⁵ The difference between Nero's earlier and later reign is well attested by historians. Jeffers, *Greco-Roman World*, 318.
⁶⁶ Troftgruben, *Conclusion Unhindered*, 22.
⁶⁷ Chrysostom, *Hom. Acts*, 1 (*NPNF1-*11:1). This may have been said for rhetorical effect but Schaff (note 3) says that Chrysostom had "made the same complaint" at Antioch.
⁶⁸ Johannes Quasten, *Patrology* (4 vols; repr., Westminster, MD: Christian Classics, 1950–86), 3:440.
⁶⁹ Chrysostom, *Hom. Acts*, 1 (*NPNF1-*11:2). Since Chrysostom (just a few verses earlier) refers to 2 Tim. 4:10 "Only Luke is with me," he could be reading this verse into the end of Acts.

what was of "immediate importance" and the rest would have been known by oral tradition.[70] In other words, if there were more pressing things of importance surely Luke would have written about them, but he did not. Closer to the end of Acts Chrysostom asks: "But of his affairs after the two years, what say we? (The writer) leaves the hearer athirst for more: the heathen authors do the same (in their writings), for to know everything makes the reader dull and jaded. Or else he does this, not having it in his power to exhibit it from his own personal knowledge."[71] He laments Luke's lack of knowledge while speculating that this could be a literary device designed to leave the reader wanting more or that he really did not know anything beyond the two years.

As a result, we can conclude that Chrysostom is not aware of any new information post-Acts 28.[72] Cadbury highlights Chrysostom's point that the "sequel would have been no different in kind from what has already been told."[73] Any further information beyond Acts 28 would have included the same kind of struggles throughout Acts. It appears then that Chrysostom was left wondering why the book ended as it did but also with the impression that Luke was not aware of any events beyond Acts 28:31. At any rate, by the end of the fourth century CE, it is clear that the ancient interpreters did not have any concrete information on the end of Acts beyond the simple explanation that Luke wrote about the events that he had knowledge of.

Modern Interpretation of the Enigma

In modern times we find no shortage of interpretations concerning the end of Acts. Beginning with the early nineteenth century, it is interesting that many of the conclusions about Paul's fate and the end of Acts mirror that of the ancient writers.[74] For example, Michaelis stated that Acts was written from Rome "in company with St. Paul, shortly before the close of the book."[75] There is also a growing concern to place the events at the close of Acts within a historical framework. For instance, Ebrard reasoned that it was "not after the lapse of these two years Paul suffered martyrdom,

---

[70] The "sacred writers ever addressed themselves to the matter of immediate importance … it was no object with them to be writers of books: in fact, there are many things which they have delivered by unwritten tradition." Chrysostom, *Hom. Acts*, 1 (*NPNF1*–11:2). Cadbury, *Luke-Acts*, 322, says that this "implies that it was an intentional, even conventional, secular custom thus to stop in mid course."

[71] Chrysostom, *Hom. Acts*, 55 (*NPNF1*–11:326). Pervo, *Acts*, 688, and Troftgruben, *Conclusion Unhindered*, 22, discuss this passage. Subsequently, Chrysostom muses on the texts from Romans 15:22, 23 in a similar way as the author of the *Muratorian fragment* did.

[72] Chrysostom, *Hom. Acts*, 55 (*NPNF1*–11:326).

[73] Cadbury, *Luke-Acts*, 322. "Why didst thou wish to learn what happened after these two years? Those too are such as these: bonds, tortures, fightings, imprisonments, lyings in wait, false accusations, deaths, day by day." Chrysostom, *Hom. Acts*, 55 (*NPNF1*–11:327).

[74] Troftgruben, *Conclusion Unhindered*, 8–11. The earliest interpretation remained virtually unchallenged until the nineteenth century.

[75] Johann D. Michaelis, *Introduction to the New Testament* (trans. Herbert Marsh; 2nd edn; 4 vols; London: F & C Rivington, 1802), 3:327. Otherwise Luke as a "credible historian" would have "related some other particulars relative to St. Paul, or would at least have mentioned the event of his imprisonment, in which the Christian reader was highly interested" (3:327).

but that he was set free at his first trial before Nero, and then perished in a second imprisonment."[76]

Before the advent of complicated literary explanations, questions were asked following a similar line of reasoning as the ancients. For example, Ebrard wonders why Luke closes his book this way since there is no record of the "process against Paul," a final address to Theophilus, nor a formal wrap up conclusion to the work.[77] Ebrard simply explains that Luke has "detailed the events as far as they had developed" while providing us an indication of when he composed his work.[78] Although he suggests that Acts 28:31 represents the "last narrated event" this does not offer us proper closure since "we naturally expect a reference to the beginning of the book, and to Theophilus."[79]

The ancient view that Luke was not aware of the events post-Acts 28 continued into the early twentieth century. Harnack observed how throughout "eight whole chapters" Luke "keeps his readers intensely interested in the progress of the trial of St Paul, simply that he may in the end completely disappoint them—they learn nothing of the final result of the trial!"[80] Subsequently, he insists that "neither is the slightest reference made to the martyrdom of St Paul."[81] Harnack's argument merits repeating:

> We are accordingly left with the result: that the concluding verses of the Acts of the Apostles, taken in conjunction with the absence of any reference in the book to the result of the trial of St Paul and to his martyrdom, make it in the highest degree probable that the work was written at a time when St Paul's trial in Rome had not yet come to an end.[82]

A similar but nuanced approach to the preceding interpretation gained popularity during the nineteenth and early twentieth century—the idea that Luke was prevented from finishing his two-volume work.[83] One version of this view is that Luke somehow left things unfinished due to a "mechanical reason like the filling of a papyrus role to the limit."[84] A second view is that Luke died before he could finish

---

[76] Johannes H. A. Ebrard, *Biblical Commentary on the New Testament* (trans. David Fosdick; 5 vols; New York: Sheldon, 1866), 3:412.
[77] Ibid.
[78] Ibid. This is a very important clue for the time of composition. Again, Ebrard (3:412) points to the main "question" that concerns the "substance of the concluding verses" that leave the "account regarding Paul unfinished; the decision of his appeal to the Emperor must have been stated, if it had taken place when Luke concluded."
[79] Ibid., 3:412–13.
[80] Harnack, *Date of Acts*, 95. He compares this glaring omission with that of the gospels ending with the trial of Jesus before Pilate in Jerusalem.
[81] Ibid., 97. Similarly, Rackham, *Acts*, 51, exclaims: "It seems incredible that if S. Luke had known it, he should have not mentioned it."
[82] Harnack, *Date of Acts*, 99 (originally all in italics).
[83] For survey of these views see Troftgruben, *Conclusion Unhindered*, 12–14.
[84] Hemer, *Acts*, 386. For an early example of this see Arnold Rüegg, "Die Lukasschriften und der Raumzwang des antiken Buchwesens," *TSK* 69 (1896): 94–101—although Rüegg thought that "Luke was content to stop because he intended a 3rd volume" (as noted by Troftgruben, *Conclusion Unhindered*, 12 [n. 15]). Hemer (386) states that there is "every reason to suppose that the ending was intended, whatever the motive for it." Harnack, *Date of Acts*, 96–7, had rejected this explanation as well.

Acts.[85] A third view is that Luke lost his "more complete" ending.[86] Similarly, a fourth view is that Luke planned on writing a third volume but it was "not completed or lost."[87] A fifth view that remains a popular explanation is that Luke did, in fact, know about Paul's death but, for various "literary" reasons, he intentionally fabricated the end of Acts.[88]

Contemporary Interpretation of the Enigma

During the latter part of the twentieth century, variations of the ancient and modern explanations continued to be repeated and repackaged while in some cases new perspectives developed from literary criticism.[89] And yet the common thread of the contemporary interpretations stems from Baur and the Tübingen school who presupposed that Luke was aware of Paul's fate at the time of his writing.[90] With the support of modern literary criticism, especially narrative and composition criticism, it is now commonly thought that Luke wrote his conclusion to Acts in order to fulfil some higher literary purpose.[91] For some, the "solution must therefore be

---

[85] Johannes De Zwaan, "Was the Book of Acts a Posthumous Edition?," *HTR* 17 (1924): 95–153. See also Hans Lietzmann, *The Founding of the Church Universal* (trans. Bertram L. Woolf; 2nd edn; London: Lutterworth, 1950), 78, and Blaiklock, *Acts*, 195. Although this is possible—and we cannot rule out of hand that it is not—the problem with this and other speculations is that "our actual ending, however difficult, bears the marks of deliberation." Hemer, *Acts*, 387 (n. 52).

[86] Troftgruben, *Conclusion Unhindered*, 12. Loisy, *Actes*, 103–4, 120, 940–54.

[87] Troftgruben, *Conclusion Unhindered*, 13 (and esp. his n. 13). Ramsay, *St. Paul*, 23, based his view on the opening line of Acts thinking that πρῶτος λόγος as a "*First Discourse*" implies a third volume otherwise Luke would have used the term πρότερος "*Former Discourse*." Blaiklock, *Acts*, 195, muses whether "another book" was planned beginning with Paul's "release or acquittal in Rome, and proceeding with the story of further evangelism," but it was "never written." See also Jacques Winandy, "La finale des Actes: Histoire ou Théologie," *ETL* 73 (1997): 106.

[88] See "Fabrication" below. Troftgruben, *Conclusion Unhindered*, 14–16. The root of these explanations stem from nineteenth-century German scholarship, such as Ferdinand C. Baur's, *Paul the Apostle of Jesus Christ: His Life and Works, His Epistles and Teachings* (2 vols; repr., Grand Rapids: Baker, 2010), 226–52, chapter 9 on Paul's imprisonment and martyrdom, and is still popular in recent times. See Haenchen, *Acts*, 732 and Holloway, "Inconvenient Truths," 418–33.

[89] See Troftgruben, *Conclusion Unhindered*, 22–35.

[90] Baur, *Paul*, 226–52; Philip Davies, "The Ending of Acts," *ExpTim* 94 (1983): 334; Pervo, *Acts*, 688. A perfect example is openly stated by Pervo, *Acts*, 688: "The close of Acts is fictitious in that it chooses to abandon its principal story line on a high note rather than follow it into failure and contradiction." Pervo admits to Haenchen's influence in the preface (xv), therefore it is not surprising to read Haenchen's, *Acts*, 732, earlier conclusion that Luke's "apologetic attempt" was "hopeless from the beginning."

[91] E.g., Daniel Marguerat, "The Enigma of the Silent Closing of Acts (28:16–31)," in *Jesus and the Heritage of Israel: Luke's Narrative Claim Upon Israel's Legacy* (ed. David P. Moessner; Luke the Interpreter of Israel Series 1; Harrisburg, PA: Trinity Press International, 1999), 284–304; idem, *Historian*, 205–30; Puskas, *Conclusion*, 137–40; Troftgruben, *Conclusion Unhindered*, 179–88; David P. Moessner, "'Completed End(s)ings' of Historiographical Narrative. Diodorus Siculus and the End(ing) of Acts," in *Die Apostelgeschichte und die hellenistische Geschichtsschreibung: Festschrift für Eckhard Plümacher zu seinem 65. Geburtstag* (ed. Cilliers Breytenbach and Jens Schröter; Ancient Judaism and Early Christianity: AGJU 57; Leiden: Brill, 2004), 193–221. Fitzmyer, *Acts*, 792 (n. 2), says the end of Acts "is that which is planned by Luke for his literary composition." Holloway, "Inconvenient Truths," 419–20, challenges the explanations that rely upon the "internal logic" of the narrative (here 419). He finds this approach to be problematic because it "does not so

literary"⁹² rather than dealing with the so-called "speculative historical questions."⁹³ But why should historical enquiry take a back seat to literary criticism, especially given the lack of a literary consensus?

Fabrication

As discussed above, the explanation that Luke was aware of Paul's death but intentionally left that out and therefore fabricated (or falsified) his ending was developed as early as the nineteenth century in Germany.⁹⁴ This basic theory grew in popularity via Haenchen who claimed that "Luke thus presupposes Paul's martyrdom."⁹⁵ Essentially, scholars here explain Luke's silence on Paul's death because it would otherwise (1) be considered unedifying;⁹⁶ (2) imply Paul's guilt;⁹⁷ (3) implicate Christians who abandoned Paul;⁹⁸ (4) blame the Roman Empire for Paul's death;⁹⁹ and (5) parallel the death of Jesus too closely.¹⁰⁰ All of these scholars presuppose a late date and dismiss the most straightforward and ancient explanation that Luke was not aware of Paul's death at the time of writing.

More recently, Holloway refers to other ancient histories, such as 2 Maccabees, that seem to leave out key events such as the death of Judas (see 1 Macc. 9:1-22).¹⁰¹ However, several objections can be made for this line of argument. First, as Holloway admits there is the problem that we do not know exactly when 2 Maccabees was written—its final form arrives "sometime after" 124 BCE based on the "date of its prefatory letter in 1:1-9."¹⁰² Moreover, 2 Maccabees is also an "epitome of Jason of Cyrene's longer

---

much explain *why* Luke decided to end his narrative on such a[n] ambivalent note as it documents *how* Luke attempted all along to prepare his reading for such an ending" (his emphasis).

⁹² Pervo, *Acts*, 688. Recall my note 14 from Chapter 2 on the importance of the historical context and interpretation.

⁹³ Puskas, *Conclusion*, 28. Here Puskas laments that "there has been too much preoccupation with the more speculative historical questions but no consensus has been reached on the significant literary concerns."

⁹⁴ See Baur, *Paul*, 226-52; Haenchen, *Acts*, 732; Pervo, *Acts*, 688-90.

⁹⁵ Haenchen, *Acts*, 732; Pervo, *Acts*, 688, and Puskas, *Conclusion*, 32 (n. 82), says that Acts 20:25, 38 "seems to presuppose his death around A.D. 64." See further, Armstrong, "Ernst Haenchen," forthcoming.

⁹⁶ Barrett, *Acts*, 2:1249, claims that the "end of the story was omitted because it was not edifying." See also Holloway, "Inconvenient Truths," 423-33.

⁹⁷ See Schneckenburger, *Der Apostelgeschichte*, 124-33, 244-53, who builds on Baur's, *Paul*, 5-14, 226-52, reconstruction of Jewish and Gentile Christian relations. Cf. also Haenchen, *Acts*, 15-24.

⁹⁸ Barrett, "End of Acts," 549-50; idem, *Acts*, 2:1236, 1248-50. You can see how this view developed based on the contemporary texts: E.g., *1 Clem.* 5:2, 5; 2 Tim. 1:15-18; 4:16; Phil. 1:15-17.

⁹⁹ Karl Schrader, *Der Apostel Paulus* (5 vols; Leipzig: Christian Ernst Kollmann, 1830-6), 5:573-4. Similarly, Paul W. Walasky, "*And so we came to Rome*": *The Political Perspective of St. Luke* (SNTSMS 49; Cambridge: Cambridge University Press, 1983), 62-3, contends that Luke is trying to protect Rome's reputation.

¹⁰⁰ Haenchen, *Acts*, 732, suggests that although Luke "presupposes Paul's martyrdom" he did not "see it as his task to enhance devotion to the martyrs." Where Haenchen (732) reasoned that Luke wanted to "spare the Church martyrdom" earlier Adolf Jülicher, *An Introduction to the New Testament* (trans. Janet P. Ward; London: Smith, Elder, & Co., 1904), 439, thought that Luke was not aware of the later churches' devotion to martyrdom. See Troftgruben, *Conclusion Unhindered*, 16 (n. 29) here and also pp. 15-16 on these five common explanations (and their problems).

¹⁰¹ Holloway, "Inconvenient Truths," 430-2.

¹⁰² Ibid., 432.

five-volume" and we "do not know when Jason ended his work."[103] This chronological uncertainty seems to minimize the value of comparing Judas's defeat of Nicanor in 161 BCE as the last recorded event in 1 Maccabees with Acts (Paul's imprisonment). The time lag between the end of Paul's imprisonment (*c.* 62) and the writing of Acts (62–63 CE) is conceivably very short compared to 2 Maccabees.

Second, if the omission of Judas's death in 2 Maccabees is intentional there exists a clear motive for doing so (i.e., avoiding the death of the hero). In Acts, there is no clear motive for omitting the death of Paul given Luke's own tendency to narrate the suffering and martyrdom of his characters—and this is corroborated with Paul's own teaching. Besides, Paul's trial formulates a significant part of the plot of Acts that is left unfinished.[104]

Third, Holloway's argument breaks down even further in light of the combined omissions that can be dated with relative certainty in relation to the end of Acts. It does not seem reasonable to compare the omission of the death of Judas in 2 Maccabees with the omission of not only the death of Paul (and Peter and James) in Acts but also the fire of Rome, Nero's persecution, and the Jewish War in such a short span of time (see Chapter 8). It is certainly *possible* that Luke omitted the death of Paul—along with other key events in world history—as an "inconvenient truth" but it does not make it a logical necessity. It seems to be a rather *convenient* interpretation to argue that "whatever happened to Paul" contradicted Luke's "larger theological narrative."[105]

Last, Holloway refers to less persuasive examples such as the comparison between the end of Acts with the end of 2 Kings that leaves the Jewish King Jehoiachin "being well treated in exile."[106] Davies essentially relates the story of Jehoiachin—as the end of the Davidic line—with Luke's emphasis on Jesus as the "Davidic King."[107] Somehow the life and death of Paul as a part of the "new kingdom" and as the "prisoner and servant of the son of David" directly relates back to the end of 2 Kings.[108] In fairness, Davies is not definitive in his conclusion; he merely suggests that "for Luke, the 'historian' of the new kingdom, the OT history of the old kingdom ends in a way which *may* have provided inspiration for the ending of Acts."[109] Although his proposition is possible, Davies's short essay is entirely speculative and undeveloped.

Altogether these views remain popular explanations. For example, Lüdemann calls the ending of Acts "bizarre ... Luke knows that the Roman state executed Paul" and he "fails to report it."[110] Instead of giving reasonable consideration that the author of Acts may not have been aware of Paul's death at the time of writing, Lüdemann assumes that he was.[111] Where is the evidence to support this hypothesis? Lüdemann describes

---

[103] Ibid.
[104] See Conrad H. Gempf, "Luke's Story of Paul's Reception in Rome," in *Rome in the Bible and the Early Church* (ed. Peter Oakes; Grand Rapids: Baker Academic, 2002), 42, on the significance of the omitted trial.
[105] Holloway, "Inconvenient Truths," 433.
[106] Ibid., 432 (n. 53). See, Davies, "The Ending of Acts," 334–5.
[107] Davies, "The Ending of Acts," 335.
[108] Ibid.
[109] Ibid. (my emphasis).
[110] Lüdemann, *Acts*, 349.
[111] Lüdemann, *Acts*, 347. "[H]is trial—to say nothing of the possibility of his being found guilty—must be expunged from the record to allow for a properly basic heroic ending." See also Pervo, *Acts*, 688.

Luke's picture as a "theologically grounded (but deliberately unhistorical) picture of the Roman state . . . it casts serious doubt on Luke's veracity in general and on the credibility of this account. Luke again turns out to be a cunning propagandist with a theological bias."[112] Although Lüdemann's explanation is entirely possible, nevertheless, it is fraught with assumptions about the "chief" literary "motive" of Acts—that Rome should continue its "hands-off" policy towards Christianity.[113] Given Nero's "policy" in the summer of 64 CE, any literary motive to paint Christianity as a legitimate religion after this event seems a little too late for the "immense multitude" of exterminated Christians in Rome.[114]

Foreshadowing and Silence

Another common literary explanation stems from the "fabrication" view discussed above but emphasizes how Acts somehow provides "hints" in the text that Paul had long been "processed" by Caesar (Nero) and that everyone was aware of the outcome (i.e., Acts 20:25, 38; 21:13). Those who assume this foreshadowing in the text infer that "arguments for an early date" arise from the "unwarranted" assumption that the "Lucan writings must have been completed before Paul's trial or death or before the destruction of Jerusalem."[115] Ironically, a few pages later Fitzmyer observes how "modern interpreters have long been puzzled by the failure of NT writers to mention the destruction of Jerusalem by the Romans in A.D. 70."[116] An argument from silence with regard to the destruction of Jerusalem and other important events does not

---

[112] Lüdemann, *Acts*, 349.

[113] Ibid., 347. Since Cadbury and Dibelius may be regarded as "the seminal figures in Lukan research" for the past century it is worth a moment's reflection on their methodology in light of Lüdemann's comments. Bonz, *Legacy*, 1. For Cadbury, *Luke-Acts*, 48, the recognition of motive is central, but Lüdemann's hypothesis remains highly speculative given the historical framework of Acts. Cadbury explains that the author's motive is "never strictly historical, but always aetiological, and frequently apologetic" (48). In other words, the central motive is to present, defend, and confirm the faith of its readers. He also taught that motive is "not so much a creative as a molding force" (48). The motives operating in oral tradition impacted the character of the written "material long before it came to the hands or ears of Luke" (48). On a similar scale, Dibelius was very much focused on discovering motive (cf. Dibelius, *Studies*, 4, 11, 144–5). The application of these earlier theories of motive criticism survive in more recent works such as Marguerat, *Historian* and once more in his more recent work "Paul's End," 332 (Marguerat states that "the same reluctance to expose the internal dissensions within Christianity—*drove* the author of Acts to remain silent about Paul's end"; my emphasis). This goes beyond the parameters of Dibelius and especially Cadbury. Further, Barrett questions Marguerat's attempt to present "Luke as a writer of sophisticated literary skill." Barrett, review of *The First Christian Historian*, 257. "Was he such a writer? I do not think so" (257). It seems negligent to draw conclusions of an ancient narrative based on authorial motives alone.

[114] Tacitus, *Ann*. 15.44.2, 4; Lampe, *Valentinus*, 401; Parker, "'Former Treatise,'" 53; Cadbury, *Luke-Acts*, 48; Kamp et al., *Writing History!*, 77. See also Greene and Moore's, *Archaeology*, 155, fifth criterion for the historical dating process that seeks to evaluate any perceived authorial motive.

[115] Fitzmyer, *Acts*, 52. See also idem, *Luke*, 54–7. It is equally important to "avoid the opposite conclusion as well—that Luke-Acts could not have been completed before Paul's trial or death." Karl L. Armstrong, "The End of Acts and the Jewish Response: Condemnation, Tragedy, or Hope?," *CurBR* 17 (2019): 72.

[116] Fitzmyer, *Acts*, 55. See also Chapter 8.

provide proof that they did not happen by the time of Luke's writing. However, in a dispute of probabilities, such arguments should not be left out.[117]

This is especially true in light of the hypothetically possible but unprovable argument that Luke has foreshadowed Paul's death. Fitzmyer (and others) claim that Luke's failure to account for Paul's death was because it was foreshadowed (cf. Acts 20:25, 38; 21:13).[118] Fitzmyer maintains that the "best way" to account for this ending (and here he quotes Hanson) "is that his [Luke's] readers knew the rest of Paul's story."[119] This hypothesis is over a century old, with Bartlet who assumed that it was not necessary for Luke to mention Paul's execution because, for Luke's readers, the consequences of prosecution under Nero were obvious.[120] There are serious problems with these theories and consequently they should remain just that—theoretical possibilities.

Perhaps the most straightforward criticism is that the end of Acts could easily have been completed *before* Paul's trial and death and the "destruction of Jerusalem."[121] Paul's death *may* be foreshadowed in Acts (esp. 20:25) however, neither Paul's actual trial nor any details concerning his death are recorded in Acts (or in any of the variants).[122] Additionally, although Cadbury did not commit to a specific date of Acts,

---

[117] See Mittelstaedt, *Lukas als Historiker*, 17–21 (esp. his closing remarks on p. 21). See also Kamp et al., *Writing History!*, 77 and "Principles for Interpreting Sources" in Chapter 2.

[118] Fitzmyer, *Acts*, 52–3 and 674–6. Bruce contends that when Luke "wrote, he probably knew" that Paul's Miletus prediction (Acts 20:25) "had come true." Bruce, *Acts* (3rd edn), 9–10. See also Mount, *Pauline Christianity*, 128, who claims this speech is "foreshadowing Paul's death." See also Gerhard Schneider, *Die Apostelgeschichte II: Kommentar zu Kap. 9, 1–28, 31* (Freiburg: Herder, 1982), 300; Larkin, *Acts*, 18, and Jervell, *Die Apostelgeschichte*, 515. Puskas, *Conclusion*, 32, thinks that Acts "seems to presuppose his death." More recently, Riesner, "Paul's Trial," 395, maintains that "Luke alludes *clearly* to the martyrdom of the apostle" in the Miletus speech (Acts 20:23-25, 37-38) and "speaks strongly against such a date of composition" (my emphasis). Here Riesner (395) is arguing against Robinson, *Redating the New Testament*, 88–92, and Mittelstaedt, *Lukas als Historiker*, 165–220, who maintain that Luke-Acts was written during Paul's captivity (60–62 CE).

[119] Fitzmyer, *Acts*, 53, citing Richard P. C. Hanson, "The Provenance of the Interpolator in the 'Western' Text of Acts and of Acts Itself," *NTS* 12 (1966): 228, and J. H. Crehan, "The Purpose of Luke in Acts," in *Studia Evangelica II: Texte und Untersuchungen zur Geschichte der altchristlichen Literatur* (ed. F. L. Cross; TU 87; Berlin: Akademie-Verlag, 1964), 361–2. Note Crehan's corrected reference here since it is missing in Fitzmyer and referenced incorrectly elsewhere.

[120] Bruce, *Acts* (1983), 535, refers to Bartlet, "St. Paul's Fate at Rome," 464–7, who is writing in response to William M. Ramsay, "Two New Testament Problems. I. St. Paul's Fate at Rome," *Exp* 5 (1913): 264–84. Bartlet does not think Paul survived Nero's persecution in 64 and so argues against Ramsay and "any theory of St. Paul's release from the imprisonment" (467). In light of Nero's infamy Bartlet (465) presupposes the silence of Paul's death in Acts and how Luke's readers would understand Agrippa's comments (Acts 26:32): "'This man might have been set free, if he had not appealed to Caesar;' but he had, and the reigning Caesar was Nero!" Since Nero was this Caesar and an "abnormal monster" Luke's readers would be "relying upon the Christian estimate of Nero after 64 A.D. to guide their reading" (466 and 465). Bartlet also factors "Paul's doubly recorded foreboding at Miletus that he would never again see the Ephesian elders" (465). His argument is reasonable except for at least two major problems (that continue to be repeated)—that Acts was written after 64 CE and clearly foreshadows Paul's death. Gary W. Trompf, "On Why Luke Declined to Recount the Death of Paul: Acts 27–28 and Beyond," in *Luke-Acts: New Perspectives from the Society of Biblical Literature Seminar* (ed. Charles H. Talbert; New York: Crossroad, 1984), 232–4, later modifies Bartlet's earlier theory and argues for a deliberate ending to Acts.

[121] Fitzmyer, *Acts*, 52.

[122] See Chapter 7 and 8.

he was adamant there is no "decisive proof that Luke was not written before the fall of Jerusalem."[123]

Beyond Cadbury's point, there has never been a decisive argument against the early dating proponents who, like Rackham, maintain the incredulity of Luke not mentioning Paul's death if he knew it.[124] Elsewhere Rackham remarks how from Acts 19:21 onwards, matters have been "working up to a crisis" and that there is "not even a single anticipatory hint or allusion to the fate of St. Paul."[125] Additionally, Macgregor later emphatically states that Paul's "whole progress from Corinth to Jerusalem reads in Luke's account like a march to martyrdom."[126] In light of this "march to martyrdom" what possible literary explanation can justify Luke's silence?[127]

There are other more recent variations of this fabrication/foreshadowing theory. Since Marguerat's solution presupposes the death of Paul, then in some respects it can be viewed as a similar branch of argument—albeit with a twist. His proposition is that Luke is using a rhetorical procedure (i.e., narrative suspension) to explain this silence.[128] He claims that "Luke wishes to reinterpret the memory of the apostle's martyrdom, by inverting the structure of the expected trial (Acts 27-28), and to ensure the perpetuation of his missionary work in the present."[129] Marguerat's application of narratological criticism leads him to conclude that the Acts narrative is "intentionally ambivalent."[130]

However, the book of Acts is anything but ambivalent—the narrative is intentionally filled with trials, suffering, martyrdom, and miracles. Furthermore, it was Harnack who, over a century ago, explained that the "contrary impression" of Peter and Paul's "presupposed" death in Acts is given, thus challenging Marguerat's "rhetoric of silence."[131] Recently, Troftgruben considered Marguerat's rhetoric of silence "questionable" because ancient literature does not "explicitly speak of

---

[123] Cadbury, "Identity," 2:358.
[124] Rackham, *Acts*, 51. A falsified ending provides an easy alternative but creates far more problems than it solves.
[125] Rackham, "Plea," 78. Although some argue that Luke alludes to Paul's death in Acts (i.e., Riesner, "Paul's Trial," 398; Acts 20:23-25, 37), this is nothing beyond what he wrote in his own letters (i.e., 1 Cor. 9:15; 15:31-32, 2 Cor. 1:8-10; 7:3, 11:23-26; Gal. 2:19-20; 6:14, 17; Rom. 6:8, 12:1, 14:8; esp. Phil. 1:21; Col. 3:3; and later 2 Tim. 4:6).
[126] G. H. C. Macgregor, *Interpreter's Bible. IX. The Acts of the Apostles, the Epistle to the Romans* (Nashville: Abingdon, 1952), 350.
[127] Recall "Principles for Interpreting Sources" in Chapter 2.
[128] Cf. Marguerat, *Historian*, 229-30, and his earlier essay "Et quand nous sommes entrés dans Rome: L'énigme de la fin du livre des Actes (28, 16-31)," *RHPR* 73 (1993): 1-21 that was published in English in idem, "Enigma," 284-304; idem, "The End of Acts (28:16-31) and the Rhetoric of Silence," in *Rhetoric and the New Testament: Essays from the 1992 Heidelberg Conference* (eds. Stanley E. Porter and Thomas H. Olbricht; JSNTSup 90; Sheffield: JSOT, 1993), 74-89; and in his chapter "The Enigma of the End of Acts (28:16-31)" in *Historian*, 205-30. For his most recent treatment see idem, "Paul's End," 305-32. Parsons, *Acts*, 366, considers Acts to be either "characterized by 'suspended' ending" (i.e., J. Lee Magness, *Sense and Absence: Structure and Suspension in the Ending of Mark's Gospel* [SemeiaSt 15; Atlanta: SBL, 1986]) or Marguerat's, "Enigma," 284-304, "Rhetoric of Silence."
[129] Marguerat, *Historian*, 229-30.
[130] Ibid., 230.
[131] Harnack, *Date of Acts*, 97.

such a convention for narrative endings."[132] Troftgruben's detailed criticism of this rhetorical device leads him to rightfully conclude that Marguerat's "proposal that the ending of Acts implies particular outcomes (for both Paul and the reader) is flawed."[133]

Why would an author be content to foreshadow Paul's death (or "invert" his trial) when elsewhere the founder and followers of the gospel story have already been presented in their suffering and death as heroes and examples to follow in Luke-Acts and other New Testament writings?[134] Jesus's death was clearly foreshadowed (e.g., Mk 9:12; Lk. 24:46) and vividly described in all four gospel accounts, and in Luke's version especially (23:26-49)—so why not Paul's death if he had known? Beyond this, Paul, in Acts as well as in his letters, illustrates sufficient danger to such a degree that a foreshadowed death is really a moot point.[135] Should we now consider Paul's "undisputed" letters as posthumous writings? Further, how could we reasonably assume that a close companion of Paul (Col. 4:14; Phlm. 24; 2 Tim. 4:11) and careful writer (Lk. 1:3) would fail to record Paul's fate at this time?[136]

It seems that the foreshadowing theories are incredibly assumptive and lacking in solid evidence. Consider Walton who contends that the Miletus speech in Acts shows "significant parallels to other farewell speeches, especially from Jewish contexts."[137] He also finds the argument where Paul is dead by the time Acts is written to be "inconclusive."[138] His counter-argument seems entirely defensible with regard to the popular reference to Acts 20:25, 38 for evidence of foreshadowing. Simply put, these verses convey only that "Luke's Paul is uncertain about his future" and that he will not be returning to Ephesus.[139] And since Paul clearly continues his journey by visiting many places and making many speeches post-Ephesus—during the remaining eight chapters of Acts—how can we reasonably consider this to be Luke's "narrative farewell for Paul?"[140] Therefore, rhetorical explanations for the silence at the end of the narrative must remain theories at best.

---

[132] Troftgruben, *Conclusion Unhindered*, 34-5. He postulates that the use of silence in rhetoric occurred but "no ancient rhetorician applies these ideas explicitly to the practice of concluding narratives" (35 [n. 101]; Aristotle, *Poetics*, 7:3).

[133] Troftgruben, *Conclusion Unhindered*, 169 (162-9). He explains that the "openness of the ending cannot be pinned down to such predictable results" (169).

[134] Marguerat, *Historian*, 229-30.

[135] In Romans, Paul asks for prayer "that I may be delivered from those in Judea who refuse to believe" (Rom. 15:31). Why else would Paul write that unless he was genuinely worried about what might happen in Jerusalem? Recall Collingwood's, *Idea*, 218, advice on rethinking the thoughts of the past. See also "Principles for Selecting Events" from Chapter 2.

[136] Regardless, the author clearly has great respect for Paul as the hero of his narrative. Commenting on Paul's fate at the end of Acts, Munck claims it is a "reasonable assumption that this question is not answered because it could not be answered." Therefore, it is "unlikely that he [Luke] would have deliberately avoided an account of Paul's death." See Munck, *Acts*, 53-4.

[137] Walton, *Leadership and Lifestyle*, 202.

[138] Ibid.

[139] Ibid. Consider also Rom. 15:23 where Paul wanted to visit Spain and stop in Rome along the way. The language in Acts 20:25, 38 may therefore only convey generalizations and desires and not definitive statements that will certainly come to pass.

[140] Walton, *Leadership and Lifestyle*, 202.

Theological and Political Explanations

Another common perspective on the end of Acts is that it provides a sufficient literary or spiritual/theological explanation. This is especially prevalent among the commentaries such as that of Marshall's who suggests that the "fate of Paul is secondary to that of the gospel... Nothing that men can do can stop the progress and ultimate victory of the gospel."[141] Williams suggests that "Acts ends at 28:31, but the story of Jesus goes on wherever his Spirit finds men and women ready to believe, to obey, to give, to suffer, and if need be, to die for him."[142]

Other dedicated studies on the end of Acts broadly represent both a literary and theological approach to the conclusion of Acts 28:16-31.[143] For example, Puskas's expressed methodology is that of "composition criticism with insights gleaned from narrative criticism."[144] He approaches the text of Acts 28:16-31 by analysing both the structure and literary forms of the pericope.[145] He focuses upon the theological significance of Paul "as one like Jesus engaged in the work of Jesus."[146] He concludes with this axiom: "The mission of Paul in Acts sets forth an agenda of world-wide mission for the church. In Acts 28, Luke seems to be telling his readers/auditors: to be identified with Christ and his church, one must also do the work of Christ and his church."[147] This may be valuable for a theological interpretation on Acts (that can also be found in many of the commentaries); however, this does not add to our knowledge of Acts in its historical context.[148]

Furthermore, Puskas *assumes* the death of Paul and the destruction of Jerusalem as bygone events and, like Troftgruben (see "Linkage" below), states that a "date near the end of the first century (A.D. 80-90) is assumed for the composition of Luke-Acts."[149] It seems arbitrary to draw moral and theological value from a text that aims to provide an accurate report (Lk. 1:3) but then intentionally conceals the trial and death of Paul (its main character in the second half of the book) as well as other major historic events.[150] On the positive side, however, Puskas's insights indirectly remove

---

[141] Marshall, *Acts*, 447.
[142] Williams, *Acts*, 17. See also Willie J. Jennings, *Acts* (Belief: A Theological Commentary on the Bible; Louisville, KY: Westminster John Knox Press, 2017), 242–57.
[143] See Puskas, *Conclusion*, 140, for a similar view that is expressed by many commentaries.
[144] Ibid., 30.
[145] Ibid., 33–63. While Puskas, *Conclusion*, 145–70, provides some valuable exegetical insights the book is lacking in modern grammatical, linguistic, text-critical and historical considerations. Besides the BDAG, there are minimal resources along these lines and barely any attention to the significant matters of textual criticism or the more "speculative historical questions" (28). See ibid., 32 and Matthew L. Skinner, review of *The Conclusion of Luke-Acts: The Significance of Acts 28:16-31*, by Charles B. Puskas, *RelSRev* 35 (2009): 189. Compare Puskas with Keener's, *Acts*, 4:3717–75, treatment on the end of Acts.
[146] Puskas, *Conclusion*, 115 (see also 115–35, 139); Skinner, review of *Conclusion*, 189.
[147] Ibid., 140.
[148] Where Williams, *Acts*, 17, is typical of the commentaries, Bock, *Acts*, 706, gives greater attention to the historical context of Paul's situation at the end of Acts.
[149] Puskas, *Conclusion*, 32, does not find Pervo's, *Dating Acts* second-century date convincing.
[150] Ibid., 32 (n. 82). Most notably the fire of Rome and the destruction of Jerusalem. Omissions of this nature would render Acts as a deliberate and delusional fabrication of reality. From the perspective of historiography, the date of Acts greatly impacts our interpretation of its text(s). Recall Chapters 1 and 2; Tyson, *Marcion*, 1–2; Pervo, *Dating Acts*, viii; Keener, *Acts*, 1:401.

some of the "abruptness" of the ending of Acts by showing its literary significance as a completed and fitting ending that connects the narrative back to Luke.[151]

There are a number of sub-theories and explanations on the end of Acts that are briefly worth mentioning. One view is that the end of Acts represents some form of narrative climax with Paul's arrival in Rome, thus fulfilling the beginning of Acts 1:8.[152] Another perspective is that Paul's Jewish encounter in Rome (and the lack of response to the Gospel) represents the book's narrative climax.[153] A further view sees the close of Acts as a similarly completed ending but fatally disregards the unanswered events generated in the narrative.[154] Last, Mauck insists that "Luke-Acts was written as a legal defense of Paul as he awaited trial before Nero."[155] At the very least we can say with Puskas that Luke "defends Paul."[156]

The problem with such interpretations is that they raise more questions about the end of Acts rather than providing solid answers. The common root is that they assume a later date where Paul is dead, Rome and the church are decimated, the Jews, Jerusalem, and its Temple are destroyed, and somehow Luke as a historical and theological writer (via some advanced literary tactic) has opted to leave all of this out of his narrative.[157]

Linkage

Troftgruben's interpretation of the conclusion of Acts consists of a theological approach with literary (esp. narrative) criticism as its aid.[158] He surveys the close-of-Acts perspectives among ancient, modern, and more recent scholars and provides a

---

[151] See Keener's, *Acts*, 4:3716–18, list of Puskas's comparisons where he concludes: "Certainly Acts 28:17–31 provides a fitting climax to Luke's work" (4:3718). A fitting climax to Acts is also consistent with a pre-70 date.

[152] In Acts 1:8 Jesus promised his disciples: "you will be my witnesses . . . unto the ends of the earth." The idea that this represents some form of Gentile or Roman narrative climax is widespread. Bock, in 2007, declares how "Luke chose to end his book here because his point was the arrival of the word to the highest levels of Rome." Bock, *Acts*, 758. Pervo, *Acts*, 686, similarly states: "'The ends of the earth' (Acts 1:8) is realized in a mission that has no limits." Nevertheless, see Robert C. Tannehill, *The Narrative Unity of Luke-Acts: A Literary Interpretation* (2 vols; Minneapolis: Fortress, 1990), 2:17–18, 108–9, and 356. Troftgruben, *Conclusion Unhindered*, 24, highlights a variant of the Roman narrative climax view "not because it fulfills the promise of 1:8, but because it signifies the spread of the gospel to the capital of the Gentile world." See also his note 57 and his reasons that mitigate the validity of such views (25–6). See also Moessner, "'Completed End(s)ings,'" 218–21, who considers the close of Acts as fulfilling the promise of Acts 1:8 and the mission to the Jews.

[153] See Troftgruben, *Conclusion Unhindered*, 25 and Chapter 6 of this volume.

[154] See Moessner, "'Completed End(s)ings,'" 193–221, and Troftgruben's, *Conclusion Unhindered*, 34 and 161–2, critique of this explanation.

[155] J. W. Mauck, *Paul on Trial: The Book of Acts as a Defense of Christianity* (Nashville: Thomas Nelson, 2001), 226. See also Omerzu, *Der Prozess des Paulus, et passim*.

[156] Puskas, *Conclusion*, 137.

[157] The tension is felt by Keener, *Acts*, 4:3762, who states that "Luke is not denying Paul's eventual execution." He (4:3763) further says that he has "written on the assumption that Paul was dead when Luke wrote." Then he claims a post-70 CE date is "likelier than not" pending the date of Mark but then he back-peddles somewhat and states that it is "not possible to be dogmatic on this point" (4:3763). Further he (4:3763) points to the commentators and the "internal evidence" that point to Paul's "eventual martyrdom"—but logically Paul's death (and other key events) either happened before or after Luke wrote Acts—there is no other option available.

[158] Troftgruben, *Conclusion Unhindered*, 5.

helpful analysis that identifies some of the problems and advantages of each view.[159] Instead of focusing on *why* the book of Acts ends, his goal is to focus on *how* it ends.[160]

He believes that the conclusion of Acts is a "question of narrative interpretation" and specifically "narrative closure" that seeks to understand the "question about an ancient writing."[161] Subsequently, he engages the enigma with the principles of narrative *closure* and *openness* as a means to understand the endings of ancient works in general and, correspondingly, Acts in particular.[162] Beyond his comparison with other endings in Greco-Roman literature, he offers a familiar blend of existing theological, exegetical and/or literary explanations discussed in the previous two sections.[163]

Troftgruben maintains that the questions relating to *how* Acts concludes are "not so simply answered."[164] However, his solution is assumptive and raises more issues than it solves—he insists that this is a "question of narrative interpretation, which requires a response informed by narrative criticism."[165] This solution seems tendentious given the fact that all of the ancient interpreters until modern times discussed the ending of Acts at face value while asking reasonable questions concerning the silence of Paul's fate. So after nearly twenty centuries of interpretation where Luke is seen as writing only about the events he was aware of, how can modern principles of narrative criticism offer the right answers to the questions the ancients were asking? What about the "extraordinary darkness" we face when we grasp the abrupt ending that Cadbury spoke of?[166]

As argued in Chapter 2, historians factor not only what is present in a document but also what is absent—and what Luke (as the historian) leaves out of Acts (either by lack of knowledge or by choice) speaks volumes. A narrative interpretation *may* very well supply a *theory* on the ending of a book in the ancient world (as compared with the endings of other ancient works), but the theory falls short of demonstration

---

[159] Ibid., 7–36. Troftgruben (8–28) provides an analysis of the following viewpoints: (1) Luke knew no more; (2) Luke was prevented from finishing; (3) the ending was deliberately abrupt; (4) the ending was an intentional and fitting conclusion.

[160] Ibid., 1–6.

[161] Ibid., 35. Troftgruben (8–28) cites three key studies that effectively launched the quest for a narrative closure approach to the end of Acts: Jacques Dupont, "La conclusion des Actes et son rapport à l'ensemble de l'ouvrage de Luc," in *Les Actes des Apôtres: Traditions, redaction, théologie* (ed. J. Kramer; BETL 48; Leuven: Leuven University Press, 1979), 359–404; Hermann J. Hauser, *Strukturen der Abschlusserzählung der Apostelgeschichte (Apg 28, 16–31)* (AnBib 86; Rome: Biblical Institute, 1979), and Puskas, "Conclusion."

[162] Troftgruben, *Conclusion Unhindered*, 60. With respect to the end of Acts (144–78) he finds evidence for both narrative closure and openness.

[163] Cf. Puskas, *Conclusion, et passim*.

[164] Troftgruben, *Conclusion Unhindered*, 35. Perhaps a better question to ask is not so much *how* or *why* Acts ends the way it does, but rather "What is the ending of Acts?" and "How does the ending add to our knowledge of its historical context and especially its date?"

[165] Ibid., 35. Troftgruben (37) states that the "narrative criticism" he employs "is an interpretive approach that focuses on the narrative (or literary) features of a text." This methodology may be sufficient for studying an ancient novel or epic, but it seems insufficient when it comes to interpreting the end of Acts since it has always been a matter of historical inquiry. On narrative criticism see Mark A. Powell, *What is Narrative Criticism?* (Minneapolis: Fortress, 1990); Marianna Torgovnick, *Closure in the Novel* (Princeton, NJ: Princeton University Press, 1981), 198–9, 209; Mark A. Powell, "Narrative Criticism: The Emergence of a Prominent Reading Strategy," in *Mark as Story: Retrospect and Prospect* (eds. K. R. Iverson and C. W. Skinner; SBLRBS 65; Leiden: Brill, 2011), 19–43.

[166] Cadbury, *Acts in History*, 3.

because the content and genre of Acts, along with the historical context of the people in Acts, are vastly different from the literature Troftgruben finds comparable in many significant ways.

While he recognizes the genre debate and identifies the four genres that "nearly all scholars associate Acts with"—prose fiction, biography, epic, and historiography—there still remains a methodological deficit in his approach.[167] While he looks at the endings of various literature that are "contemporaneous with Acts," he fails to consider the content of those endings that are in many ways anachronistic.[168] Although he examines historiography "most fully since it is the genre to which Acts is most often compared" he finds that the ending of Acts is "most comparable to the endings of certain epic narratives" (esp. Homer's *Iliad*, Virgil's *Aeneid*).[169]

He proposes that the narrative "openness" and "closure" finds a "linkage" that "connects the story of the narrative (i.e., Acts) to another, subsequent story."[170] Acts then is an "expansive saga" that continues beyond the end "in similar ways Homer's *Iliad* envisions events that occur beyond the end of the narrative: the death of Achilles and the fall of Troy, events that occur later on in the Epic Cycle."[171]

From the outset, there are significant difficulties with his methodology, starting with the rather precarious nature of comparing Acts in the first century CE with Homer's works that are easily dated several centuries earlier.[172] Another serious issue is that a large contingent of scholarship considers Acts to be some form of historiography or

---

[167] Troftgruben, *Conclusion Unhindered*, 4. See his note 12 on the diversity of genre studies and more recently Smith and Kostopoulos, "Genre," 392, who note the "more gourmet choices such as 'collected biography' or 'apologetic historiography.'" See also Burridge, "Genre," 3–28 and Pitts, *Genre*, 165.

[168] Troftgruben, *Conclusion Unhindered*, 5. He (6) chooses Heliodorus, Achilles Tatius and Chariton for prose fiction, Plutarch's *Lives* (esp. *Cato Minor*) for biography, Homer's *Iliad* and *Odyssey* and Virgil's *Aeneid* for epic, and for historiography he uses Herodotus, Thucydides, Sallust, 1–4 Kingdoms and Josephus (see his chapter 3 [61–113]). Acts is *somewhat* "contemporaneous" with Sallust, Plutarch, Josephus, and Virgil, but Acts is certainly not contemporaneous with some of the other works—especially Herodotus, Thucydides, 1–4 Kingdoms and Homer's *Iliad* (eighth to sixth century BCE) which he particularly relies on.

[169] Troftgruben, *Conclusion Unhindered*, 6 (and his chapter 5 [144–78]).

[170] Ibid., 169.

[171] Ibid., 176, also 177, 187. In his analysis he also looks to Sallust's *Jugurtha* and identifies two of the main characters (Marius and Sulla) who "follow the path of power, corruption, and demise in subsequent Roman history, but Sallust's narrative ends midway along this path" (160). He compares *Jugurtha* with Acts and claims that both "conclude with broken cycles: the narratives allude to events that would complete their respective cycles" (cf. *Bell. Jug.* 63:6; 95:3-4 with Acts 20:24-25, 38; 21:13). And yet, this presupposes that the Miletus speech is a clear allusion to the event (of Paul's death). This allusion is far from clear and hypothetical at best. Recall "Foreshadowing and Silence" above. See also Pervo, *Acts*, 689–90 who compares *Jugurtha* with the end of Acts.

[172] See Barbara Graziosi, *Inventing Homer: The Early Reception of Epic* (Cambridge: Cambridge University Press, 2002), 91 (see esp. her chapter on "The date of Homer" [90–124]). The late dating advocates ascribe a date of around the "middle of the sixth century" BCE and the early group consider a date in the eighth century BCE. A third group considers a date somewhere in between based on the "fall of Egyptian Thebes in 663, and the destruction of Babylon in 688" CE (92). Meanwhile Herodotus lived *c.* 484–*c.* 425 BCE; Thucydides *c.* 460–*c.* 400 BCE and Plutarch wrote in the two decades before his death in 125 CE. Sallust lived 86–*c.* 35 BCE while Virgil wrote somewhere between 29 and 19 BCE.

biography, but certainly not epic.¹⁷³ More recently Adams, in his dedicated study on the genre of Acts, remarks that "it is apparent that Acts is *not an epic*. There are very few formal features that support this claim."¹⁷⁴ Furthermore, although Adams considers there to be "some generic relationship between Acts and ancient novels . . . there are a number of areas in which Acts and novels differ."¹⁷⁵ Without getting into a detailed study on genre, these observations seem entirely reasonable.

This makes Troftgruben's comparisons troublesome from the start since Acts is some form (or blend) of historiography or biography. How can we take two very different texts, with different genres, written by very different authors (that in some cases are hardly contemporaneous [esp. Homer]) and find parallels with the ends and formulate a credible interpretation? While Troftgruben claims that his study is "not an argument" for the genre of Acts, this is a tendentious point in his argument unless we can prove the minority position that the genre of Acts (or its ending) is epic.¹⁷⁶ He claims that the "conclusion to Acts implies that the narrative, *like other epic narratives*, relates the historic beginnings of a particular movement."¹⁷⁷ Therefore, his approach remains problematic since, in some measure, he considers Acts as epic literature despite the evidence to the contrary.

While his focus is on narrative criticism his disclaimer is that it "may also be a question of source criticism or historical events, certainly. This study, however, is primarily concerned with the final stage of the text."¹⁷⁸ Although the sources of Acts

---

[173] See Troftgruben, *Conclusion Unhindered*, 4 (n. 12). Although there are some who classify Acts as epic literature, such as Bonz, *Legacy*, 163, who, after deciding (without argument) that Luke is "writing at the end of the first century" CE, claims that "in the early Roman imperial period there is only one genre in which audiences expect to find supernatural beings intermingling with human characters in historical stories. That genre is epic." See also Dennis R. MacDonald, *Does the New Testament Imitate Homer? Four Cases from the Acts of the Apostles* (New Haven: Yale University Press, 2003) and idem, "Paul's Farewell to the Ephesian Elders and Hector's Farewell to Andromache: A Strategic Imitation of Homer's Iliad," in *Contextualizing Acts: Lukan Narrative and Greco-Roman Discourse* (eds. Todd C. Penner and Caroline Vander Stichele; SymS 20; Atlanta: SBL, 2003), 189–203. Part of the problem is due to the fact that there continues to be a variety of views on the genre of Acts. Recall my Chapter 3 and Palmer, "Monograph," 1:1–29; idem, "Acts and the Historical Monograph," 373–88; Phillips, "Consensus?" 365–96; Balch, "Μεταβολη Πολιτειων," 139–88. More recently, see the overview of genre research in: Sean A. Adams, *The Genre of Acts and Collected Biography* (SNTSMS 156; Cambridge: Cambridge University Press, 2013), 1–22.
[174] Adams, *Genre of Acts*, 170 (my emphasis). See also Burridge, "Genre," 3–28, and the conclusions of Smith and Kostopoulos, "Genre," 409–10 and also Pitts, *Genre*, 1–2, 165–74.
[175] Adams, *Genre of Acts*, 170. This challenges the views of Pervo and others who say that "the best generic fit for Acts" is as a novel (170).
[176] Troftgruben, *Conclusion Unhindered*, 181 (see also 170). It is problematic to isolate the end of Acts as epic—which is what Troftgruben's study implies: "In terms of literary closure, Luke's ending is best compared to the endings of famous epic works" (181).
[177] Ibid., 181 (my emphasis). A very serious and subsidiary problem of method relates to the application of modern principles of narrative openness and closure. For example, Troftgruben (30 [see also 7 and 37]) relies on Tannehill, *Narrative Unity*, 2:353–7, who in turn employs Torgovnick's "categories of narrative closure (circularity, parallelism) and openness (incompletion) to examine the ending of Acts." However, Torgovnick, *Closure*, 10, in her book chooses to examine eleven very modern novels in order to give a "roughly historical or chronological sense of the developments in the novel since 1848." This is highly problematic from a chronological standpoint and also because Acts is not a novel.
[178] Troftgruben, *Conclusion Unhindered*, 35 (n. 103). He is correct in saying that the end of Acts is neither to "entertain readers" or "narrate a life of Paul" or "narrate history for history's sake" (181).

is a contested issue it is nevertheless critical that we do not bypass those issues before engaging the "final stage" of the text. We must also ask, "What is the final stage of the text of Acts and which manuscripts or textual family is Troftgruben referring to?"[179] Although this represents a much greater issue in Acts scholarship, no study on Acts (including its end) can afford to ignore the major text-critical issues (see Chapter 7).[180]

Additionally, interpreting the end of Acts is a question of understanding the historical events that are found both inside (and outside) of Acts.[181] Since Acts contains a number of historic persons, places, and events—and is not simply a grand epic like Homer's *Iliad* or Virgil's *Aeneid*—any defensible interpretation requires serious consideration of the historical context. So Troftgruben's narrative solution seems to be more open to criticism because it focuses on the "final stage" of the text (that is difficult to define given the textual variation in Acts) to the neglect of the historical context.

My greatest contention with Troftgruben's thesis relates directly to the date of Acts and his dismissal of scholarly views that see the end of Acts as a result of Luke's lack of further knowledge (or that he ran out of sources).[182] While he claims that these "explanations make sense of the abruptness of Acts 28, and the narrative's preoccupation with Paul in chapters 20–28" and also accounts for the "we" passages of Acts, he claims that "both proposals have problems."[183] For him a major roadblock for the *Luke knew no more* perspective directly relates to my argument—that the "majority of scholars date Luke-Acts much later," which he relegates to 80–90 CE.[184] Unfortunately, it is all too common to parrot the political compromise 80–90 CE range (or later) as if it is a closed case.

If an early date of Acts can be maintained (or if a date range of 80–90 CE can be dismantled) then Troftgruben's argument breaks down and this roadblock can be

---

However, the end does relay many historical events relating to Paul in Rome in a well-detailed geographical context.

[179] It seems that he equates the final stage of the text with the critical editions NA/UBS.

[180] See Ropes, "Text of Acts," 3:i–cccxx, 1–371; Head, "Problem," 415–44; Porter, "Developments," 31–67; Delobel, "Luke-Acts," 83–107; Tuckett, "Early Text," 157–74, and more recently Armstrong, "Variants," 87–110.

[181] See "Principles for Selecting Events" in Chapter 2.

[182] Troftgruben, *Conclusion Unhindered*, 9. See also Wendt, *Die Apostelgeschichte* (8th edn), 31–2; Cadbury, *Luke-Acts*, 321, and more recently, Walasky, *Political Perspective*, 77. Troftgruben (10) challenges the idea that Luke ran out of sources after the final events in Acts since there is "no compelling evidence that Luke used sources for composing Acts." Although the identification of specific sources is a matter of ongoing debate very few (if any) scholars (historically or recently) would deny that Luke used sources; see Dupont, *Sources*; Porter, *Paul in Acts*, 10–46, and Chapter 3 of this volume.

[183] Troftgruben, *Conclusion Unhindered*, 9–10.

[184] Ibid., 10. He (10) also claims that the "Luke knew no more" view does "not explain why Luke did not 'finish' the book at a later date." This concern is only valid for a late date and many argue that the end of Acts did *not* need finishing, as Troftgruben himself maintains on the next page (11) when he says these "features show that the ending of Acts is hardly haphazard" (see also his conclusion: 179–88). There are several reasons why Luke did not or could not "finish" it at a "later date" (10). He may have (1) run out of sources or (2) died in Rome along with Peter or Paul as a result of Nero's persecution or (3) was otherwise inhibited or (4) that he was content to leave it as is. Cadbury's, *Luke-Acts*, 321, point in relation to the "omission caused by the abrupt end of Acts" is still valid. "Perhaps the author's information here came to an end. Then his source, whether his own information or the writings of others, must be credited with this abrupt silence."

safely removed allowing the ancient and un-enigmatic interpretation—that "Luke knew no more"—to be reinstated to its rightful place.[185] The other major roadblock for Troftgruben is the "ominous tone" of Paul's Miletus speech (Acts 20:17-38), the "several parallels to earlier material in the narrative,"[186] and a "concluding summary" (Acts 28:30-31) "like those found earlier in Acts" (5:14; 6:7; 9:31; 11:21; 16:5; and 19:20).[187] However, the Miletus speech does not present any significant barrier to an early date of Acts. The latter two points simply reflect Luke's writing style and only affirm that he was cognizant that he was writing a conclusion to his two-volume work.[188] An intentional ending should be no surprise given an intentional beginning.

Conclusion: The Un-Enigmatic End of Acts

As compelling and creative as the modern and contemporary interpretations are for the end of Acts, the consistent and most ancient interpretation concerning Luke's silence at the end of Acts seems to offer a more acceptable explanation and correlates with an early date.[189] It may seem trendy to bypass the hard questions of history in favour of narratological and theological concerns, but in the end there really needs to be a consideration of all three aspects of Luke as an author.[190] In Chapter 7, the ancient interpretation of Luke's silence is expanded into a study of the variants at the end of Acts that challenges the literary-critical solutions further still. But first, there is one further matter concerning the end of Acts that deserves our attention.

---

[185] Troftgruben, *Conclusion Unhindered*, 8 and (on page 9) admits the earliest approaches "make sense of the abruptness of Acts 28" and the "narrative's preoccupation with Paul" in Acts 20–28.
[186] Ibid., 11. He refers to Dupont, "La Conclusion," 359–404, and Puskas, *Conclusion* and other examples (see Troftgruben's note 12).
[187] Ibid., 11. As noted by Kirsopp Lake and Henry J. Cadbury, "The Acts of the Apostles: English Translation and Commentary," in *The Beginnings of Christianity*, 4:349.
[188] Troftgruben, *Conclusion Unhindered*, 11.
[189] According to Reinfandt, "Reading Texts," 51, the choice between "acceptable ('true') and unacceptable ('false') interpretations" remains a subjective, but necessary process.
[190] E.g., Puskas, *Conclusion*, 28. Haenchen, *Acts*, 90, explains that there is an "uncommonly close tie in Luke between theology, historiography and literary prowess." See further Ziemann and Dobson, "Introduction," 1–20, and my note 14 in Chapter 2.

6

The End of Acts and the Jewish Response

Introduction

Perhaps one of the most misinterpreted aspects in the history of end-of-Acts interpretation that directly impacts one's view on the date relates to Paul's engagement with the Jews in Acts 28:17-28.[1] Among the conflicting views, it is found that scholars fall into one of three general categories (with some overlap) that suggest some degree of Jewish condemnation, tragedy, or hope. A tragic or condemning interpretation tends to reflect a post-64 CE state of affairs where a more hopeful interpretation reflects a date before the Jewish War, the destruction of Jerusalem, and the Great Fire of Rome. Recent trends demonstrate a more hopeful prognosis than prior assessments with regard to Luke's attitude towards the Jews—and this is good news for those who date Acts early. This trend is supported by recent studies regarding the wisdom background for the text of Isa. 6:9-10 in light of the growing recognition and appreciation for an increasingly Jewish portrait of Paul in Acts.

For Tuckett, the subject of "Luke's attitude to Jews and/or Judaism" is "perhaps one of the most controversial in contemporary Lukan studies."[2] The post-Second World War reaction produced many overgeneralizations that are still repeated today, such as Haenchen who plainly states that "Luke has written the Jews off."[3] Meanwhile a less

---

[1] Little has changed since L. M. Wills's, "The Depiction of the Jews in Acts," *JBL* 110 (1991): 631, assessment that Luke's attitude towards the Jews has been "anything but clear in recent scholarship." This chapter is a modified version of an earlier essay. See Armstrong, "Jewish Response," 209–30.

[2] Christopher M. Tuckett, *Luke* (NTG; Sheffield: Sheffield Academic, 1996), 50.

[3] Ernst Haenchen, "The Book of Acts as Source Material for the History of Earliest Christianity," in *Studies in Luke-Acts* (eds. Leander E. Keck and J. Louis Martyn; Nashville: Abingdon, 1966), 278. Other scholars who echo this view include: O'Neill, *Theology of Acts*, 90; Rosemary R. Ruether, *Faith and Fratricide: The Theological Roots of Anti-Semitism* (New York: Seabury, 1974), 89; Jack T. Sanders, "The Jewish People in Luke-Acts," in *Luke-Acts and the Jewish People: Eight Critical Perspectives* (ed. J. B. Tyson; Minneapolis: Augsburg, 1988), 53; Michael J. Cook, "The Mission to the Jews in Acts: Unravelling Luke's 'Myth of the Myriads,'" in *Luke-Acts and the Jewish People: Eight Critical Perspectives* (ed. Joseph B. Tyson; Minneapolis: Augsburg, 1988), 122. Some also charge Luke with anti-Semitism: Jack T. Sanders, "The Salvation of the Jews in Luke-Acts," in *Luke-Acts: New Perspectives from the Society of Biblical Literature Seminar* (ed. C. H. Talbert; New York: Crossroad, 1984), 116; Cook, "Myriads," 123; Ruether, *Faith and Fratricide*, 64–116. See, more recently, Bonz, "Revision," 151; Pervo, *Acts*, 685, and Simon Butticaz, "'Has God Rejected His People?'" (Romans 11.1). The Salvation of Israel in Acts: Narrative Claim of a Pauline Legacy," in *Paul and the Heritage of Israel: Paul's Claim Upon Israel's Legacy in Luke and Acts in the Light of the Pauline Letters* (eds.

condemning rejection motif is promulgated by Tannehill as he concludes that Luke presents the Jews as "a tragic story."⁴ Given such a mélange of interpretation it is no surprise that Luke-Acts has come under "critical scrutiny in recent years."⁵

More recently, Keener explains that, against "many interpreters," Acts 28:16-31 "does not teach a final rejection of Israel."⁶ Like Immanuel, we ask similar questions: "What is Luke's position regarding the Jews in Acts? Is he anti-Jewish? Are the Jews lost forever, especially after Paul's quotation and interpretation of Isaiah in Acts 28:23-28?"⁷ Which view accurately reflects the story of Paul's engagement with the Jews in Acts 28:17-28? And how does such a view inform our understanding of the date of Acts?

This recent and notable shift in the interpretation concerning the Jewish response at the end of Acts directly impacts the dating debate. Views that see the Jews as condemned in Acts in general (and the end in particular) reflect a post-70 CE date of Acts where Jerusalem and its Temple are destroyed. This is also true for those who see the Jews in Acts as a "tragic" story rather than condemned completely. Conversely, a more hopeful view that sees evidence of a more favourable attitude towards the Jews in Acts and an acceptance of the gospel more accurately reflects a pre-70 CE date.⁸

At first glance, the end of Acts does seem to leave the reader on a "triumphant" note concerning the Gentile mission, but also a sense of "tragedy" or "condemnation" concerning a lack of Jewish response to Paul's gospel.⁹ While some emphasize the recurrent themes of Jewish rejection (or condemnation), others focus upon the success of the Gentile mission while remaining hopeful with regard to the Jewish response. Regardless, the common thread seems to be that the end of Acts formulates some kind of narrative climax that corresponds to a certain date of Acts—either Jewish *tragedy*, Gentile *triumph*, or at times a blend of both themes.

David P. Moessner et al.; LNTS 452; Luke the Interpreter of Israel 2; London: T&T Clark, 2012), 162. Still others claim that it is an "unjustified conclusion" that "God has abandoned his people because of their unbelief" which is the "first step towards Christian antisemitism." Dunn, *Acts*, xii.

⁴ Robert C. Tannehill, *The Shape of Luke's Story: Essays on Luke-Acts* (Eugene, OR: Cascade Books, 2005), 124; idem, "Israel in Luke-Acts: A Tragic Story," *JBL* 104 (1985): 69–85; idem, "Rejection by Jews and Turning to Gentiles: The Pattern of Paul's Mission," in *Luke-Acts and the Jewish People: Eight Critical Perspectives* (ed. K. H. Richards; Minneapolis: Augsburg, 1988), 130–41 and idem, *Narrative Unity, et passim*.

⁵ Tuckett, *Luke*, 50.

⁶ Keener, *Acts*, 4:3714 (see also 4:3718 and 2:2098); Tuckett, *Luke*, 62–4; E. P. Sanders, "Reflections on Anti-Judaism in the New Testament and in Christianity," in *Anti-Judaism and the Gospels* (ed. W. R. Farmer; Harrisburg, PA: Trinity Press International, 1999), 265–86; Babu Immanuel, *Repent and Turn to God: Recounting Acts* (Eugene, OR: Wipf & Stock, 2004), 157; Bock, *Acts*, 755, and more recently Jennings, *Acts*, 245.

⁷ Immanuel, *Repent*, 156. Cf. also Tuckett, *Luke*, 50–64; Butticaz, "Rejected," 162–3.

⁸ One of the reasons commonly cited for dating Acts early is the fact that the early Jerusalem church was still in contact with the Temple establishment, Synagogues, Pharisees, and Sadducees which would make a date of Acts after the Jewish rebellion in 66 CE difficult and incomprehensible after Jerusalem's destruction in 70 CE along with the Temple (cf. Chapter 1).

⁹ Troftgruben, *Conclusion Unhindered*, 26, states that many view the end of Acts as containing a "definitive theological message about the lack of response to the gospel by the Jews." E.g., Tannehill, "Tragic Story," 85.

Jewish Condemnation

There are several *degrees* as to how some interpret the so-called "tragic" response of Israel to the gospel at the end of Luke-Acts. The most severe is outright condemnation. Jack Sanders explains how the view that "Luke condemns 'the Jews'" and "'writes them off' is almost as old as critical New Testament scholarship."[10] The history goes back to Overbeck (= DeWette) who "took such a view" after rejecting the Tübingen school's explanation that the intention of Acts was to "reconcile apostolic Jewish Christianity and Pauline Gentile Christianity."[11]

A few decades later Loisy, contra Tübingen, continued Overbeck's view as did Haenchen in more recent times.[12] Haenchen picks up where Loisy left off, arguing that Paul's pronouncement to the Jews in Rome (Acts 28:28) represents a *final* rejection of the Jews who are replaced by the Gentiles, who will listen.[13] Following Haenchen, Conzelmann proposes that "Luke no longer counts on the success of the Christian mission with 'the Jews' . . . the situation with the Jews was hopeless."[14] Conzelmann also insists that the "turning away from the Jews and turning toward the Gentiles is final."[15]

It seems that Ruether, in a similar fashion to Haenchen and Conzelmann, also holds a condemning view.[16] Like Ruether, Sanders does not see much hope for the Jews in Luke-Acts.[17] One of his key arguments is that the verb πείθω ("to convince/persuade")

---

[10] Sanders, "Jewish People," 51–75 (53). It is clear that the conclusions of some in this camp are simply a repeat of the previous generation. For instance, the first four pages of Sanders's, "Jewish People," 51–4, argument reveals only four references that are not dependent upon Haenchen's viewpoint, and two of them—Wilhelm M. L. DeWette, Kurze Erklärung der Apostelgeschichte (ed. Franz Overbeck; 4th edn; Leipzig: Hirzel, 1870) and Loisy, *Actes*—are the progenitors of Haenchen's viewpoint. Recall my Chapter 2; Porter and Robinson, *Hermeneutics*, 10, and Rudolf Bultmann's dictum, *New Testament and Other Basic Writings* (ed. and trans. S. M. Ogden; Philadelphia: Fortress, 1984), 145, that "no exegesis is without presuppositions."

[11] Sanders, "Jewish People," 53. See also, Baur, *Paul*, 1:6; Dewette, *Apostelgeschichte*, xxxxxxi.

[12] Alfred Loisy, *Les évangiles synoptiques* (2 vols; Près Montier-en-Der: publ. by author, 1907), 2:652; idem, *Actes*, 118; and Ernst Haenchen, "Judentum und Christentum in der Apostelgeschichte," *ZNW* 54 (1963): 155–87.

[13] Haenchen, "Judentum und Christentum," 185 (see also 165–6, 171, 173–5).

[14] Conzelmann, *Acts*, 227.

[15] Ibid.

[16] Ruether, *Faith and Fratricide*, 64–116 (89–90). Ruether wrongly considers Acts 13:45-48 as a representative "formula in Acts for Jewish rejection versus gentile faith" (90). Ruether fails to include the greater context of Acts 13 where Paul not only addresses his fellow Israelites (v. 16), but also that "many of the Jews and devout proselytes followed Paul and Barnabas" (v. 43). They were also (in v. 43) "persuading them to continue in the grace of God" (ἔπειθον αὐτοὺς αὐτοὺς προσμένειν τῇ χάριτι τοῦ θεοῦ). Ruether further recounts Paul's situation where the "Jewish religious community of Rome confronts him" and explains how their "rejection of the gospel then constitutes the culminating 'rejection of the Jews' and 'election of the Gentiles'" (90). On the contrary, the end of Acts does not paint such a clear picture of Jewish rejection (cf. esp. Acts 28:24, 30).

[17] Sanders, "Salvation," 104, considers it the "standard view" that the Jews "no longer have the opportunity to accept the gospel" in Acts 28. See also, Jacob Jervell, *Luke and the People of God: A New Look at Luke-Acts* (Minneapolis: Augsburg, 1972), 44; Hans Conzelmann, *The Theology of St. Luke* (New York: Harper & Brothers, 1960), 163, and Haenchen, *Acts*. Sanders (108) works through the less "condemning" views of Jervell, *People of God*, 63, and E. Franklin, *Christ the Lord: A Study in the Purpose and Theology of Luke-Acts* (Philadelphia: Westminster, 1975), 114–15, who think that there is some hope for Israel and that "Paul's final statement is not a rejection of the Jews" (quotation is Franklin's). See also Sanders, "Jewish People," 52, who outlines the two main camps of opinion: some Jews accept while others do not, or Luke "condemns all the Jewish people collectively

rarely constitutes conversion.[18] While he provides only three examples (Acts 13:43; 18:4; and 28:23-24), it is also clear that his understanding of πείθω is deficient (cf. "Jewish Tragedy" below). He further claims that "there is precious little conversion to Christianity in the diaspora according to Acts."[19] This is strange, as he dismisses the evidence of the "great crowd of Jews" who "believed" in Borea and that of Acts 21:20.[20] Here the verb in question (πιστεύω) means "to believe something to be true and, hence, worthy of being trusted—to believe, to think to be true, to regard as trustworthy."[21] Therefore, the clause πόσαι μυριάδες εἰσὶν ἐν τοῖς Ἰουδαίοις τῶν πεπιστευκότων reads: "how [many] thousands are among the Jews [who] have believed."

Sanders also highlights the repeated "hostility of the Jewish people to the purposes of God" that is so "vehemently denounced" and presented "ad nauseam throughout the rest of Acts right up to the concluding scene."[22] He argues that the theme of Jewish rejection is entirely pervasive in the Gospel while culminating in the "most infamous act of rejection possible by murdering Jesus."[23] As some have pointed out, it is simply not true that Luke's gospel blames "the Jews" for the murder of Jesus.[24] Rather, Luke points to a narrower audience—the Jewish leadership as the ones responsible for Jesus's death (Lk. 22:1-6, 52, 66-71; 23:1, 2).[25]

There are scholars who still hold to this condemning view such as Bonz, who claims that Luke placed "a sharpened version of Paul's original words in the apostle's mouth at the very close of Luke-Acts."[26] Part of her thesis relies on the speculative premise that Luke had time to "rethink this problem from a considerably later and more wholly

---

for their obstinacy in the face of divine proffering of salvation and for their participation in the execution of Jesus."

[18] Sanders, "Salvation," 108.
[19] Ibid., 109.
[20] Ibid., 111; Cook, "Myriads," 102-23.
[21] L&N 31:35. Porter, *Verbal Aspect*, 260-70, suggests this heavily marked verb in the stative aspect represents a complex state of affairs. Further to this, the head term for this word group in Acts 21:20 is μυριάς which is a "very large number, not precisely defined" (BDAG). The interrogative πόσος is an "interrogative of quantity of objects or events, usually implying a considerable amount—how many" (L&N 59:5 and Rom. 11:12). Accordingly, πόσος defines (modifies) μυριάς ("thousands")—at the same time τῶν πεπιστευκότων (inflected = "believers") qualifies the scope of μυριάδες. The distributional preposition ἐν is the specifier (along with τοῖς) for the head term Ἰουδαίοις. See Karl L. Armstrong, "The Meaning of ὑποτάσσω in Ephesians 5:21-33: A Linguistic Approach," *JGRChJ* 13 (2017): 152-71, with regard to my linguistic framework.
[22] Sanders, "Salvation," 110. Cook, "Myriads," 122, is another proponent of the *condemning* view as he insinuates how Luke's argument is that the Jews essentially get what "they deserve and what retribution demands."
[23] Sanders, "Salvation," 116-17. See also idem, "Jewish People," and Cook, "Myriads," 123. This interpretation is a dangerous and unjustified misapplication of prophetic texts to other groups as noted by Mary C. Callaway, "A Hammer that Breaks Rock in Pieces: Prophetic Critique in the Hebrew Bible," in *Anti-Semitism and Early Christianity: Issues of Polemic and Faith* (eds. Craig A. Evans and Donald A. Hagner; Minneapolis: Fortress, 1993), 21-38 (esp. p. 38).
[24] Keener, *Acts*, 1:941-2.
[25] See Robert Maddox, *The Purpose of Luke-Acts* (SNTW; Edinburgh: T&T Clark, 1982), 45. Further to this point, Craig A. Evans, *To See and Not Perceive: Isaiah 6:9-10 in Early Jewish and Christian Interpretation* (JSOTSup 64; Sheffield: JSOT Press, 1989), 123-5, refutes the charge that Luke's use of Isa. 6:9-10 is anti-Semitic. He (123) points to Sanders's oversight of "intra-Jewish polemic and sectarian controversy" while noting the very real hatred the Pharisees had towards the Sadducees (cf. also 1 Enoch 38.5, 95.3; *m. Sanh.* 10.1, *b. Ber.* 58a).
[26] Bonz, "Revision," 143-51 (151).

Gentile perspective."[27] Bonz argues based on the "past tense" of ἀποστέλλω ("to send"), that "this last warning" turns "into a solemn pronouncement" (Acts 28:28).[28] However, in the Acts narrative, the Gentile *and* Jewish mission continues on (cf. Acts 28:30-31).[29] Bonz does not seem to consider this as she states in her conclusion: "With this pronouncement, Luke's narrative essentially ends, making Paul's words of judgment against Jewish unbelief no longer an interim reflection but the final word—and not only Paul's final word but God's final word as well."[30] Contrary to Bonz, the Acts narrative does not end until v. 31, which is "God's final word" in Luke-Acts.

Since then, Butticaz draws upon Bonz claiming that Acts 28:25-27 "appears to be the final judgement against the Jews who oppose the gospel."[31] Similarly, Pervo perceives "a shift toward invoking the passage [Acts 28:26-27=Isa. 6:9-10] to condemn the Jews in general."[32] This line of reasoning fails to account for (1) the grammatical issues discussed above, (2) the evidence for a mixed Jewish response in verse 24, (3) the inclusive and welcoming nature of verse 30, and especially (4) the wisdom background of Isa. 6:9-10 in light of (5) the Jewish portrait of Paul in Acts.[33]

Jewish Tragedy

This camp of scholars, though not as extreme as Jack Sanders et al., still interprets the end of Acts as some form of Jewish "tragedy" or rejection of the gospel.[34] Jervell

---

[27] Ibid., 151. Here the connection between date and interpretation is most evident. Earlier, O'Neill, *Theology of Acts*, 93, argued that Acts reflects "a theology which developed in the second century" (see also, Tyson, *Marcion*; Pervo, *Dating Acts*; and idem, *Acts*, 685). Bonz's (via O'Neill's and others') view is assumptive and precarious given the strong evidence for a much earlier date of Acts. See Mittelstaedt, *Lukas als Historiker*; Keener, *Acts*, 1:383–401; Porter, "Dating," 553–74; Schnabel, *Acts*, 27–8, 1062–3 and Armstrong, "A New Plea," (2017): 79–110.

[28] Bonz, "Revision," 151. This proposition suffers from a fatal neglect of the well-established research on Greek tense form and function. Cf. Frank Stagg, "The Abused Aorist," *JBL* 91 (1972): 222–31; Porter, *Verbal Aspect*, 29, 76–83, 98–102; Rodney J. Decker, *Temporal Deixis of the Greek Verb in the Gospel of Mark with Reference to Verbal Aspect* (SBG 10; New York: Peter Lang, 2001), 26. As the least marked tense, the aorist in Acts simply formulates the narrative background as noted by Martin M. Culy and Mikeal C. Parsons, *Acts: A Handbook on the Greek Text* (Waco, TX: Baylor University, 2003), xv–xvi. The meaning of verse 28 is such that the "gospel has been sent to the Gentiles *even* they will listen." The conjunction καὶ in this case is adverbial, giving the sense of "even" or "also." Cf. Porter, *Idioms*, 211.

[29] Troftgruben, *Conclusion Unhindered*, 127.

[30] Bonz, "Revision," 151.

[31] Butticaz, "Rejected," 162; Bonz, "Revision," 151.

[32] Pervo, *Acts*, 685.

[33] See Craig A. Evans, "The Text of Isaiah 6:9-10," *ZAW* 94 (1982): 415–18; C. A. Evans, "Isaiah 6:9-10 in Early Jewish and Christian Interpretation," (PhD diss., Claremont Graduate University, California, 1983); idem, *Perceive*; Barry M. Foster, "The Contribution of the Conclusion of Acts to the Understanding of Lucan Theology and the Determination of Lucan Purpose" (PhD diss.; Trinity International University, Illinois, 1997); Donald E. Hartley, *The Wisdom Background and Parabolic Implications of Isaiah 6:9-10 in the Synoptics* (StBibLit 100; New York: Peter Lang, 2006); John J. Kilgallen, "Acts 28, 28–Why?" *Bib* 90 (2009): 176–87; Rikki E. Watts, "Isaiah in the New Testament," in *Interpreting Isaiah: Issues and Approaches* (eds. D. G. Firth and H. G. M. Williamson; Downers Grove, IL: InterVarsity Press, 2009), 213–33; and Magnus Zetterholm, *Approaches to Paul: A Student's Guide to Recent Scholarship* (Minneapolis: Fortress, 2009), *et passim*.

[34] Jervell, *People of God*, 41–74, 63–9.

thinks that Luke has in effect declared an end to the Jewish mission—not because it was a failure, but because it was a success. Furthermore, Jervell thinks that the Isaiah quotation is directed to the unrepentant Jews only, so he does not see a problem per se because there are "repentant" Jews who do accept the Christian message.[35]

Since then, Tyson, who engages Jervell, provides an overview for understanding the fundamental problem of why the Jews are portrayed in Acts the way they are.[36] He is certain that this problem is, to a large extent, tied to the end of Acts along with the major themes throughout the book.[37] He explains that "Luke-Acts must also deal with a historical problem, namely the problem that most Jews did not become Christians."[38] Tyson's perspective offers a tragic, but less condemning view when it comes to the difficulties apparent in Acts 28. With regard to Paul's second meeting with the Jews (Acts 28:24), he admits that "the reaction of the Jews is not one of total rejection, but of partial acceptance."[39] He also notes the important difference (and distance created) between Paul's use of "our" vs "your ancestors" (28:17, 25) as well as the debate on ἐπείθοντο (Acts 28:24).

Tyson relays Bruce's caution that "the imperf. does not necessarily imply that they were actually persuaded."[40] Likewise, Tannehill thinks that some of Paul's hearers "were in process of being persuaded but had made no lasting decision."[41] Meanwhile, Williams (based on the imperfect tense) thinks that the "possibility remains that the process of conversion went on until some were converted."[42] Still others argue they were in fact "persuaded," which can be substantiated through a linguistically informed understanding of tense, mood, and aspect.[43] The verb πείθω here in the imperfective aspect means "to convince someone to believe something and to act on the basis of what is recommended—to persuade, to convince."[44] If πείθω does not connote persuasion, then the clause οἱ δὲ ἠπίστουν (which is directly dependent upon the previous clause) would not make any sense.[45] Therefore, it seems to me that there are substantial reasons here to mitigate the level of Jewish rejection.

---

[35] Ibid., 63–9.
[36] Joseph B. Tyson, "The Problem of Jewish Rejection in Acts," in *Luke-Acts and the Jewish People: Eight Critical Perspectives* (ed. J. B. Tyson; Minneapolis: Augsburg, 1988), 124–37.
[37] Tyson suggests that "almost all scholars agree" that Paul's meeting with the Jews in Acts 28:17-28 represents a "narrative event of special prominence" but some consider this to be a "special problem" because Paul "rejects Jews in a way that is incompatible" with earlier themes in Acts. See Tyson, "Jewish Rejection," 124.
[38] Idem, *Images of Judaism in Luke-Acts* (Columbia: University of South Carolina Press, 1992), 182.
[39] Ibid., 175. Idem, "Jewish Rejection," 137, considers both acceptance and rejection motifs in Luke-Acts and shows that while Luke "ends with Paul preaching the gospel in Rome, 'openly and unhindered' (Acts 28:31), not far from his mind is the rejection by that final group of Jews Paul tried to convince." Hence, he (137) considers the "problem of Jewish rejection" to be "more significant than the story of Gentile acceptance." His concluding viewpoint is that "the mission to the Jews has been a failure" (137) and later he says "it has been terminated" (latter quotation is from Tyson, *Images*, 176).
[40] Bruce, *Acts* (3rd edn), 540. Tyson, *Images*, 180. Bruce (540) takes ἐπείθοντο (Acts 28:24) in the sense that they "gave heed."
[41] Tannehill, *Narrative Unity*, 2:347. Marshall, *Acts*, 444–5, also notes a lack of a definitive conversion.
[42] Williams, *Acts*, 453.
[43] Evans, *Perceive*, 125–6; Longenecker, *Acts*, 570.
[44] L&N 33:301.
[45] Additionally, the imperfective aspect suggests that the "convincing" is "in progress" while the indicative mood of the verb is used to "grammaticalize simple assertions about what the writer

According to other Jewish *tragedy* proponents like Maddox, the end of Luke-Acts reveals a negative "anti-Jewish orientation" where "the Jews are excluded."[46] Although Maddox recognizes that "many Jews became disciples of Jesus" and "many others became believers in him," Luke "nevertheless stands over against Judaism as an organized community, which he regards as unbelieving."[47] For Maddox, the final scene of Acts presents a clear contrast between "Isaiah's words to 'this people'" (v. 26) and "the Gentiles, who 'will actually listen'" (v. 28).[48]

Tannehill is perhaps the best known and often quoted proponent of the Jewish rejection/tragedy motif in Luke-Acts.[49] The following is a summary of his viewpoint: "Jewish rejection dominates the final scene in Acts and is emphasized in other major scenes of the narrative. The story of Israel, so far as the author of Luke-Acts can tell it, is a tragic story."[50] Tannehill explains that since this theological problem is given so much weight in the Acts narrative (as it was in Rom. 9-11), this "is a sign of the importance of scriptural promises to the Jewish people for the implied author."[51] Although he promotes a Jewish rejection motif in Acts, he does offer some glimmer of hope for the Jews.[52]

There are a few other scholars who fit into the tragedy camp such as Pao who claims that in Lk. 4:16-30 the "dawn of the new age as characterized by the Isaianic New

---

or speaker sees as reality, whether or not there is a factual basis for such an assertion." See Porter, *Idioms*, 21 and 51 respectively; and also idem, *Verbal Aspect*, 163-77. While πείθω occurs fifty-two times in the NT, it occurs four times in Luke (11:22; 16:31; 18:9; 20:6) and seventeen times in Acts (5:36-37, 39; 12:20; 13:43; 14:19; 17:4; 18:4; 19:8; 19:26; 21:14; 23:21; 26:26, 28; 27:11; 28:23-24). In every single case the context suggests the persuasion produced some kind of action or result. For example, Acts 14:19 graphically suggests that the crowd was amply persuaded (πείσαντες τοὺς ὄχλους)—enough to stone and almost kill Paul! Therefore, it seems clear in Acts 28:24a that the basic sense of οἱ μὲν ἐπείθοντο τοῖς λεγομένοις is that "some were convinced by what he said."

[46] Maddox, *Purpose*, 42-3. Maddox does highlight the positive Gentile theme, especially the last two verses, but observes the Jewish rejection throughout (citing Haenchen and Conzelmann).

[47] Ibid., 46.

[48] Ibid.

[49] For example, Tannehill is cited at least eleven times by Peterson, *Acts*, 717-25, on the last few verses of Acts. Peterson (717) reproduces Tannehill's view as he claims how this "final statement about the Jewish lack of response to the gospel is certainly pessimistic."

[50] Tannehill, *Shape*, 124. See also idem, "Tragic Story," 69-85, and idem, *Narrative Unity*, 2:354-7. Tannehill, *Shape*, 145, highlights the "increasing emphasis on Jewish rejection in the Pauline portions of Acts" which represents a grand theological problem for Tannehill (see also *Shape*, xvi, 145-65 and "Rejection," 130-41).

[51] Tannehill, *Shape*, 145. The role of an "implied author" also implies the concept of an "implied reader" which is an important but debated concept; see Wayne C. Booth, *The Rhetoric of Fiction* (2nd edn; Chicago: University of Chicago Press, 1983), 137-40; Susan R. Suleiman, "Introduction: Varieties of Audience-Orientated Criticism," in *The Reader in the Text: Essays on Audience and Interpretation* (eds, S. R. Suleiman and I. Crosman; PLL 617; Princeton: Princeton University Press, 1980), 3-45; and also Jane P. Tompkins, "An Introduction to Reader Response Criticism," in *Reader-Response Criticism: From Formalism to Post-structuralism* (ed. Jane P. Tompkins; Baltimore: Johns Hopkins University Press, 1980), ix-xxvi. Troftgruben, *Conclusion Unhindered*, 42, via Robert M. Fowler, "Who is 'The Reader' in Reader Response Criticism?," *Semeia* 31 (1985),13, raises the question as to what degree do "texts influence (direct, control, manipulate) readers?" and vice versa (see n. 20). Troftgruben (43) observes how "texts are scarcely without influence in the reading process." Additionally, Mikeal C. Parsons and Richard I. Pervo, *Rethinking the Unity of Luke and Acts* (Minneapolis: Fortress, 1993), 77-8, explain the inherent problem of "identifying an implied author with a real historical author"—especially with regard to the "implied author of Acts" and of Luke.

[52] Tannehill, *Narrative Unity*, 2:357.

Exodus is announced" and in Acts 28:25-28 the "rejection of the prophetic movement by the Jews is noted by a lengthy quotation from Isaiah 6."[53] He substantiates the "connection between the rejection by the Jews and the mission to the Gentiles" by appealing to Acts 13:46, 18:6b and 28:28.[54] Last, Puskas presents a similar tragic view that goes back to O'Neill.[55] Although such perspectives present the Jewish rejection motifs in a more balanced manner than the previous group of scholars, they do not seem to factor many examples of Jewish conversion and acceptance.

Jewish Hope

While the first two groups interpret the Jewish response at the end of Acts with varying levels of doom, this group is more hopeful and does not consider the issue to be a closed case. For example, Skarsaune explains that the mission to the Jews is not finished—and the patristic evidence further points to this fact.[56] Likewise, Marshall is optimistic and does not consider the Jewish rejection to be final.[57] Meanwhile, Soards notes how the "results of Paul's efforts were mixed, and as they [the Jews] quarrelled among themselves Paul had the last word, which he spoke to those who disbelieved."[58] He also notices how in "form and function the concluding remarks, vv. 25b-28, are comparable to 13:46-47; 18:6, but these verses are generally similar to other polemical remarks made in speeches" (see Acts 7:4b).[59] Consequently, here he argues against

---

[53] David W. Pao, *Acts and the Isaianic New Exodus* (WUNT 2/130; Tübingen: Mohr Siebeck, 2000), 109. He explains how "the early Christian community" is "the true heir of the Israelite traditions" (Pao, *New Exodus*, 37–69 [here 69]). See also his concluding chapter: "The Transformation of the Isaianic Vision: The Status of the Nations/Gentiles" (217–48).

[54] Ibid., 243. Here, Pao (243 [n. 88]) leaves a (small) window open for the Jewish mission (cf. also Porter, *Paul in Acts*, 186; Tannehill, "Rejection," 83–101). With regard to the end of Acts, Pao (104) declares that the "theme of the rejection of the Christian message by the Jews reaches its climax" (along with Tannehill, this is repeated by Peterson, *Acts*, 716–18). This view is not new as O'Neill, *Theology of Acts*, 90, explained how the "Church is shown to be at last facing the destiny to which God was leading it, by finally turning from the Jews to the Gentiles" (see also 93).

[55] Puskas, *Conclusion*, 116 (n. 35), argues that the "Jewish indifference to Paul's preaching" is because of the "traditional disobedience of the Jews reflected in the unbelief of their fathers to the message of the prophets" (see also 112–14, 127; Acts 7:51-53; 28:25b-28; Lk. 6:22-23; 11:47-50; 13:33-34; O'Neill, *Theology of Acts*, 76 (n. 1), and Franklin, *Christ the Lord*, 114–15. Puskas, *Conclusion*, 137–40, rests most of his conclusions upon the success of the gospel and the Gentile mission in Rome.

[56] Oskar Skarsaune, "The Mission to the Jews—A Closed Chapter?," in *The Mission of the Early Church to Jews and Gentiles* (eds. J. Ådna and H. Kvalbein; WUNT 127; Tübingen: Mohr Siebeck, 2000), 82.

[57] Marshall, *Acts*, 445. He refers to Rom. 11:25-32 and suggests that this indicates that Paul was looking "for a change of heart on their part in due time." Cf. also his note on Lk. 13:35 in idem, *The Gospel of Luke* (NIGTC; Exeter: Paternoster, 1978), 577. Peterson, *Acts*, 719 (n. 105), disagrees (re: Acts 28:28) and states that Marshall has misread "the text in its context . . . and that he is missing the point of Acts 28:30-31" (however, Peterson [as noted above] is heavily influenced by Tannehill).

[58] Marion L. Soards, *The Speeches in Acts: Their Content, Context, and Concerns* (Louisville: Westminster/John Knox, 1994), 131.

[59] Ibid., 132. Maddox, *Purpose*, 44, holds a contrary view where the verses are "not merely parallel: there is a progressive intensification of the theme" [cf. also Soards, *Speeches*, 132]). However, Soards (132) further reasons via David P. Moessner, "Paul in Acts: Preacher of Eschatological Repentance to Israel," *NTS* 34 (1988): 96–104, that here there is a clear Jewish "eschatological remnant illustrating non-believing Israel's peril but also the continuing possibility of repentance and belief."

"those readings of Acts which find the door to salvation closed to Israel at the end of Acts."[60]

Others have also challenged the rejection motifs in favour of a more hopeful interpretation. Gempf explains how it is "completely unlikely" that the story of Paul in Rome is an "attempt by Luke to disown any continuing attempts to evangelize the Jews."[61] Gempf further contends that a more "careful reading of the story" shows that "Christianity has not rejected the Jews, although Jews have rejected Christianity."[62] Meanwhile, Litwak compares Rom. 11 and Acts 28:16-31 and proposes that "both Pauls agree on several points regarding Jewish response to the gospel."[63] At the end of Acts, Litwak sees Paul "as an Israelite: at one with the people of Israel and in sympathy with them and the customs of the fathers."[64] He estimates that this account should "not be read as a final, decisive rejection for Jews as a whole, as that is contrary to the pattern already established in Acts and the first half of Acts 28:24."[65] If anything, the end of Acts offers a message of hope and reconciliation.

The popular *tragic* Jewish position proposed by Tannehill has recently been challenged by O'Toole.[66] In his rebuttal, O'Toole highlights Luke's narration of Paul's loyalty to Judaism in Acts (i.e., Acts 21:24).[67] He contends that Luke actually redefines Israel,[68] and that the statement "about salvation for the Gentiles in v. 28 does not diminish the openness of v. 31."[69] In his conclusion O'Toole argues that the "structure of Acts 28:16-31 surely emphasizes the quotation from Isaiah" but the emphasis rests on "salvation being sent to the gentiles" (v. 28) and Paul's "freedom to receive and

---

[60] Soards, *Speeches*, 132.
[61] Gempf, "Reception," 59. He (60) refers to the inclusive "all" found in Acts 28:30 and Paul's pattern of going to the Synagogue first.
[62] Ibid., 60. He (63) is optimistic in the sense that the Jews in Rome are not as "anti-Christian as we might have expected. Instead, to our surprise, they seem quite open and even interested."
[63] Kenneth Litwak, "One or Two Views of Judaism: Paul in Acts 28 and Romans 11 on Jewish Unbelief," *TynBul* 57 (2006): 229. He infers (229) that the historical Paul and the Paul of Luke "see a mixed response among Jews, the developing of a faithful remnant, and in both texts 'provoking to jealousy' is a critical element."
[64] Litwak, "Judaism," 232. He argues against Barrett that Acts 13:46 does not represent "'a decisive and radical turning-point in Paul's mission'... The Jews are never abandoned, but the rejection of the gospel by some of them 'provided the occasion,' though not the cause, for the mission to the Gentiles" (Litwak [233] cites Barrett, *Acts*, 657). Litwak (233) posits that Acts 28:24 and 28:30 "frame the citation from Isaiah 6 and indicate that some, including Jews, continue to respond positively to Paul's preaching" (see also Witherington, *Acts*, 804).
[65] Ibid., 233. Litwak (234) sees the last scene with Paul in Acts as a mixed response while challenging the prevalent view that "Paul will no longer preach to Jews at all" (237-9; Acts 28:28). He does this (and I think successfully) by noting the problems of this view against the background of Paul's expressed desire in Romans 11 "to continue to win Jews to an acceptance of Jesus" (237; Acts 17:2).
[66] Robert F. O'Toole, "The Christian Mission and the Jews at the End of Acts of the Apostles," in *Biblical Exegesis in Progress: Old and New Testament Essays* (eds. J. L. Ska and J. N. Aletti; AnBib 176; Rome: Editrice Pontificio Istituto Biblico, 2009), 371-96 (372). He (372) refers to Barrett, *Acts*, 1246, who writes in response to Tannehill, saying this "seems to be too simple an analysis of Acts."
[67] O'Toole, "End of Acts," 378. O'Toole (373) uses composition criticism (vs Tannehill's narrative criticism) which is a "specification of redaction criticism." The purpose of this method is to "determine what the final author (editor) wanted to say to his readers or, if one wishes, what the present text tells us" (372).
[68] Ibid., 376-9.
[69] Ibid., 382-3.

preach to all of his visitors" (vv. 30-31).⁷⁰ The purpose of Isa. 6:9-10 at the end of Acts relates to "God's guiding what happens and challenges the Roman Jews and Luke's reader to value rightly the Christian message."⁷¹

Troftgruben also challenges those who see the end of Acts as a final blow to the Jews. First, he states that throughout Acts Paul "makes a concentrated effort to minister to Jews, a practice that he continues in the ending" (Acts 28:17).⁷² Second, he highlights the mixed response of the Jews to Paul's preaching (vv. 24-25a).⁷³ Third, although Troftgruben considers the Isaiah quotation (28:26-27) to be "forceful," the purpose "may be aimed at generating a response from the hearers (i.e., repentance) rather than finalizing their rejection."⁷⁴ His fourth point relates to the "all" inclusive nature of Paul's welcoming in Acts 28:30-31.⁷⁵ He concludes by stating that the "message of Acts 28:16-31 concerning the Jews appears more ambiguous than decisive."⁷⁶ I heartily agree with Troftgruben and the other scholars who see in Luke's narrative a more hopeful and reconciliatory theme that seems to be entirely reflective of a pre-70 date of Acts.

Isaiah 6:9-10 in Light of the Jewish Portrait of Paul in Acts

Two additional factors need to be taken into consideration with regard to the interpretation of the Jewish response at the end of Acts. The first is the notoriously

---

⁷⁰ Ibid., 392.

⁷¹ Ibid., 392.

⁷² Troftgruben, *Conclusion Unhindered*, 27.

⁷³ Ibid., 27. Spencer, *Acts*, 239, and Alexander, *Ancient*, 215, similarly emphasize the mixed response of the Jews. Elsewhere Troftgruben (126) notes how "many features of Acts 28:16-31 call into question the idea that vv. 25b-28 conclude all hope for the Jews" based on the fact that there are "Jews still being persuaded by the message of Jesus" (127; Acts 28:24). Here there appears to be some crossover with Tannehill, *Narrative Unity*, 2:347, who "indicates that there is still hope of convincing some Jews in spite of what Paul is going to say about the Jewish community in Rome."

⁷⁴ Troftgruben, *Conclusion Unhindered*, 27. See also 127–30 and Loveday C. A. Alexander, "Reading Luke-Acts from Back to Front: The Unity of Luke-Acts," in *The Unity of Luke-Acts* (ed. J. Verheyden; BETL 142; Leuven: Leuven University Press, 1999), 442. Troftgruben (27 [n. 72]) explains how Paul's "turning" to the Gentiles (Acts 13:46-47; 18:6) is "followed by continued ministry among the Jews. If Paul has not followed through by decisively abandoning the Jewish people earlier in the narrative, is there anything to indicate that he will do so here (cf. 28:30-31)?" As a result, the point of Acts 28:25b-28 is "to sense the tragedy of Paul's words" (130).

⁷⁵ Troftgruben, *Conclusion Unhindered*, 27-8. See also Richard J. Cassidy, "Paul's Proclamation of Lord Jesus as a Chained Prisoner in Rome: Luke's Ending is in His Beginning," in *Luke-Acts and Empire: Essays in Honor of Robert L. Brawley* (eds. David Rhoads et al.; PTMS 151; Eugene, OR: Pickwick, 2011), 147, and Jennings, *Acts*, 246, who nicely captures the Spirit of the Isaiah text from the viewpoint of Jewish hope. Strangely enough, it seems that many advocates of the *condemnation* camp either bypass or argue against the inclusive elements in Acts 28. It was Dupont, "La Conclusion," 377, who previously corrected Haenchen's, *Acts*, 726, and others' view that v. 30 could not include the Jews. Here Dupont considers a restrictive interpretation of πάντας unjustified. In Acts 28:30 the adjective πάντας (here in predicate structure) clearly denotes an extensive use which is "often translated all" (Porter, *Idioms*, 119). It appears that Dupont is correct—especially since "all" the major translations similarly reflect this extensive use. Some scholars (i.e., Bonz, "Revision," 151 [n. 31]) seem to have missed Dupont's dated (but correct) observation.

⁷⁶ Troftgruben, *Conclusion Unhindered*, 28.

complex nature of the Isaiah passage found in Acts 28:26-27 (Isa. 6:9-10), and second is the Jewish background of Paul in Acts.[77] Starting with the first issue, Evans comments on how Luke's inclusion of Isa. 6:9 "Go to this people, and say" is "particularly appropriate" due to the overall missionary tone of Acts.[78] Subsequently, Evans claims that according to Luke "what prompted Paul's recitation of this Old Testament text was the response of unbelief" (Acts 28:24).[79] Accordingly, the thrust of the text is no longer about the "threat of final hardening, but is a promise of ultimate forgiveness."[80]

Beyond the hope of Israel motif, the often misunderstood fattening (or hardening) motif of Isa. 6:9-10 is also vital for understanding its purpose in the context of the New Testament in general, and the end of Acts in particular.[81] Hartley explains how this text (Isa. 6:9-10) "which is part of the commissioning of Isaiah, is most likely programmatic for the entire prophecy."[82] Hartley examines the hermeneutical and philosophical underpinnings of many interpretations and discovers that they are loaded with presuppositions.[83] He finds that Isa. 6:9-10 "outlines divine fattening of the

---

[77] Hartley, *Wisdom Background*, xiii, admits that Isa. 6:9-10 "by any definition or estimation, is a difficult text to understand."

[78] Evans, *Perceive*, 121. Evans (115) observes how the first appearance of Isa. 6:9-10 in Luke-Acts is a paraphrase of Mk 4:12 (Lk. 8:10b) while the second quote (which is roughly based on the LXX) appears in Acts 28:26-27 (cf. Bock, *Acts*, 755, as he notes the exceptions). Evans (121) explains (that Luke's use of the LXX here is not significant because that is "the only version of the Old Testament that the Evangelist ever uses" (see also Pao, *New Exodus*, 103).

[79] Evans, *Perceive*, 121. In other words, Paul (in v. 25) is addressing the unbelievers in v. 24: "The Holy Spirit was right in saying to your fathers through Isaiah the prophet." Afterwards, in v. 28 Paul subsequently "admonishes his fellow unbelieving Jews" when he states: "Let it be known to you that this salvation of God has been sent to the Gentiles, they will listen." Evans, *Perceive*, 121. Likewise, Spencer, *Acts*, 240, claims that "Paul links his present audience with '*your* [rebellious] ancestors' whom Isaiah denounced—thus distancing himself from '*our* ancestors' whom he had openly embraced in the previous scene" (original emphasis; cf. also Bock, *Acts*, 755 and Acts 28:17, 25). After explaining Paul's Jew first program, Spencer (240) claims that since the "days of Isaiah up to the time of Paul, God's gracious plan to save Jews as well as Gentiles has remained in force. Prophetic warnings have always been designed to prepare God's people for renewal; judgement leads to hope—the 'hope of Israel.' There is no reason to think that this hope has suddenly been abandoned at the end of Acts."

[80] The Rabbis indicate that Isa. 6:9-10 [=1QIsaa] "implies the gracious extension of a final offer of repentance." Evans, "Isaiah 6:9-10," 418. More recently, Kilgallen, "Acts 28, 28–Why," 186, similarly proposes that Acts 28:26-28 is "a speech ordered to repentance and faith" and is "not a condemnation or abandonment of Jews." Cf. also the similar conclusion of "repentance" in Geoffrey D. Robinson, "The Motif of Deafness and Blindness in Isaiah 6:9-10: A Contextual, Literary, and Theological Analysis," *BBR* 8 (1998): 186. Butticaz nuances his position by explaining that Acts 28:27b reflects a similar pronouncement of a "salvation for Israel" that is "peppered throughout the diptych of Luke-Acts" (see Butticaz, "Rejected," 162–3, and Lk. 13:34-35; 21:24; Acts 3:21).

[81] Since Hartley's thesis (*Wisdom Background*, xiii) is on the "congenital nature of the fatness of the heart" his insights illuminate this particularly complex issue. Hartley (24) refers to Evans's 1983 thesis as a "watershed work on obduracy and the use of Isa. 6:9-10" (refer also to Foster, "Contribution," for his extensive treatment of Isa. 6:9-10 in Acts 28:23-28).

[82] Hartley, *Wisdom Background*, 1. The fact that Isa. 6:9-10 appears at critical junctures throughout the NT further confirms its significance (1). Hartley (24) points to Romans 9–11 and Heb. 3:8, 13, 15; 4:7 and suggests that "Jewish hardening . . . serves as a warning to Christians who can harden themselves and suffer the same fate . . . The hardening of Isa. 6:9-10 serves the same purpose for believers in the NT (Acts 28)."

[83] Ibid., 55. He claims that the historical and philosophical question of freedom is the central bias that impacts the interpreter's view of this passage: "this view of freedom is usually unstated, seldom critically examined, yet serves as a guiding hermeneutic that dictates how Isa. 6:9-10, and passages like it, can or cannot be construed" (97). If we are convinced that Acts portrays a separation between

heart as a prevention of perception, knowledge, and understanding."[84] Therefore this "fattening of the heart" represents the identification of a deprivation in wisdom where the purpose is not to condemn the Jews and "write them off."[85] Consequently, Luke's concluding remark is simply a reflection of the "church's experience in general, and of the Pauline mission in particular"—certainly nothing that justifies a condemning view towards the Jews at the end of Acts.[86]

A secondary issue relates to "Paul and Judaism" in Acts, or as E. P. Sanders explains "should one not say, 'Paul and *the rest* of Judaism,' since Paul himself is surely Jewish?"[87] Niebuhr rightly claims that Paul (during his last years in Roman custody) was "regarded as a Jew by those who came to see him in prison."[88] At the same time, Paul also "considered himself a Jew" aside from his view of Christ as the "only judge he would have to confront" and "not the emperor."[89] Paul's letters also reveal that he clearly thought of himself as thoroughly Jewish (i.e., Phil. 3:5-6).[90] Concurrently, Paul (according to Luke) states: "I am a Jew, born in Tarsus of Cilicia, but brought up in this city, educated under Gamaliel, strictly according to the law of our fathers, being zealous for God just as you all are today" (Acts 22:3; cf. also Acts 21:39). With regard to Acts, the portrait of Paul is thoroughly Jewish.[91]

Therefore, if there is an anti-Jewish or literary plan in Acts to present the Jews as a rejected or condemned people, which would substantiate a post-70 CE context, why is Paul consistently presented as not only a Jew but as a Jewish (Christian) *hero* in Acts? Luke gives priority to the Jewish mission city after city, synagogue after synagogue—something which accurately reflects the missional impulse of Paul and "prevails all the way to its close" (Acts 3:26; 13:46; 17:2, 11, 12; 28:17-31).[92] At the same time, Luke (in

---

Paul and Judaism, paired with a growing and consistent theme of Jewish rejection, then naturally the Isaiah passage will be presented as the final blow (the reverse is also true). Melanie Johnson-DeBaufre, "Historical Approaches: Which Past? Whose Past?," in *Studying Paul's Letters* (ed. J. A. Marchal; Minneapolis: Fortress, 2012), 18, is correct in that "what we see depends on where you stand."

[84] Hartley, *Wisdom Background*, 98. Along with hearing and seeing, these terms "serve as a circumlocution for *the prevention of wisdom*" (98; original emphasis).

[85] Haenchen, "Source Material," 278.

[86] Evans, *Perceive*, 121.

[87] E. P. Sanders, *Paul and Palestinian Judaism: A Comparison of Patterns of Religion* (Philadelphia: Fortress, 1977), 1 (original emphasis); see also Pamela Eisenbaum, "Jewish Perspectives: A Jewish Apostle to the Gentiles," in *Studying Paul's Letters* (ed. J. A. Marchal; Minneapolis: Fortress, 2012), 135–54.

[88] Karl-Wilhelm Niebuhr, "Roman Jews under Nero: Personal, Religious, and Ideological Networks in Mid-First Century Rome," in *The Last Years of Paul: Essays from the Tarragona Conference, June 2013* (eds. Armand Puig i Tàrrech et al.; WUNT 352; Tübingen: Mohr Siebeck, 2015), 89.

[89] Niebuhr, "Roman Jews," 89.

[90] Porter, *Apostle*, 27, relays how Paul at "several places in his letters . . . chronicles his ethnic and religious background in Judaism." See also Porter's seven reasons (pp. 27–30).

[91] Paul is a devout Jew even if we factor the incident where Jews from Asia had falsely accused him and had him arrested in Jerusalem (Acts 21:27-36). See Porter, *Apostle*, 48. The issue that led to his arrest relates to the assumption by the Jews from Asia (v. 27) that Paul was teaching heresy and had brought "Trophimus the Ephesian" into the Temple (v. 29)—they were not calling into question Paul's Jewish identity. The nature of the accusation reinforces the fact that they considered Paul to be Jewish; otherwise there would be no point in accusing a gentile of heresy. While noting the complexities Keener, *Acts*, 3:3150, explains that Paul is a "*Jewish* Roman citizen and so could not be accused of profaning the temple by his own presence" (emphasis original). See also Keener's discussion on the accusation (3:3144–50).

[92] Butticaz, "Rejected," 160.

Acts) emphasizes Paul's "Jew first principle" (i.e., Rom. 1:16; 9:1-5; 10:1) that was not without results.[93] Finally, beyond the text, the archaeological record indicates that the Jewish response to the gospel in Rome was quite substantial.[94]

Conclusion: The End of Acts and the Jewish Response

It seems there are far greater reasons to see Luke's attitude towards the Jews in Acts and their response at the end as a far more hopeful situation than is often painted by the first group of (condemnation) scholars who overgeneralize the issue of Jewish rejection to the neglect of complex evidence.[95] Although the second (tragedy) group of scholars approach the rejection motifs in a more balanced and less extreme fashion than the former, there is still a tendency to overplay the rejection motif while minimizing the clear cases of Jewish acceptance. The condemnation and rejection motifs are further deflated by an understanding of the wisdom background of Isa. 6:9-10 in light of the Jewish portrait of Paul in Acts. The real Jewish "tragedy" from the perspective of Acts 28 is that some, but not all, rejected Paul's message of salvation, as many Gentiles did as well.

It seems that the best interpretation envisions a mixed but hopeful Jewish response at the end of Acts; and this is consistent with a pre-70 CE date of Acts. Otherwise how can we reconcile the picture of a Jewish Paul consistently and, in many cases, successfully reaching out to his kinsmen immediately after his conversion in Damascus (Acts 9:20) to the last verse in Rome (Acts 28:31) with the destruction of the Temple and the wholesale slaughter of his fellow Jews in Jerusalem?[96] The incredibly macabre picture of Rome in ashes, along with the multitudes of Christians that were killed under Nero in 64 CE makes a later date for Acts increasingly difficult to maintain. Luke is a skillful writer but it seems highly improbable that we can reconcile this hopeful and peaceful portrait at the end of Acts with a post-64 CE historical context.

---

[93] For example, in Thessalonica it was Paul's εἰωθὸς ("custom") as he went "into the synagogue, and on three Sabbath days he reasoned with them from the Scriptures" (Acts 17:2). See also Spencer, *Acts*, 240; Gempf, "Reception," 60, and Troftgruben, *Conclusion Unhindered*, 27 (n. 72). That Paul was rejected from the synagogue is no indication that he was not Jewish. The problem was that he was teaching an aberration of Judaism (Acts 21:28).

[94] Although NT scholarship views the church in Rome as predominantly gentile the material evidence points to another reality. Within the confines of Rome is the XIV Augustan region known as "Trastevere" where Jews are known to have lived since the first century CE. Lampe states "with great certainty" that Trastevere is also "an early Christian residential quarter" (cf. Lampe, *Valentinus*, 42 [also 38, 44–5]). Given that Roman Christianity likely "emerged from the Roman synagogues" it is entirely plausible that many of the Jews who lived in this region converted to Christianity (Acts 28:24a). See Lampe, "Roman Christians," 117, and also my Chapter 8.

[95] For example, Evans, *Perceive*, 123–4, bluntly states how "[J.] Sanders does not fail to assess the items adequately; *he does not address them at all*" (emphasis added).

[96] See Chapter 8.

7

The End of Acts and the Comparable Age of Its Variants

Introduction

As we have seen in the last two chapters, the end of Acts provides no shortage of discussion and debate.[1] While the two most recent monographs on this subject have suggested narrative and literary-critical solutions for the ending, many of the historical and textual matters remain unaddressed.[2] Their efforts have in some ways advanced scholarship, but one critical aspect of the so-called enigma has remained untouched—the textual variants of Acts 28.[3] Scholars who rely solely on the "text" of Acts found in the Nestle-Aland (or UBS) are limiting themselves to one set of manuscripts while excluding the "Western" and other textual variations.[4] These variants, however we

---

[1] This chapter (including the Appendix) is a modified version of Armstrong, "Variants," 87–110.
[2] E.g., Troftgruben, *Conclusion Unhindered* and Puskas, *Conclusion*.
[3] My methodology here draws from classical and recent approaches to papyrology and textual criticism (recall "Principles for Sources and Textual Criticism" from Chapter 2). As far as papyrology, interpretation, and the transcription of the texts, my manuscript research draws from the INTF database and the examples found in Stanley E. Porter and Wendy J. Porter's, *New Testament Greek Papyri and Parchments: New Editions: Texts* (Mitteilungen aus der Papyrussammlung der Österreichischen Nationalbibliothek [Papyrus Erzherzog Rainer]; Neue Serie XXIX; Folge [MPER XXIX]; Berlin: de Gruyter, 2008) and Eric G. Turner's, *Greek Papyri: An Introduction* (Oxford: Clarendon, 1968), esp. pp. 54–73. See "Appendix: The Manuscript Record for Acts 28:11-31."
[4] For example, consider Troftgruben's, *Conclusion Unhindered*, 35 (n. 103), reliance on "the final stage of the text" or Puskas's, *Conclusion*, 25, dismissal of the Western variants in favour of the "the superior Alexandrian text." Meanwhile others ignore the variants entirely, e.g., Williams, *Acts*, 446–55. This problem is a widespread issue in Acts scholarship in general. Concerning the "Western" text, Ropes, "Text of Acts," 3:vii, laments that "it is unfortunate that no better name should be at hand." It has been well-established that the Western tradition is "misnamed, since it is not particular to 'the west.'" Porter, "Developments," 31 (n. 3). See also Günther Zuntz, "On the Western Text of the Acts of the Apostles," in *Opuscula Selecta: Classica, Hellenistica, Christiana* (Manchester: Manchester University Press, 1972), 189, and Tuckett, "How Early," 70. Some scholars have seriously called into question the validity of text-types, most notably Parker who, *Introduction*, 171, notes how the Western text-type differs "from each other almost as much." Meanwhile Stanley E. Porter, *How We Got the New Testament: Text, Transmission, Translation* (Grand Rapids: Baker Academic, 2013), 57, observes how the discipline is in a "state of flux" where the "methods of categorizing and using manuscripts are undergoing serious revaluation." I am in general agreement with Elliott's, *Textual Criticism*, 7, emphasis on the text-types as "family allegiances between mss" and Eldon J. Epp's, "The Twentieth

choose to categorize them, are not simply "scraps on the cutting room floor" as they can also "function as 'windows' into the world of early Christianity, its social history, and the various theological challenges it faced."[5]

Shortly after the Second World War, Kenyon made a statement that is still relevant today—that the issue of the Alexandrian and Western texts remains "the outstanding issue in the criticism of the New Testament."[6] In his excellent summary, Delobel states that it is "not an exaggeration to pretend that the 'Western' text is the most complicated matter in the field of New Testament textual criticism."[7] And yet, none of the recent approaches to the end of Acts address this issue in detail or provide a first-hand encounter with the actual manuscripts themselves. A critical study on the end of Acts should first assess and engage the "centuries-old riddle" of the variants no matter how "secondary" they appear to be.[8] Second, all of the variants of Acts 28:11-31 should be studied together in light of the historical events relating to Acts in general, but especially those tied to its end. Substantial pieces of the puzzle will be forfeited when we neglect the historical context as well as the variants.[9]

The goal of this chapter is by no means an attempt to solve the puzzle of the ending, nor the ongoing problem of the text(s) of Acts. It is much more modest—to understand the significance of the variants in light of the ever-present "Western" tendency for expansion.[10] Subsequently, the question of the silence at the end of

---

Century Interlude in New Testament Textual Criticism," in *Studies in the Theory and Method of New Testament Textual Criticism* (eds. E. J. Epp and G. D. Fee (Grand Rapids: Eerdmans, 1993), 83–108, classification as "clusters" in a looser sense as the variants in the Appendix of this volume show.

[5] Cf. Hill and Kruger, "Introduction," 1–19 (5) in reference to Ehrman's principle in "Text as Window," 361–79. I am well aware that the traditional text-types are being redefined and, in some cases, thrown out entirely. Regardless of how we classify these variants, they still represent the earliest sources for the history of early Christianity. See "The New Quest for the 'Western' Text" below.

[6] Frederic G. Kenyon, *The Text of the Greek Bible: A Students' Handbook* (London: Duckworth, 1949), 171. Cadbury, *Acts in History*, 149, describes the two texts in Acts as "so similar as to be not independent, so different as not to be merely the accumulation of usual variants in copying." He (149) goes on to say how this "has posed to scholars a difficult if not insoluble problem. How did two such texts arise?" See more recently Porter, "Developments," 31–67.

[7] Delobel, "Luke-Acts," 83–107 (106). Metzger, *Text*, 293, considers the "evaluation of the 'Western' type of text" to be "one of the most persistent problems in New Testament textual criticism." Epp relays how the Western/Alexandrian textual controversy "really has not been resolved" and the obvious bias from Westcott and Hort continues through to the Alands who obviously "pre-judged" the D-text manuscripts and in a sense they had been already "sent into exile." Epp, "Traditional 'Canons,'" 79–127 (99–100).

[8] See Delobel, "Luke-Acts," 106, and Head, "Problem," 415, respectively.

[9] Prior to the Second World War, historical concerns took centre stage in Acts studies as exemplified by the massive (and still useful) work of Frederick J. Foakes Jackson and Kirsopp Lake, eds., *The Beginnings of Christianity* (5 vols; London: Macmillan, 1920–33). Afterwards, the pendulum swung from historical concerns to an unbalanced emphasis on the theology and literary motives of Luke. Since the 1990s, attempts have been made to revisit the historical context of Acts once more. See David W. J. Gill et al., "Preface," in *The Book of Acts in Its Ancient Literary Setting* (ed. Bruce W. Winter and Andrew D. Clarke; 5 vols; BAFCS 1; Grand Rapids: Eerdmans, 1993), 1:ix–xii.

[10] Although there are many studies on the Western theological tendencies, some have challenged Eldon J. Epp's earlier thesis *The Theological Tendency of Codex Bezae Cantabrigiensis in Acts* (Cambridge: Cambridge University Press, 1966), and since then have not found any great differences between the author of Acts and the Western variants. Cf. Strange, *Problem*, 26–7 (65), and Charles K. Barrett, "Is there a Theological Tendency in Codex Bezae?," in *Text and Interpretation: Studies in the New Testament Presented to Matthew Black* (eds. Ernest Best and R. McL. Wilson; Cambridge: Cambridge University Press, 1979), 15–27 (25–7). However, it seems that

Acts that was introduced in Chapter 5 is revisited once more, but this time with an examination of the manuscript record (see "Appendix: The Manuscript Record for Acts 28:11-31"). It is proposed that these variants provide additional evidence in support of Epp's proposition that the Alexandrian and Western texts are comparable in age.[11] A further deduction is that the age of these variants, along with the Alexandrian, is decidedly early (pre-70 CE), directly challenging post-70 CE advocates.[12]

The "Western" Front

In terms of Acts scholarship, all is not "quiet on the 'Western' front."[13] The history of discussion behind the two versions of Acts is extensive, and many scholars have put their hand to the plough in the quest to provide a cogent solution.[14] Recent trends in text-critical scholarship suggest that the time is ripe for revisiting theories with regard to the origins and development of the text of Acts.[15] Although the grander problem of the origin of the text(s) of Acts will not be solved here, the variants found in Acts 28:11-31 shed light onto an early period in the textual history of Acts.[16] Given the textual diversity in Acts, as well as the Western tendency of expansion, it is exceptional that the Western scribe(s) fail to add any significant information with regard to the fate of Paul, the fate of the Roman church, and the destruction of Rome.[17] All of these factors lend support to an early date of Acts.

Epp, at the very least, generated greater attention towards the variants of Acts at a key turning point in Acts scholarship. See George D. Kilpatrick, review of *The Theological Tendency of Codex Bezae Cantabrigiensis in Acts*, by Eldon J. Epp, *VC* 24 (1970): 166-70.

[11] Epp, "Traditional 'Canons,'" 100, claims that a "defensible argument can still be made for their comparable age."

[12] The Alexandrian family is usually considered to be earlier than the Western, but this chapter argues that both are essentially early.

[13] Delobel, "Luke-Acts," 83. This popular phrase hails from Erich M. Remarque, *Im Westen nichts Neues* (Berlin: Ullstein 1928).

[14] See Kenyon, "Western Text," 299. I agree (in principle) with Ropes's, "Text of Acts," 3:viii, original 1926 assessment that "a definite Western text, whether completely recoverable in its original form or not, once actually existed."

[15] There have been several studies on the broader "texts" of Acts: Ropes, "Text of Acts," 3:i-cccxx, 1-371; Kenyon, "Western Text," 287-315; Bruce M. Metzger, *A Textual Commentary on the Greek New Testament* (2nd edn; New York: United Bible Societies, 1994), 222-36; Barrett, *Acts*; Marie-Emile Boismard, "The Text of Acts: A Problem of Literary Criticism," in *New Testament Textual Criticism: Its Significance for Exegesis—Essays in Honour of Bruce M. Metzger* (eds. Eldon J. Epp and Gordon D. Fee; Oxford: Clarendon, 1981), 147-57; Joël Delobel, "Focus on the 'Western' Text in Recent Studies," *ETL* 73 (1997): 401-10; idem, "Luke-Acts," 83-107; Head, "Problem," 415-44; Porter, "Developments," 31-68; Strange, *Problem*, 1-34; Tuckett, "How Early," 69-86; more recently idem, "Early Text," 157-74; and Holger Strutwolf et al., *Die Apostelgeschichte. ECM III* (4 vols; Stuttgart: Deutsche Bibelgesellschaft, 2017).

[16] Where Metzger, *Text*, 207, sees "the reconstruction of the history of a variant reading" as a "prerequisite to forming a judgement about it," Kenyon, *Greek Bible*, 253, sees the comprehension of the history of the NT text as "the final goal of textual criticism."

[17] As discussed below (and in Chapter 8), these factors are magnified by proximity and chronology. At the end of Acts (28:14-16), Paul goes to Rome in 60-61 CE and stays there under house arrest for the subsequent two-year period (28:16, 30). This brings us to approximately 63 CE which is only a year (or so) away from Rome's Great Fire that occurred in July of 64 CE and Nero's subsequent persecution of the Christians. Although the exact year of Paul's death is debated it likely occurred

Since there are multiple variants, roughly comprising at least two versions (or editions) of Acts, we must go beyond a tacit rejection of the "lesser" variants by Committee decisions.[18] Meanwhile, a tacit acceptance of the eclectic text leaves out a valuable piece of textual history and clues to the puzzle we find at the end of Acts.[19] Therefore, one way to move the discussion forward with regard to interpreting the end of Acts is to factor in important research on the development of the text(s) of Acts along with a study of the variants themselves. Since there is so much textual diversity in Acts it seems paramount that this issue is addressed, otherwise we are only dating the Alexandrian family of texts.[20]

This text-critical problem with Acts is unavoidable. Strange insists that it is "forced upon the reader of Acts" and "decisions about the text affect conclusions about the work in all its aspects."[21] This *problem* has been noted for a long time. Concerning the Western text, Ropes, in 1926, asserts that "we should be the poorer, for those fragments of its base, which it enshrines like fossils in an enveloping rock-mass, would probably have perished, and we should have lost these evidences of a good text of extreme antiquity, vastly nearer in date to the original autographs than any of our Greek manuscripts."[22]

Over seventy years later, Delobel's 1999 survey of this issue *actualized* what Ropes *hypothesized*—Delobel claims that it was not until the mid-1980s that scholarship began to engage the Western front once more:[23]

> Apart from a few stubborn "heretics," most editors and exegetes during the preceding decades had based their text-critical decisions on the explicit or silent assumption that the "Western" text is the result of some form of corruption of

---

close to 64 CE and no later than the end of Nero's reign in 68 CE. Since all of this happened in Rome and within a very short span of time it seems incredible that the scribe(s) would not capitalize on these well-known events in history or the fate of Paul (the book's main character).

[18] Vaganay, *Introduction*, 88 and 169, refers to the presuppositions of the UBS editorial committee as well as their bias against the Western text (while it is also clear that Vaganay [and Amphoux] are biased in favour of the Western text). The first and second committee was made up of Kurt Aland, Matthew Black, Bruce Metzger, and Allen Wikgren while the third added Carlo Maria Martini. Metzger, *Commentary* (2nd edn), 235, admits how the Committee "more often than not" preferred "the shorter, Alexandrian text." He also claims "the information incorporated in certain Western expansions may well be factually accurate, though not deriving from the original author of Acts" (235). Head, "Problem," 419, also explains how this Alexandrian "consensus is clearly reflected in the texts of the favoured modern editions of the Greek New Testament (NA^{26}, UBS^3)."

[19] While Marshall includes a brief note on the *stratopedarch* found in the expanded verse 16 of some Western texts and verse 29, he does not refer to the Western omissions found in Acts 28:11, 12-14a, or the addition of verse 19, and the extended verse 31. Marshall, *Acts*, 439–47 (446).

[20] Troftgruben, *Conclusion Unhindered*, 35 (n. 103). He is correct in saying that the end of Acts is neither to "entertain readers" or "narrate a life of Paul" or "narrate history for history's sake"— however, the end does relay many historical events relating to Paul in Rome in a well-detailed geographical context. Troftgruben, *Conclusion Unhindered*, 181.

[21] Strange, *Problem*, 1. Recall Chapter 5 with regard to the assumptions of Troftgruben and Puskas.

[22] Ropes, "Text of Acts," 3:ix. More recently, Parker claims that the early second-century Western text of Acts (and possibly earlier) can be found among the Old Latin, Syriac, and D text. Parker, "Codex Bezae," 43–50 (48–9).

[23] Delobel, "Luke-Acts," 83.

the original text, which is more faithfully represented by the Alexandrian text-tradition. Everything seemed to be "quiet on the Western front." But all of a sudden, the hostilities started again.[24]

Delobel credits the "impressive" study by Boismard and Lamouille as a primary reason for the shift in focus away from a pure Alexandrian development to a reconsideration of the Western text once more.[25] For example, Barbara Aland explains that when she first wrote her methodology, she assumed the "established" view was that the Western text is a later revision of the book of Acts—"but this is not so."[26]

There have been numerous attempts to provide a solution to the distinct and divergent "traditions" or "text-types."[27] The first position, credited to Blass, is that the author of Acts "issued two editions of each of his works."[28] Blass's theory is that Luke originally wrote his gospel in Palestine but "issued a new edition" when he went to Rome with Paul; Luke then wrote two copies of Acts—one for Theophilus and another "with substantial differences, for the church at large."[29] For Blass the Western text of Acts is earlier, while the Gospel is later.[30] The major critique against this view is that it has "not always been clear why the author made the changes that he did."[31] Where Blass's position was later adapted by Boismard and Lamouille, Tavardon builds on Boismard-Lamouille's work and sees the Alexandrian text as the work of a redactor, thus promoting the Western text as "more primitive."[32]

Like the first, the second theory involves "two different but related editions" except that the second view argues that the Alexandrian text came first.[33] It is possible that the Alexandrian text could have been expanded upon and improved while forming the Western edition, though few scholars accept this possibility. The third position—the

---

[24] Ibid. The opposition from pro-Western scholars is so great that it almost "looks like a conspiracy against the dominant critical text" (96). See also Delobel, "Focus," 401–10.

[25] Ibid., 83; Boismard and Lamouille, *Le Texte Occidental*. Unfortunately, I did not have adequate time or access to the most recent third critical edition: Patrick Faure. *Les Actes des Apôtres: Texte occidental reconstitué* (EBib 79. Leuven: Peeters, 2019).

[26] "Dem ist aber nicht so." Barbara Aland, "Entstehung, Charakter und Herkunft des Sog. Westlichen Textes Untersucht an der Apostelgeschichte," *ETL* 62 (1986): 5–65 (6). Apparently it was Boismard and Lamouille's, *Le Texte Occidental* that shifted her viewpoint. Cf. Delobel, "Luke-Acts," 83.

[27] It is very likely that two editions (or versions) of Acts exists. See Barrett, *Acts*, 1:26, and Metzger, *Commentary* (2nd edn), 222.

[28] See Kenyon, "Western Text," 299. According to Kenyon (299), the two-edition view goes back at least as far as Jean Leclerc in 1684 (and Semler had also suggested that Hemsterhuis was of a similar view). In 1871, Lightfoot revived the theory but it was not until Friedrich Blass (in 1895) presented this idea in full detail.

[29] Ibid., 299; Porter, "Developments," 33.

[30] See Kenyon, "Western Text," 299; Porter, *New Testament*, 62; Boismard and Lamouille, *Le Texte Occidental*, 1:ix; Marie-Emile Boismard and Arnaud Lamouille, "Le texte occidental des Actes des Apôtres. À propos d'Actes 27, 1–13," *ETL* 63 (1987): 48–58; and Boismard, "Problem," 147–57. For the original proposal, see Blass, *Acta Apostolorum*, 24–32, and idem, *Philology of the Gospels*, 96–137.

[31] Porter, "Developments," 34.

[32] Delobel, "Luke-Acts," 96, and Paul Tavardon, *Le texte alexandrin et le texte occidental des Actes des Apôtres: Doublets et variantes de structure* (CahRB 37; Paris: Gabalda, 1997), 1–41.

[33] Porter, "Developments," 34.

"revision" or "interpolation" theory—is perhaps the most popular. This view suggests that the "early period of textual transmission was more fluid, and this resulted in a number of interpolations being added to the text, possibly by revisers."[34] Westcott, Hort, Kenyon, Dibelius, and Ropes all held to this view. The variant readings could have begun as early as the first draft of Acts was written in the early 60s CE.[35] Meanwhile, Clark proposed a fourth view that the Alexandrian text, which came later, was the result of abbreviation due to the "stichometric arrangement" of the Western text.[36] Lastly, a fifth position involves theories of translation that attempt to explain the Western text's "growth in length."[37]

There are a few more theories worth mentioning that represent a blending of the previous viewpoints. For example, Delebecque proposes that Luke first wrote the Alexandrian draft of Acts around 62 CE. The Western text was Luke's second, improved edition completed a few years later in 67 CE. His view is a blend of Ropes and Aland due to the Alexandrian priority. Delebecque also joins rank with Blass who ascribes "the Western text to the same author and dating it in the first century."[38] Meanwhile, Amphoux claims that the Western text of the gospels "is the most anciently accessible form of the text" and that the Alexandrian text "is the result of editorial work" from around 175 CE.[39]

A few years after Delebecque, Strange hypothesized that the final revised published versions was a result of two earlier drafts. He believes that Acts was a posthumous edition (as the end of Acts shows that Luke never completed it).[40] He does so based on Rackham's observation that the "textual variety" arose from early drafts or perhaps even Luke's death.[41] Strange thinks that Luke's gospel was published after his death while his Acts was not (as there is no evidence of them ever being together either by scroll or codex).[42] He further speculates that Acts was needed after Marcion because it undermined his views (he considers the anti-Judaic content to be the result of pro-Marcion influence).[43]

---

[34] Porter, "Developments," 34.
[35] Meanwhile, Strange, *Problem*, 185–9, thinks Luke left marginal notations in his first draft which later became the Western text. Delobel, "Luke-Acts," 105, agrees with Strange's view in that the Western readings are "(narrative or theological) commentary." The various Bezan correctors suggest an evolution of the text where marginal notations may have entered the text early on. Cf. Parker, "Codex Bezae," 43–50 (esp. 48), and Delobel, "Luke-Acts," 91–2.
[36] Albert C. Clark, *The Descent of Manuscripts* (Oxford: Clarendon, 1918) and idem, *The Primitive Text of the Gospels and Acts* (Oxford: Clarendon, 1914) later modified his position in idem, *The Acts of the Apostles: A Critical Edition, with Introduction and Notes on Selected Passages* (Oxford: Clarendon, 1933) to show the "conscious editorial effort" by the editor who "created the Alexandrian text." Cf. Porter, "Developments," 35. See further Kenyon's, "Western Text," 287–315, critique of Clark.
[37] Porter, "Developments," 35. Porter argues for Alexandrian priority while the Western text evinces later editorial activity.
[38] Delobel, "Luke-Acts," 88. Delebecque, *Les Deux Acte*, 376, dates the Alexandrian to 61–63 CE and the Western by *c.* 67 CE (p. 380).
[39] Delobel, "Luke-Acts," 94. Amphoux's work on the gospels supports an early date of the text.
[40] Strange, *Problem*, 176–8.
[41] Ibid., 177.
[42] Ibid., 181–2.
[43] Ibid., 183.

This I find highly problematic for similar reasons as Tyson/Knox's theory (as argued in Chapters 1 and 2). In the end, he seems to be saying that prior to Luke's death there were two drafts: (1) the non-Western and (2) an annotated "copy" (by Luke)—both of which gave rise to the later second-century published versions.[44] Head outlines the "several weaknesses" of Strange's hypothesis first by challenging his erroneous view that since there are no earlier references to Acts, it did not exist until the "middle of the second century."[45] Second, Head explains (with perhaps an accidental pun?) that it is "rather strange" that somehow "two forms of Luke's notes were kept, quite independently, across over eighty years, but never published or referred to."[46] On the positive side, Strange helped to reignite the conversation while providing valuable research for the theories on the development of the Western text while also providing an excellent appendix of the extant witnesses for Acts.[47] Last, the view that Luke left his work unfinished is not a new one.

More recently in 2009, the work of Rius-Camps and Read-Heimerdinger has significantly "disquieted" the Western front further.[48] Using principles of discourse analysis, Read-Heimerdinger proposes that Codex Bezae (05) is earlier than the Alexandrian text and not "the work of an enthusiastic and fanciful scribe who embellished the original text represented by the Alexandrian manuscripts."[49] In their combined work they "highlight the inner coherence of Bezae in Acts" drawing attention to the "distinct message communicated by its narrator, in the hope that the manuscript's witness to the concerns of the early Church might once more be recognized and valued."[50] In many ways, Rius-Camps and Read-Heimerdinger's conclusions support both the intrinsic value and an early date of the Western variants of Acts 28:11-31, as they believe that their extended Bezan text is one that "preserves a voice of the Church in the first decades of its existence."[51]

Although the debate regarding the age and stages of Bezae's development continues, it is clear that Bezae represents a concrete expression of the later developing Western tradition.[52] It seems reasonable to suppose that the (pre-Bezae) Western text preserves

---

[44] Ibid., 175, 189.
[45] Cf. Head, "Problem," 427 (n. 71).
[46] Head, "Problem," 428.
[47] Strange, *Problem*, 1–34. For an updated list see http://www.uni-muenster.de/INTF.
[48] Delobel, "Luke-Acts," 95. See Josep Rius-Camps, *Commentari als Fets dels Apòstols* (4 vols; Barcelona: Facultat de Teologia de Catalunya/Herder, 1991–2000); Jenny Read-Heimerdinger, *The Bezan Text of Acts: A Contribution of Discourse Analysis to Textual Criticism* (JSNTSup 236; London: Sheffield Academic, 2002) and their combined work in Josep Rius-Camps and Jenny Read-Heimerdinger, *The Message of Acts in Codex Bezae: A Comparison with the Alexandrian Tradition* (4 vols; LNTS 415; London, T&T Clark, 2009).
[49] Read-Heimerdinger, *Bezan Text of Acts* (abstract). This is not the place to debate her synchronic approach; the point of agreement here is that the text of Bezae is a very early witness. She proposes that the Bezan text is earlier because it "displays an exceptional degree of linguistic consistency and a coherence of purpose which is essentially theological, with a marked interest in a Jewish point of view." Delobel, "Luke-Acts," 95, conveys how Rius-Camps, *Commentari*, also defends the "primitive character" of the Western text.
[50] Rius-Camps and Read-Heimerdinger, *The Message of Acts*, 4:12.
[51] Ibid., 4:ix.
[52] See Parker, *Introduction*, 288 and 298; Porter, "Developments," 66–7. Earlier David C. Parker, *Codex Bezae: An Early Christian Manuscript and its Text* (Cambridge: Cambridge University Press, 1992), 284, relayed how the Bezan text "is not a defined text …We have not a text, but a genre."

an earlier version of the text of Acts. Who the author (or authors) of this version is, and just how early it is, remains a matter of ongoing debate. Nevertheless, the Western text is, at the very least, the "earliest commentary" on the primitive text available.[53]

Delobel claims the textual problem stems from the second century, "the period during which the text may be supposed to have enjoyed [the] most freedom and to have suffered most corruption."[54] He maintains that although "imaginative constructions are to be welcomed" every "theory can only be hypothetical."[55] The inevitable deduction is that both pro-Western and pro-Alexandrian views must remain theories because the textual evidence is mixed and for at least two major reasons. First, because the "earliest papyri for Acts are from the third century" and second because many of them exhibit Western tendencies (i.e., P^{29}, P^{38}, and P^{48}).[56] Consequently, we must not confuse our hypotheses with facts—or our "building" will be "no stronger than its basement."[57]

Tuckett provides a more recent assessment of this text-critical problem while engaging the Alands, and especially Barbara Aland's definitive article on the subject.[58] Aland, after examining Bezae (D 05) and notable papyri—P^{38} and P^{48} especially—postulates that somewhere during the second century variants began to appear.[59] Later in the third century, these variants developed into something more significant, as the similarities between Codex 614 and some early manuscripts reveal.[60] Some infer that the text carried in Codex 614 and its sister text 2412 (twelfth/thirteenth century) should be used to "establish the stage of the text prior to the early third century."[61]

---

[53] So Head, "Problem," 444. See also Zuntz, "Western Text," 196, and his comments on the Western "paradigmatic expansions" that "give concrete directions for Christian life, as it was meant to be lived in the early Christian communities" (as noted by Head, "Problem," 444). See also Armstrong, "Variants," 95, 98.

[54] Delobel, "Luke-Acts," 96.

[55] Ibid.

[56] Ibid., 103. See my note 59 below (esp. Comfort and Barrett's remarks).

[57] Ibid., 98–106 (102).

[58] See Aland and Aland, *New Testament*, 54–64 and Aland, "Charakter und Herkunft," 5–65. Barbara Aland claims that the Western text "cannot be traced back to a period earlier than the early third century." Cf. Tuckett, "How Early," 70. While Boismard considers the Western text to be the original, Aland considers it to be a corruption of the Alexandrian text, which "remained much closer to the autographs." Delobel, "Luke-Acts," 91.

[59] Porter, *New Testament*, 63, considers the age of P^{38} to be close to 300 CE while P^{48} can be dated to the late third century. Cf. Metzger, *Commentary* (2nd edn), xix and Aland and Aland, *New Testament*, 98–9. Philip W. Comfort and David P. Barrett, *The Complete Text of the Earliest New Testament Manuscripts* (Grand Rapids: Baker Books, 1999), 135, suggest P^{38} is "late second or early third century" while (via Sanders) they state that the form is close to P. Oxy. 843 (late second century), P. Oxy 1607 (late second or early third century), and that other "comparable examples of this kind of handwriting can be seen in P. Oxy. 37 (ca. 200), P. Oxy. 405 (ca. 200), and P. Oxy. 406 (early third century)." Perhaps further research on the form and hand of such texts (i.e., P^{38}) may push the date back further. They also state that P^{38} (in addition to D, P^{29}, and P^{48}) is "representative of the 'Western' form of the Book of Acts" (135).

[60] Aland's *Hauptredaktor*, the ancient Western redactor/editor, produced the extra Bezan material. Tuckett, "How Early," 70.

[61] See Tuckett, "How Early," 75. At the same time, the similarities between 614 and 2412 are compelling (see Aland and Aland, *New Testament*, 137). Acts 28:29, for example, is almost exactly the same in 614 (including the diaeresis above the ι's)—except συζήτησϊν contains a marked ϋ. Similar to Aland, Kenyon, "Western Text," 314, earlier considered 1571 and 1165 each to be an "unquestionably Western text of Acts" and this shows how "texts of this type existed in Egypt in the fourth century." Meanwhile, Tuckett, "How Early," 75, considers 614 to be a "Byzantine manuscript rather than 'Western.'" See also Kurt Aland and Barbara Aland, *Text und Textwert der Griechischen Handschriften*

The Western tradition then is best understood as a series of developmental stages; and although related, the earlier texts should not be directly equated with the fifth-century Codex Bezae (D) (05).[62] It was not until sometime later in the fourth or fifth century that Codex D became the refined product of this Western development.[63]

The better, external evidence for the early Western text is found in P^{38}, not simply because it is more Western than 614, but because the manuscript is far older (c. third century).[64] Furthermore, despite a recent change in consensus with regard to the Western readings found in the very fragmentary P^{29}, the Western branch in P^{48} continues to be upheld.[65] This is very compelling evidence for the age of these early variants because there are only six early papyri (P^{29}, P^{38}, P^{45}, P^{48}, P^{53}, and P^{91}) and one third-century parchment (0189) to begin with.[66] Furthermore, although P^{45} shows the "greatest affinity" with the Alexandrian uncials (א, A, B, C), the gospels (Matthew, Luke, and John) exhibit a mix of Alexandrian and Western traditions.[67] Since there are only seven manuscripts that are earlier than the third century, it is very difficult to relegate the Western textual family to the bottom of the scrap-pile since it is represented well among the early manuscripts of Acts.[68]

There are further reasons to turn back the clock on the Western tradition. For example, nearly a century ago, Sanday discovered that there are "close points of contact with fourth century patristic quotations" both in the Gospels *and* in Acts.[69] The alleged agreement between the D text and Irenaeus's *Against Heresies* is of particular interest

---

des Neuen Testaments III: Die Apostelgeschichte (2 vols; Berlin: de Gruyter, 1993), 1:135. Further, Strange, *Problem*, 11, considers 383 and 614 to be a Byzantine text-type with some Western readings. Strange's assessment is reasonable based on my analysis of Acts 28:11-31.

[62] Tuckett, "How Early," 70–1.

[63] Some date Bezae earlier, while some prefer later. See Barrett, *Acts*, 1:5.

[64] Tuckett, "How Early," 72 and 75. Sanders dated the fragment "as early as 200–250 CE" (Tuckett, 71) and Henry A. Sanders, "A Papyrus Fragment of Acts in the Michigan Collection," *HTR* 20 (1927): 1–19.

[65] Tuckett, "Early Text," 169, claims that although P^{48} has been "carelessly written," it has a "form of the text that is strongly 'Western' in its readings." That P^{29} exhibits Western readings has come under greater scrutiny in recent years despite the earlier views (see 160–2 and his note 16 on p. 160). See also Porter, "Developments," 41, who sees P^{29} not as a Western text but indicative of "another tradition" or "possibly a freer paraphrase."

[66] Tuckett, "Early Text," 157 (n. 1). Comfort, *Manuscripts*, 64 and 79, notes that while P^{53} and P^{91} are both "proto-Alexandrian," the latter is "too fragmentary to be sure."

[67] Comfort, *Manuscripts*, 66. Comfort (65) relays how Kenyon in his *editio princeps* thought the original order was Western (Matthew, John, Luke, Mark, and then Acts). See Frederic G. Kenyon, *Chester Beatty Biblical Papyri II/1: The Gospels and Acts, Text* (London: Walker, 1933); and *II/2: The Gospels and Acts, Plates* (London: Walker, 1934). It may be worth following up with a detailed study of the version of Acts in P^{45}, especially where Colwell, *Studies in Methodology*, 118–19, showed how the scribe did not copy word for word (i.e., P^{75}) but phrase per phrase while freely omitting material. Royse, *Scribal Habits*, 197, also found that the scribe had a "marked tendency to omit portions of the text, often (as it seems) accidentally but perhaps also deliberately pruning." For the latest list of manuscripts and evidence for the Western order of the Gospels see Crawford, "A New Witness," 1–7, and his discovery via the concordance table of a sixth-century mss (GA 073+74) that also reflects the Western order.

[68] Tuckett, "How Early," 74.

[69] William Sanday et al., *Novum Testamentum Sancti Irenaei Episcopi Lugdunensis* (Oxford: Clarendon, 1923), clxv.

for the date of the Western text.[70] Souter determined that the "Greek text of Acts, even in its surviving fragments, shows striking observations about Irenaeus' text of the gospels."[71]

Subsequently, Sanday explains that although Turner does not "specify any precise date" he "clearly suggests that the translation is considerably early."[72] Sanday then suggests that there is a "distinct possibility that the Latin version of Irenaeus was already accessible to Tertullian when he wrote his treatise against the Valentinians in AD 207. If that is so, its date might be represented as ±200."[73] A few years later, Ropes, who agrees with this assessment, argues that a "copy of Acts used by Irenaeus was, like his copies of the Gospels and the Pauline epistles, a Greek manuscript with a thorough-going 'Western text,' showing but few departures from the complete 'Western' text."[74]

More recently, Barrett claims that Irenaeus is the "first Christian author extant to quote Acts explicitly. He does so frequently and at length."[75] Barrett, through his list of examples, shows that there is "no doubt that Irenaeus is often in agreement with readings found in D, in the Old Latin MSS, in the Harclean, or in combinations of these."[76] Similarly, Tuckett concludes by stating it is "clear how the judgement of Ropes and others [i.e. Barrett, Souter] has been reached: there is clearly a significant level of agreement between the text of Acts presupposed by Irenaeus and the D text of Acts."[77]

Last, there are many prominent third-, fourth-, and fifth-century patristic manuscripts that use the D text.[78] One of the most notable is Chrysostom (347–407 CE) whose sermons, that showcase Western (and Byzantine) variants, are the "only complete

---

[70] This is remarkable because we have a second-century writer who employs Western readings. The traditional view (contra Aland, "Charakter und Herkunft," 43–56) has been defended by Barrett, *Acts*, 1:15–18 and Tuckett, "How Early," 76–82. According to Delobel, "Luke-Acts," 103, the Latin translation of Irenaeus's book is considered to be "a faithful one."

[71] Sanday et al. *Sancti Irenaei*, clxiv. In his analysis, Souter explains how the "translator wrote in Africa in the period 370 to 420" CE. See Sanday et al., *Sancti Irenaei*, xcvi. Sanday (lxiv) agrees with Souter's assessment. Souter relays the earlier opinion of Hort who also suggested that the "true date of the translation is the fourth century. The inferior limit is fixed by the quotations made from it by Augustine about 421" (lxv). See Brooke F. Westcott and Fenton J. A. Hort, *Introduction to the New Testament in the Original Greek* (Cambridge: Macmillan, 1882), 160. Ropes, "Text of Acts," 3:clxxxvii, accepts Souter's translation estimate of 370 to 420 CE.

[72] Sanday et al., *Sancti Irenaei*, lxiv (Sanday refers to Turner's work on pp. 229–52). Based on Turner's comments, Sanday gives the Latin translation a third-century dating.

[73] Ibid., lxiii. He cautions that it should not be dated "too near the actual completion of the Greek Irenaeus" because there is evidence of development between the Greek and Latin versions (1xiii).

[74] Ropes, "Text of Acts," 3:clxxxvii.

[75] Barrett, *Acts*, 1:15. He (1:16–17) compares the D text with Irenaeus (*Haer*. 3).

[76] Ibid., 1:16 and Parker, "Codex Bezae," 48–9.

[77] Tuckett, "How Early," 82. Delobel thinks that the date of the *Hauptredaktion* may be subject to change pending further research on the "longer readings in Irenaeus." Delobel, "Luke-Acts," 104. He goes on to say the *Hauptredaktion* would only "need a (somewhat) earlier dating" and "not the rejection of the theory as such" (104). Remarkably, Irenaeus mirrors the Western theological tendencies such as the modified Apostolic degree with the absence of "things strangled," the added Golden rule, and the longer reading in Acts 15:29 (Tuckett, "How Early," 85). All of this evidence from Irenaeus leads him to a second-century date for the Western text (or earlier). Tuckett's research (and the earlier work of Ropes, Souter, Westcott, and Hort), challenges Aland's assessment (86).

[78] Clement of Alexandria, Tertullian, Origen, Cyprian (third century), Eusebius of Caesarea, Lucifer of Cagliari, Athanasius of Alexandria, Cyril of Jerusalem (fourth century), Chrysostom, Jerome, Augustine, Cyril of Alexandria, Speculum, and the Venerable Bede (fifth century). Eusebius of Caesarea shows a curious "mixture of Old Uncial and Western readings," Barrett, *Acts*, 1:18–20 (19).

commentary on Acts that has survived from the first ten centuries."[79] Therefore, it seems very likely that the D text has roots that date "before and perhaps long before, the year 150" CE.[80]

The New Quest for the "Western" Text

However, there are some scholars who would question the earlier perspective on the age of the Western text. Since the release of the third volume of the *Editio Critica Maior* in 2017, the editors of the ECM claim that the "Western" front has been silenced. In fact, Wachtel concludes that

> The quest for the "Western text" has failed. What we have instead are variants in different kinds of texts. If there are agreements between Irenaeus' citations and variants in 05, this does not mean that the "Western text" goes back to the second century, but rather that these particular variants do. Thus the notion of a second century "Western text" should be abandoned once and for all.[81]

This is a bold conclusion that seems to overturn much of the current research on the history of the development of the texts of Acts.[82]

---

[79] Quasten, *Patrology*, 3:440. Chrysostom's text is "basically Antiochian, as one might be expected, but shows from time to time awareness of Western variations." Barrett, *Acts*, 1:20. Chrysostom uses an Alexandrian version of Acts 28:11-16 that is similar to Codex 614, but with the addition of verse 29.

[80] Ropes, "Text of Acts," 3:ccxliv. Ropes (along with Jackson and Lake) concludes that the Western text (ironically) hails from the East and "perhaps in Syria or Palestine" (3:ccxlv). They further suggest that the reviser's aim was to "improve the text, not to restore it, and he lived not far from the time when the New Testament canon in its nucleus was first definitely assembled" (3:ccxlv). Zuntz, "Western Text," 214, argues that the "re-written text of Acts" was in use in the church community at Edessa "as early as about A.D. 100." For those who expect a longer period "between original and rewriting," he offers this counter-question: "How long a period must be supposed to have elapsed between the re-writing of Q by Mark, and of Mark by the other Synoptics?" (214 [n. 1]).

[81] Klaus Wachtel, "On the Relationship of the 'Western Text' and the Byzantine Tradition of Acts—A Plea Against the Text-Type Concept," in *Die Apostelgeschichte. ECM III/3*, 147. Holger Strutwolf, "Der Text der *Apostelgeschichte* bei Irenäus von Lyon und der sogenannte 'Westliche Text,'" in *Die Apostelgeschichte. ECM III/3*, 180, comes to the same conclusion. For a contrary view, see Tuckett, "How Early," 69–86; idem, "Early Text," 157–74.

[82] Wachtel's conclusion should be tempered here by Wasserman and Gurry's wise caution on the delicate relationship between historical knowledge and textual criticism (in reference to Evans, *Defence*, 110). They point out that we are only relying upon a fragment of the records that once existed, and the method for the ECM (CBGM) in particular is using only "about one-third of our extant Greek manuscripts." See Tommy Wasserman and Peter J. Gurry, *A New Approach to Textual Criticism: An Introduction to the Coherence-Based Genealogical Method* (SBLRBS 80; Atlanta: SBL, 2017), 112–13. Although this selection includes the best of manuscripts "they are still a selection not only of what once was but even of what we now have. The significance of this selectivity of our evidence means that our textual flow diagrams and the global stemma do not give us a picture of exactly what happened" (113). In light of their caution, and given the volume of research on the texts of Acts, I question Wachtel's definitive and positivistic conclusion on the failure of the Western text.

However, even if the findings of the ECM are found to be correct, there still remains the issue of Acts containing a significant number of textual variants that go back at least as early as the second century, as noted by Wachtel above. In other words, we still have comparably ancient sources in addition to the initial or *Ausgangstext*, regardless of whether or not these texts have "sufficient coherencies" to demonstrate a definable textual family (cluster or type).[83] From the perspective of historiography, these variants, however one chooses to define them, collectively represent a very early witness to the narrative.

With regard to the *failure* of the Western text, there are several reasons why such a conclusion should remain tentative at best and these issues relate directly to methodology.[84] In their application of the *Coherence Based Genealogical Method* (CBGM), the editors seem to minimize the value of the Western text based on a lack of *coherence* between variants.[85] However, one of the distinctive issues with the Western text is the problem of multiple languages and translation, and this is significant because the ECM cannot accommodate non-Greek evidence.[86] Epp further explains some of the difficulties with the "D-text" cluster:

---

[83] Klaus Wachtel, "Notes on the Text of the Acts of the Apostles," in *Die Apostelgeschichte. ECM III/1.1*, 31 (and 28).

[84] Even Wachtel, "'Western Text,'" 148, recognizes the need to pursue other methodologies and avenues of research with regard to the "vexing problems" caused by the "phenomena labeled 'Western.'"

[85] Wachtel, "Notes," 31. In 1999, the CBGM, or "Münster Method," was developed by Gerd Mink at the Münster Institute who with "singular clarity recognized the philological opportunities offered when the data can be recorded and analysed digitally." Parker, *Textual Scholarship*, 84–5. David C. Parker, "Is 'Living Text' Compatible with 'Initial Text'? Editing the Gospel of John," in *The Textual History of the Greek New Testament: Changing Views in Contemporary Research* (eds. Klaus Wachtel and Michael Holmes; SBLTCS 8; Leiden: Brill, 2012), 21, claims that the CBGM (along with phylogenetic analysis) makes "Lachmannian stemmatics work for the first time." The CBGM is about establishing relationships between variants by tracing manuscripts for agreements and divergencies. See Gerd Mink, "Contamination, Coherence, and Coincidence in Textual Transmission: The Coherence-Based Genealogical Method (CBGM) as a Compliment and Corrective to Existing Approaches," in *The Textual History of the Greek New Testament: Changing Views in Contemporary Research* (eds. Klaus Wachtel and Michael Holmes; SBLTCS 8; Leiden: Brill, 2012), 141–216 (149), and also Klaus Wachtel and Michael Holmes, "Introduction," in *The Textual History of the Greek New Testament: Changing Views in Contemporary Research* (eds. Klaus Wachtel and Michael Holmes; SBLTCS 8; Leiden: Brill, 2012), 1–12. In his dedicated study, Gurry in his conclusion, states that the CBGM is a "valuable tool for reconstructing the text of the New Testament and for studying its textual history." See Peter J. Gurry, *A Critical Examination of the Coherence-Based Genealogical Method in New Testament Textual Criticism* (NTTSD 55; Leiden: Brill, 2017), 221, and his earlier overview "How Your Greek NT Is Changing: A Simple Introduction to the Coherence-Based Genealogical Method (CBGM)," *JETS* 59 (2016): 675–89, and also his co-authored work: Wasserman and Gurry, *Approach*.

[86] Epp, "Traditional 'Canons,'" 87. Wasserman and Gurry, *Approach*, 117, commenting on Mink, "Contamination," 148, observe how in spite of the "abundance of data included in the CBGM" the "method could still include additional types of variants and witnesses." Wasserman and Gurry subsequently advise that the CBGM "should seek ways to incorporate all the evidence of the lectionaries, versions, and patristic sources where currently cited in the ECM" (118). Regardless of the important "advances, it is not a magic wand that will solve all our text-critical problems" (112). See further pp. 111–22 and Gurry's, *Examination*, 206–18, discussion on the limitations and suggested improvements for the CBGM.

The most distinctive variants involved words, phrases, clauses, and even full sentences ... that alter a scene, a context, a description, a sequence, an apparent motivation, or an expressed viewpoint. When such notions are written in Latin, but especially Syriac or Coptic, syntax differences often will disallow word-for-word equivalence, and there are other disjunctions, but in most cases it will be obvious whether the same idea is being expressed regardless of the language and in spite of minor differences.[87]

Since the Western Greek witnesses reflect the "relationship between translations," Wachtel acknowledges the problem with the CBGM that it "does not provide tools appropriate for studying this strand of transmission."[88] Despite this drawback, he states that it "goes without saying that the present edition dispenses with a theory of two texts of Acts."[89]

A further weakness of the CBGM rests on the "lack of an adequate definition of what is meant by *coherence*."[90] While CBGM provides a more *coherent* view of the history of the text and details the ancestry of manuscripts, it "does not address the question [of] how they align with the history of copying the NT writings in the framework of Christian culture."[91] Furthermore, the "individual traits of a manuscript are completely overlooked, because variants are studied in isolation apart from their original contexts."[92] In fact, Mink admits that the focus is not on the manuscripts "as

---

[87] Cf. Eldon J. Epp, "Textual Clusters: Their Past and Future in New Testament Textual Criticism," in *The Text of the New Testament in Contemporary Research: Essays on the Status Quaestionis* (eds. Bart D. Ehrman and Michael W. Holmes; 2nd edn; NTTSD 42; Leiden/Boston: Brill 2013), 566.

[88] Klaus Wachtel, "Notes," 31. He (31) further admits that the CBGM can be "applied only if sufficient coherencies are extant." Additionally, he explains that an "essential reason why the CBGM cannot be applied to the phenomena of the 'Western text' is the fact that a substantial part of this tradition is transmitted in versions." See also Gurry, *Examination*, 27.

[89] Wachtel, "Notes," 32. Here he quotes Parker, *Introduction*, 298, who does not allow for any consideration of text-types. Parker is certainly not alone, but the perceived fall of text-types is far from consensus and requires a much greater discussion since it seriously impacts how we evaluate external evidence among other criteria. Cf. Elliott, *Textual Criticism*, 7, and Epp "Interlude," 83–108; and more recently Stanley E. Porter, "The Domains of Textual Criticism and the Future of Textual Scholarship," in *The Future of New Testament Textual Scholarship: From H. C. Hoskier to the 'Editio Critica Maior' and Beyond* (ed. Garrick V. Allen; WUNT 417; Tübingen: Mohr Siebeck, 2019), 131–53. Porter finds the arguments offered by the ECM (via the CBGM) against text-types "odd" and "unconvincing"—and I agree—especially "when two of the three recognized text types are essentially retained" (139 [n. 36]). The two being the "hard to deny" Byzantine text and the "'Western' cluster of variants." See Wasserman and Gurry, *Approach*, 9, and pp. 7–10 in context.

[90] Porter and Pitts, *Fundamentals*, 90 (n. 2, original emphasis). They (n. 2) further observe that coherence becomes a "mathematical calculation, rather than a literary concept that appreciates the possible means for variants within a given manuscript." See also Porter, *New Testament*, 32–3. Others have noted problems with the ECM. For example, Elliott states that "nowhere are we informed how and on what principles the ECM text was established." Elliott, *Textual Criticism*, 477. Citing Housman, he asks that critical editors be "called to account and asked for his reasons" (p. 557). Elliott further highlights the small number of changes in 1 Peter and James (post-NA/UBS), and the consistent reliance on Sinaiticus and Vaticanus (p. 505)—the text then is essentially a fully eclectic fourth-century text (p. 508).

[91] Wachtel and Holmes, "Introduction," 9.

[92] Porter and Pitts, *Fundamentals*, 90 (n. 2).

physical artifacts" but on the "texts they carry, whose sequence of variants can be compared with DNA chains."[93]

Still, there is the issue of "relating the initial text to the original text"—if the goal is to reconstruct the latter, there will be a deficiency due to the gap in transmission history.[94] Additionally, another issue is that the CBGM does not begin with text-types. Rather, it looks for an emerging structure based on the textual "relationships between all witnesses and thus determine their places in the transmission history."[95] Although the method claims to involve external and internal criteria, there seems to be an unhealthy imbalance on the "texts" via internal considerations instead of the manuscripts themselves.[96] In the end, there are sufficient reasons to continue the quest for the Western text of Acts.

Evaluation of the End of Acts Variants

In the final analysis, it seems that on the one hand there is sufficient evidence to show an early origin of the Western textual variants (or however we define them). On the other, there remains a general lack of consensus concerning theories of what came first and how the text(s) of Acts developed.[97] Even among pro-Alexandrian scholars, there are those who suggest that the Western text has its roots in the early second century (or earlier).[98] There are also a growing number of scholars who are finding sufficient value in studying the variants for their intrinsic worth and the light they can shed on the historical development of the text beyond a need to establish an initial or original text.[99]

---

[93] Mink, "Contamination," 146. CBGM finds "relationships between preserved witnesses, that is, between texts as transmitted by manuscripts, not between manuscripts as historical artifacts" (p. 202). Cf. also Wachtel, "Notes," 31. This seems problematic because manuscripts are definably historic artifacts.

[94] Porter and Pitts, *Fundamentals*, 90 (n. 2 [see also 1–6]). The concept of an original text is much debated in textual criticism. Eldon J. Epp, "The Multivalence of the Term 'Original Text' in New Testament Textual Criticism," *HTR* (1999): 280, explains how the term *original* has "exploded into a complex and highly unmanageable multivalent entity." Some text critics are adamant that the best we can hope for is an initial text (*Ausgangstext*). See Elliott, *Textual Criticism*, 7. For further study see Holger Strutwolf, "Original Text and Textual History," in *The Textual History of the Greek New Testament: Changing Views in Contemporary Research* (eds. Klaus Wachtel and Michael Holmes; SBLTCS 8; Leiden: Brill, 2012," 23–41, and most recently Porter, "Domains," 131–53.

[95] Mink, "Contamination," 148. Meanwhile, Klaus Wachtel, "Conclusions," in *The Textual History of the Greek New Testament: Changing Views in Contemporary Research* (eds. Klaus Wachtel and Michael Holmes; SBLTCS 8; Leiden: Brill, 2012), 222, suggests the method is not a cure for contamination, but a way to live with it (or understand it). Gurry, *Examination*, 207, notes how contamination "may remain a problem for which the only solution for the CBGM is evidence from outside the CBGM."

[96] Wachtel, "Conclusions," 224, states that the method applies "internal criteria predominantly" while deriving "tendencies regarding ancestor relationships on this basis." Although Mink allows for the inputted internal and external criteria to be corrected, starting without text-types is disconcerting. Mink, "Contamination," 149.

[97] Delobel, "Luke-Acts," 106.

[98] Epp, "Issues," 17–76 (38, 41). Ropes, "Text of Acts," 3:x, saw the second-century development of the Western text as a "monument of the life and thought of that period, an historical source, although one not easily reconstructed with completeness and accuracy."

[99] Elliot, *Textual Criticism*, 18; Epp, "Traditional 'Canons,'" 100; and Parker, *Textual Scholarship*, 26–7.

So, from a source perspective what is the value of these variants in Acts 28:11-31 and "what do they suggest"? Perhaps it is better to ask, "What do they *not* suggest"?[100] The goal of this chapter was to understand the significance of the variants in light of the known Western tendencies.[101] These tendencies, though often debated, exhibit one unifying characteristic since Westcott and Hort onwards, and that is *expansion*.[102] However, as we can see in the manuscript record the differences among the manuscripts with respect to Acts 28:11-31 are relatively *colourless* (see Appendix). In previous chapters, we have acknowledged that the end of Acts begs for an answer to whatever happened to Paul and his appeal to Caesar and the upcoming trial (Acts 25:11).[103] At the same time, this triumphant ending begs for at least a scribal note concerning the catastrophic events that soon followed. And yet not one single extant manuscript of Acts says anything about them. Given the variety of conclusions regarding the end of Acts, it requires a careful assessment of the "extant evidence, drawing only such conclusions as seem to be warranted by it."[104] So what conclusions can be drawn from the evidence?

The greatest observation is, in fact, a negative one. The so-called Western variants do *not* present any major theological, social, cultural, or historical differences as compared with the Alexandrian text. Given the generally accepted tendency for Western scribe(s) to expand on the text of Acts, intrinsic probabilities imply that a Western editor would capitalize on the storyline and present a much more colourful ending to Acts. However, the variants at the end of Acts, with a few more details and differences, nevertheless paint a similar picture of the hero of the story, Paul, in house arrest and awaiting trial in Rome (Acts 28:16, 30).[105] This supports an early date of Acts because we have an entire collection of variants that all point to the same period in history—pre-64 CE.

Since modern times, a variety of literary or narrative solutions have been offered, but these do not account for the colourless expansions in light of Roman and Jewish history in the mid-60s CE. Is it reasonable to suppose that the later versions of Acts were published well into the late first or early second century, decades apart from the first draft while betraying no major differences in the end of the narrative? No, it is more reasonable to suggest that the variants are comparable in age. The gap between the first draft and the later stages of its transmission is minor, represented by months and years, not decades.

Not only is the author of Acts (in 28:11-31) silent with regard to the fate of Paul, the terrible events that affected the Roman Empire, the city of Rome, and the church in the mid-60s CE, the Western scribes and editors are also equally silent.[106] The earliest

---

[100] See "Appendix: The Manuscript Record for Acts 28:11-31."
[101] Recall Head's, "Acts," 415, observation on the Western *Tendenz*.
[102] See Westcott and Hort, *Original Greek II*, 122-6, 174; Ramsay, *St. Paul*, 24-7; Hemer, *Acts*, 55; and Strange, *Problem*, 4, 38-56.
[103] See Fitzmyer, *Acts*, 52.
[104] See Pherigo, "Close of Acts," 277.
[105] Tajra claims the concentration on "legal terminology and procedure can only lead to the conclusion that Luke has given a legally realistic account of Paul's judicial history in Acts." Harry W. Tajra, *The Trial of St. Paul: A Juridical Exegesis of the Second Half of the Acts of the Apostles* (WUNT 2/35; Tübingen: Mohr Siebeck, 1989), 1-2.
[106] See my Chapter 8 and Hemer, *Acts*, 365-410.

and simplest explanation—that Luke knew no more—should now be given greater attention because of the combined silence of *all* the variants.[107] Unfortunately, great literary efforts, that are often divorced from a study of the variants and the historical context of Acts 28, have been given to explain away this silence through various literary methodologies and theories of foreshadowing without addressing the foundation of history and lower criticism first.[108]

If a scribe would take the time to provide additional details about Paul's imprisonment with regard to the captain of the guard (τῷ στρατοπεδάρχῳ) in Acts 28:16, how could the same scribe fail to narrate Paul's martyrdom, the dying multitudes of Christians and victims of the Great Fire of Rome, the Jewish War with Rome, or the destruction of Jerusalem and its Temple?[109] There is not so much as a marginal notation anywhere in any textual strata of Acts. The burden of proof must be shifted back to scholars who claim that the end of Acts evinces sophisticated literary devices not only by the original author, but also across the entire manuscript record.

Is it realistic to argue that all of these scribes, writing from different geographical areas, faithfully maintained the same silence throughout the first and second century? Surely the later Western redactor(s) and scribes would say something of the obvious about Paul, his trial and death, or the destruction of the Temple or Jerusalem itself? How completely out of context is the picture of Paul's peaceful relationship with the Roman authorities and his free preaching—that spans the entire manuscript record—given the events that followed the narrative![110]

The city of Rome takes centre stage in Acts 28 and yet every textual variant examined in the Appendix fails to mention the city's greatest disaster—the fire of Rome in 64 CE that turned nearly 70 per cent of the city into ashes, along with a sizable portion

---

[107] Recall Rackham's, *Acts*, li; idem, "Plea," 76–87, incredulity of Luke's silence with regard to Paul's death that was introduced in Chapter 1. Cf. also Troftgruben, *Conclusion Unhindered*, 8–11; Muratorian fragment (lines 35–9); Clement, *1 Clem.* 5:2-7; Chrysostom, *Hom. Act.* 55 and Eusebius, *Hist. Eccl.* 2.22:1, 6-8; 3.1:3.

[108] Perhaps the greatest interpretative (and methodological) failure of some is that they develop their hypotheses based on a supposed *majority* view on the date of Acts between 80 and 90 CE—that has been recently dismissed by *every* major monograph on the subject and continues to be dismissed in the most recent essays. See Mittelstaedt, *Lukas als Historiker*; Pervo, *Dating Acts*; Tyson, *Marcion*; Porter, "Early Church," 72–100, idem, "Dating," 553–74; Armstrong, "A New Plea," (2017): 79–110; idem, "Variants," 87–110. See also Keener, *Acts*, 1:382–40.

[109] It has long been observed how Western readings regularly "impinge on historical questions." See Head, "Problem," 419. And yet, with all the propensity to fill in the "historical" blanks elsewhere, the scribes (or redactor) of these variants remain silent with regard to the major events that tragically affected both Jews and Christians along with the people Jerusalem and Rome. The earliest redactor or Aland's *Hauptredaktor* could have been from Rome as he seemed to be aware of very specific political and military situations unique to the Imperial city. Cf. Tuckett, "How Early," 70. The στρατοπεδάρχος (Acts 28:16) in particular gives an "impression of authenticity." Cf. Kenyon, "Western Text," 310; Bruce, *Acts* (1983), 528–9, and Ramsay, *St. Paul*, 347–8. That the "stratopedarch" in the Western text of Acts 28:16 is the Praetorian Prefect Afranius Burrus is interesting but speculative. See Witherington, *New Testament History*, 788.

[110] Marguerat, *Historian*, 34–5, notices the positive attitude in Acts towards Rome versus the negative portrayal in Revelation: "It is the goal of Paul's mission for the former [in Acts] and the symbol of evil for the latter." Likewise, Tajra *Trial of St. Paul*, 164, recognizes the "positive tone on which Acts ends." The Western additions in Acts 28 are also favourable to Rome suggesting a time that was prior to Nero's conflagration policy against Christians.

of its general population, in addition to the Christians who were murdered during Nero's subsequent persecution.[111] No credible historian, whether ancient or modern, much less the "first Christian historian," could invent such an ending if these events had already passed.[112] If such a fabricated ending can be justified by popular literary theories then the book of Acts should then be relegated to a fictional class of literature that ignores the historical context.

Conclusion: The End of Acts and the Comparable Age of Its Variants

Whatever date one ascribes to the text(s) of Acts 28:11-31, they are comparable in age, especially when factoring the modest expansions that betray no clear knowledge of the aftermath of Paul (the book's protagonist), nor the destruction of Rome and Jerusalem (the book's central locations), nor the Jewish Temple (the book's central institution).[113] Given all the Western tendencies for expansion, there is not one reference to these tragic events anywhere in the manuscript record of Acts, nor are there any clearly significant theological expansions that reflect a later stage of the church's life or theology. These observations further strengthen Epp's observation regarding the "comparable age" of the B and D text clusters.[114] Given the lack of expansion, it is proposed that the age of the variants should be dated within relative proximity to the events of the mid- and late 60s CE that impacted Rome, Judaea, and the church in remarkable ways. It is to these terrifying and cataclysmic events in world history that we now turn.

---

[111] See Chapter 8.
[112] Gasque, *History*, 160, relays how Meyer was perhaps the first to give Luke the title, "'the historian' par excellence" before Dibelius called Luke the "first Christian historian" (as noted by Marguerat, *Historian*, 12, and Marshall, *Luke: Historian and Theologian*, 49).
[113] Paul is the central character in Acts: Acts 8:1; 9:1-30; 11:25-30; 12:25; chapters 13–15 and especially from 15:40 all the way to the end in 28:31. Rome is a central location: Acts 2:10; 18:2; 19:21; 23:11; 25:25, 27; 27:1; 28:11, 14, 16-17. Jerusalem is also central: Acts 1:4, 8, 12, 19; 2:5, 14; 4:5, 16; 5:16, 28; 6:7; 8:1, 14, 25-27; 9:2, 13, 19-21, 26-28; 10:39; 11:2, 22, 27; 12:25; 13:13, 27, 31; 15:1-4; 16:4; 18:22; 19:21; 20:16, 22; 21:4, 11-17, 31; 22:5, 17-18; 23:11; 24:11, 17; 25:1-24; 26:4, 10, 20 and is mentioned in 28:17 where Paul's engagement with the Jews in Rome occurs approximately five years before the Jewish War in 66 CE. The Temple as well plays a key role in the narrative: Acts 2:46; 3:1-10; 4:1; 5:20-25, 42; 21:26-30; 22:17; 24:6, 12, 18; 25:8; 26:2.
[114] Epp, "Traditional 'Canons,'" 100.

8

Acts in Its Jewish and Greco-Roman Historical Contexts

Introduction

Since the first chapter, there has been a consistent attempt to place the book of Acts in its proper historical context.[1] The last chapter presented argues that this context is consistent with a pre-70 date of Acts while challenging the credibility of the various literary explanations that often start with the assumption that Acts must have been written later. Such literary explanations focus primarily on the presumed death of Paul to the almost wholesale neglect of other key events.[2]

The Great Fire of Rome in July of 64 CE was an event that devastated a large portion of the eternal city and Nero's subsequent persecution, according to non-Christian sources, saw "multitudes" of Roman Christians slaughtered with notorious barbarity. Most scholars in the middle and especially late dating camps completely ignore this aspect of Christian and Roman history. There has also been much discussion about the prophecy of Jerusalem's destruction in Luke's gospel where it is often assumed, rather than argued, that this reference is proof that Luke (and by extension Acts) is clearly written *after* this event. In a sense, this final chapter is a tale of two cities—Rome and Jerusalem—where the assumptions and literary explanations regarding the Christian history in Acts are re-examined once more in the context of Jewish and Greco-Roman history.

This re-examination of the book of Acts is resolutely consistent with a time that is not only before the siege of Jerusalem in 70 CE, but also before the death of Paul and

---

[1] Recall my note 14 on the historical context in Chapter 2. Gill et al., *Ancient Literary Setting*, ix–xiii, make this distinction in their preface.

[2] In addition to the death of Paul (*c*. 63–64 CE), the Great Fire of Rome (64 CE), and the destruction of the Jewish Temple (70 CE), many other significant historical events are *not* clearly detailed in Acts: (1) the deaths of the other two great apostles: James (62 CE) and Peter (*c*. 64 CE); (2) the Jewish Revolt in 66 CE; (3) the death of Nero in 68 CE; (4) the destruction of Jerusalem in 70 CE; (5) the Roman Triumph in 71 CE; (6) the eruption of Mount Vesuvius and the destruction of Pompeii and Herculaneum in 79 CE (Acts 28:13-14). Cf. Hemer, *Acts*, 365–410. Tajra, *Martyrdom*, 199, finds "a few facts about Paul's final days"—(1) that Paul died in Rome; (2) Paul died during Nero's reign (54–68 CE); (3) Paul was martyred.

the fire of Rome in July of 64 CE.³ Such events in Jewish, Roman, and Christian history are far too cataclysmic to be ignored—or relegated to a footnote—in favour of yet another speculative literary explanation. Hence my chosen date is somewhere between 62 and 63 CE.

Acts in History

Before diving into a discussion of the fall of Jerusalem and the fire of Rome, it seems appropriate to briefly discuss the historicity of Acts as this relates to our ability to connect the events in the narrative within the broader spectrum of history.[4] Since there continue to be scholars who assume, to varying degrees, the fictional character of Acts, it is important not to make a similar mistake and assume its historicity.[5] For example,

---

[3] There is some debate as to the exact date of Paul's death but historians are clear it happened before the end of Nero's reign in 68 CE and very likely a few years beforehand; that was either just before or during the Neronian persecution in 64 CE. Tajra, *Martyrdom*, 199, pins the death of Paul (by execution) as "quite certain" to have occurred specifically in Rome (and not in any other city) and during Nero's reign (54–68 CE). He concludes (199) that the "likeliest juridical schema" involves (1) Paul's release from house arrest at the end of the two years (62 CE, Acts 28:30), and (2) a "short period of freedom" with the possibility of a trip to Spain, (3) Paul was arrested for a second time and endured a harsher captivity, (4) he was tried according to "extra ordinem procedure," and (5) following the via Ostiense, was "led outside the city walls" and "beheaded by a speculator" (63/64 CE). Tajra also concludes he was buried in a columbarium "very near his locus passionis" (199). Based on all of the sources, and with some archaeological evidence, this location is considered very close to this section of the via Ostiense, where the basilica "San Paolo fuori le mura" (St. Paul Outside the Walls) now stands. See the second-century account of Gaius in Eusebius, Hist. eccl. 2.25.7 and Riesner, "Paul's Trial," 407; G. Giorgio Filippi, "Die Ergebnisse der neuen Ausgrabungen am Grab des Apostels Paulus," *MDAI(RA)* 112 (2005–2006): 277–92. On a similar chronology to Tajra (especially the date of 62 CE as the end of Paul's first Roman imprisonment and his death "around 63/64" instead of a few years later with Peter in 67/68 CE) see Riesner, "Paul's Trial," 406 (here 407); Lothar Wehr, *Petrus und Paulus, Kontrahenten und Partner: Die beiden Apostel im Spiegel des Neuen Testaments, der Apostolischen Väter und früher Zeugnisse ihrer Verehrung* (Münster: Aschendorff, 1996), 359; and Pherigo, "Close of Acts," 277–84 (278).

[4] See Chapter 2 and "Principles for Sources and Textual Criticism." Greene and Moore, *Archaeology*, 155, suggest (as their third criterion for historical dating) that we factor the "author's record of accuracy." Hemer's, *Acts*, 1, observation with regard to Acts is just as relevant today as he states that the "question of its historicity has been strangely neglected" and not answered definitively. And yet, his work remains foundational to this question. As regards the historical reliability of Acts in general, refer to the earlier studies by Ramsay, *St. Paul*, and idem, *Recent Discovery*; Lake et al., eds., *Beginnings of Christianity*; Cadbury, *Luke-Acts*; idem, *History*; Dibelius, *Studies*. For more recent discussion see Hengel, *Acts*, 1–68; Bruce, *Acts* (3rd edn), 27–34; Marshall, *Luke: Historian and Theologian*; idem, *Acts*, 35–6; Gasque, *History*; Marguerat, *Historian*; Porter, *Paul in Acts*; and the collection of essays in BAFCS; Charles K. Barrett, "The Historicity of Acts," *JTS* 50 (1999): 515–34; and Keener, *Acts*, 1:166–220. For more critical (or sceptical) views see Haenchen, *Acts*; Conzelmann, *Acts*; Pervo, *Acts*; and Lüdemann, *Acts*.

[5] E.g., Haenchen, *Acts*; Pervo, *Acts*; idem, *Profit with Delight*; Lüdemann, *Acts*; and MacDonald, "Paul's Farewell," 189–203. Haenchen's perspective is discussed in more detail below. Helga Botermann, a German historian of classical antiquity, writes: "I have been shocked for many years concerning the manner in which New Testament scholars treat their sources. They have managed to question everything to such a degree that both the historical Jesus and the historical Paul are hardly discernible any longer. If classical scholars were to adopt their methods, they could take their leave immediately. They would not have much left to work with . . . If classical scholars analyzed their sources as 'critically' as most New Testament theologians do, they would have to close the files of Herodotus and Tacitus." Cf. Helga Botermann, "Der Heidenapostel und sein Historiker.

Alexander cuts to the chase and asks "whether or not Acts should be read as 'history.'"[6] A little further she asks: "Does Acts give an accurate picture of the events it narrates?—or more simply, 'Is Acts true?'"[7] The answers to these questions are not a simple "yes" or "no," but a matter of ongoing debate and require a much greater discussion than can be allotted here. These questions do, however, require some consideration because of the relationship between the events in the narrative of Acts and their relationship to history.

In Chapter 1, it was suggested that one's views on the date of Acts are directly related to the book's perceived historical reliability.[8] This seems to be the general trend, although some scholars perceive its relative historicity while also subscribing to a later date:

> Today there are few who support the early date for Acts championed by Rackham. To reject the early date does not in itself deny the historical value of the book, the question remains open. A date as late as 150 is fairly generally abandoned. AD 90 or thereabouts is more probable—and this is neither early enough to forbid the intrusion of legend, nor late enough to be out of touch with facts.[9]

Although Barrett's erudition on Acts is generally commended, his assertion here seems problematic.[10] On this point I am inclined to agree with Pervo—that such comfortable parameters sound more like a "political compromise" and that a date in the "80's requires a great deal of explaining away."[11]

Zur historischen Kritik der Apostelgeschichte," *ThBeitr* 24 (1993): 62–84 (64, 73). Translation from Schnabel, *Mission*, 1:23.

[6] See Alexander, *Ancient*, 133. This question goes back at least to Baur and the Tübingen school. See William Baird, *History of New Testament Research. 1. From Deism to Tübingen* (Minneapolis: Fortress, 1992), 244–93.

[7] See Alexander, *Ancient*, 133. She says this is a "perfectly right and proper question to ask of any narrative" (133). Hemer, *Acts*, 15, ponders the question as to whether Acts is essentially reliable or not, or somewhere in between. He figures that "inquiry is overlaid with conflicts of presupposition." As well, the quest to "prove the historicity of Acts" is far too simplistic (206). See also Hemer's first chapter on "Acts and Historicity" (1–29).

[8] Recall my note 3 from Chapter 1.

[9] Barrett, "The Historicity of Acts," 515–34 (530).

[10] For example, according to Kosso, *Knowing the Past*, 51, the first criterion for assessing the credibility of a text is the "ancient author's access to the event." Additionally, Greene and Moore's, *Archaeology*, 155, second criterion for historical dating is "the distance (in time and place) of the author from the events described." See "Principles for Sources and Textual Criticism" in Chapter 2. If Acts is dated somewhere in the 90s CE then it seems that the author is fairly out of touch with the events within the narrative. In similar terms, Porter, "Dating," 565, claims a late date implies that the NT books were "second-generation or later documents, without direct contact with the events or people that they purport to represent." Therefore, against Barrett's view there seems to be a diminishing historical "credibility" for Acts as it is dated increasingly later (especially *c.* 90 CE).

[11] Pervo, "Suburbs," 31 and 46 respectively. See also Porter, "Dating," 553–74 (568). With regard to the NT books in general the "middle dates are less argued dates than a settled-upon compromise between the perceived extremes of the early dates—which usually implies a level of conservatism and orthodoxy unacceptable to many scholars" (565). Dupont, *Sources*, 168 (n. 1), in his final comment says that a "traditional affirmation is not necessarily erroneous. At the level of critical thought, the reasons which make one opinion preferable to another are more important than the fact of knowing whether this opinion has been put forward by ecclesiastical or academic authorities."

Barrett's point that the relative historicity of Acts is compatible with a later date is feasible to a certain degree, where some of the events may still be considered factual and datable. However, at the same time the relative historicity of *any* historical document that fabricates its narrative in order to hide the fate of its main character (Paul), along with the destruction of the city he is residing in (Rome), the subsequent murder of the people he was at great pains to reach (Christians), and the destruction of his people's holy city (Jerusalem) should be called into question and placed into the realm of historical fiction at best.[12]

The relative historicity of Acts is also related to our understanding of sources (recall Chapters 2 and 3). If one's views on the date of Acts are directly related to the book's perceived historical reliability to some degree, then by reasonable extension the book's perceived historical reliability also relates to one's perceived reliability of the author's sources.[13] In simpler terms, a decidedly historical (or unhistorical) view of Acts also directly impacts one's view of sources. If we take stock of the extensive historiography on the date of Acts, it seems that late dating advocates tend to classify Acts as unhistorical and the author's sources as unreliable. Acts is then subject to parallels with romance novels, Homeric works, and later historians (notably Josephus)—and in some cases, Acts is considered to be no more than the author's literary invention or imagination.[14]

Nevertheless, even the most critical (and overtly sceptical) scholars recognize a measure of historicity for Acts and recognize the author is clearly relying on some form of a source (or sources) and did not invent all of the stories and speeches in the narrative for some imaginative purpose. For example, although Haenchen is hesitant to name specific sources, he does not dismiss the likelihood of such sources either.[15] He does not reject outright even the long-standing Antioch source theory but challenges its veracity while also weighing the possibility of Paul's companions as legitimate sources of information.[16]

---

[12] If Paul goes to Rome in 60–61 CE and stays there under house arrest for the subsequent two-year period this brings us close to 63 CE—just within a year of Rome's Great Fire in July of 64 CE and Nero's subsequent persecution of Christians. Paul's death was arguably close to this time. The Jewish revolt began in 66 CE while Jerusalem was levelled in 70 CE.

[13] Pervo, *Dating Acts*, 1, is absolutely correct in his lament at just how far away the issue of dating early Christian texts and sources are from the "cutting edge" in order to "make the subject exciting only to a highly impressionable freshman." He refers to Wendt, *Die Apostelgeschichte* (8th edn), who gave substantial attention to the sources of Acts and then to Haenchen, *Acts*, who sent "reams of source theory up the chimney" (1). Pervo also refers to Talbert, *Reading Acts*, 2, who "efficiently dispenses with questions about the sources and date of Acts before he has completed the first page" (*Dating Acts*, 1). Questions of source and date must return to the forefront of any serious discussion on the interpretation of Acts.

[14] Keener, *Acts*, 1:199, thinks that "on the whole, scholars seem more appreciative than not of Acts as a legitimate source for historical reconstruction"—although he notes this appreciation is anything but unanimous. Cf. also Marguerat, *Historian*, 2–7. For a decidedly unhistorical view of Acts, see MacDonald, "Paul's Farewell," 189.

[15] Haenchen, *Acts*, 86. Although Marshall, *Acts*, 36, with regard to the publication of Haenchen's *Die Apostelgeschichte* (1956), says that up to that point "anyone who thought that R. Bultmann represented the ultimate in historical scepticism as regards the New Testament was in for a rude shock." Haenchen's scepticism is well known but nevertheless he has made an indelible imprint on Luke-Acts scholarship. See Armstrong, "Ernst Haenchen," (forthcoming).

[16] Haenchen, *Acts*, 87, 369. Recall the "Antioch Source Theories" from Chapter 3.

For Haenchen, it was not a simple matter of choosing between a "travel-journal and the chronicle of Antioch."[17] He thought they were both oral and written traditions that originated with certain Christians and their associated church communities. For Luke there were "various possibilities of collecting the required material."[18] He could connect with the "most important Pauline communities" (i.e., Philippi, Corinth, Ephesus, Antioch) or he might even travel to Jerusalem.[19] He could have asked "other Christians travelling to these places" or "written to the congregations in question and asked them for information."[20]

If we compare Haenchen with Hengel it is clear that Hengel is far more optimistic in his assessment concerning the "historical reliability of Acts" and yet he does agree "substantially" with Haenchen as regards to "Luke's method of collecting data."[21] According to Hengel, Luke is the first theologian whose approach was to go back and examine *ad fontes* "the primitive Christian sources (cf. Lk. 1:1),"[22] asking questions of those who "handed on the traditions, and evaluating critically his sources."[23]

With regard to the historical reliability of Acts, Hengel has much to say, although he is not naive concerning some of the errors and inaccuracies in Acts.[24] But this is no surprise due to the fact that the events took place over the course of some thirty-plus years.[25] For him, the author can be compared to his contemporaries:

> Luke is no less trustworthy than other historians of antiquity. People have done him a great injustice in comparing him too closely with the edifying, largely fictitious, romance-like writings in the style of the later acts of apostles, which freely invent

---

[17] Haenchen, *Acts*, 86. Over the course of his publications Haenchen came to question (in greater intensity) the itinerary/travel-journal hypothesis proposed by Dibelius—initially he supported it, but later rejected it.
[18] Ibid.
[19] Ibid., 86. Haenchen (503) thinks that Luke "probably received the information concerning Philippi—directly or indirectly—from an eyewitness of the Pauline mission . . . He may have received not only information about the founding of the community and the expulsion of the Apostle, but also stories which circulated about Paul in Philippi."
[20] Ibid., 86. His view on the process of gathering information is reasonable.
[21] Donelson, "Cult Histories," 3.
[22] Hengel, *Acts*, 63.
[23] Donelson, "Cult Histories," 3; Hengel, *Acts*, 61–3. Against Haenchen, Hengel (65) proposes that "Luke makes use of two strands of source material" although "we can no longer make a consecutive reconstruction of them." The first is the so-called Antiochene or Hellenist source which he thinks derives from Stephen, Philip, and the "reports about Barnabas and Paul's early days" (65). The second is from a "collection of stories about Peter" (66). Essentially, Luke used these sources to "make a careful selection from them to serve the purpose of his narrative." Hengel, *Acts*, 66. The flow of the narrative moves from the Jewish-Christian community in Jerusalem (that is given "central significance") to "Paul's world-wide mission to the Gentiles" (66).
[24] Hengel, *Acts*, 35 and 112. He claims that the "chronological arrangement is substantially better than that in the gospels, though it too has errors and inaccuracies" (35). Although Acts is "incomplete, fragmentary and misleading" at times, he reminds us that we cannot place Paul in his proper geographical or historical setting without this source (38). We would be in the dark about much of Paul's life without Acts (i.e., Paul's origins in Tarsus, link with Jerusalem, the significance of Antioch and Barnabas, the sequence of Paul's letters, his missionary activity—all this and more would be "completely or largely unknown to us without Acts" (39).
[25] Ibid., 35 (see his chapter on "Acts as a Historical Source").

facts as they like and when they need them. There is a great gulf between him and the later romances about the apostles.[26]

Hengel remarks how Acts at "many points" is "connected with other contemporary historical sources."[27] Some of these points of connection—Josephus, Suetonius, and the Gallio inscription at Delphi that dates Paul's stay in Corinth—enable us to develop a chronology for Paul and our earliest sources for Christianity.[28]

There are also other avenues to evaluate the historicity of Luke-Acts. Hengel claims that if we go by "ancient standards, the relative reliability of his account can be tested in the gospels by a synoptic comparison with Matthew and Mark."[29] Hengel sees the author as an *editor* emphasizing the parts he considered worthy while shrinking the others to fit his authorial need. Luke combines "separate historical traditions to serve his ends" while on the other he can "separate matters that belong together" if this achieves a "meaningful sequence of events."[30] Hengel is also right in saying that "one can hardly accuse [Luke] of simply having invented events, creat[ing] scenes out of nothing and depict[ing] them on a broad canvas, deliberately falsifying his traditions in an unrestrained way for the sake of cheap effect."[31] Based on the "standards of

---

[26] Ibid., 60 (see also p. 12).

[27] Ibid., 39.

[28] Ibid. See also Cadbury, *Acts in History*, 115; David W. J. Gill and Bruce W. Winter, "Acts and Roman Religion," in *The Book of Acts in Its Graeco-Roman Setting* (eds. David W. J. Gill and Conrad Gempf; 5 vols; BAFCS 2; Grand Rapids: Eerdmans, 1995), 98–103; Lampe, *Valentinus*, 14; John McRay, *Archaeology and the New Testament* (Grand Rapids: Baker, 2008), 227; Keener's section on "Claudius's Expulsion of Jews from Rome" (*Acts*, 3:2697-714) and his discussion on Gallio with reference to Acts 18:12-17 (3:2760-79). Keener explains that "despite a small number of detractors, most scholars agree that the Gallio inscription allows us to pinpoint to within a year or two the time when Gallio was in Corinth" (3:2761). Jerome Murphy-O'Connor, *St. Paul's Corinth: Texts and Archaeology* (Collegeville, MN: Liturgical Press, 2002), 161, insists that our "only means of dating the presence of this official in Corinth" is this "badly broken inscription containing a letter of the Emperor Claudius." This lynchpin in Pauline Chronology was a letter written after Claudius had been acclaimed emperor for the twenty-sixth time. Hence the upper limit is the twenty-seventh year, which is dated between January 25 and August 1 of 52 CE. Murphy-O'Connor proposes that the letter was written in the late spring or early summer of 52 (164) based on Seneca's statement that his brother did not finish his term of office—hence, "it is impossible to place Gallio's encounter with Paul (Acts 18:12-17) in the latter part of the proconsular year A.D. 51–52" (167). Therefore, Gallio's encounter with Paul "must have taken place between July and September A.D. 51" (167). See also, Jerome Murphy-O'Connor's, "Paul and Gallio," *JBL* 112 (1993): 315–17, terse and persuasive rebuttal of Dixon Slingerland's, "Acts 18:1–18, the Gallio Inscription, and Absolute Pauline Chronology," *JBL* 110 (1991): 439–49, seven-year window theory. Last, see Campbell's, *Framing Paul*, 182–9, recent treatment on Pauline chronology where he argues that Paul's letters do in fact provide an "absolute chronology" with respect to 2 Cor. 11:32-33 (quotation from 182).

[29] Hengel, *Acts*, 61. Similarly, Keener, *Acts*, 1:181, explains how in the third gospel Luke "preserves the basic substance of his sources where we can compare them." See also Craig S. Keener, *The Historical Jesus of the Gospels* (Grand Rapids: Eerdmans, 2012), 85–94. As a consequence, we have "no reason to assume that he acted completely differently" in Acts from his first work, or that he invented his narrative "largely out of his own head." Hengel, *Acts*, 61. Since Christianity was based on a series of events that were not only eschatological but also historical, its proclamation had to be narrative (41).

[30] Hengel, *Acts*, 61. Evidently, "All of this" says Hengel, "can be found in the secular historians of Greek and Roman antiquity" (61).

[31] Ibid. The suppositional thinking that sees the author as painting a falsified picture continues without justification. Cf. Pervo, *Acts*, 688 and Lüdemann, *Acts*, 347–9.

antiquity" there is a sense that Luke-Acts "always remains within the limits of what was considered reliable" at the time.[32]

Furthermore, it seems reasonable to suppose that the author's "assurance" in the preface (Lk. 1:3) is no "mere convention" as it reflects a "real theological and historical programme."[33] Accordingly, Hengel maintains that the author does "not set out primarily to present his own 'theology,'" but rather an honest recollection of the events described in the book.[34]

> We only do justice to the significance of Luke as the first theological "historian" of Christianity if we take his work seriously as a source, i.e. if we attempt to examine it critically, reconstructing the work which he tells by adding and comparing other sources. The radical "redaction critical" approach so popular today, which sees Luke above all as a freely inventive theologian, mistakes his real purpose, namely that as a "Christian" historian he sets out to *report the events of the past* that provided the foundation for the faith and its extension (original emphasis).[35]

These reported "events of the past" are measurable and datable on the *outside* while on the *inside* they represent something far greater as Hengel indicates.[36]

The events narrated in Acts provide nothing short of the foundation of the faith of the early church (Acts 2:1-41).[37] And yet these events should not be divorced from the significant events that occurred within the broader context of history.[38] Furthermore, in general, the first Christian authors did not "claim to be inspired writers, like the prophets of the OT. Their authority did not rest on a theory of inspiration, but on the truth-claim contained in the eschatological saving event which they presented."[39] The

---

[32] Hengel, *Acts*, 61.
[33] Ibid. He contends that this assurance "cannot be measured by the standards of a modern critical historian" (61). Recall the discussion on "The 'We' Passages and the Prologue" from Chapter 3.
[34] Ibid., 68.
[35] Ibid., 67-8.
[36] Recall "Principles for Selecting Events" from Chapter 2 and Collingwood, *Idea*, 213. There is a tendency for Acts scholars to focus on the inside of the event and begin the process of interpretation without doing the hard work of assessing the external/outside of the event. At the same time, it is also possible to assess the external and bypass the internal meaning as well.
[37] In Acts 2:13 we have an early case of interpreting the inside of an event. On the *outside* Luke describes this miraculous experience of speaking in other tongues (v. 4). This supernatural interchange of speaking and understanding leads some to the *inside* interpretation (or better charge) that "they have had too much wine" (v. 13). The counter-interpretation (also on the inside) is that this is an outpouring of God's Spirit and they are not drunk due to the early time of day (vv. 15-21). The inside nature of this event can be set aside for the moment in favour of the *outside* interpretation that this group of early Christians heard a sound (v. 2), saw "tongues of fire" (v. 3), spoke in "other tongues" (v. 4), while the crowd also "heard this sound" (v. 6) and their "own language being spoken." While other explanations of each aspect of this experience may be offered something momentous occurred to the disciples and the crowd in Jerusalem that was worth recording by Luke. The crowd witnessed this event and immediately began the process of interpretation asking "What does this mean?" (12)—while Luke (via Peter's speech in 2:14-21) explains what was happening from Joel 2:28-32.
[38] Munslow, *Deconstructing History*, 45.
[39] Hengel, *Acts*, 19, but see Brian S. Rosner, "Acts and Biblical History," in *The Book of Acts in Its Ancient Literary Setting* (eds. Bruce W. Winter and Andrew D. Clarke; 5 vols; BAFCS 1; Grand Rapids: Eerdmans, 1993), 1:65-82.

outside of the events happened first, and the subsequent *inside* interpretation of those events occurred in light of the OT writings (e.g., Acts 2:16, 22-24). Although we cannot know with certainty what happened in the past, our sources allow us to construct what happened within the greater narrative of history.[40]

There are further reasons to assign a measure of credibility to Luke as a historian. The traditions of early Christianity were handed down "not with anonymous communities but with well-known individual authoritative bearers of tradition."[41] Additionally, there is an established paper trail of sources for Acts that involves recognized people, places, and events. As Hengel explains, the "history of earliest Christianity in the first sixty or seventy years down to the time of the composition of the four gospels did not get lost in any anonymous, unbounded and imaginary setting; it can still be traced."[42]

Perhaps the most applicable point to this discussion in particular, and the date of Acts in general, is the question of Luke's intention and impression that was introduced in Chapter 3 to present a reliable account for Theophilus (Lk. 1:3).[43] Rosner asks a similar question: "Did Luke intend to write history?" and points to the fact that Acts has

> so many features in common with the Old Testament historical works strongly suggests that Luke was writing what he conceived to be a historical work. The conclusion that Luke wrote as a historian does not of course settle the question of whether he was a reliable writer. That would depend on the state of his sources, the soundness of his historical judgment, and so on.[44]

This entire discussion on the historicity of Acts in general, and Rosner's point in particular, does not answer Alexander's initial question of whether or not Acts is "true." And yet, if we consider Luke's intention to write history, his proximity to his sources, and the relative accuracy of the people, places, and events he records, this surely places his two-volume work in a different class of writing than an ancient novel or epic.[45]

---

[40] Munslow, *A History*, 7; Tosh, *Pursuit* (6th edn), x, 10.
[41] Hengel, *Acts*, 26.
[42] Ibid., 27.
[43] Recall "The 'We' Passages and the Prologue" from Chapter 3.
[44] Rosner, "Acts and Biblical History," 1:81.
[45] See Alexander, *Ancient*, 133; Hemer, *Acts*, 1–29. So far it has been argued that Acts is historical in the sense that it represents some form of historiography or biography, but certainly not epic. See Adams, *Genre of Acts*, 1–22, 170–1; Phillips, "Consensus?," 384–5; Palmer, "Monograph," 1:1–29; Smith and Kostopoulos, "Genre," 390–410; Pitts, *Genre*, 1–2. Additionally, Porter, *Paul in Acts*, 188, recognizes that Acts is "primarily a book of ancient historiography." On the contrary, MacDonald, "Paul's Farewell," 189–203 (189), via his "mimesis criticism" claims that the author "intended to write" anything but an "accurate history" that "only the most credulous could consider historically plausible." He dismisses Luke's sources as "incredibly naïve" and that he was "a sophisticated, clever and creative author of fiction" (189). He further states that a "growing number of scholars [without naming them] . . . have argued that Luke had no intention of writing history" (189). In the next paragraph he (189) refers to Bonz, *Legacy*, 26, and her problematic theory that Luke-Acts is a "prose epic modelled after Vergil's *Aeneid*." MacDonald says she is "generally on the right track, but she does not take her insight far enough" (190). He then suggests that Paul's farewell address (Acts 20:17-38) is in fact a "strategic rewriting of a famous episode in Homer's Iliad" (190). See also MacDonald, *Homer?* and idem, *Homeric Epics*. Recall also Troftgruben's comparisons with Homer's *Iliad* and Virgil's *Aeneid* with the end of Acts in Chapter 5.

The Fall of Jerusalem: Dividing the Early and Middle Groups

While the early and middle groups are inclined to place a higher value on the historicity of Acts and generally view the author in some way as an associate of Paul, late dating advocates tend to place a lower historical value on Acts.[46] They consider the author to be a "redactional theologian" while connecting their dates with dependency on Josephus, changing relations between Jews and Christians (via the curse of the Minim), Domitian's persecution, or "cultural or theological kinship to various features of a later date."[47] As identified in Chapter 1, the key divide between the early and middle groups rests on the relationship between Luke and the fall of Jerusalem in 70 CE.[48] Those who argue for a date after the fall of Jerusalem claim that Lk. 21:20-24 shows a "post-70 editing of Mark."[49] However, the prediction of Jerusalem's destruction as a *vaticinium ex eventu* is not decisive, especially given the city's history.[50]

Although the silence of Jerusalem's destruction in Acts does not prove an early date, Dodd's essay (along with the conclusions of Rackham, Torrey, and Hemer) has successfully challenged the arguments that support a post-70 CE date as too simplistic.[51] In Mk 13:2, Jesus pronounces judgement upon the Temple and the "abomination of desolation" in Mark 13:14 is replaced by "Jerusalem surrounded by camps" in Lk. 21:20.[52] Fitzmyer explains how this "Marcan apocalyptic prophecy, alluding to Dan 9:27 or 12:11, about the coming desolation of the Temple has given way to a description of a siege and capture of the city of Jerusalem itself."[53]

At first glance, the theory of Luke's post-70 CE editing of Mark does merit attention. However, an analysis of the prophetic language of Luke challenges this simple interpretation starting with the widespread LXX usage of ἐρήμωσις (destruction/desolation) in Lk. 21:20 as part of the phrase "the Abomination of Desolation" (τὸ βδέλυγμα τῆς ἐρημώσεως) from Mk 13:14.[54] In his analysis, which remains largely

---

[46] See Armstrong, "A New Plea," (2017): 91–4.
[47] So Hemer, *Acts*, 373. This tendency is common for dating the NT in general. See Porter, "Dating," 565.
[48] Fitzmyer, *Acts*, 54, in his summary claims that the "reasons for a post-70 dating are drawn mostly from the Lucan gospel." See Schäfer, *History of the Jews*, 123–33, and his chapter 7, "The First Jewish War (66–74 CE)." See also Mittelstaedt, *Lukas als Historiker*, 68–164, and his valuable insights on the destruction of Jerusalem. See also Steve Mason, *A History of the Jewish War: AD 66–74* (Cambridge: Cambridge University Press, 2016), et passim.
[49] Hemer, *Acts*, 374.
[50] Besides, a fulfilled prophecy carries a far greater literary force in the ancient world. See Hemer, *Acts*, 375; Bock, *Acts*, 27; Porter, *When Paul Met Jesus*, 78, and the example from Cassius Dio in "The Great fire of Rome" below.
[51] Dodd, "Jerusalem," 47–54; Hemer, *Acts*, 375; Torrey, *Composition*, 69–70. Pervo, *Dating Acts*, fails to engage Dodd's convincing arguments.
[52] The word κυκλόω "surround/encircle" or "to move around an object" is very popular in the LXX with ninety-five occurrences and only four in the NT (Lk. 21:20; Jn 10:24; Acts 14:20 and Heb. 11:30). See BDAG/L&N 15.146 and also Dodd, "Jerusalem," 48. In Hebrews 11:30 κυκλόω is used in a military sense regarding the walls of Jericho: "Πίστει τὰ τείχη Ἰεριχὼ ἔπεσαν κυκλωθέντα ἐπὶ ἑπτὰ ἡμέρας." Similarly, περικυκλόω (περι + κυκλόω) is found only once in Lk. 19:43 (in a military context) as compared to sixteen times in the LXX.
[53] Fitzmyer, *Acts*, 54.
[54] Although many scholars point to Luke's "redaction" of Mk 13:14 in Lk. 21:20, one could argue that the central "prophetic" description is common to all three synoptic gospels. For example, the phrase

ignored by middle and late dating advocates, Dodd argues persuasively against Luke's supposed "editing" of Mark stating that the "term 'editing' is in fact inapplicable."[55] Dodd explains that Luke in 21:21b-22 and 23b-24 is either "following a different source, or 'writing out of his own head.'"[56] Meanwhile in verses 21a and 23a Luke is "not 'editing' Mark but simply copying him. It is only in [verse] 20 that it is plausible to speak of him as 'editing' Mark 13:14."[57] Where Mk 13:14a reads "<u>When you see</u> the 'abomination of desolation'" (<u>Ὅταν δὲ ἴδητε</u> τὸ βδέλυγμα τῆς ἐρημώσεως) Lk. 21:20a writes "<u>When you see</u> Jerusalem surrounded by armies" (<u>Ὅταν δὲ ἴδητε</u> κυκλουμένην ὑπὸ στρατοπέδων Ἰερουσαλήμ).

With regard to Luke's "editing" in 21:20 Dodd says that it can "hardly" be argued that the "mere expression κυκλουμένην ὑπὸ στρατοπέδων, describes Titus's siege so precisely that it must necessarily be a 'vaticinium ex eventu.' If you want to say in Greek 'Jerusalem will be besieged,' the choice of available expressions is strictly limited, and κυκλοῦσθαι ὑπὸ στρατοπέδων, is about as colourless as any."[58] So in effect Luke (in 21:20) wished to modify Mark's usage here because otherwise it would be "unintelligible to the public he had in view."[59] We have every reason to suspect that Luke was capable of redacting his sources for his own needs.[60]

Another facet of the dividing wall between the early and middle groups involves the phrase "your house is abandoned" in Lk. 13:35 that some say can only make sense *after* the destruction of Jerusalem.[61] It seems that a number of scribes found this verse so familiar that they added ερημος (ἐρήμωσις) from Jer. 22:5 after ὑμῶν.[62] This prophetic language (or better, the language of prophets) very easily reflects Jer. 22:5 where the force of the words is even stronger: "But if you will not obey these words, I swear by myself, says the LORD, that this house will be for desolation" (ἐὰν δὲ μὴ ποιήσητε τοὺς λόγους τούτους, κατ' ἐμαυτοῦ ὤμοσα, λέγει κύριος, ὅτι εἰς ἐρήμωσιν ἔσται ὁ οἶκος οὗτος).[63]

"stone upon stone" λίθον ἐπὶ λίθον is found in Lk. 19:44 while the corresponding phrase λίθος ἐπὶ λίθον is identical to both Mk 13:2 and Mt. 24:2. The only difference is that the first stone in Lk. 19:44 is in the accusative case, where Mark and Matthew's usage is nominative.

[55] Dodd, "Jerusalem," 48.
[56] Ibid.
[57] Ibid.
[58] Ibid., 48. One would think that Luke would make some reference to στρατόπεδον rather than στρατοπέδων if he was looking back on the event since the actual siege was by "the" Roman army; or at the very least some imagery indicative of the Roman army or its legions perhaps.
[59] Ibid., 48–9. At this point in history, this would be a natural choice for any Greek speaking Jew or Christian (49). Dodd further cites several key passages where variants of ἐρήμωσις is found in the LXX (i.e., Jer. 4:7; 7:34; 51:6; etc). Where there are some twenty-six references in the LXX (Lev. 26:34-35; 2 Chron. 30:7, 36:21; 1 Esd. 1:55; Jdt. 8:22; 1 Macc. 1:54; etc), only three are found in the NT—curiously, they are the synoptic "desolation" passages (Mk 13:14; Mt. 24:15; and Lk. 21:20).
[60] See "Principles for Selecting Facts" in Chapter 2.
[61] Fitzmyer, *Acts*, 54.
[62] D, N, Δ, Θ, Ψ, f^{13}, 33, 700, 892, 1241, 1424, pm, it, vg^d, sy$^{c.p.h}$; and the Latin Irenaeus.
[63] A similar sentiment is expressed earlier in Jer. 12:17: (ἐὰν δὲ μὴ ἐπιστρέψωσιν, καὶ ἐξαρῶ τὸ ἔθνος ἐκεῖνο ἐξάρσει καὶ ἀπωλείᾳ). See also Lam. 2:7: "The Lord has rejected his altar, he has abandoned his sanctuary, he has shattered in the hand of the enemy the walls of her palaces" (Ἀπώσατο κύριος θυσιαστήριον αὐτοῦ, ἀπετίναξεν ἁγίασμα αὐτοῦ, συνέτριψεν ἐν χειρὶ ἐχθροῦ τεῖχος βάρεων αὐτῆς·).

Whether "your house" in Lk. 13:35 means Jerusalem or the Temple makes little difference for the purposes of dating Acts.[64] The fact that Luke borrows directly (or indirectly) from Jeremiah or Lamentations is sufficient to show that this is not some unique and never before heard of indictment against Jerusalem or its Temple. It can easily be interpreted as an indictment that was borrowed from the OT prophecies on the destruction of Jerusalem. In fact, given the political circumstances of Israel leading up to 66 CE this language is entirely predictable and, in some ways, expected.[65]

Another argument for a post-70 date of the third gospel is that Luke in 19:43-44 "alludes to Roman earthworks of the sort described by Josephus" (cf. *War* 6.150, 156).[66] However, this line of reasoning is rather precarious for at least two reasons. The first is that there is no credible evidence to suppose that Luke is dependent upon the writings of Josephus, as was argued in Chapter 4. The second reason relates to the manner of ancient siege tactics against a walled city, such as Jerusalem.

Dodd rightfully explains that the military operations described in Lk. 19:42-44 are "no more than the regular common-places of ancient warfare."[67] The prophecy of the destruction of Jerusalem is simply a reflection of the earlier LXX account of Nebuchadnezzar's siege in 586 BCE and the siege of other cities as well.[68] We do not need to scour the much later works of Josephus in order to find Luke's sources. Some of the exact same military language that Luke uses is found in the LXX of Isa. 29:3; 37:33; Ezek. 4:1-3; 21:27; 26:8; Jer. 27:29; 41:1; and also 1 Macc. 15:13-14.[69] This can hardly be coincidental given Luke's frequent use of the LXX.[70]

---

[64] Leon Morris, *The Gospel According to St. Luke* (TNTC; Grand Rapids: Eerdmans, 1977), 229, claims that many "hold the house to be the Temple, but it is more probably Jerusalem as a whole."

[65] See Schäfer, *History of the Jews*, 117, on the "progressive deterioration" of the political situation in Judea during 44–66 CE.

[66] Fitzmyer, *Acts*, 54. Josephus uses χωμάτων from line 150 and χώματα from line 156 where Luke uses a different word altogether—χάραξ (see my note 69 below on the difference). Regardless the LXX of Ezek. 21:27 uses both χάραξ and χῶμα and there are twelve occurrences for χῶμα, three in Exod. 8:12-13; the rest are found in (Josh. 8:28; Job 14:19; 17:16; 20:11; 22:24; 28:6; Hab. 1:10; Isa. 25:2; Ezek. 21:27; and Dan. [Theodotion] 12:2). The LEH defines χῶμα as "earth thrown up" or a "mound (thrown up against the walls of cities in order to take them)."

[67] Dodd, "Jerusalem," 49.

[68] According to Dodd, "Jerusalem," 50, Luke's phrase in 19:44 (καὶ ἐδαφιοῦσίν σε καὶ τὰ τέκνα σου) is "commonplace of Hebrew prophecy" and has intriguing parallels in the LXX with (Hos. 10:14; 14:1; Nah. 3:10; Isa. 3:25-26; Ps. 137:9 [136:9 LXX]; cf. Mk 13:17 and Lk. 21:23).

[69] Isaiah 29:3 recounts the Assyrian advance on Judea: καὶ κυκλώσω ὡς Δαυιδ ἐπὶ σὲ καὶ βαλῶ περὶ σὲ χάρακα and the later promise of safety in 37:33: οὐδὲ μὴ κυκλώσῃ ἐπ' αὐτὴν χάρακα. Ezekiel 4:2 warns of the coming Babylonian siege: χάρακα καὶ δώσεις ἐπ' αὐτὴν παρεμβολὰς καὶ τάξεις τὰς βελοστάσεις κύκλῳ·, and in Ezek. 21:27 the King of Babylon decides whether to attack Ammon or Judah: ἐγένετο τὸ μαντεῖον ἐπὶ Ιερουσαλημ τοῦ βαλεῖν χάρακα ... τοῦ βαλεῖν χάρακα ἐπὶ τὰς πύλας αὐτῆς καὶ βαλεῖν χῶμα καὶ οἰκοδομῆσαι βελοστάσεις, while Ezek. 26:8 describes the siege of Tyre: καὶ ποιήσει ἐπὶ σὲ κύκλῳ χάρακα. Jeremiah 27:29 writes: παρεμβάλετε ἐπ' αὐτὴν κυκλόθεν ... ἀνταπόδοτε αὐτῇ κατὰ τὰ ἔργα αὐτῆς and later in 41:1 states: καὶ Ναβουχοδονοσορ βασιλεὺς Βαβυλῶνος καὶ πᾶν τὸ στρατόπεδον αὐτοῦ. 1 Maccabees 15:13-14 further uses such military terms: παρενέβαλεν Ἀντίοχος ἐπὶ Δωρα ... καὶ ἐκύκλωσεν τὴν πόλιν. See Dodd's full list of examples in "Jerusalem," 50-1 (and also his note 6 on p. 50). The earlier and basic use of the χάραξ "stake/barricade" in Lk. 19:43 is especially noteworthy because this is the only occurrence in the NT and that the LXX *always* uses this form (with fifteen references). Josephus (*War* 5.269) uses a later Hellenistic form χαράκωμα (χάραξ + χῶμα) "palisade" whereas Luke does not. See also Xenophon, *Hist. Hellenica* 5.4.39 and *Hist. Anabasis* 5.2.26.

[70] Rosner, "Acts and Biblical History," 1:80, says the "semitic cast of the books is best explained in terms of the linguistic influence of the LXX, that is the use of deliberate Septuagintalisms."

Furthermore, Josephus's *Jewish War* (written c. 75-79 CE) describes some very specific "eye-witness" details that go far beyond Luke's very brief and simple account. These details include the inner Jewish faction fighting inside the walls, the "horrors of pestilence and famine," cannibalism, and the fire that destroyed the Temple and a large part of the city.[71] Josephus's account is clearly looking back on the siege from the vantage point of having several years to process his sources and reflect on his own involvement.

Josephus spared no details, writing not only a lengthy, but also an exceptionally barbaric account. Such details are nowhere to be found in Luke-Acts. For example, one starving woman cooked and ate her own infant (*War* 6.201-13).[72] Josephus further describes how the "whole city instantly rang with the abomination, and each, while picturing the horror of it, shuddered as though it had been perpetrated by himself. The starving folk longed for death and felicitated those who had gone to their rest ere they had heard or beheld such evils" (*War* 6.212-13).[73] This represents but one small section of Josephus's graphic account of the siege. In comparison, Luke's description is very brief and very similar to the well-known account of the Babylonian siege of Jerusalem in 586 BCE.

Furthermore, Lk. 19:44 cannot be used as evidence for looking back at the siege of 70 CE: "and they will dash you to the ground and your children within you" (καὶ ἐδαφιοῦσίν σε καὶ τὰ τέκνα σου). Dodd explains that "among all the barbarities which Josephus reports, he does not say that the conquerors dashed children to the ground."[74] In fact Josephus (*War* 6.418-19) says instead: "those under seventeen were sold" (οἱ δ' ἐντὸς ἑπτακαίδεκα ἐτῶν ἐπράθησαν) and "of the rest, those over seventeen years of age he sent in chains to the works in Egypt, while multitudes were presented by Titus to the various provinces, to be destroyed in the theatres by the sword or by wild beasts" (*War* 6.418).[75] Regardless, however one may interpret the phrase in Lk. 19:44 (ἐδαφιοῦσίν σε καὶ τὰ τέκνα σου), it shows that it is not specific to "anything that happened in 66–70" CE since it is "commonplace of Hebrew prophecy."[76]

---

[71] Cf. Dodd, "Jerusalem," 49.

[72] Josephus (*War* 6.208) writes: "With these words she slew her son, and then, having roasted the body and devoured half of it, she covered up and stored the remainder." See Thackeray et al., *Josephus*, 3:437. There is an account of this happening with a painful twist during the siege of Samaria where this woman cries out to the King of Israel who was "passing by on the wall" (2 Kgs 6:26). She explains her ordeal: "This woman said to me, 'Give up your son so we may eat him today, and tomorrow we'll eat my son.' So we cooked my son and ate him. The next day I said to her, 'Give up your son so we may eat him,' but she had hidden him" (2 Kgs 6:28-29, NIV).

[73] Thackeray et al., *Josephus*, 3:437.

[74] Dodd, "Jerusalem," 50.

[75] Thackeray et al., *Josephus*, 3:496–7.

[76] Dodd, "Jerusalem," 50. For example, Hosea (10:14) is warning Israel of coming destruction by recalling the time when Shalman destroyed the house of Arbel and "mothers were dashed to the ground with their children" (μητέρα ἐπὶ τέκνοις ἠδάφισαν). Compare also Hos. 14:1 (ἐν ῥομφαίᾳ πεσοῦνται αὐτοί, καὶ τὰ ὑποτίτθια αὐτῶν ἐδαφισθήσονται, καὶ αἱ ἐν γαστρὶ ἔχουσαι αὐτῶν διαρραγήσονται) with Mk 13:17 (οὐαὶ δὲ ταῖς ἐν γαστρὶ ἐχούσαις καὶ ταῖς θηλαζούσαις ἐν ἐκείναις ταῖς ἡμέραις). See also Nah. 3:10; Isa. 3:25-26; and Ps. 137:9 (136:9 LXX).

Rather than assuming that Luke (and Acts) was written after the destruction of Jerusalem and showing the prophecies as "proof," the linguistic evidence demonstrates the opposite.[77]

> It appears, then, that not only are the two Lucan oracles composed entirely from the language of the Old Testament, but the conception of the coming disaster which the author has in mind is a generalized picture of the fall of Jerusalem as imaginatively presented by the prophets. So far as any historical event has coloured the picture, it is not Titus's capture of Jerusalem in A.D. 70, but Nebuchadnezzar's capture in 586 B.C. There is no single trait of the forecast which cannot be documented directly out of the Old Testament.[78]

In the future, scholars who insist on a post-70 CE date of Luke-Acts need to marshal better evidence that these prophecies are not simply the language of the prophets, but that they somehow demonstrate that Luke is offering a very specific and unambiguous reflection of the actual siege and destruction of Jerusalem. However, the likelihood of this occurring seems remote considering how the *entire* narrative of Luke-Acts reflects the language of a city going about its business with its Temple still standing with all of its establishments in operation, including an active Sanhedrin (συνέδριον) and the office of the High Priest (ἀρχιερεύς).[79]

It is worth recounting a brief summary of the aftermath of the Jewish rebellion against Rome as this does not seem to be a significant factor for the middle and late dating groups. Schäfer explains how the "consequences of the first great war of the Jews against Rome were extremely far-reaching and their significance for the future history of Judaism can hardly be over-estimated."[80] He then describes how the "immediate political consequences were drastic" as Judaea became an "independent Roman province" after the war.[81] As far as the population of Judea was concerned, entire communities were desolated, with modern researchers estimating that up to one-third of the Jewish population of Palestine was killed.[82] One wonders, how Luke in Acts 28:21 could take the time to account for the lack of letters from Judea concerning Paul

---

[77] For various reasons (that remain largely unsubstantiated), late dating advocates assume a post-destruction state of affairs. Tyson, *Marcion*, 140 (n. 58), for example, gives only a single passing reference to Dodd's article.
[78] Dodd, "Jerusalem," 52. As far as the gospel of Mark, the "prototype" of "coming disaster" is the "sacrilege of Antiochus" in 168–167 BCE (see p. 53).
[79] See the συνέδριον in Lk. 22:66; Acts 4:15; 5:21, 27, 34-35, 41; 6:12, 15; 7:54; 22:30; 23:1, 15, 20, 28; and 24:20. It is rather curious that Luke uses this term (συνέδριον) only once in his gospel whereas he prefers to use the term chief priests (ἀρχιερεύς), often in combination with the teachers of the law (γραμματέων).
[80] Schäfer, *History of the Jews*, 135.
[81] Ibid.
[82] Schäfer, *History of the Jews*, 135. Schäfer (135) claims that both Josephus and Tacitus report "massive casualties amongst the population." Josephus (*War* 6.420) with some expected exaggeration writes: "The total number of prisoners taken throughout the entire war amounted to ninety-seven thousand, and of those who perished during the siege, from first to last, to one million one hundred thousand" (see Thackeray et al., Josephus, 3:497 and *War* 6.420–434 for more details on the aftermath).

to the Jews in Rome, but somehow fail to mention that many of their friends and family had been slaughtered and that their homeland was razed to ground?

As a result this also produced "catastrophic economic consequences" beyond the already exploited rural populace who were now "impoverished even further."[83] Essentially, the land in Jerusalem and all of Judea became "the property of the emperor" (i.e., Vespasian).[84] Another consequence from the war was the "major upheaval in Jewish religious life" since the Temple cult had been at the centre of Judaism for centuries.[85] Its destruction called for a "fundamental rethink, a radical new beginning."[86] Again, this is something that Luke is absolutely blind to (both in his gospel and in Acts). Given the central importance of the Temple in Luke-Acts there can be no rational explanation for a post-70 date—unless one can clearly demonstrate that (1) Luke carefully crafted the entire narrative of Luke-Acts based on pre-70 sources *and* (2) that it was politically and theologically advantageous to do so. In my reading and research on this tenuous subject neither has been rationally and satisfactorily accomplished.

This subsequent radical restructuring of the Temple cult also meant the end of the office of High Priest (Lk. 3:2; 22:50, 54). After the Temple's destruction, the High Priesthood "disappeared for good" along with the "orderly 'functioning' of the Temple cult."[87] One of the more obvious and visual changes that immediately impacted the post-70 CE Jewish population was that the old Temple tax "now had to be paid in the form of the *fiscus Judaicus* to the temple of Jupiter Capitolinus in Rome."[88] This was a powerful gesture that symbolized "where Jewish loyalty must now be directed."[89]

According to Udoh, before 70 CE when "Vespasian converted the temple tax into a poll tax imposed on all Jews, the Jews in Palestine did not pay an annual 'head' tax."[90] Josephus (*War* 7.218) writes that "On all Jews, wheresoever resident, he [Vespasian] imposed a poll-tax of two drachms [δύο δραχμὰς], to be paid annually into the Capitol as formerly contributed by them to the temple at Jerusalem."[91] Schäfer explains how this represented "less a financial burden—the Temple tax was two drachmas—than an unprecedented and dispiriting humiliation for the pious orthodoxy (the *chasidim*)."[92] For a post-70 CE date of Luke-Acts, an omission of this critical change in taxation is exceptionally baffling.[93] Last, along with the demise of the High Priesthood the next most significant "state and religious institution"—the Sanhedrin—also "disappeared"

---

[83] Schäfer, *History of the Jews*, 135.
[84] Ibid., 135. Josephus (*War* 7.216) writes that "Caesar sent instructions to Bassus and Laberius Maximus, the procurator, to farm out all Jewish territory" (Thackeray et al., *Josephus*, 3:567).
[85] Schäfer, *History of the Jews*, 136.
[86] Ibid.
[87] Ibid.
[88] Ibid.
[89] Anne Fitzpatrick-McKinley, "Synagogue Communities in the Graeco-Roman Cities," in *Jews in the Hellenistic and Roman Cities* (ed. John R. Bartlett; London: Routledge, 2002), 55–87 (75).
[90] Cf. Fabian Udoh, "Taxation and Other Sources of Government Income in the Galilee of Herod and Antipas," in *Galilee in the Late Second Temple Period and Mishnaic Periods* (eds. David A. Fiensy and James R. Strange; Life, Culture, and Society 1; Minneapolis: Fortress, 2014), 378.
[91] See Thackeray et al., *Josephus*, 3:567–69 and Cassius Dio, *Hist.* 65.7.2
[92] Schäfer, *History of the Jews*, 136.
[93] See also Lk. 20:1, 22-26 (and also Mk 12:17; Mt. 22:21).

along with the Sadducees.⁹⁴ The contacts between the early Jerusalem church and these essential Jewish institutions can only suggest a time before they were eradicated.⁹⁵

Therefore, the burden of proof must remain with those who consider Luke to be writing at a time after the destruction of Jerusalem, its people, its economy, and its beloved Temple.⁹⁶ Fitzmyer's observation is somewhat ironic, but it presents the solution to this key division in the debate as he states: "Modern interpreters have long been puzzled by the failure of NT writers to mention the destruction of Jerusalem by the Romans in A.D. 70."⁹⁷ Instead of being puzzled by this omission, the easiest and by far the most logical solution in light of the combined evidence is that the NT writers did not mention this fact in history simply because it had not happened yet.⁹⁸ To insist that such an epic event in Jewish, Roman, and Christian history had already occurred but was not important enough for the NT writers to openly and clearly mention seems to represent a profound case of special pleading. The alternative is far more logical and requires fewer loopholes in the interpretation.

Acts and the City of Rome

Not only is Jerusalem of central importance to Acts, but the city of Rome plays a key role in the narrative as well, especially towards the end (Acts 2:10; 18:2; 19:21; 23:11; 25:25, 27; 27:1; 28:11, 14, 16-17).⁹⁹ Acts reveals a geographical and thematic shift in importance from Jerusalem to Rome (Acts 19:21), where Paul awaits the outcome of his appeal to Caesar while remaining under house arrest (Acts 28:30-31).¹⁰⁰ Since Paul is left in Rome without any clear indication of the outcome of his trial or his fate, it is necessary to consider the end of Acts in light of the most significant events in the history of Rome and the church in the mid-60s CE.¹⁰¹ The Great Fire of Rome, the subsequent persecution of Roman Christians under Nero, and the martyrdom of

---

⁹⁴ Schäfer, *History of the Jews*, 136. The Sanhedrin was "headed by the High Priest and, despite the growing influence of the Pharisees, was undoubtedly dominated largely by the aristocratic and economically influential Sadducee families" (136).

⁹⁵ Unless one subscribes to the unhistorical notion that Luke intentionally falsified his narrative to reflect some idyllic pre-70 CE status of the Temple (along with all of its elements). Even the prayer forms in Acts reflect the Temple and not the synagogue which lends to the conclusion that Acts does not exhibit any "elements from post-70 developments in Jewish and Christian worship." Cf. Falk, "Jewish Prayer," 4:267.

⁹⁶ This was certainly front-page news across the Roman Empire, but especially in Rome. The Arch of Titus (constructed in 82 CE) demonstrates just how "widespread this event was known in antiquity." See Karl L. Armstrong, "The End of Acts 28 and the Fate of the Historical Apostle Paul" (MA diss., Acadia Divinity College, Wolfville, NS, 2013), 14, and Schäfer, *History of the Jews*, 130–1.

⁹⁷ Fitzmyer, *Acts*, 55.

⁹⁸ I look forward with anticipation to Jonathan Bernier's forthcoming *Rethinking the Dates of the New Testament* (Grand Rapids: Baker).

⁹⁹ See Keener's "Continuing Ministry in Rome" in *Acts*, 4:3714–75.

¹⁰⁰ Recall "Luke's Concern with Geography, Travel, and Lodging" from Chapter 3. It was deduced that Luke is either from Rome or Rome was his current address at the time of writing. A third possibility is that his intended audience (i.e., Theophilus) is in Rome. Since the city of Rome is central to the narrative, the author, and recipients it is reasonable to expect at least a footnote to the terrible events that transpired within a year or so after the end of Acts.

¹⁰¹ Rhee, *Early Christian Literature*, 12. For alternative literary explanations, see Chapter 5.

Paul are far too significant events to be brushed aside by the middle and late dating advocates.[102] Therefore, these events must be placed in their proper historical context, which accurately reflects a time before 64 CE.

The Great Fire of Rome

The Great Fire of Rome in July of 64 CE represents one of the most significant aspects of the date of Acts for at least two reasons. First, it was the ancient city's worst recorded disaster and, second, the last recorded event in Acts (i.e., Paul in Rome) is dated just before the fire—and Luke says nothing.[103] There are no allusions and no hints anywhere in the textual record to this catastrophic event. Furthermore, there can be no discernible literary, political, or theological motive for such an omission either.[104] Although this event is but one piece of the larger historical context, the experience of Paul described in the texts of Acts 28:11-31, and Luke-Acts as a whole, reflects a time prior to the city's greatest disaster.[105]

No one knows where Paul stayed in Rome,[106] but there are a few clues that describe his accommodations, starting with Acts 28:16. We learn that after arriving in Rome "Paul was permitted to live by himself, with the soldier who was guarding him" (ἐπετράπη τῷ Παύλῳ μένειν καθ' ἑαυτὸν σὺν τῷ φυλάσσοντι αὐτὸν στρατιώτῃ).[107] A further description in verse 23 says "they [Jewish Leaders, v. 17] came to him into

---

[102] See Mittelstaedt, *Lukas als Historiker*, 165–220; Lampe, "Roman Christians," 111–29; Peter Oakes, "Using Historical Evidence in the Study of Neronian Christian Groups and Texts," in *The Last Years of Paul: Essays from the Tarragona Conference, June 2013* (eds. Armand Puig i Tàrrech et al.; WUNT 352; Tübingen: Mohr Siebeck, 2015), 131–51; Barrett et al., *The Emperor Nero: A Guide to the Ancient Sources* (Princeton: Princeton University Press, 2016), 149–70; and Stephen Dando-Collins, *The Great Fire of Rome: The Fall of the Emperor Nero and His City* (Cambridge, MA: Da Capo Press, 2010), *et passim*. While the Great Fire of Rome and the subsequent persecution are frequently discussed by early dating advocates, it is often dismissed (or not even considered at all) by those preferring a later date of Acts.

[103] See Mittelstaedt, *Lukas als Historiker*, 208–18 (Der Brand von Rom und die Verfolgung unter Nero). Oakes, "Historical Evidence," 131, states that the "only narrative account of Christians in Rome, in a text that is probably fairly close to this period, is that of Luke in Acts 28." Oakes (134) further claims that the "archaeology of the centre of Rome supports and clarifies the literary accounts of the fire of 64 CE and its effects." See also John Pollini, "Burning Rome, Burning Christians," in *The Cambridge Companion to the Age of Nero* (eds. Shadi Bartsch et al.; Cambridge: Cambridge University Press, 2017), 213–36.

[104] Kosso, *Knowing the Past*, 51, explains how the meaning of a text is "often revealed only in context with other claims about the past such as about related events or the author's motives." See also Greene and Moore's, *Archaeology*, 155, fifth criterion for the historical dating process and Kamp et al., *Writing History!*, 77; Cadbury, *Luke-Acts*, 48; and Dibelius, *Studies*, 4, 11, 144–5.

[105] Although major fires in the city were "regular events," the fire of 64 CE was the "most spectacular of these." See Tim G. Parkin and Arthur J. Pomeroy, *Roman Social History: A Sourcebook* (Routledge Sourcebooks for the Ancient World; London: Routledge, 2007), 239.

[106] Cf. Keener, *Acts*, 4:3727–32, and his insightful section on "Apartments in Rome." Lampe, "Roman Christians," 118, while commenting on the various places both Jews and Christians were known to live in Rome highlights the fact that the "topographical results cohere with the situation in the year 64 CE" (i.e., the time of the Great Fire).

[107] Some of the later expanded Western variants such as found in Codex 614 read after (εἰς Ῥώμην), "the centurion delivered the prisoners to the captain of the guard; but Paul was permitted to live by himself outside of the barracks with a soldier guarding him" (ὁ ἑκατόνταρχος παρέδωκε τοὺς δεσμίους τῷ στρατοπεδάρχη· τῷ δὲ παύλῳ ἐπετράπη μένειν καθ' ἑαυτὸν ἔξω τῆς παρεμβολῆς).

his lodging in great numbers" (ἦλθον πρὸς αὐτὸν εἰς τὴν ξενίαν πλείονες οἷς)[108] and verse 30 says that "He [Paul] lived there two whole years in his own rented house" (Ἐνέμεινεν δὲ διετίαν ὅλην ἐν ἰδίῳ μισθώματι).

Mealand has established that the word μίσθωμα (v. 30) is used in the sense of "payment in general" and there are many examples where it "specifically refers to the payment of rent."[109] Along with ἀκωλύτως (v. 31) and διετία, the three words together "regularly appear in ancient papyri dealing with the leasing of property" and are found in "ancient leases."[110] Additionally, it seems plausible that Paul's "rented accommodation ... gave him unrestricted use of it."[111] For example, P. Oxy. 14.1641, dated to Nero's fourteenth year (May 11, 68 CE), refers to the "lease of a house which is to be used without let or hindrance."[112] As a result, the picture of Paul's unhindered accommodation is one of availability, affordability, and accessibility for his visitors. Therefore, how does our understanding of Paul's lodging in Acts relate to (1) his ability to afford such accommodations and (2) the cost and availability of housing in Rome before and after the fire?

Granted, any estimation of Paul's socio-economic status at the time of his Roman sojourn and his ability to afford rent must remain tentative.[113] However, it is reasonable to extend a recent and "moderate thesis" that Paul and his family were "most likely among the artisan-business class of the ancient world who had some success in their occupation as tent makers."[114] This is supported by the picture of Paul in Corinth (Acts 18:1-3), along with Priscilla and Aquila, who (in v. 3) were "tentmakers by trade" (σκηνοποιοὶ τῇ τέχνῃ).[115] Although it is difficult to place exactly where and when Paul lived for those two years in Rome (c. 60–61 CE; Acts 28:30), his choice of accommodations after 64 CE would have decreased dramatically and would call into question his ability to entertain the "many" (πολύς of v. 23) and "all" (πάντας of

---

Hemer, *Acts*, 200, thinks the stratopedarch may prove "important to the historical puzzles surrounding the end of Acts."

[108] ξενίαν is "a place of temporary lodging for a person away from home—guestroom, lodging for guest [sic], place to stay in" (cf. L&N 7:31, and Phlm. 22).

[109] Mealand, "Close of Acts," 585.

[110] Ibid., 590 and 595.

[111] Ibid., 595.

[112] Cf. http://www.trismegistos.org/text/21951. Compare the ἀκολούτως in line six with ἀκωλύτως in Acts 28:31. It is unlikely that ἀκολούτως derives from a different verb than ἀκωλύτως. See Mealand, "Close of Acts," 592 (n. 16). There are hundreds of papyri that relate to renting and the leasing of property.

[113] The adjective ἴδιος (v. 30) seems to suggest he did not rely on the support of family, friends, or associates (though Phil. 4:10-23 [N.B. vv. 18 and 22]). There is also no indication that he worked to support himself in Rome especially given his house arrest (Acts 28:17, cf. Herod Agrippa's case in Josephus, *Ant.* 18.235).

[114] Cf. Andrew W. Pitts, "Paul in Tarsus: Historical Factors in Assessing Paul's Early Education," in *Paul and Ancient Rhetoric: Theory and Practice in the Hellenistic Context* (eds. Stanley E. Porter and Bryan R. Dyer; Cambridge: Cambridge University Press, 2016), 43–67.

[115] For some of the textual problems and versional renderings of σκηνοποιός see Ronald F. Hock, *The Social Context of Paul's Ministry: Tentmaking and Apostleship* (repr., Minneapolis: Fortress, 2007), 20. Meanwhile, Murphy-O'Connor, *St. Paul's Corinth*, 195-6, offers a snapshot of what Paul's workshop would have entailed: a downstairs shop, basic tentmaking tools, with modest upstairs living quarters.

v. 20) of the visitors, and especially his ability to afford his own rented house for that length of time after the fire.[116]

The material context of Rome in the time of Nero before July of 64 was radically different than it was during the city's complex and systematic rebuilding phase. Narrow streets, coupled with crowded timber tenement housing, were always a concern for city officials and residents.[117] The city centre changed forever when the fire broke out over July 18 and 19, somewhere in the shops of the Palatine "with their flammable booths," and burned for nine days, spreading north across the Capitoline and as far as the Esquiline.[118] The severity of the damage was so great, Tacitus stated that out of fourteen regions "only four remained intact."[119] Everything from temples to tenement housing vanished, along with many of the city's fleeing inhabitants.[120]

Nero's subsequent and extensive rebuilding campaign began with a revised building code for spacious streets and tenements with "courtyards and porticos," height limits, and the use of "fire-resistant stone."[121] Some of Nero's largest post-conflagration building projects, such as the Domus Aurea (Golden House), required a massive

---

[116] Keener, *Acts*, 4:3730, states that housing was "much more expensive in Rome than elsewhere." Earlier, Bradley Blue, "Acts and the House Church," in *The Book of Acts in Its Graeco-Roman Setting* (eds. David W. Gill and Conrad Gempf.; 5 vols; BAFCS 2; Eerdmans: Grand Rapids, 1995), 156, remarks on the "high cost of housing" in Rome. Blue (155) explains how the average Roman would have lived in an *insula* (a multiple unit building) versus the 3 per cent wealthy fortunate who lived in a *domus*. See also James E. Packer, "Housing and Population in Imperial Ostia and Rome," *JRS* 57 (1967): 62, and Jerome Carcopino, *Daily Life in Ancient Rome: The People and the City at the Height of the Empire* (ed. Henry T. Rowell; trans. Emily O. Lorimer; New Haven: Yale University Press, 2003), 23. The wealthy property owners would lease the upper storeys of their *insula* for approximately 2,000 *sesterces* to a "middle-manager for a five year term and give him the rent of the ground floor *domus*" (Blue, 156 and Packer, 86). This would not be economically possible for the average Roman since they earned just three *sestertii* per day (156 [n. 141]). Carcopino, *Daily Life*, 56, states, "So intolerable was the burden of rent that the sub-tenants of the first lessee almost invariably had to sub-let in their turn every room in their *cenaculum* which they could possibly spare."

[117] Barrett et al., *Nero*, xv–xvi. Before the fire of 64 CE the ancient writers were "very conscious of the absence of beauty in the streets of Rome." See Laurence et al., *City*, 117. Apparently, Rome was known for its "ugly buildings and narrow winding streets or *vici*" and unlike Pompeii and the other colonies it was "filled up rather than laid out" (117). Additionally, Parkin and Pomeroy, *Roman Social History*, 239, observe how the "practice of constructing the upper storeys of apartment buildings with timber frames would have lightened the load on the lower floors, but increased the fire risk."

[118] Barrett et al., *Nero*, 149.

[119] "Rome is divided into fourteen regions, among which only four remained intact. Three were burned to the ground, and of the other seven there were only a few houses left, which were severely damaged and half-burnt." Tacitus, *Ann*. 15.40 (cited by Lampe, *Valentinus*, 47). The destruction was "so complete that in most of the devastated areas only piles of ashes and useless rubble remained, and most streets were impassable." Dando-Collins, *Great Fire*, 99. Cf. also Parkin and Pomeroy, *Roman Social History*, 239.

[120] Barrett et al., *Nero*, 149. Fuelled by the wind, the speed of the fire hemmed in many of those trying to escape (p. 154). The exact death toll remains unknown but later writers say that "countless persons perished" (καὶ ἄνθρωποι ἀναρίθμητοι). Cassius Dio, *Hist. Rom*. 62.18.2.

[121] Barrett et al., *Nero*, 149, 151. After the fire there began a "new form of urbanism" with "rows of measured streets with broad thorough fares, a restriction on the height of buildings, open spaces, and the addition of colonnades in front of the apartment blocks." See Laurence et al., *City*, 117, and Tacitus, *Ann*. 15.43. Rome's "shady, winding streets, and towering buildings" had been replaced with "broad streets with colonnades and lower buildings" (117–18, and Tacitus, *Ann*. 15.38). The "new Rome" was later described by Tacitus (*Ann*. 15.41) as a "city of beauty" (118).

amount of land that was expropriated.¹²² His extravagant building projects added to the "constant theme in Roman literature" of the "high cost of rental housing in the city."¹²³ Parkin and Pomeroy observe how this cost is partly the "result of the density of the urban population (usually estimated at a million or more) crammed into a limited space, [and] partly the high risk of investing in housing."¹²⁴ Paul in some measure, along with the "poor," would "no doubt be seriously affected, since proper planning to discourage overcrowding would lead to a shortage of accommodations and pressure to increase rents."¹²⁵

In consideration of this, it seems that the language of Acts 28:11-31 reflects an earlier time when tenement housing was both available and more affordable.¹²⁶ Although this interpretation is by no means decisive, it is firmly supported by the substantial omission of the fire in *any* textual strata of Acts.¹²⁷ Given the established propensity for expansion among the Western and Byzantine traditions, it seems very strange that neither the text nor any of the variants in Acts 28:11-31 show an awareness of the city's greatest disaster.¹²⁸ Given the steady stream of datable events in Acts, it seems extremely unlikely that Luke would fail to mention one of the "best known historical events."¹²⁹

This last point on the Great Fire of Rome is worth considering further in light of the many narrative solutions put forward concerning the end of Acts (Chapter 5). First, since the author of Acts readily describes significant events in Roman history like the Jewish expulsion (Acts 18:2), or the "severe famine" (Acts 11:28), and incidental details relating to historical figures (i.e., Sergius Paulus, Acts 13:7), why is the Great Fire omitted? Second, there does not appear to be any conceivable, rational "motive" for

---

122 Suetonius, *Ner.* 31.1–2; Barrett et al., *Nero*, 151. It is hard to imagine in today's dollars the enormous cost of this project. McRay, *Archaeology*, 345, notes that this included a 120 foot "gilded bronze statue" of Nero on the property (cf. Suetonius, *Ner.* 31.1). The statue stood approximately southwest of the Domus Aurea just in front of the Temple of Venus and Rome and the Coliseum. Barrett et al., *Nero*, 160 (n. 27), refer to Pliny (*Nat. Hist.* 34.45–47) who apparently saw a "model of it and noted its resemblance to the emperor." The entire surrounding vestibule was so spacious that its "triple portico was a mile long" and contained a pool "the size of a sea"—and was surrounded by "tilled fields, vineyards and woods" (160, Suetonius, *Ner.* 31.1). As far as the structure, "everything was overlaid with gold and studded with precious stones and mother-of-pearl. The dining rooms had ceilings made of ivory panels that could rotate for flowers to be scattered from above, and were fitted with pipes for dispensing perfume. The principle dining room had a dome that, day and night, was continuously revolving like the heavens" (160, Suetonius, *Ner.* 31.2).
123 Parkin and Pomeroy, *Roman Social History*, 239.
124 Ibid.
125 Barrett et al., *Nero*, 151.
126 It is highly unlikely that Luke mentioned Paul's rental situation in order to indicate his affluence given the well-established concern for the appropriation of wealth in Luke-Acts (cf. Lk. 5:11, 28; 6:24-26; 12:33; 16:1-13; 18:18-23; 24-30; 21:1-4; Acts 2:41-47; 4:36–5:11; 6:1-7; 11:12-30; 24:17; 20:30-35).
127 See "Appendix: The Manuscript Record for Acts 28:11-31." See also "Principles for Interpreting Sources" in Chapter 2.
128 Westcott and Hort, *Original Greek II*, 122–6.
129 See here Dando-Collins, *Great Fire*, 1 and also Joseph J. Walsh, *The Great Fire of Rome: Life and Death in the Ancient City* (Baltimore: Johns Hopkins University Press, 2019), 1 on the "greatest of the Great Fires." This omission is especially inconsistent given Luke's well established attention to time and detail in Luke-Acts (recall Chapter 3 and Lk. 1:5, 39; 2:1; 4:25; 17:26-28; Acts 5:37; 7:2-47; 11:28; and 18:2).

the author to omit this information.¹³⁰ Third, other contemporary writers that discuss the Great Fire, such as Cassius Dio, provide an example of what we should expect from Acts, if it is to be dated after the fact.

Cassius Dio (*c*. 155–235 CE) claimed the Great Fire was "without parallel earlier or later, apart from the Gallic sack. The entire Palatine Hill, the theater of Taurus, and some two-thirds of the rest of the city went up in flames, and the loss of life was incalculable."¹³¹ Moreover, in the context of the Roman people blaming and "cursing" Nero (v. 3), Cassius made it a point to remind his readers of the Oracle spoken in the time of Tiberius that tells of Rome's future destruction: "Thrice three hundred years having run their course of fulfillment, Rome by the strife of her people shall perish."¹³² In stark contrast to Cassius Dio, we find a favourable attitude towards both Rome and Nero in Acts.¹³³

In reference to Nero, a further Sibylline prophecy was circulating among the people that said, "last of the sons of Aeneas, a mother-slayer will govern" ("ἔσχατος Αἰνεαδῶν μητροκτόνος ἡγεμονεύσει").¹³⁴ Given the author's tendency in Acts to frequently incorporate prophecies from the LXX in his narrative (notably in Acts 28:26-27=Isa. 6:9-10), it seems reasonable to expect some prophetic dialogue directed towards Rome or its leaders if Acts was written after the fire, and especially the subsequent Neronian persecution.¹³⁵ Taken together, the cumulative evidence indicates that the texts of Acts 28:11-31 reflect a time prior to Rome's greatest disaster.

Post-Fire Persecution under Nero

Along with the fall of Jerusalem and the Great Fire of Rome, another facet of the debate identified in the historiography of dating Acts is the persecution of Christians that happened after the fire (*c*. 64 CE).¹³⁶ The relationship between the two related events requires some contextualizing. Whereas the fire itself "marked an important turning point in Nero's reign," it generated "political repercussions that went far beyond the immediate effects of the fire itself."¹³⁷ The popular image of the crazed ruler playing his

---

[130] Cadbury, *Luke-Acts*, ix, 32; Greene and Moore, *Archaeology*, 155.
[131] Cassius Dio, *Hist. Rom.* 62.18.2 (and not 62.17 in Barrett et al., *Emperor Nero*, 159). See the full account in Cassius Dio, *Hist. Rom.* 62 (chapters 16–18). Compare Cassius Dio's account with Tacitus, *Ann.* 15.38–43. For an extensive discussion of the known sources see the chapter on "The Great Fire" in Barrett et al., *Emperor Nero*, 149–70.
[132] Cassius Dio, *Hist. Rom.* 62.18.3 and Cassius Dio, *Dio's Roman History* (trans. Earnest Cary and Herbert B. Foster; 9 vols; LCL; London: William Heinemann, 1914–55), 8:117.
[133] E.g., Acts 25:11; 28:20; Porter, *When Paul Met Jesus*, 78.
[134] Cassius Dio, *Hist. Rom.* 62.18.4 and Cary and Foster trans., *Dio's Roman History*, 8:116–17. Cassius Dio considers whether this was spoken beforehand as a prophecy (v. 4), but goes on to say that Nero was in fact the last of the Julian line "from Aeneas" (ἀπὸ Αἰνείου).
[135] Tacitus, *Ann.* 15.44.2, 4. Marguerat notes the positive attitude in Acts towards Rome versus the negative portrayal in Revelation: "It is the goal of Paul's mission for the former [in Acts] and the symbol of evil for the latter [Revelation]. The capital of the Empire is the target of the narrative from Acts 19:21 onwards whereas from Revelation 13 onwards it is silhouetted behind the metaphors of evil." Marguerat, *Historian*, 34–5.
[136] Hemer, *Acts*, 371.
[137] Barrett et al., *Emperor Nero*, 150.

harp while Rome burned is not an entirely accurate picture of history. Moreover, his reputation as an infamous despot did not happen overnight.[138] In fact it took "some time for it to emerge that Nero's appointment as emperor was a disaster."[139]

Before 64 CE, Nero had already exhibited "erratic and autocratic behaviour" but it was the "devastation of the fire" that "caused an enormous drop in his broader popularity."[140] Many scholars split Nero's rule into two distinct periods: "the early period, until 62, when he allowed himself to be guided by the philosopher Seneca and by the head of the Praetorian Prefect Burrus; and the later period, when he ruled on his own. The early period saw a more balanced, enlightened rule, including several popular reforms."[141] It was not until the later period that Nero was "characterized by the eccentric rule of a despot."[142] Nero increasingly saw himself an "artist" and "left the Empire in the hands of freedmen while he conducted a concert tour through Greece."[143] He began to become increasingly paranoid in his rule and "viciously murdered anyone who seemed to threaten him," including his mother, wife, and stepbrother.[144] However, the blame that he placed on the Christians was not immediate and it came *after* Nero's initial and substantial relief efforts.

It is generally understood by historians that Nero did in fact deserve "some credit for the vigorous measures of relief which he instituted for the homeless, and the rules which he laid down for the more scientific reconstruction of the devastated areas."[145] Tacitus recounts how the populace were at first pleased because

> vital supplies were shipped up from Ostia and neighboring municipalities, and the price of grain was dropped to three sestertii. These were measures with popular appeal, but they proved a dismal failure, because the rumour had spread that, at the very time that the city was ablaze, Nero had appeared on his private stage and sung about the destruction of Troy, drawing a comparison between the sorrows of the present and the disasters of old. (*Ann.* 15.39.2–3)[146]

It was not only the rumours described by Tacitus that caused the suspicion of the populace, but also Nero's appropriation of some "120 acres of the burnt-out region

---

[138] Tacitus, *Ann.* 15.39.2.
[139] David Potter, *Emperors of Rome: The Story of Imperial Rome from Julius Caesar to the Last Emperor* (London: Quercus, 2007), 66.
[140] Barrett et al., *Emperor Nero*, 150.
[141] Jeffers, *Greco-Roman World*, 318. Max Cary and Howard H. Scullard, *A History of Rome: Down to the Reign of Constantine* (rev. edn; London: Macmillan, 1992), 358, describe how the government under Nero—with the aid of Seneca and Burrus—"followed a cautious but efficient administrative routine . . . and outside his family he had spilt hardly any blood." Witherington, *New Testament History*, 278, similarly describes Nero's first five years as "relatively moderate."
[142] Jeffers, *Greco-Roman World*, 318.
[143] Ibid. It is said that he loved Greek culture so much that he "declared all of Greece free" (318).
[144] Ibid., 318; Eusebius, *Hist. Eccl.* 2.25.2.
[145] Cary and Scullard, *History of Rome*, 359.
[146] Cited from Barrett et al., *Emperor Nero*, 156. On this passage they (156 [n. 13] remark how Tacitus on the one hand kept an "open mind about Nero's responsibility for the fire" but that he also gave credit for the ways Nero tried to improve the well-being of the people (esp. as compared to other sources).

between the Palatine and Esquiline hills" for his own pleasure with his "sumptuous new palace, the Domus Aurea."[147] As a result, the people began to set the blame on Nero directly for trying to acquire this land for next to nothing in addition to his scandalous singing about the destruction of Troy.[148]

The question as to whether Nero was guilty of setting the fire in the first place is something ancient and modern historians debate. For example, Suetonius (*Ner.* 55) discusses the rumours and thinks that he did start the fire as he planned on naming the rebuilt city "Neropolis."[149] Tacitus is more cautious and seems to leave the door of Nero's culpability open in comparison to other sources. At any rate the evidence that he was responsible for starting the fire is inconclusive and circumspect.[150]

Nevertheless, the people increasingly pointed the finger at Nero as the one "responsible for the disaster" and he found his "scapegoats" by blaming the already "unpopular Christians."[151] Nero then began to target members of the Christian community with the aid of Tigellinus, his Praetorian prefect.[152] An "unknown number" of victims were "condemned on mere profession of faith, and burnt or otherwise tortured to death."[153] Tacitus (*Ann.* 15.44.4) says that "an immense multitude" was convicted while Clement, using a similar phrase, claims that "a great multitude" was

---

[147] Cary and Scullard, *History of Rome*, 359. Recall my note 122.
[148] Ibid.
[149] Suetonius, *Ner.* 55; Barrett et al., *Emperor Nero*, 151.
[150] Barrett et al., *Emperor Nero*, 151-2, explain that it was a full moon on the night of the fire (which is not ideal for committing public arson) and that "neither outbreak started in the area that Nero would develop for his Domus Aurea. The energetic measures he took to prevent the spread of the fire, as described by Tacitus, speak against the notion of its being deliberately set." Nero's own Domus Transitoria was destroyed and it broke out again near Tigellinus's estates six days later. It seems that Tacitus (*Ann.* 15.39) is "cautious, observing that the claim began as a rumour," unlike Suetonius, *Ner.* 38.2, or Cassius Dio, *Hist. Rom.* 62.16.1-2. Cf. Barrett et al., *Emperor Nero*, 152. Meanwhile, Jeffers, *Greco-Roman World*, 318, thinks that Tacitus "seems to believe the rumours that Nero ordered the fire" even though there is "no hard evidence for this."
[151] Barrett et al., *Emperor Nero*, 161. Cary and Scullard, *History of Rome*, 359, similarly report that once the rumours took hold the people "persisted in its belief that Nero was the real culprit, while his ruthless cruelty excited pity for the victims and thus increased his unpopularity." Cf. also Jeffers, *Greco-Roman World*, 31. Lampe, "Roman Christians," 118, may be correct in his theory that if Christians settled in the "perimeter regions" such as Trastevere and Porta Capena it becomes "all the more plausible that Nero would choose them as scapegoats, accusing them of arson."
[152] Cary and Scullard, *History of Rome*, 359. Cary and Scullard consider the Christians in Rome as "newly formed" but Christianity thrived long before Paul entered Rome in c. 60-61 CE. Lampe, *Valentinus*, 42, for example identifies Trastevere (XIV Augustan region) as an "early Christian residential quarter" (see also pp. 42-5). Trastevere was situated "west of the Tiber river across from Tiber Island." See Lampe, "Roman Christians," 118, and Philo, *Legat.* 155, 57. Brown and Meier, *Antioch and Rome*, 103, state that the "contention that Christianity reached Rome in the early 40s remains unverifiable probability; that it had reached Rome by the late 40s or early 50s is virtually certain." Meanwhile, Peterson, *Acts*, 709, via Tajra, *Martyrdom*, 76-7, thinks that Christians were in Rome by the end of Tiberius's reign (which extended to 37 CE). Additionally, Claudius's datable expulsion of 49 CE (Acts 18:2) further provides evidence of Christianity in Rome. Also, Acts 28:14-15 provides evidence that there were in fact Christians at Puteoli, the Forum of Appius and Three Taverns by the time Paul reached Italy. Last, and this is admittedly speculative but during the early account of the church's birth at Pentecost in Jerusalem Luke records that there were Jews from Rome (Acts 2:10). With regard to Tigellinus, Potter, *Emperors of Rome*, 68, explains how after joining Nero's inner circle he would "prove a loyal confederate in encouraging the worst of Nero's vices, and was rewarded in AD 62 by being made prefect of the Praetorian Guard."
[153] Cary and Scullard, *History of Rome*, 359.

put to death at this time (*1 Clem.* 6.1).¹⁵⁴ This translates into what Jeffers describes as hundreds or even "perhaps several thousand" Christians in Rome who "lost their lives in this persecution."¹⁵⁵ Lampe claims that this dual witness of Tacitus and Clement is a "coincidence that can hardly be explained by imputing rhetorical exaggeration to both authors."¹⁵⁶

Among all of the accounts, Tacitus's chapter of the Annals is "one of the most intensely studied passages of classical literature" that outlines what was arguably "the first Christian 'persecution.'"¹⁵⁷ Just before he describes the nature of the persecution, Tacitus (*Ann.* 15.44.1) makes it clear that there was an intense religious quest for appeasement and for answers via the Sibylline books, while prayers were offered to Vulcan (the god of fire), Ceres, and Proserpina along with "propitiatory ceremonies" that were "performed for Juno by married women."¹⁵⁸ Subsequently, Tacitus explains the process of how Christians became implicated:

> But neither human resourcefulness, nor the emperor's largesse, nor appeasement of the gods could stop belief in the nasty rumor that an order had been given for the fire. To dispel the gossip, Nero therefore found culprits, on whom he inflicted the most exotic punishments. These people were hated for their shameful offenses, people whom the common people called Christians. The man who gave them their name, Christus, had been executed during the rule of Tiberius by the procurator Pontius Pilatus. The pernicious superstition had been temporarily suppressed, but it was starting to break out again, not just in Judea, the starting point of that curse, but in Rome as well, where all that is abominable and shameful in the world flows together and gains popularity.¹⁵⁹

---

[154] See my note 53 in Chapter 5. On Tacitus 15.44 see Schnabel, "Trial," 192–3.

[155] Jeffers, *Greco-Roman World*, 318.

[156] Lampe, *Valentinus*, 82. Kosso, *Knowing the Past*, 82, explains the added value of an independent witness when two pieces of "textual evidence" are written by "different authors." Similarly, Mark Leone and Constance Crosby, "Epilogue: Middle Range Theory in Historical Archaeology," in *Consumer Choice in Historical Archaeology* (ed. Suzanne M. Spencer-Wood; New York: Plenum, 1987), 399, explain the value of independent data that is provided by "different individuals, at different times, for different purposes." Naturally, data arising from different literary sources that corroborate with the material remains constitute superior evidence (such as the fire of Rome).

[157] Barrett et al., *Emperor Nero*, 166 and 161 respectively.

[158] Formal banquets were held where the image of the god was set before the dining guests (as was common in Roman religious life). Ritual feasts held for female gods were called *sellisternia* and that for the male gods *lectisternia*. Apparently, the Sibylline books that were inside the Temple of Apollo on the Palatine managed to survive the fire. See Barrett et al., *Emperor Nero*, 166 (n. 35 and n. 37). One wonders how many countless pagan, Jewish, or Christian manuscripts (including Luke's or even Paul's) perished in the fire (except for those in the few unaffected regions such as Trastevere or Porta Capena). See Lampe, "Roman Christians," 117–19.

[159] Tacitus, *Ann.* 15.44.2–3; Barrett et al., *Emperor Nero*, 166–7. With regard to the "shameful offenses" this may refer to the second-century rumours alleging cannibalism or infanticide (n. 39). *Chrestiani* was apparently the original reading before it was corrected to *Christiani* (the *e* was erased with an *i* added). Exactly which hand made the change is debated but it seems likely that it had something to do with the *i* in Christus in the next verse (Tacitus, *Ann.* 15.44.3). It is rather interesting that "in Antioch the disciples were first called Christians" (πρώτως ἐν Ἀντιοχείᾳ τοὺς μαθητὰς Χριστιανούς, see Acts 11:26). There is some variation for Χριστιανός and of particular interest is that Χρηστιανούς with the η is found in the original reading of ℵ* and also 81. See also Keener's, *Acts*, 2:1847–50, discussion on the Latin political background of this term.

It is especially unfortunate for the purpose of dating Acts that Tacitus does not give any precise indication as to how much time passed between the fire and the punishment.[160] However, there is every reason to suspect that the time between the fire, the "nasty rumour," "gossip," and the subsequent punishment was probably a matter of days—or perhaps a few weeks at most—but it is very likely that the persecution happened by the end of the summer of 64 CE.[161]

The historical value of this account is strengthened by the fact that Tacitus is clearly no fan of Christianity (or Judaism for that matter—see *Hist.* 5.5.1) but also because he describes the persecution in relation to the death of Christ under Pontius Pilate:[162]

> And so, at first, those who confessed were apprehended, and subsequently, on the disclosures they made, a huge number were found guilty—more because of their hatred of mankind than because they were arsonists. As they died, they were further subject to insult. Covered with hides of wild beasts, they perished by being torn to pieces by wild dogs, or they would be fastened to crosses and, when daylight had gone, set on fire to provide lighting at night. Nero had offered his gardens as a venue for the show, and he would also put on circus entertainments, mixing with the plebs in his charioteer's outfit or standing up in his chariot. As a result, guilty though these people were and deserving exemplary punishment, pity for them began to well up because it was felt that they were being exterminated not for the public good but to gratify one man's cruelty.[163]

The cruelty of this account is self-evident and requires no further comment.[164]

---

[160] Barrett et al., *Emperor Nero*, 166–7 (n. 38). It is also uncertain as to exactly who the Christians were brought before. Perhaps it was Ofonius Tiggelinus, Nero's "sinister praetorian prefect," or the "prefect of the city" or even the *praefectus vigilum* who was in charge of the "Imperial fire service, who could deal with cases of arson" (n. 38).

[161] My interpretation could be wrong but in light of the magnitude of the tragedy, the human suffering and the people's want of answers it seems reasonable to conclude that justice would be sought rather quickly (Tacitus, *Ann.* 15.44.1). Furthermore, the time-period must have been short given Nero's decisiveness on the relief efforts and his increasingly autocratic nature—plus the fact that Tacitus (*Ann.* 15.44.2 and 4) does not indicate any lengthy judicial process. The account progresses rather quickly from confession to apprehension and subsequent death (verse 4).

[162] This provides a measure of evidence for the significant existence of Christianity in Rome by 64 CE. Recall my note 152 above.

[163] Tacitus, *Ann.* 15.44.4–5; Barrett et al., *Emperor Nero*, 167–8. Tacitus's (*Hist.* 5.5.1) comments on the Christian "hatred of mankind" reflect his views elsewhere towards the Jews as well: "The customs of the Jews are base and abominable. . . . [T]oward every other people they feel only hate and enmity" (166). See also Lampe's, "Roman Christians," 119, section C on the "'Bad Press' about the Christians."

[164] "So horrific was their treatment that it elicited popular sympathy." Barrett et al., *Emperor Nero*, 162. There are other sources such as Suetonius (*Ner.* 16.2.2): "The Christians, devotees of a new and abominable superstition, were subjected to punishment" (168). Notice his view of the Christians is very similar to Tacitus (*Ann.* 15.44.2) but does not go into any further details about the punishment. Still, this means we have two independent and corroborating non-Christian references to the same event. Meanwhile, Lactantius (*De mort. pers.* 2.5–7) refers to the death of Peter and Paul in Rome and Nero's attempt to wipe out Christianity but does not provide a specific post-Great Fire persecution account. See Barrett et al., *Emperor Nero*, 168–9. Last, Eusebius (*Hist. Eccl.* 2.25.1–5) has much to say about Nero as the enemy of the Christian faith. In verse 2 he writes (169–70): "it is possible for anyone who so wishes to see from them the loutish qualities of the

What does require further comment is that this account of the Roman persecution is notoriously difficult, if not impossible to corroborate with the friendly and peaceful relations between the Christians and the Roman authorities in the Acts narrative.[165] While commenting on the peaceful "tone" of Acts, Rackham highlights how Nero's "cruel and bloody persecution" impacted "the whole Church."[166] Up to this point there had been some localized persecutions with "few deaths."[167] However, the "wholesale slaughter under Nero must have marked an epoch in the relations of the Church and the Empire."[168]

Accordingly, Luke's description in Acts 28:30-31 would "not only have been difficult to write but actually misleading."[169] Rackham's argument is sound because a late date—even a date past 64—creates even more problems because in Acts there is a "very obvious ... apologia for Christianity to the Roman authorities" that "would serve excellently—before 64 A.D."[170] However, after the summer of 64 CE, Nero's persecution "altered the whole relation of Church and Empire ... the Emperor had declared war; Christianity had become a *religio illicita*; and St. Luke's arguments were thrown away."[171]

Under closer examination, the persecution of 64 CE does not harmonize with the pro-Roman sentiment in Acts by any stretch of the imagination. Furthermore, the distinction between Nero's earlier and later reign is also critical for interpreting the date of Acts. After 62 CE any *appeal* to Caesar seems risky and no one (especially a Christian) in their right mind would attempt an appeal after 64 CE given Nero's reputation along with the grisly details of the persecution discussed above.[172] Any author, especially a Christian one, would lose all credibility if they were to narrate such an appeal to Nero or present such a friendly attitude towards the Roman government

---

bizarre man's insanity. Driven on by this, he brought about the destruction of countless men one after the other" along with the murder of his "closest relatives and friends." Eusebius speaks only of the persecution in "general terms" as does Tertullian (*Apol.* 5.3) "with no reference to the fire or the horrific punishments" that we read in Tacitus's account (170 [n. 48]).

[165] There does not appear to be any plausible motive for this dichotomy. Cf. Reinfandt, "Reading Texts," 51; Greene and Moore, *Archaeology*, 155.
[166] Rackham, "Plea," 81.
[167] Ibid.
[168] Ibid.
[169] Ibid.
[170] Ibid., 83. Setting aside their views on the date of Acts, this case in point corresponds well to the motive criticism of Cadbury, *Luke-Acts*, 48, and Dibelius, *Studies*, 144–5. See also Kosso, *Knowing the Past*, 51.
[171] Rackham, "Plea," 83.
[172] Ibid., 83, explains that up to this time in "individual cases they had asserted the innocence or harmlessness of the Christian teachers. But an appeal had been made to Caesar at Rome." In Acts 25:11, Paul spoke two simple words in Greek (or perhaps in Latin) to the Roman Procurator Festus: "I appeal to Caesar" (Καίσαρα ἐπικαλοῦμαι). In turn, Festus echoes Paul's choice in v. 12: "To Caesar you have appealed; to Caesar you will go." This process was known as the *provocatio* not the later *appellatio* as in the case of modern English law where the sentence or verdict could be changed. See Barrett, *Acts*, 2:1131; Tajra, *Trial of St. Paul*, 144–7; Adrian N. Sherwin-White, *Roman Society and Roman Law in the New Testament* (Oxford: Oxford University Press, 1963), 68–70; and Witherington, *Acts*, 724–6. Peterson, *Acts*, 649, explains that at this time Nero "was not yet guilty of the sort of injustices for which he later became famous." Since Paul knows he does not stand a chance of surviving a (lower) Jewish court he plays, as Barrett, *Acts*, 2:1131, calls it, his "trump card." And yet, after 64 CE Paul (or any Christian for that matter) would realize his chances of surviving an appeal to Nero would be extremely unlikely. Cf. Bartlet, "St. Paul's Fate at Rome," 465–6.

after 64 CE. A far more plausible scenario is that Acts was written prior to Nero's persecution and moral slide into a tyrannical autocracy.[173]

Conclusion: Acts in Its Jewish and Greco-Roman Historical Contexts

These events in history that have been discussed in this chapter are far too significant and contemporaneous with the last event in Acts to ignore. We are left with Paul the "unhindered" Jewish-Christian protagonist under house arrest in Rome engaging Jews and Gentiles alike. Within the next two to three years Rome is utterly destroyed by fire in July of 64 CE along with multitudes of Christians that may have included Luke and Paul. A couple of years later in 66 CE, the Jews rebel against Rome. In 70 CE the city of Jerusalem, and their beloved Temple, are destroyed, and much of its population are either killed or sent into slavery. Luke says nothing. Therefore the book of Acts was written before all of these events took place. The various attempts to explain all of these omissions from Luke's narrative, however creative, are divorced from the Jewish and Greco-Roman historical contexts.

---

[173] Harnack, *Date of Acts*, 99. Harnack's position (99) sums up the arguments for an early date well: "Not only is the slightest reference to the outcome of the trial of St Paul absent from the book, but not even a trace is to be discovered of the rebellion of the Jews in the seventh decade of the century, of the destruction of Jerusalem and the Temple, of Nero's persecution of the Christians, and of other important events that occurred in the seventh decade of the first century."

9

Conclusion: Dating Acts in Its Jewish and Greco-Roman Contexts

The date of Acts is a paradox in many ways. While the so-called majority of scholars think that Acts was written somewhere between 70 and 90 CE, the *vast* majority of those who have written the most extensively and recently on the subject are absolutely convinced that this range is simply an untenable and convenient political compromise. At the same time, the arguments in favour of a post-90 CE date are easier to dismantle. There are simply far too many problems with this range as my arguments (along with those before me) have shown.

Several critical methodological flaws can be identified among the various approaches to the date of Acts in general, and especially among the most recent monographs (esp. Pervo and Tyson). Assessing the date of Acts should never be reduced to comparing texts between completely different authors, purposes, and genres, and then claiming a date. The problem is far more complex and requires attention to several areas of research. We must consider relevant contemporary sources and texts within their historical context.

Unfortunately, Pervo's application of intertextuality fails to adequately address the notoriously problematic textual record of Acts or provide a satisfactory account of its place in history. Meanwhile, Tyson's method remains largely undefined while his conclusions rest on several shaky assumptions that are easy to refute, such as his view that Luke-Acts is a reaction to Marcion. Last, while Mittelstaedt provides several compelling historical arguments for an early date, there are some valuable arguments and areas of research that he does not address.

Dating any historical document requires attention to several factors (i.e., literary, textual, source, and material) and in many cases these remain largely untouched among the so-called majority middle and late dating positions. Where methodological deficiencies have been identified, a historiographical approach to the date of Acts meets these deficiencies by providing an appropriate framework for addressing the date of Acts in its Jewish and Greco-Roman contexts. An analysis of the historiography on the date of Acts, supplemented with textual criticism and modern grammatical insights, will advance the debate substantially in new ways while also modernizing and reinforcing the existing arguments in favour of an early date of Acts.

We also need to be aware that our source theories impact the way we date Acts—or any historical document for that matter. Since there is strong evidence that Luke is the author of Acts and a companion of Paul, this allows us to date Acts in accordance with Paul's life and death. What is more difficult to process is the fact that Luke's personal style and mind are visible throughout Acts, making it difficult to determine his sources with precision. However, this realization only strengthens the position of Lukan authorship and his relationship to the datable elements in the narrative.

Accordingly, the "we" (and they) passages clearly point towards Luke's incorporation of other written or oral sources with those of his own. Furthermore, the "we" passages should be redefined to consider the possibility of a sixth "we" passage that occurs before the others in the Western text of Acts 11:28 while the last "we" passage (Acts 28:1-16) should be extended to verse 29 (and possibly 31). Additionally, it is likely that this early Western variant arose from Antioch first and, in due course, launched the known traditions connecting Antioch with the author of Acts.

It is also likely that Luke is presenting himself in the prologues as a participant in the narrative, to some degree, rather than giving a simple literary impression. It further seems clear that Luke, in addition to his own memories, makes use of written sources that must have included some measure of a broadly-defined itinerary, or at the very least some personal notes that were kept by the author and likely supplemented by others connected with the churches in Acts. Luke's attention to matters of geography, lodging, and politics also increases our ability to date Acts as well as indicate the form of the sources he employed in the narrative.

Subsequently, it appears that Luke, in addition to his own notes and memories, relied on Barnabas as his source from Antioch. Together, this data undergirds the source material in the middle half of Acts (*c.* 11:19–15:39) while Paul (along with Luke, Silas, or Timothy) provided the Rome source for the last section of Acts (*c.* 15:40–28:31). My analysis also reaffirms that there is no clear evidence that Luke used Paul's letters and, even if this were to be proven, it does not preclude an early date of Acts. Similarly, it has also been demonstrated that the long-held theory that Luke relies on the writings of Josephus should be thrown out entirely. All of these points increase our ability to place Acts into a much earlier chronological framework.

Moreover, an exploration of the relationship between the date of Acts and the ancient, modern, and contemporary interpretations of the end of Acts leads to the discovery that many of the recent literary explanations often *assume* a post-70 CE date. The nineteenth-century premise of fabrication morphed into later theories of foreshadowing and, more recently, Marguerat's *rhetoric of silence* or Troftgruben's *linkage*. The common root with all such rhetorical explanations is that they assume, rather than argue, a later date where Paul is dead, the city of Rome and the church are decimated, and many of the Jews in Judea and Jerusalem, along with its Temple, are destroyed.

Somehow Luke as a historical and Jewish-Christian writer (via some advanced literary tactic) has opted to abandon his plot and leave all of this out of his narrative in favour of an epic ending that loosely mirrors pagan literature from several centuries earlier. Moreover, all of these interpretations bypass the most ancient interpretation that Luke's silence at the end of Acts is due to a lack of further knowledge. This straightforward interpretation remains the most compelling choice among other options in light of the combined literary and historical evidence.

Conclusion

The discussion on the Jewish response to the gospel in Acts (and Acts 28:17-28 specifically) offers additional reasons for an early date while offering insight into the interpretation of Acts in general. Simply stated, a tragic, condemning, or otherwise negative view of the Jewish response in Acts more aptly reflects a post-70 CE historical context whereas a more hopeful situation supports a pre-70 CE view. After sifting through layers of argumentation, and considering the wisdom background of Isa. 6:9-10 in light of the Jewish portrait of Paul in Acts, it becomes clear that the Jewish response to the gospel in Acts is in fact far more hopeful than previously espoused. Such a hopeful view is logically inconsistent with a text written during and after the fall of Jerusalem.

Despite the general lack of consensus concerning theories of what came first and how the texts of Acts developed, there is sufficient evidence to show an early origin of the Western text (or however we choose to define these variants). In fact, a further implication is that the texts of Acts are comparable in age since none of the variants at the end of Acts show any significant expansion reflecting a later (post-64 CE) state of affairs. In the very place where extra scribal details should be expected we do not find any major theological, social, cultural, or historical differences, and not one single reference to the tragic events that soon followed the narrative. This is exceptional given the well-established Western tendency for expansion. Another implication is that a study of the variants magnifies the already problematic literary solutions to the end of Acts.

After a brief discussion on the question of the historicity of Acts, it was proposed that the fall of Jerusalem and its aftermath (which has long divided the early and middle groups) presented what I consider to be decisive evidence that Acts was written before 70 CE. It was amply demonstrated that Dodd's conclusion is correct—the Lukan texts and prophecies with regard to Jerusalem's destruction and its Temple in 70 CE simply reflect that which can already be found in the LXX.

Moreover, it was further argued that the language of Luke clearly reflects a literary and historical context prior to 70 CE and not the depth and details found in Josephus's much later account, *Jewish War*. Meanwhile, it seems that the middle group also failed to satisfactorily explain why Luke and Acts unequivocally reflect the language of an unscathed Jerusalem. The city, along with its Temple organization and officers, is narrated as functioning in every respect, including its worship practices and prayers, as if nothing had happened. A post-70 CE date of Acts is doubtful given the historic aftermath of the Jewish rebellion and all of its catastrophic effects on the Jewish population, politics, economics, and religious practices.

Perhaps even more decisive than the fall of Jerusalem is the last recorded event in Acts. Paul is in Rome under house arrest, yet Luke says nothing of the Great Fire that devastated this very city in July of 64 CE, nor does he say anything about the subsequent persecution of Christians in Rome under Nero. Given the untold thousands of casualties to both the Roman and Christian population that is well attested by several non-Christian authors, it remains extremely far-fetched that any rational motive could exist for Luke's silence on what happened to Rome and its populace in 64 CE.

A rational explanation for such an omission is also unlikely if we factor Luke's frequent use of the Jewish prophetic tradition (LXX) in light of the contemporaneous application of the non-Christian prophetic texts at the time (i.e., Cassius Dio). In line with Rackham and Harnack, the Roman persecution remains entirely at odds with the friendly and peaceful relations between the Christians and the Roman authorities in Acts. Hence, those who support a post-64 CE date of Acts need to not only substantiate these grand historical omissions, but they *also* need to explain why Acts contains many pro-Roman elements in the narrative, complete with an appeal to a famously murderous (post-64 CE) tyrant by Luke's main character (Paul in Acts 25:11).

In the final analysis, we are left with a series of unexplainable absences in the narrative of Acts that clearly point to its place in history before 64 CE. The most notable absences are the death of Paul, the destruction of Rome (along with large tracts of its general population as well as the multitudes of Christians who were murdered at Nero's request), the destruction of Jerusalem (along with its Temple), while Palestine suffered the destruction of approximately one-third of its Jewish population. We are also left with a series of unexplainable realities in Acts—an unscathed Jerusalem with its unscathed Temple establishment complete with unscathed Jewish and Christian relations with Rome. At the book's end we find an unscathed and unhindered Paul in an unscathed Rome, liberally and legally proclaiming his gospel while he awaits an audience with an even-tempered Nero.

An early date of Acts may not be popular given the current scholarly status quo but in the end its date, like that of any historical problem, must not rest on untested literary theories and assumptions. Instead, the date should be based on historiography—the ways that historians, however imperfectly and subjectively, have interpreted the sources and available evidence. This process should always include an awareness of the historical context of the sources for both the ancient writers and those commenting on the issue into the present day. An interpretation of the cumulative research discussed finds that the book of Acts should be securely dated just prior to 64 CE (*c.* 62–63 CE).

Appendix

The Manuscript Record for Acts 28:11-31

Despite the changing trends in NT textual criticism, one unifying principle among text critics is that studying the manuscripts remain a prerequisite for making any judgements about a text, or the history of its development.[1] This is somewhat ironic because text critics often have divergent views on everything from choosing a variant to the overall goals of the discipline.[2] Where some scholars emphasize the need to compare actual manuscripts instead of a set of readings, should not the goal be to include a consideration of both?[3] Consequently, the following three sections will catalogue the extant papyri, majuscules, and minuscules of Acts (that may or may not include 28:11-31) and compare them with the NA^{28}.

The overall goal here is to assess what the variations and changes may or may not suggest in light of the well-established Western tendencies of expansion.[4] At the end of Acts we simply do not find the level of variation that we can reasonably expect from Western scribes, and this is exceptional given the magnitude of the events that occurred soon after the final scene in Acts (see Chapter 8).

(A) Manuscripts with an Alexandrian Ending

The first manuscript on the docket is P^{74}—which is commonly considered to be the best surviving Acts manuscript to date.[5] The Alands considered P^{74} to be a top manuscript of a "very special quality" used for establishing the original text.[6] Accordingly, it

---

[1] Metzger, *Text*, 207; Porter, "Developments," 32, 36; Parker, *Codex Bezae*, 1.
[2] For a helpful comparison of the traditional and socio-historical goals for the discipline, see Porter and Pitts, *Fundamentals*, 1–6.
[3] Porter, "Developments," 36. Other methods (such as the CBGM) deal primarily with texts and not the manuscripts. See Wachtel, "Notes," 28.
[4] See Chapter 7.
[5] P^{74} is a sixth- or seventh-century manuscript (from the Bodmer collection in Geneva) that contains a large portion of Acts. Fitzmyer, *Acts*, 47.
[6] Category I, so Aland and Aland, *New Testament*, 101. Their scale of quality (cf. 106) ranges from 1 (being the best) to 5 (being the worst). Barrett, *Acts*, 1:3, further notes the "general agreement with ℵ A B, that is, the Old Uncial, or Alexandrian text." For criticism of the circular nature of the Alands' categories see Metzger and Ehrman, *Text*, 238, and also James K. Elliott, "The Early Text of the Catholic Epistles," in *The Early Text of the New Testament* (eds. Charles E. Hill and Michael J. Kruger; Oxford: Oxford University Press, 2012), 204–24 (209).

is no surprise that the (reading) text of Acts 28:11-31 (P⁷⁴) is basically the same as the NA²⁸ starting with verse 11: [μ]ετὰ δὲ τρις (*l.* τρεῖς) μῆνας [ἀ]νήχθημεν πλο[ί]ῳ παρακεχιμακότ[ι] ἐν τῇ νήσῳ ἀλεξανδρίνῳ παρασήμῳ διοσκοροις· (*l.* διοσκούροις).⁷ Folio 184 contains verse 12 and most of verse 13 as well. P⁷⁴ has τρις instead of τρεῖς at the end of verse 12. Verses 14-15 are very fragmentary but seem to reflect the NA²⁸. At the bottom of the fragment (folio 184) one can see [Τρ]ιῶν [ταβερνῶν]. Verse 16 reads: [μέ]νιν (*l.* μένειν) καθ' ἑαυτὸ[ν] σὺν τῷ φυλάττοντι αὐτὸν στρατιώτ[η] and starts with ἐγένετο in verse 17. P⁷⁴ shows part of ἀπεστάλη and σωτήρι[ον] from Acts 28:28 (folio 187).

The subsequent fragment contains only two words from verse 30 and the remaining verse 31: [π]ρὸς αὐτόν κηρύσσων (the NA²⁸ states that verse 29 is missing from P⁷⁴). The final folio is missing vv. 29-30 and includes the rest of verse 31: [π]ρὸς αὐτόν· κηρύσ[σ]ων τὴν βασιλείαν [τ]οῦ θυ· καὶ διδάσκων [τ]ὰ περὶ τῆς βασιλιάς (*l.* βασιλειας) [ι]υ χυ μετὰ πάσης σωτηρίας ἀκωλύτως·.⁸ The πράξις [απ]οστόλων follows underneath a series of symbols and what looks like a tally count for the scribe. It is doubtful that the non-Alexandrian verse 29 was originally part of this manuscript.

The next manuscript to examine is the fourth-century Codex Sinaiticus א (01).⁹ Although 01 is known for some Western readings, it follows the NA²⁸ very closely with regard to verses 11, 16, 19, 28-31 with no Western variants in the whole chapter.¹⁰ The fifth-century Codex Alexandrinus (A) (02), like Sinaiticus, once contained the whole Bible and then some. It contains the book of Acts right up until 28:30: ἔμεινεν δὲ δίαιτιαν ὅλην ('Ἐνέμεινεν in the NA²⁸). The text does not show any signs of the Western variants.

The fourth-century B (03) Codex Vaticanus is also a "primary witness for the Alexandrian or Old Uncial text."¹¹ Verse 11 reads: Μετὰ δὲ τρεῖς μῆνας ἀνήχθημεν ἐν πλοίῳ παρακεχειμακότι ἐν τῇ νήσῳ, Ἀλεξανδρίνῳ, παρασήμῳ Διοσκούροις.¹² Vaticanus contains verses 12-14 while including καὶ οὕτως εἰς τὴν Ῥώμην ἤλθαμεν.¹³ Verse 15 is the same as the NA²⁸ except that the article οἱ is missing before ἀδελφοὶ and has the *nomem sacrum* for θεῷ. Verse 16 is the same with σὺν τῷ φυλάσσοντι αὐτὸν στρατιώτῃ. Verse 28 reads οὖν ὑμῖν ἔστω ὅτι instead of οὖν ἔστω ὑμῖν ὅτι. Although verse 29 is absent in B (03), there is a large space between ἀκούσονται (v. 28) and Ἐνέμεινεν (v. 30).¹⁴ Verses 30 and 31 are the same with Πράχεις απολοστόλον at the end.¹⁵

---

⁷ The first ἐν is missing before πλοίῳ. Some of the Western versions omit Μετὰ δὲ τρεῖς μῆνας and παρασήμῳ Διοσκούροις. See also Boismard and Lamouille, *Le Texte Occidental*, 424. Διοσκούροις is the usual Attic spelling of the word where ου represents the Hellenistic form. Cf. Barrett, *Acts*, 2:128.

⁸ P⁷⁴ has τῆς βασιλιάς instead of τοῦ κυρίου and σωτηρίας instead of παρρησίας (NA²⁸).

⁹ For a descriptive list of the majuscules, see Aland and Aland, *New Testament*, 107-28 and Barrett, *Acts*, 1:4-7.

¹⁰ It is no surprise to find the διοσκούροις in verse 11 (316v) with no expanded verse 16 or the additional verse 29. In verse 16 it has μενιν instead of μένειν (NA²⁸) with πράξεις αποστόλων at the very end.

¹¹ Cf. Barrett, *Acts*, 1:5. For its Egyptian roots see Ropes, "Text of Acts," 3:xlvi-xlviii.

¹² Notice the variant spelling τρεῖς instead of τρίς in P⁷⁴.

¹³ οὕτως is missing in some Western texts. Cf. Boismard and Lamouille, *Le Texte Occidental*, 424.

¹⁴ Though speculative, it is possible the scribe was aware of v. 29.

¹⁵ Note the spelling variation of Πράχεις in 03 as compared with P⁷⁴.

E (08), with its biblical majuscule hand, is a sixth- or seventh-century Graeco-Latin Majuscule that ends with Acts 26:29 ὁ δὲ Παῦλος (224v) and starts again with Acts 28:26 πορεύθητι πρὸς τὸν λαόν.[16] Hence, the earlier (pre-verse 26) variants cannot be examined. Verse 28 reads: γνωστὸν οὖν ἔστω ὑμῖν ὅτι τοῖς ἔθνεσιν ἀπεστάλη τὸ σωτήριον τοῦ θεοῦ· αὐτοὶ καὶ ἀκούσοντα[ι].[17] E shows a true omission for verse 29 between ἀκούσοντα[ι] (verse 28) and Εμινεν (Ενέμεινεν) from verse 30.[18] Verse 31 is identical to the NA[28] except that it reads παρρησία instead of παρρησίας. The final words are written below verse 31: Πράχεις τῶν ἁγίων απολστόλον.

The ninth-century codex Athous Laurensis (Ψ, 044) does not contain the expanded verse 16 or verse 29.[19] 048, the "category II" fifth-century double palimpsest, includes the Alexandrian παρασήμῳ Διοσκούροις and not the expanded verse 16, 19, or verse 29.[20] 33, the ninth-century Byzantine (category V) minuscule, does not contain verse 29.[21] 1175, the tenth-century manuscript, contains the Διοσκούροις of verse 11, but not the extra variants in verse 16, 19, or the extra verse 29.[22] Similarly, the ninth-century Codex 2464 and the tenth-century Codex 1739 include the Alexandrian Διοσκούροις in verse 11 and not the extra variants in verse 16, 19, or the extra verse 29.[23] Codex 81, which is dated to 1044 CE, reflects the same Alexandrian text as 1739 and 2464 with the addition of πράξεις τῶν αποστόλων at the end (56v).[24]

(B) Manuscripts without Acts 28:11-31

This section is somewhat of a grey area because, unfortunately, most of the earliest papyri (and majuscules) do not include Acts 28:11-31 (irrespective of Alexandrian, Western, or a mix of readings): P[8], P[29], P[33], P[38], P[41], P[45], P[48], P[50], P[53], P[56], P[57], P[91], P[112], P[127], 04, 05, 057, 076, 077, 095, 096, 097, 0140, 0165, 0175, 0189, 0236 (Greek and Coptic), 0244 and 0294.[25] Since P[29] is counted among "the witnesses to the Western text," it is unfortunate that only Acts 26:7-8 and verse 20 remain.[26] Likewise, the sixth-century fragment P[33] does not contain anything from Acts 28 at all, only Acts 7:6-10; 7:13-18; 15:21-24; 15:26-32. The Western fragment P[38] (which is known to be related to Codex

---

[16] Latin is on the left of the manuscript with Greek on the right. E's physical dimensions are 27.0 × 22.0 cm with 227 leaves.
[17] τοῦτο is missing from ἀπεστάλη [τοῦτο] τὸ σωτήριον.
[18] The ι is likely buried between the parchment pages. Verse 30 is the same except for Ἐμινεν instead of Ἐνέμεινεν (NA[28]). The last few letters of εἰσπορευομένους is hard to decipher.
[19] The last word of verse 31 is usually ἀκωλύτως. Here it is found with a variant spelling and is followed by an ἀμήν.
[20] Aland and Aland, *New Testament*, 118.
[21] This manuscript has been indexed for Acts (INTF).
[22] Folio 52v includes the extra ἀμήν and the signature πράξεις αποστόλων.
[23] There may be evidence of redaction due to the large space between verse 28 and 30 in 033, 1175, 1739 (and 03).
[24] The last word of verse 13 shows: ποτιευλούς·|corrector: ποτιολούς (INTF). The final word ἀποστόλων is written as a unique *nomen sacrum*. The ἀ has the breathing mark and a long, flowing accent, followed by two π's with large dots above them.
[25] Majuscule 066 does contain Acts 28:8-17 and shows no sign of Western expansion or omission.
[26] Cf. Barrett, *Acts*, 1:2. A Western version of Acts 28:11-31 is likely.

614) is dated to around the year 300 CE or earlier, and only includes Acts 18:27–19:6; 19:12-16.[27]

Meanwhile P[41], the very fragmentary eighth-century papyrus, which includes a Coptic translation, only contains approximately Acts 17:28–22:17. P[45], a papyrus dated to the "first half of the third-century," contains only Acts 4:27–17:17.[28] Another early third-century papyrus, P[48], exhibits a Western "type of text" where only Acts 23:11-17 and 23:25-29 survived.[29] P[50] (fourth to fifth century) contains only Acts 8:26-30; 8:30-32; 10:26-27; 10:27-30; and 10:30-31. The third-century papyrus, P[53], includes only Acts 9:33–10:1. P[56], a fifth- to sixth-century papyrus, includes only Acts 1:1-11. The fourth- (to fifth-) century papyrus P[57] contains only Acts 4:36–5:2; 5:8-10. The third-century papyrus, P[91], includes only Acts 2:30-37, 46-47; 3:1-2. P[112] (fifth century) contains only Acts 26:31-32; 27:6-7. P[127] (fifth century) has only Acts 10:32–17:10.[30]

All of these fragmentary papyri are missing Acts 28:11-31, therefore we cannot know with certainty what variants the ending contained. However, given that three of the earliest six papyri exhibit Western readings (P[29], P[38], P[48]), and the proto-Alexandrian P[91] is too fragmentary to be sure, the propensity is certainly there that they may have contained Western variants.[31] The same goes for the list of majuscules that do not contain Acts 28:11-31. The whole of chapter 28 is missing, or destroyed, in every single case (recall list above).

Perhaps the most disappointing for this study is that although Codex D (= Bezae, 05) is an extremely important manuscript for the greater textual discussion, it is unfortunately missing the rest of Acts after chapter 22, v. 29b onwards. It is highly likely that Bezae once contained Western variants in Acts 28 as it is "the most important representative of the so-called Western text."[32] Second, and equally disappointing to this discussion, is that the difficult to read fifth-century palimpsest Codex Ephraemi Rescriptus C (04) does not contain Acts 28:5 onwards, since it is also known for its Western readings.[33]

Last, 0166 is a tiny fragment worth mentioning that includes a few words from Acts 28:30 and part of the first word in verse 31. The text is reproduced here as follows:][δι] ετί[αν ὅλην ἐν] [ἰ]δίῳ [μισθώμα]τι καί [ἀπεδέχε]το πάν[τας τοὺς] εἰσπορευ[ομέ]νους πρὸ[ς αὐτόν] κηρύσ[σων τὴν][. It is anyone's guess if this fragment once contained verse 29 or any other Western variants.[34] We can only speculate as to the number of variants, Western or otherwise, that were once a part of these ancient texts.

---

[27] P[38] could be dated earlier (see my note 59 in Chapter 7 on the issue).
[28] David P. Barrett and Philip Wesley Comfort, *The Text of the Earliest New Testament Greek Manuscripts* (2 vols; Grand Rapids: Kregel, 2019), 1:138.
[29] Barrett, *Acts*, 1:3. Recently, Comfort and Barrett, *Earliest New Testament*, 2:346, have dated P[48] to the "early third century."
[30] According to Tuckett, "Early Text," 157 (n. 1), there is "considerable text-critical interest" in P[127]. See more recently Wachtel, "Notes," 31, who explains that P[127] and Bezae "feature the same paraphrasing expansions of the 'Western' text."
[31] Recall the discussion above: Tuckett, "How Early," 74, and Comfort, *Manuscripts*, 64 and 69.
[32] Barrett, *Acts*, 1:6.
[33] Cf. Barrett, *Acts*, 1:5, and Ropes, "Text of Acts," 3:lv.
[34] Jas 1:11 is found on the verso (INTF).

(C) Manuscripts with a Western Ending

This section examines the manuscripts that exhibit some form of Western and non-Alexandrian readings of Acts 28:11-31. Beyond the known Latin and Syriac manuscripts that contain some of these variants,[35] the following Greek manuscripts meet this criterion: H (014), L (020), P (025), 18, 323, 383, 424, 614, 630, 945, 1241, 1505, and 2412.[36] First is H (014), the ninth-century Byzantine codex Mutinensis (43 leaves, 33.0 cm x 23.0 cm). This is an important majuscule because it only contains the book of Acts; it exhibits the Alexandrian text παρασήμῳ Διοσκούροις and the expanded verse 16: εἰς Ῥώμην· ὁ ἑκατόνταρχος παρέδωκεν τοὺς δεσμίους τῷ στρατοπεδάρχῳ τῷ δὲ παύλῳ· ἐπετράπει (the remaining text here matches the NA[28]).[37] The text of verse 29 reads: καί ταῦτα αὐτοῦ εἰπόντος· ἀπῆλθον οἱ Ἰουδαῖοι, πολλὴν ἔχοντες ἐν ἑαυτοῖς συζήτησιν·.[38]

Codex Angelicus L (020) is a ninth-century Byzantine text. Angelicus has the Διοσκούροις from verse 11 (NA[28]) and the expanded verse 16 with a few spelling errors/variants: παρέδωκε(ν), στρατοπα(ι)δάρχῳ and στρατιώτ(ι). The text of (verse 29) folio 42v, Col. 2 (lines 5-9) reads: καί ταῦτα αὐτοῦ εἰπόντος· ἀπῆλθον οἱ Ἰουδαῖοι· πολλὴν ἔχοντες· ἐν ἑαυτοῖς συζητησιν· (the straight upright letters suggests a later biblical majuscule style).[39] The scribe makes use of ligatures or what appears to be *combination* letters, as is common to minuscule mss., such as found on line 5 where τοῦ, from αὐτοῦ, is morphed into one symbol.[40]

Many of the ninth-century (and later) minuscules include Western variants.[41] Since the majority of the 2,853 plus minuscules have not been examined in detail, it is very likely that a good portion of them contain Western variants.[42] Codex 614 (thirteenth

---

[35] The following manuscripts contain the expanded version of verse 16: gig, p, sy[h2], and sa. Verse 29 is also found in vg[d] and sy[h2]. In some manuscripts (p, vg[mss] and sy[h]) verse 31 has this extended Latin ending: *dicens quia hic est Christus Jesus filius dei per quem incipiet totus mundus iudicari.*

[36] The following manuscripts include some version of the expanded text that includes the στρατοπέδαρχος found in Acts 28:16: 1241 (στρατοπεδάρχῳ), 18, 323, 614, 630, and 945 (στρατοπεδάρχη). Verse 29 is found in: P (025) (ninth century, folio 248, col. 1); 323 (very decorative and clear, twelfth century); 383 (very clear, thirteenth century); 945 (eleventh century); 424 (eleventh century); 630 (twelfth to thirteenth century). Notice how σύζήτησιν in 630 has the ϋ but not ϊ (cf. 614 and 2412). 1241, the very decorative twelfth-century text, includes verse 29 (note the decorative picture of Paul with a halo, 137r). See also the decorative thirteenth-century manuscript 1505 that shows v. 29 but the αὐτοῦ εἰπόντος is reversed (136v).

[37] Compare this with 614's reading below: ἐπετράπη μένειν καθ' ἑαυτὸν ἔξω τῆς παρεμβολῆς.

[38] The book ends with: πράξεις τῶν ἁγίων ἀποστόλων.

[39] Cf. Porter and Pitts, *Fundamentals*, 47. Here 020 has the same Greek text as 614 and 2412.

[40] Where 2412 contains the extra diaeresis, 020 shows no accent or diaeresis markings at all. There is an abrasion here along with ἔ[χο]ντες on line 7.

[41] Aland and Aland, *New Testament*, 128.

[42] See Ibid., 128; Vaganay, *Introduction*, 22; and Parker's, *Introduction*, 171-4, discussion on Byzantine manuscripts and text-types in general. The lack of attention to the minuscules has long been observed. Wisse, for example, remarks how "lower criticism seems to have become the study of what to do when Codex Vaticanus and P[75] disagree," while "a study of the minuscules could change this situation." Frederick Wisse, *The Profile Method for Classifying and Evaluating Manuscript Evidence* (SD 44; Grand Rapids: Eerdmans, 1984), 5, as noted by Michael Holmes, "From Nestle to the Editio Critica Maior: A Century's Perspective on the New Testament Miniscule Tradition," in *The Bible as Book: The Transmission of the Greek Text* (eds. Scot McKendrick and Orlaith O'Sullivan; London: Oak Knoll Press, 2003), 129. For an up-to-date list of manuscripts visit http://

century) has been frequently discussed as a known Western manuscript.[43] Due to its "special textual character" and its (potential) relationship to D (05), the Alands considered this to be a "category III" manuscript.[44] Categories aside, the quality of agreement between 614 and 05 is too low; therefore, it seems best to think of it as a mixed Byzantine witness.[45]

For example, 614 shows a blend of textual families with some striking similarities with the NA[28]. Acts 28:11 in 614 is the same as in the NA28 with the παρασήμῳ Διοσκούροις, which reflects the Alexandrian tradition. Verse 12 is also the same except ἡμέρας τρεῖς is found in reverse order in 614 (metathesis).[46] Verse 13 has περιελθόντες instead of περιελόντες. Meanwhile, verse 14 begins to show some textual cross-pollination that is different from the NA[28]. It has ἐπ αὐτοῖς instead of παρ' αὐτοῖς, ἐπιμείναντες instead of ἐπιμεῖναι, and εἰς Ραμην ἤλθομεν instead of εἰς τὴν Ῥώμην ἤλθαμεν. Verse 15 has ἡμῶν εξηλθον instead of ἡμῶν ἤλθαν and ἄχρις Απφιου instead of ἄχρι Ἀππίου. Most notable is how verse 16 contains this extra, sizable text following εἰς Ῥώμην: ὁ ἑκατόνταρχος παρέδωκε τοὺς δεσμίους τῷ στρατοπεδάρχῃ· τῷ δὲ παύλῳ ἐπετράπη μένειν καθ' ἑαυτὸν ἔξω τῆς παρεμβολῆς.[47]

Verse 19 also contains this extra variant after Ἰουδαίων and before ἠναγκάσθην: καὶ ἐπικραζόντων αἶρε τὸν ἐχθρὸν ἡμῶν (and cried out, "Away with our enemy").[48] Further additions in verse 19 of Codex 614 follow κατηγορῆσαι (κατηγορεῖν in the NA[28]): ἀλλ ἵνα λυτρώσωμαι τὴν ψυχὴν μου ἐκ θανάτου· (but in order that I might free my soul from death). Verse 28 is the same except it has an interesting *nomen sacrum*: σ ρ̄ ιον for σ(ωτή)ριον.[49] The additional verse 29 is also found in 614 (80v): καὶ ταῦτα αὐτοῦ εἰπόντος ἀπῆλθον οἱ Ἰουδαῖοι· πολλὴν ἔχοντες ἐν ἑαυτ[οῖς] συζήτησϊν.[50]

There are several interesting peculiarities about verse 29. First, the scribe is attentive to all accents, breathing marks, and diaeresis marks. One sits above the first Ἰ in Ἰουδαῖοι and the second is found in συζήτησϊν. Also, ἑαυτοῖς is missing the second half of the

---

www.uni-muenster.de/INTF. As of April 23, 2020, the current number of minuscules registered in the Gregory-Aland Kurzgefasste Liste is 2956. However, the actual number is lower (2,853) because some of these manuscripts have been removed from the Liste for a variety of reasons (e.g., a manuscript is discovered to be a part of another one and the two are then combined into one number). Many thanks to Gregory Paulson at INTF for providing this info in a timely fashion.

[43] This *second order* witness (so NA[28]) resides in Milan, Italy at the Biblioteca Ambrosiana. It includes 276 leaves and is approximately 25.0 cm × 18.0 cm (INTF).

[44] Aland and Aland, *New Testament,* 106, 133. 2412 agrees with 614 in 96.62 per cent of the mutually extant passages (322). Barrett, *Acts,* 1:26, highlights the strong textual relationship with 614, P[38] (*c.* 300 CE) and P[48] (third century).

[45] Parker, *Introduction,* 290. Concerning the similarities see Aland and Aland, *New Testament* 107, 133, 149, and Tuckett, "How Early," 74–6.

[46] Cf. Comfort, *Manuscripts,* 292 and Porter and Pitts, *Fundamentals,* 115.

[47] This text is the same as the NA[28] plus this Western addition noted above: Ὅτε δὲ εἰσήλθομεν εἰς Ῥώμην, [plus Western variant] ἐπετράπη τῷ [δε] Παύλῳ μένειν καθ' ἑαυτὸν [plus Western variant: ἔξω τῆς παρεμβολῆς] σὺν τῷ φυλάσσοντι αὐτὸν στρατιώτῃ.

[48] Longenecker, *Acts,* 571.

[49] The superscript line is far above the ρ. Evidently, even the word salvation carried sacred significance.

[50] "And having said these things, the Jews departed, having a great dispute among themselves." See also 614's *editio princeps*: A. V. Valentine-Richards and John M. Creed, *The Text of Acts in Codex 614 (Tisch. 137) and its Allies* (Cambridge: Cambridge University Press, 1934), 60.

word (οἷς).⁵¹ Since the last letter of line 18 is a τ, and the following word συζήτησϊν begins with a σ, it is easy to see how the copying error occurred (due to ὁμ.). Verse 30 is mostly the same except it has the conjunction ουν instead of δὲ plus ἰουδαίους τε καὶ ἕλληνας·.⁵² Verse 31 reveals an interesting error with a triad of *nomina sacra*: κυ κυ ιυ (κυρίου, κυρίου, Ἰησοῦ).⁵³

---

[51] Valentine-Richards and Creed, *Codex*, 60. The original editors of 614 assumed the full ἑαυτοῖς in their reading (see also NA²⁸ v. 29 apparatus).

[52] Ἰουδαίους τε καὶ ἕλληνας is probably a theological insertion that seeks to clarify the adjective πάντας (here in attributive structure). Cf. Porter, *Idioms*, 119.

[53] The correct reading should be κυρίου Ἰησοῦ Χριστοῦ. There is plenty of scholarship regarding *nomina sacra*, however, perhaps one of the best treatments is found in Comfort, *Manuscripts*, 199–253, and Robert A. Kraft, "The 'Textual Mechanics' of Early Jewish LXX/OG Papyri and Fragments," in *The Bible as Book: The Transmission of the Greek Text* (eds. Scot McKendrick and Orlaith O'Sullivan; London: Oak Knoll Press, 2003), 51–72, who carefully (and I think successfully) challenges some of the prevalent theories, esp. Colin H. Roberts, *Manuscript, Society and Belief in Early Christian Egypt* (London: Oxford University Press, 1979), on the origins of the *nomina sacra*.

Bibliography

Abrams, Philip. *Historical Sociology*. Shepton Mallet, UK: Open, 1982.
Adams, Sean A. *The Genre of Acts and Collected Biography*. SNTSMS 156. Cambridge: Cambridge University Press, 2013.
Adams, Sean A. "The Relationships of Paul and Luke: Luke, Paul's Letters, and the 'We' Passages of Acts." In *Paul and His Social Relations*, edited by Stanley E. Porter and Christopher D. Land, 125–42. Pauline Studies 7. Leiden: Brill, 2013.
Aland, Barbara. "Entstehung, Charakter und Herkunft des Sog. Westlichen Textes Untersucht an der Apostelgeschichte." *ETL* 62 (1986): 5–65.
Aland, Kurt, and Barbara Aland. *The Text of the New Testament*. Translated by Erroll F. Rhodes. 2nd ed. Grand Rapids, MI: Eerdmans, 1989.
Aland, Kurt, and Barbara Aland. *Text und Textwert der Griechischen Handschriften des Neuen Testaments III: Die Apostelgeschichte*. 2 vols. Berlin: de Gruyter, 1993.
Alexander, Loveday C. A. *Acts in Its Ancient Literary Context: A Classicist Looks at the Acts of the Apostles*. LNTS 289. London: T&T Clark, 2005.
Alexander, Loveday C. A. "Luke's Preface in the Context of Greek Preface Writing." *NovT* 28 (1986): 48–74.
Alexander, Loveday C. A. *The Preface to Luke's Gospel: Literary Convention and Social Context in Luke 1.1–4 and Acts 1.1*. SNTSMS 78. Cambridge, MA: Cambridge University Press, 1993.
Alexander, Loveday C. A. "Reading Luke-Acts from Back to Front: The Unity of Luke-Acts." In *The Unity of Luke-Acts*, edited by J. Verheyden, 419–46. BETL 142. Leuven: Leuven University Press, 1999.
Ankersmit, Frank R. *History and Tropology: The Rise and Fall of Metaphor*. Berkeley: University of California Press, 1994.
Ankersmit, Frank R. *Narrative Logic: A Semantic Analysis of the Historian's Language*. The Hague: Martinus Nijhoff, 1983.
Ankersmit, Frank R., Ewa Domanska, and Hans Kellner, eds. *Re-Figuring Hayden White*. Stanford, CA: Stanford University Press, 2009.
Archer, R. L. "The Epistolary Form in the New Testament." *ExpTim* 63 (1952): 296–8.
Argyle, Aubrey W. "The Theory of an Aramaic Source in Acts 2:14–40." *JTS* 4 (1953): 213–14.
Armstrong, Karl L. "The End of Acts and the Comparable Age of Its Variants." *FN* 31 (2018): 87–110.
Armstrong, Karl L. "The End of Acts and the Jewish Response: Condemnation, Tragedy, or Hope?" *CurBR* 17 (2019): 209–30.
Armstrong, Karl L. "The End of Acts 28 and the Fate of the Historical Apostle Paul." MA diss., Acadia Divinity College, Wolfville, NS, 2013.
Armstrong, Karl L. "The Impact of Ernst Haenchen on the Interpretation of Acts." In *Luke-Acts in Modern Interpretation*, edited by Stanley E. Porter and Ron C. Fay. Grand Rapids, MI: Kregel, forthcoming.

Armstrong, Karl L. "The Meaning of ὑποτάσσω in Ephesians 5:21–33: A Linguistic Approach." *JGRChJ* 13 (2017): 152–71.
Armstrong, Karl L. "A New Plea for an Early Date of Acts." *JGRChJ* 13 (2017): 79–110.
Armstrong, Karl L. "A New Plea for an Early Date of Acts." PhD diss., McMaster Divinity College, Hamilton, ON, 2019.
Atauz, Ayse D. *Eight Thousand Years of Maltese Maritime History: Trade, Piracy, and Naval Warfare in the Central Mediterranean*. Gainesville: University Press of Florida, 2008.
Aune, David E. "Luke 1:1–4: Historical or Scientific Prooimion?" In *Paul, Luke, and the Graeco-Roman World: Essays in Honour of Alexander J. M. Wedderburn*, edited by Alf Christopherson, Carsten Claussen, Jörg Frey, and Bruce Longenecker, 138–48. JSNTSup 217. Sheffield: Sheffield Academic, 2003.
Bagnall, Roger S. *Reading Papyri, Writing Ancient History*. 2nd ed. London: Routledge, 2019.
Baird, William. *History of New Testament Research. 1. From Deism to Tübingen*. Minneapolis, MN: Fortress, 1992.
Balch, David L. "Μεταβολὴ Πολιτειῶν: Jesus as Founder of the Church in Luke-Acts: Form and Function." In *Contextualizing Acts: Lukan Narrative and Greco-Roman Discourse*, edited by Todd C. Penner and Caroline V. Stichele, 139–88. SBLSymS 20. Atlanta, GA: SBL, 2003.
Barrett, Anthony, A., Elaine Fantham, and John C. Yardley. *The Emperor Nero: A Guide to the Ancient Sources*. Princeton, NJ: Princeton University Press, 2016.
Barrett, Charles K. *The Acts of the Apostles*. 2 vols. ICC. Edinburgh: T&T Clark, 1998.
Barrett, Charles K. "The End of Acts." In *Geschichte—Tradition—Reflexion: Festschrift Für Martin Hengel*, edited by H. Cancik, H. Lichtenberger and P. Schäfer, 545–55. 3 vols. Frühes Christentum. Tübingen: Mohr Siebeck, 1996.
Barrett, Charles K. "The Historicity of Acts." *JTS* 50 (1999): 515–34.
Barrett, Charles K. "Is there a Theological Tendency in Codex Bezae?" In *Text and Interpretation: Studies in the New Testament Presented to Matthew Black*, edited by Ernest Best and R. McL. Wilson, 15–28. Cambridge, MA: Cambridge University Press, 1979.
Barrett, Charles K. *Luke the Historian in Recent Study*. London: Epworth, 1961.
Barrett, Charles K. Review of *The First Christian Historian: Writing the "Acts of the Apostles,"* by Daniel Marguerat. *JTS* 55 (2004): 254–57.
Barrett, David P., and Philip Wesley Comfort. *The Text of the Earliest New Testament Greek Manuscripts*. 2 vols. Grand Rapids: Kregel, 2019.
Barth, Markus. *Ephesians*. 2 vols. AB 34A. Garden City, NY: Doubleday, 1974.
Bartlet, J. Vernon. "Two New Testament Problems. I. St. Paul's Fate at Rome." *Exp* 5 (1913): 464–67.
Baumberger, Christoph. "What is Understanding? An Overview of Recent Debates in Epistemology and Philosophy of Science." In *Explaining Understanding: New Perspectives from Epistemology and Philosophy of Science*, edited by Stephen R. Grimm, Christoph Baumberger, and Sabine Ammon, 1–34. New York: Routledge, 2017.
Baur, Ferdinand C. *Paul the Apostle of Jesus Christ: His Life and Works, His Epistles and Teachings*. 2 vols. Reprint, Grand Rapids, MI: Baker, 2010.
Beard, Charles A. "That Noble Dream." *AHR* 41 (1935): 74–87.
Benoit, Pierre. "La deuxième visite de Saint Paul à Jérusalem." *Bib* 40 (1959): 778–92.
Bentley, Michael, ed. *Companion to Historiography*. London: Routledge, 1997.
Biers, William R. *Art, Artefacts and Chronology in Classical Archaeology*. London: Routledge, 1992.

Blaiklock, Edward M. *The Acts of the Apostles: An Historical Commentary*. London: Tyndale Press, 1959.
Blass, Friedrich. *Acta Apostolorum sive Lucae ad Theophilum liber alter*. Göttingen: Vandenhoeck & Ruprecht, 1895.
Blass, Friedrich. *Evangelium secundum Lucam*. Leipzig: Teubner, 1897.
Blass, Friedrich. *Philology of the Gospels*. London: Macmillan, 1898.
Bloch, Marc. *The Historian's Craft*. Translated by Peter Putnam. New York: Vintage, 1953.
Blue, Bradley. "Acts and the House Church." In *The Book of Acts in Its Graeco-Roman Setting*, edited by David W. J. Gill and Conrad Gempf, 2:119–89. 5 vols. BAFCS 2. Grand Rapids, MI: Eerdmans 1995.
Bock, Darrell L. *Acts*. BECNT. Grand Rapids, MI: Baker, 2007.
Boismard, Marie-Emile. "Bulletin." *RB* 61 (1954): 257–318.
Boismard, Marie-Emile. "The Text of Acts: A Problem of Literary Criticism." In *New Testament Textual Criticism: Its Significance for Exegesis—Essays in Honour of Bruce M. Metzger*, edited by Eldon J. Epp and Gordon D. Fee, 147–57. Oxford: Clarendon, 1981.
Boismard, Marie-Emile, and Arnaud Lamouille. *Les Actes des deux Apôtres*. 3 vols. Paris: Gabalda, 1990.
Boismard, Marie-Emile, and Arnaud Lamouille. "Le texte occidental des Actes des Apôtres. À propos d'Actes 27, 1–13." *ETL* 63 (1987): 48–58.
Boismard, Marie-Emile, and Arnaud Lamouille. *Le texte occidental des Actes des Apôtres: Reconstitution et réhabilitation*. Rev. ed. 2 vols. EBib 40. Paris: Gabalda, 2000.
Bonz, Marianne P. "Luke's Revision of Paul's Reflection in Romans 9–11." In *Early Christian Voices: In Texts, Traditions, and Symbols—Essays in Honor of François Bovon*, edited by David. H. Warren, François Bovon, Ann Graham Brock, and David W. Pao, 143–51. BibInt 66. Boston, MA: Brill, 2003.
Bonz, Marianne P. *The Past as Legacy: Luke-Acts and Ancient Epic*. Minneapolis, MN: Fortress, 2000.
Booth, Wayne C. *The Rhetoric of Fiction*. 2nd ed. Chicago: University of Chicago Press, 1983.
Botermann, Helga. "Der Heidenapostel und sein Historiker. Zur historischen Kritik der Apostelgeschichte." *ThBeitr* 24 (1993): 62–84.
Brown, Callum G. *Postmodernism for Historians*. Harlow, UK: Longman, 2004.
Brown, Raymond E. *An Introduction to the New Testament*. New York: Doubleday, 1997.
Brown, Raymond E., and John P. Meier. *Antioch and Rome: New Testament Cradles of Catholic Christianity*. New York: Paulist, 1983.
Bruce, Frederick Fyvie. *The Acts of the Apostles: The Greek Text with Introduction and Commentary*. 3rd ed. Grand Rapids, MI: Eerdmans, 1990.
Bruce, Frederick Fyvie. *The Book of Acts*. NICNT. Reprint, Grand Rapids, MI: Eerdmans, 1983.
Bultmann, Rudolf. *New Testament and Other Basic Writings*. Edited and translated by Schubert. M. Ogden. Philadelphia, PA: Fortress, 1984.
Bultmann, Rudolf. "Zur Frage nach den Quellen der Apostelgeschichte." In *New Testament Essays: Studies in Memory of Thomas Walter Manson*, edited by Angus J. Brockhurst Higgins, 68–80. Manchester: Manchester University Press, 1959.
Burridge, Richard A. "The Genre of Acts Revisited." In *Reading Acts Today: Essays in Honour of Loveday C. A. Alexander*, edited by Steve Walton, Thomas E. Phillips, Lloyd Keith Pietersen, and F. Scott Spencer, 3–28. LNTS 427. London: T&T Clark, 2011.

Butticaz, Simon. "'Has God Rejected His People?' (Romans 11.1). The Salvation of Israel in Acts: Narrative Claim of a Pauline Legacy." In *Paul and the Heritage of Israel: Paul's Claim upon Israel's Legacy in Luke and Acts in the Light of the Pauline Letters*, edited by David P. Moessner, Daniel Marguerat, and Mikeal C. Parsons, 148–64. Luke the Interpreter of Israel 2. LNTS 452. London: T&T Clark, 2012.

Cadbury, Henry J. "Appendix C—Commentary on the Preface of Luke." In *The Beginnings of Christianity Part I: The Acts of the Apostles*, edited by Frederick J. Foakes-Jackson and Kirsopp Lake, 2:489–510. 5 vols. London: Macmillan, 1922.

Cadbury, Henry J. *The Book of Acts in History*. London: Black, 1955.

Cadbury, Henry J. "The Identity of the Editor of Luke and Acts." In *The Beginnings of Christianity Part I: The Acts of the Apostles*, edited by Frederick J. Foakes-Jackson and Kirsopp Lake, 2:349–59. 5 vols. London: Macmillan, 1922.

Cadbury, Henry J. "The Knowledge Claimed in Luke's Preface." *Exp* 24 (1922): 401–20.

Cadbury, Henry J. "Lexical Notes on Luke-Acts III. Luke's Interest in Lodging." *JBL* 45 (1926): 305–22.

Cadbury, Henry J. *The Making of Luke-Acts*. New York: Macmillan, 1927.

Cadbury, Henry J. "The Purpose Expressed in Luke's Preface." *Exp* 21 (1921): 431–41.

Cadbury, Henry J. "'We' and 'I' Passages in Luke-Acts." *NTS* 3 (1957): 128–32.

Callaway, Mary C. "A Hammer that Breaks Rock in Pieces: Prophetic Critique in the Hebrew Bible." In *Anti-Semitism and Early Christianity: Issues of Polemic and Faith*, edited by Craig A. Evans and Donald A. Hagner, 21–38. Minneapolis, MN: Fortress, 1993.

Campbell, Douglas A. *Framing Paul: An Epistolary Biography*. Grand Rapids, MI: Eerdmans, 2014.

Campbell, William S. "The Narrator as 'He,' 'Me,' and 'We': Grammatical Person in Ancient Histories and in the Acts of the Apostles." *JBL* 129 (2010): 385–407.

Campbell, William S. *The "We" Passages in the Acts of the Apostles: The Narrator as Narrative Character*. SBLStBL 14. Atlanta, GA: SBL, 2007.

Caplan, Jane. "Postmodernism, Poststructuralism, and Deconstruction: Notes for Historians." *CEH* 22 (1989): 262–8.

Caputo, John D. *Deconstruction in a Nutshell*. New York: Fordham University Press, 1997.

Carcopino, Jerome. *Daily Life in Ancient Rome: The People and the City at the Height of the Empire*. Edited by Henry T. Rowell. Translated by Emily O. Lorimer. New Haven, CT: Yale University Press, 2003.

Carr, Edward Hallett. *What is History?* 2nd ed. Reprint, London: Penguin, 1990.

Carson, Donald A., and Douglas J. Moo. *An Introduction to the New Testament*. 2nd ed. Grand Rapids, MI: Zondervan, 2005.

Carson, Donald A., Douglas J. Moo, and Leon Morris. *An Introduction to the New Testament*. Grand Rapids, MI: Zondervan, 1992.

Cary, Earnest, and Herbert B. Foster, trans. *Dio's Roman History*. 9 vols. LCL. London: William Heinemann, 1914–55.

Cary, Max, and Howard H. Scullard. *A History of Rome: Down to the Reign of Constantine*. Rev. ed. London: Macmillan, 1992.

Casey, Robert P. "Bentley's Collation of Codex Bezae." *HTR* 19 (1926): 213–14.

Cassidy, Richard J. "Paul's Proclamation of Lord Jesus as a Chained Prisoner in Rome: Luke's Ending is in His Beginning." In *Luke-Acts and Empire: Essays in Honor of Robert L. Brawley*, edited by David Rhoads, David Esterline, and Jae Won Lee, 142–53. PTMS 151. Eugene, OR: Pickwick, 2011.

Caulley, Thomas S. "Notable Galilean Persons." In *Galilee in the Late Second Temple Period and Mishnaic Periods*, edited by David A. Fiensy and James R. Strange, 151–66. Life, Culture, and Society Volume 1. Minneapolis, MN: Fortress, 2014.

Chadwick, Henry. "St. Peter and St. Paul in Rome: The Problem of the Memoria Apostolorum ad Catacumbas." *JTS* 8 (1957): 31–52.

Chance, J. Bradley. *Acts*. SHBC. Macon, GA: Smith & Helwys, 2007.

Cheng, Eileen Ka-May. *Historiography: An Introductory Guide*. London: Continuum, 2012.

Chilton, Bruce D., and Jacob Neusner. "Paul and Gamaliel." *BBR* 14 (2004): 1–43.

Church, F. F. "Rhetorical Structure and Design in Paul's Letter to Philemon." *HTR* 71 (1978): 17–33.

Clark, Albert C. *The Acts of the Apostles: A Critical Edition, with Introduction and Notes on Selected Passages*. Oxford: Clarendon, 1933.

Clark, Albert C. *The Descent of Manuscripts*. Oxford: Clarendon, 1918.

Clark, Albert C. *The Primitive Text of the Gospels and Acts*. Oxford: Clarendon, 1914.

Clark, Elizabeth A. *History, Theory, Text: Historians and the Linguistic Turn*. Cambridge, MA: Harvard University Press, 2004.

Cokayne, Karen. *Experiencing Old Age in Ancient Rome*. London: Routledge, 2013.

Collingwood, Robin G. *The Idea of History*. Oxford: Oxford University Press, 1946.

Colwell, Ernst C. *Studies in Methodology in Textual Criticism of the New Testament*. Edited by Bruce M. Metzger. NTTSD 9. Leiden: Brill, 1969.

Comfort, Philip W. *Encountering the Manuscripts: An Introduction to New Testament Paleography and Textual Criticism*. Nashville, TN: Broadman & Holman, 2005.

Comfort, Philip W., and David P. Barrett. *The Complete Text of the Earliest New Testament Manuscripts*. Grand Rapids, MI: Baker Books, 1999.

Conybeare, Frederick C. "The Commentary of Ephrem on Acts." In *The Beginnings of Christianity: Part 1: The Acts of the Apostles*, edited by Frederick J. Foakes-Jackson and Kirsopp Lake, 3:373–453. 5 vols. London: Macmillan, 1926.

Conzelmann, Hans. *Acts of the Apostles*. Hermeneia. Minneapolis, MN: Fortress, 1987.

Conzelmann, Hans. *Die Apostelgeschichte*. HNT 7. Tübingen: Mohr Siebeck, 1963.

Conzelmann, Hans. *The Theology of St. Luke*. New York: Harper & Brothers, 1960.

Conzelmann, Hans, and Andreas Lindemann. *Interpreting the New Testament: An Introduction to the Principles and Methods of NT Exegesis*. Translated by S. S. Schatzmann. Peabody, MA: Hendrickson, 1988.

Cook, Michael J. "The Mission to the Jews in Acts: Unravelling Luke's 'Myth of the Myriads.'" In *Luke-Acts and the Jewish People: Eight Critical Perspectives*, edited by Joseph B. Tyson, 102–23. Minneapolis, MN: Augsburg, 1988.

Cooley, Alison E., and M. G. L. Cooley. *Pompeii and Herculaneum: A Sourcebook*. 2nd ed. London: Routledge, 2014.

Cox, Michael. "Introduction: E. H. Carr—a Critical Appraisal." In *E. H. Carr: A Critical Appraisal*, edited by Michael Cox, 1–18. Hampshire, UK: Palgrave, 2004.

Crawford, Matthew. "A New Witness to the 'Western' Ordering of the Gospels: GA 073 + 084." *JTS* 69 (2018): 1–7.

Crehan, J. H. "The Purpose of Luke in Acts." In *Studia Evangelica II: Texte und Untersuchungen zur Geschichte der altchristlichen Literatur*, edited by F. L. Cross, 354–68. TU 87. Berlin: Akademie-Verlag, 1964.

Cullmann, Oscar. "Les causes de la mort de Pierre et de Paul d'après le témoignage de Clément Romain." *RHPR* 10 (1930): 294–300.

Cullmann, Oscar. *Peter: Disciple, Apostle, Martyr: A Historical and Theological Study*. Translated by Floyd V. Filson. 2nd ed. London: SCM, 1962.

Culy, Martin M., and Mikeal C. Parsons. *Acts: A Handbook on the Greek Text*. Waco, TX: Baylor University, 2003.
Dando-Collins, Stephen. *The Great Fire of Rome: The Fall of the Emperor Nero and His City*. Cambridge, MA: Da Capo Press, 2010.
Davies, Philip. "The Ending of Acts." *ExpTim* 94 (1983): 334–35.
Decker, Rodney J. *Temporal Deixis of the Greek Verb in the Gospel of Mark with Reference to Verbal Aspect*. SBG 10. New York: Peter Lang, 2001.
Delebecque, Édouard. *Les Deux Actes des Apôtres*. EBib 6. Paris: J. Gabalda, 1986.
Delobel, Joël. "Focus on the 'Western' Text in Recent Studies." *ETL* 73 (1997): 401–10.
Delobel, Joël. "The Text of Luke-Acts. A Confrontation of Recent Theories." In *The Unity of Luke-Acts*, edited by J. Verheyden, 83–107. BETL 142. Leuven: Leuven University Press, 1999.
Derrida, Jacques. *Of Grammatology*. Translated by G. C. Spivak. Baltimore, MD: The Johns Hopkins University Press, 1976.
Derrida, Jacques. *Writing and Difference*. Translated by Alan Bass. Chicago: University of Chicago Press, 1978.
DeWette, Wilhelm M. L. *Kurze Erklärung der Apostelgeschichte*. Edited by Franz Overbeck. 4th ed. Leipzig: Hirzel, 1870.
De Zwaan, Johannes. *De Handelingen der Apostelen*. Groningen (The Hague): Wolters, 1920.
De Zwaan, Johannes. "Was the Book of Acts a Posthumous Edition?" *HTR* 17 (1924): 95–153.
Dibelius, Martin. *Studies in the Acts of the Apostles*. Edited by Heinrich Greeven. London: SCM, 1956.
Dittenberger, Wilhelm. *Orientis Graeci Inscriptiones Selectae: Supplementum Sylloges Inscriptionum Graecarum*. 2 vols. Leipzig: S. Hirzel, 1903–5.
Dobson, Miriam, and Benjamin Ziemann, eds. *Reading Primary Sources: The Interpretation of Texts from Nineteenth- and Twentieth-Century History*. 2nd ed. RGHS. London: Routledge, 2020.
Dodd, Charles H. *The Apostolic Preaching and Its Development*. London: Hodder & Stoughton, 1936.
Dodd, Charles H. "The Fall of Jerusalem and the 'Abomination of Desolation.'" *JRS* 37 (1947): 47–54.
Dodd, Charles H. *New Testament Studies*. Manchester: Manchester University Press, 1967.
Donelson, Lewis R. "Cult Histories and the Sources of Acts." *Bib* 68 (1987): 1–21.
Donfried, Karl P. Review of *Leadership and Lifestyle: The Portrait of Paul in the Miletus Speech and 1 Thessalonians*, by Steve Walton. *JTS* 54 (2003): 253–6.
Dray, William. "Philosophy and Historiography." In *Companion to Historiography*, edited by Michael Bentley, 763–81. London: Routledge, 1997.
Droysen, Johann Gustav. *Outline of the Principles of History*. Boston, MA: Ginn, 1897.
Dubowy, Ernst. *Klemens von Rom über die Reise Pauli nach Spanien: Historisch-kritische Untersuchung zu Klemens von Rom: 1 Kor. 5, 7*. Freiberg: Herder, 1914.
Dunn, James D. G. *The Acts of the Apostles*. Grand Rapids, MI: Eerdmans, 1996.
Dupont, Jacques. "La conclusion des Actes et son rapport à l'ensemble de l'ouvrage de Luc." In *Les Actes des Apôtres: Traditions, redaction, théologie*, edited by J. Kramer, 359–404. BETL 48. Leuven: Leuven University Press, 1979.
Dupont, Jacques. "Le salut des gentils et la signification théologique du livre des Actes." *NTS* 6 (1960): 132–55.

Dupont, Jacques. *Les sources du livre des Actes: État de la question*. Bruges: Desclée de Brouwer, 1960.
Dupont, Jacques. *The Sources of Acts: The Present Position*. London: Darton, Longman & Todd, 1964.
Easthope, Antony. "Romancing the Stone: History-Writing and Rhetoric." *SH* 18 (1993): 235–49.
Eastman, David L. "Jealousy, Internal Strife, and the Deaths of Peter and Paul: A Reassessmentof *1 Clement*." *ZAC* 18 (2013): 34–53.
Ebrard, Johannes H. A. *Biblical Commentary on the New Testament*. Translated by David Fosdick. 5 vols. New York: Sheldon, 1866.
Eckey, Wilfried. *Die Briefe des Paulus an die Philipper und an Philemon: Ein Kommentar*. Neukirchen-Vluyn: Neukirchener, 2006.
Ehrhardt, Arnold. *The Framework of the New Testament Stories*. Manchester: Manchester University Press, 1964.
Ehrman, Bart D. "The Text as Window: New Testament Manuscripts and the Social History of Early Christianity." In *The Text of the New Testament in Contemporary Research: Essays on the Status Quaestionis*, edited by Bart D. Ehrman and Michael W. Holmes, 361–79. SD 42. Grand Rapids, MI: Eerdmans, 1995.
Eisenbaum, Pamela. "Jewish Perspectives: A Jewish Apostle to the Gentiles." In *Studying Paul's Letters*, edited by J. A. Marchal, 135–54. Minneapolis, MN: Fortress, 2012.
Elliott, James K. "The Early Text of the Catholic Epistles." In *The Early Text of the New Testament*, edited by Charles E. Hill and Michael J. Kruger, 204–24. Oxford: Oxford University Press, 2012.
Elliott, James K. *New Testament Textual Criticism: The Application of Thoroughgoing Principles, Essays on Manuscripts and Textual Variation*. NovTSup 137. Leiden: Brill, 2010.
Ellis, E. Earle. *The Gospel of Luke*. London: Nelson, 1966.
Elton, G. R. *The Practice of History*. Sydney: Sydney University Press, 1967.
Elton, G. R. *Reformation Europe*. London: Fontana, 1963.
Engelmann, Michaela. *Unzertrennliche Drillinge? Motivsemantische Untersuchungen zum literarischen Verhältnis der Pastoralbriefe*. Berlin: de Gruyter, 2012.
Epp, Eldon J. "Anti-Judaic Tendencies in the D-Text of Acts: Forty Years of Conversation." In *The Book of Acts as Church History: Text, Textual Traditions and Ancient Interpretations*, edited by Tobias Nicklas and Michael Tilly, 111–46. BZNW 120. Berlin: de Gruyter, 2003.
Epp, Eldon J. "Coptic Manuscript G67 and the Rôle of Codex Bezae as a Western Witness in Acts." *JBL* 85 (1966): 197–212.
Epp, Eldon J. "Issues in New Testament Textual Criticism: Moving from the Nineteenth Century to the Twenty-First Century." In *Rethinking New Testament Textual Criticism*, edited by David A. Black, 17–76. Grand Rapids, MI: Baker Academic, 2002.
Epp, Eldon J. "The Multivalence of the Term 'Original Text' in New Testament Textual Criticism." *HTR* (1999): 245–81.
Epp, Eldon J. "Textual Clusters: Their Past and Future in New Testament Textual Criticism." In *The Text of the New Testament in Contemporary Research: Essays on the Status Quaestionis*, edited by Bart D. Ehrman and Michael W. Holmes, 519–77. 2nd ed. NTTSD 42. Leiden/Boston: Brill, 2013.
Epp, Eldon J. *The Theological Tendency of Codex Bezae Cantabrigiensis in Acts*. Cambridge: Cambridge University Press, 1966.

Epp, Eldon J. "Traditional 'Canons' of New Testament Textual Criticism: Their Value, Validity, and Viability—or Lack Thereof." In *The Textual History of the Greek New Testament: Changing Views in Contemporary Research*, edited by Klaus Wachtel and Michael Holmes, 79–127. SBLTCS 8. Leiden: Brill, 2012.

Epp, Eldon J. "The Twentieth Century Interlude in New Testament Textual Criticism." In *Studies in the Theory and Method of New Testament Textual Criticism*, edited by E. J. Epp and G. D. Fee, 83–108. Grand Rapids, MI: Eerdmans, 1993.

Epp, Eldon J., and Gordon D. Fee. *Studies in the Theory and Method of New Testament Textual Criticism*. Grand Rapids, MI: Eerdmans, 1993.

Evans, Craig A. "The Christ of Faith Is the Jesus of History." In *Debating Christian Theism*, edited by James P. Moreland, Chad V. Meister, and Khaldoun A. Sweis, 458–67. Oxford: Oxford University Press, 2013.

Evans, Craig A. "Isaiah 6:9–10 in early Jewish and Christian Interpretation." PhD diss., Claremont Graduate University, 1983.

Evans, Craig A. "The Text of Isaiah 6:9–10." *ZAW* 94 (1982): 415–18.

Evans, Craig A. *To See and Not Perceive: Isaiah 6:9–10 in Early Jewish and Christian Interpretation*. JSOTSup 64. Sheffield: JSOT Press, 1989.

Evans, Ian, and Nicholas D. Smith. *Knowledge*. Cambridge, UK: Polity Press, 2012.

Evans, Richard J. *In Defence of History*. London: Granta, 1997.

Falk, Daniel K. "Jewish Prayer Literature and the Jerusalem Church." In *The Book of Acts in Its Palestinian Setting*, edited by Richard Bauckham, 4:267–301. 5 vols. BAFCS 4. Grand Rapids, MI: Eerdmans, 1995.

Faure, Patrick. *Les Actes des Apôtres: Texte occidental reconstitué*. EBib 79. Leuven: Peeters, 2019.

Fee, Gordon D. *Paul's Letter to the Philippians*. NICNT. Grand Rapids, MI: Eerdmans, 1995.

Fee, Gordon D. "Textual Criticism of the New Testament." In *Studies in the Theory and Method of New Testament Textual Criticism*, edited by Eldon J. Epp and Gordon D. Fee, 3–16. SD 45. Grand Rapids, MI: Eerdmans, 1993.

Filippi, Giorgio. "Die Ergebnisse der neuen Ausgrabungen am Grab des Apostels Paulus." *MDAI(RA)* 112 (2005–6): 277–92.

Fitzmyer, Joseph A. *The Acts of the Apostles*. AB 31. New York: Doubleday, 1998.

Fitzmyer, Joseph A. *The Gospel According to Luke I–IX*. AB 28. New York: Doubleday, 1981.

Fitzmyer, Joseph A. *Luke the Theologian: Aspects of His Teaching*. New York: Paulist, 1989.

Fitzpatrick-McKinley, Anne. "Synagogue Communities in the Graeco-Roman Cities." In *Jews in the Hellenistic and Roman Cities*, edited by John R. Bartlett, 55–87. London: Routledge, 2002.

Foakes-Jackson, Frederick J. *The Acts of the Apostles*. MNTC. London: Hodder and Stoughton, 1931.

Foakes-Jackson, Frederick J., and Kirsopp Lake. "Prolegomena II: Criticism." In *The Beginnings of Christianity Part I: The Acts of the Apostles*, edited by Frederick J. Foakes-Jackson and Kirsopp Lake, 2:122–208. 5 vols. London: Macmillan, 1922.

Foakes-Jackson, Frederick J., and Kirsopp Lake, eds. *The Beginnings of Christianity*. 5 vols. London: Macmillan, 1920–33.

Foster, Barry M. "The Contribution of the Conclusion of Acts to the Understanding of Lucan Theology and the Determination of Lucan Purpose." PhD diss., Trinity International University, Illinois, 1997.

Foucault, Michel. *The Archaeology of Knowledge*. New York: Harper & Row, 1972.

Fowler, Robert M. "Who is 'The Reader' in Reader Response Criticism?" *Semeia* 31 (1985): 5–21.
Franklin, E. *Christ the Lord: A study in the Purpose and Theology of Luke-Acts*. Philadelphia, PA: Westminster, 1975.
Frier, Bruce W. "More is Worse: Some Observations on the Roman Empire." In *Debating Roman Demography*, edited by Walter Scheidel, 139–60. Mnemosyne 211. Leiden: Brill, 2001.
Fullbrook, Mary. *Historical Theory*. London: Routledge, 2002.
Gamble, Harry Y. "The Book Trade in the Roman Empire." In *The Early Text of the New Testament*, edited by Charles E. Hill and Michael J. Kruger, 23–36. Oxford: Oxford University Press, 2012.
Garnsey, Peter, and Richard Saller. *The Roman Empire: Economy, Society and Culture*. 2nd ed. Oakland, CA: University of California Press, 2015.
Gasque, W. Ward. *A History of the Interpretation of the Acts of the Apostles*. Reprint, Grand Rapids, MI: Eerdmans, 1975.
Gaventa, Beverly R. *The Acts of the Apostles*. ANTC. Nashville, TN: Abingdon Press, 2003.
Gempf, Conrad H. "Luke's Story of Paul's Reception in Rome." In *Rome in the Bible and the Early Church*, edited by Peter Oakes, 42–66. Grand Rapids, MI: Baker Academic, 2002.
Gerber, Daniel. "Paul's Literary Activity during His Roman Trial: A Response to Udo Schnelle." In *The Last Years of Paul: Essays from the Tarragona Conference, June 2013*, edited by Armand Puig i Tàrrech, John M. G. Barclay, and Jörg Frey, 453–68. WUNT 352. Tübingen: Mohr Siebeck, 2015.
Gilchrist, J. M. "The Historicity of Paul's Shipwreck." *JSNT* 18 (1996): 29–51.
Gill, David W. J., and Bruce W. Winter. "Acts and Roman Religion." In *The Book of Acts in Its Graeco-Roman Setting*, edited by David W. J. Gill and Conrad Gempf, 2:79–103. 5 vols. BAFCS 2. Grand Rapids, MI: Eerdmans, 1995.
Gill, David W. J., I. Howard Marshall, and Bruce W. Winter. "Preface." In *The Book of Acts in Its Ancient Literary Setting*, edited by Bruce W. Winter and Andrew W. Clarke, 1:ix–xii. 5 vols. BAFCS 1. Grand Rapids, MI: Eerdmans, 1993.
Glover, Richard. "'Luke the Antiochene' and Acts." *NTS* 11 (1964): 97–106.
Goodspeed, Edgar J. *An Introduction to the New Testament*. Chicago: University of Chicago Press, 1937.
Gordon, William. *The History of the Rise, Progress, and Establishment, of the Independence of the United States of America*. 4 vols. London: Charles Dilly and James Buckland, 1788.
Goulder, Michael D. "Did Luke Know Any of the Pauline Letters?" *PRS* 13 (1986): 97–112.
Grant, Frederick C. *The Gospels: Their Origin and Their Growth*. London: Faber and Faber, 1957.
Grant, Robert M. *Heresy and Criticism: The Search for Authenticity in Early Christian Literature*. Louisville, KY: Westminster John Knox Press, 1993.
Graziosi, Barbara. *Inventing Homer: The Early Reception of Epic*. Cambridge: Cambridge University Press, 2002.
Green, Anna, and Kathleen Troup, eds. *The Houses of History: A Critical Reader in Twentieth-Century History and Theory*. New York: New York University Press, 1999.
Green, Anna, and Kathleen Troup, eds. *Houses of History: A Critical Reader in Twentieth-Century History and Theory*. 2nd ed. Manchester: Manchester University Press, 2016.
Green, Joel B., and Michael C. McKeever. *Luke-Acts and New Testament Historiography*. IBRB 8. Grand Rapids, MI: Baker, 1994.
Greene, Kevin, and Tom Moore. *Archaeology: An Introduction*. New York: Routledge, 2010.

Grimm, Stephen R., Christoph Baumberger, and Sabine Ammon eds. *Explaining Understanding: New Perspectives from Epistemology and Philosophy of Science*. New York: Routledge, 2017.

Grünstäudl, Wolfgang. "Hidden in Praise: Some Notes on 1 Clement 5.7." In *The Last Years of Paul: Essays from the Tarragona Conference, June 2013*, edited by Armand Puig i Tàrrech, John M. G. Barclay, and Jörg Frey, 375–89. WUNT 352. Tübingen: Mohr Siebeck, 2015.

Gurry, Peter J. *A Critical Examination of the Coherence-Based Genealogical Method in New Testament Textual Criticism*. NTTSD 55. Leiden: Brill, 2017.

Gurry, Peter J. "How Your Greek NT Is Changing: A Simple Introduction to the Coherence-Based Genealogical Method (CBGM)." *JETS* 59 (2016): 675–89.

Hadas, Moses, ed. *The Letter of Aristeas to Philocrates*. New York: Harper, 1951.

Haenchen, Ernst. *The Acts of the Apostles*. Oxford: Blackwell, 1971.

Haenchen, Ernst. "The Book of Acts as Source Material for the History of Earliest Christianity." In *Studies in Luke-Acts*, edited by Leander E. Keck and J. Louis Martyn, 258–78. Nashville, TN: Abingdon, 1966.

Haenchen, Ernst. "Judentum und Christentum in der Apostelgeschichte." *ZNW* 54 (1963): 155–87.

Hahneman, Geoffrey M. *The Muratorian Fragment and the Development of the Canon*. OTM. Oxford: Clarendon, 1992.

Hanson, Richard P. C. "The Provenance of the Interpolator in the 'Western' Text of Acts and of Acts Itself." *NTS* 12 (1966): 211–30.

Harnack, Adolf. *The Acts of the Apostles*. Translated by J. R. Wilkinson. London: Williams & Norgate, 1909.

Harnack, Adolf. *The Date of Acts and of the Synoptic Gospels*. Translated by J. R. Wilkinson. CTL 33. New York: Putnam's Sons, 1911.

Harnack, Adolf. *Die Apostelgeschichte*. BENT III. Leipzig: Hinrichs, 1908.

Harnack, Adolf. *Die Mission und Ausbreitung des Christentums in den ersten drei Jahrhunderten*. 4th ed. Leipzig: Hinrichs, 1924.

Harnack, Adolf. *Luke the Physician: The Author of the Third Gospel and the Acts of the Apostles*. Translated by J. R. Wilkinson. London: Williams & Norgate, 1909.

Harnack, Adolf. *Marcion: Das Evangelium vom fremden Gott*. Leipzig: Hinrichs, 1924.

Harnack, Adolf. *Zur Apostelgeschichte und zur Abfassungszeit der Synoptischen Evangelien*. BENT IV. Leipzig: Hinrichs, 1911.

Harris, Roy. *The Linguistics of History*. Edinburgh: Edinburgh University Press, 2004.

Hartley, Donald E. *The Wisdom Background and Parabolic Implications of Isaiah 6:9–10 in the Synoptics*. StBibLit 100. New York: Peter Lang, 2006.

Hauser, Hermann J. *Strukturen der Abschlusserzählung der Apostelgeschichte (Apg 28, 16–31)*. AnBib 86. Rome: Biblical Institute, 1979.

Head, Peter. "Acts and the Problem of Its Texts." In *The Book of Acts in Its Ancient Literary Setting*, edited by Bruce W. Winter and Andrew D. Clarke, 1:415–44. 5 vols. BAFCS 1. Grand Rapids, MI: Eerdmans, 1993.

Headlam, Arthur C. "Acts of the Apostles." In *A Dictionary of the Bible: Language, Literature, and Contents*, edited by James Hastings, John A. Selbie, A. B. Davidson, S. R. Driver, and H. B. Swete, 25–35. 4 vols. Edinburgh: T&T Clark, 1908.

Hemer, Colin J. *The Book of Acts in the Setting of Hellenistic History*. WUNT 49. Tübingen: Mohr Siebeck, 1989.

Hemer, Colin J. "First Person Narrative in Acts 27–28." *TynBul* 36 (1985): 79–86.

Hengel, Martin. *Acts and the History of Earliest Christianity*. Translated by John Bowden. London: Fortress, 1979.
Hengel, Martin. "The Geography of Palestine in Acts." In *The Book of Acts in Its Palestinian Setting*, edited by Richard Bauckham, 4:27–78. 5 vols. BAFCS 4. Grand Rapids, MI: Eerdmans, 1995.
Herman, Paul. *Hayden White: The Historical Imagination*. Cambridge, UK: Polity Press, 2011.
Herron, Thomas J. "The Most Probable Date of the First Epistle of Clement to the Corinthians." In *StPatr* 21, edited by E. A. Livingstone, 106–21. Leuven: Peeters, 1989.
Herzer, Jens. "Die Pastoralbriefe." In *Paulus Handbuch*, edited by F. W. Horn, 538–42. Tübingen: Mohr Siebeck, 2013.
Herzer, Jens. "Fiktion oder Täuschung? Zur Diskussion über die Pseudepigraphie der Pastoralbriefe." In *Pseudepigraphie und Verfasserfiktion in frühchristlichen Briefen*, edited by J. Frey, Jans Herzer, Martina Janßen, and Clare K. Rothschild, 489–536. WUNT 246. Tübingen: Mohr Siebeck, 2009.
Herzer, Jens. "The Mission and the End of Paul Between Strategy and Reality: A Response to Rainer Riesner." In *The Last Years of Paul: Essays from the Tarragona Conference, June 2013*, edited by Armand Puig i Tàrrech, John M. G. Barclay, and Jörg Frey, 411–31. WUNT 352. Tübingen: Mohr Siebeck, 2015.
Hill, Charles E. "The Debate Over the Muratorian Fragment and the Development of the Canon." *WTJ* 57 (1995): 437–52.
Hill, Charles E. "Introduction." In *The Early Text of the New Testament*, edited by Charles E. Hill and Michael J. Kruger, 1–19. Oxford: Oxford University Press, 2012.
Hill, Charles E. *The Johannine Corpus in the Early Church*. Oxford: Oxford University Press, 2004.
Hill, Charles E., and Michael J. Kruger, eds. *The Early Text of the New Testament*. Oxford: Oxford University Press, 2012.
Hobart, William K. *The Medical Language of St Luke*. London: Longmans, Green, 1882.
Hock, Ronald F. *The Social Context of Paul's Ministry: Tentmaking and Apostleship*. Reprint, Minneapolis, MN: Fortress, 2007.
Holloway, Paul A. "Inconvenient Truths: Ancient Jewish and Christian History Writing and the Ending of Luke-Acts." In *Die Apostelgeschichte im Kontext antiker und frühchristlicher Historiographie*, edited by Jörg Frey, Clare K. Rothschild, and Jens Schröter, 418–33. BZNW 162. Berlin: de Gruyter, 2009.
Holmes, Michael W. "From Nestle to the Editio Critica Maior: A Century's Perspective on the New Testament Miniscule Tradition." In *The Bible as Book: The Transmission of the Greek Text*, edited by Scot McKendrick and Orlaith O'Sullivan, 123–37. London: Oak Knoll Press, 2003.
Holtzmann, Heinrich J. *Lehrbuch der historisch-kritischen Einleitung in das Neue Testament*. 2nd rev. ed. Freiberg: J. C. B. Mohr (Paul Siebeck), 1886.
Hopkins, Keith. "On the Probable Age Structure of the Roman Population." *PS* 20 (1966): 245–64.
Howell, Martha C., and Walter Prevenier. *From Reliable Sources: An Introduction to Historical Methods*. Ithaca, NY: Cornell University Press, 2001.
Heuzey, Léon, and Honoré Daumet. *Mission Archéologique de Macédoine: Texte/Planches*. Paris: Firmin-Didot, 1876.
Iggers, Georg G. *The German Conception of History: The National Tradition of Historical Thought from Herder to the Present*. Rev. ed. Middletown, CT: Wesleyan University Press, 1983.

Immanuel, Babu. *Repent and Turn to God: Recounting Acts*. Eugene, OR: Wipf & Stock, 2004.
Jeffers, James S. *The Greco-Roman World of the New Testament Era: Exploring the Background of Early Christianity*. Downers Grove, IL: InterVarsity Press, 1999.
Jenkins, Keith. "An English Myth? Rethinking the Contemporary Value of E. H. Carr's *What is History?*" In *E. H. Carr: A Critical Appraisal*, edited by Michael Cox, 304–21. Hampshire, UK: Palgrave, 2004.
Jenkins, Keith. *At the Limits of History: Essays on Theory and Practice*. London: Routledge, 2009.
Jenkins, Keith. *Re-thinking History*. Reprint, London: Routledge, 2003.
Jenkins, Keith, ed. *Postmodern History Reader*. London: Routledge, 1997.
Jennings, Willie J. *Acts*. Belief: A Theological Commentary on the Bible. Louisville, KY: Westminster John Knox Press, 2017.
Jeremias, Joachim. "Untersuchungen zum Quellenproblem der Apostelgeschichte." *ZNW* 36 (1937): 205–21.
Jervell, Jacob. *Die Apostelgeschichte*. Göttingen: Vandenhoeck & Ruprecht, 1998.
Jervell, Jacob. *Luke and the People of God: A New Look at Luke-Acts*. Minneapolis, MN: Augsburg, 1972.
Johnson, Luke T. *The Acts of the Apostles*. SP 5. Collegeville, MN: Liturgical, 1992.
Johnson, Luke T. *The Gospel of Luke*. SP 3. Collegeville, MN: Liturgical, 1991.
Johnson-DeBaufre, Melanie. "Historical Approaches: Which Past? Whose Past?" In *Studying Paul's Letters*, edited by J. A. Marchal, 13–32. Minneapolis, MN: Fortress, 2012.
Jülicher, Adolf. *An Introduction to the New Testament*. Translated by Janet P. Ward. London: Smith, Elder, & Co., 1904.
Kaibel, Georg, ed. *Inscriptiones Graecae. XIV. Inscriptiones Siciliae et Italiae, additis Galliae, Hispaniae, Britanniae, Germaniae Inscriptionibus*. Berlin: Reimer, 1890.
Kamp, Jeannette, Susan Legêne, Matthias van Rossum, and Sebas Rümke eds. *Writing History! A Companion for Historians*. Amsterdam: Amsterdam University Press, 2018.
Karakolis, Christos. "Paul's Mission to Hispania: Some Critical Observations." In *The Last Years of Paul: Essays from the Tarragona Conference, June 2013*, edited by Armand Puig i Tàrrech, John M. G. Barclay, and Jörg Frey, 507–19. WUNT 352. Tübingen: Mohr Siebeck, 2015.
Keener, Craig S. *Acts: An Exegetical Commentary*. 4 vols. Grand Rapids, MI: Baker Academic, 2012–15.
Keener, Craig S. *The Historical Jesus of the Gospels*. Grand Rapids, MI: Eerdmans, 2012.
Kenyon, Frederic G. *Chester Beatty Biblical Papyri II/1: The Gospels and Acts, Text*. London: Walker, 1933.
Kenyon, Frederic G. *Chester Beatty Biblical Papyri II/2: The Gospels and Acts, Plates*. London: Walker, 1933.
Kenyon, Frederic G. *The Text of the Greek Bible: A Students' Handbook*. London: Duckworth, 1949.
Kenyon, Frederic G. "The Western Text in the Gospels and Acts." *PBA* 24 (1939): 287–315.
Kilgallen, John J. "Acts 28, 28–Why?" *Bib* 90 (2009): 176–87.
Kilpatrick, George D. Review of *The Theological Tendency of Codex Bezae Cantabrigiensis in Acts*, by Eldon J. Epp. *VC* 24 (1970): 166–70.
Knowling, Richard J. "The Acts of the Apostles." In *The Expositor's Greek Testament*, edited by W. Robertson Nicoll, 1–554. 5 vols. London: Hodder & Stoughton, 1897–1910.

Knox, John. "Acts and the Pauline Letter Corpus." In *Studies in Luke-Acts: Essays Presented in Honor of Paul Schubert*, edited by Leander E. Keck and J. Louis Martyn, 279–87. Nashville, TN: Abingdon, 1966.
Knox, John. *Marcion and the New Testament: An Essay in the Early History of the Canon*. Chicago: University of Chicago Press, 1942.
Koester, Helmut. *Introduction to the New Testament: History and Literature of Early Christianity*. 2nd ed. 2 vols. New York: de Gruyter, 1995–2000.
Kosso, Peter. *Knowing the Past: Philosophical Issues of History and Archaeology*. Amherst, NY: Humanity Books, 2001.
Kraft, Robert A. "The 'Textual Mechanics' of Early Jewish LXX/OG Papyri and Fragments." In *The Bible as Book: The Transmission of the Greek Text*, edited by Scot McKendrick and Orlaith O'Sullivan, 51–72. London: Oak Knoll Press, 2003.
Krebs, Johann T. *Observationes in Novum Testamentum e Flavio Josepho*. Lipsiae: Wendlerus Joannes, 1755.
Krenkel, Max. *Josephus und Lukas: Der schriftstellerische Einfluss des jüdischen Geschichtschreibers auf den Christlichen*. Leipzig: H. A. Haessel, 1894.
Kristeva, Julia. *The Kristeva Reader*. Edited by Toril Moi. New York: Columbia University Press, 1986.
Kruger, Michael J. *The Question of Canon: Challenging the Status Quo in the New Testament Debate*. Downers Grove, IL: InterVarsity Press, 2013.
Kümmel, Werner G. "Das Urchristentum." *ThR* 14 (1942): 81–95.
Kümmel, Werner G. "Das Urchristentum. II. Die Quellen für die Geschichte des Urchristentums." *ThR* 14 (1942): 155–73.
Kümmel, Werner G. *Introduction to the New Testament*. Nashville, TN: Abingdon Press, 1975.
Lake, Kirsopp. *The Influence of Textual Criticism on the Exegesis of the New Testament*. Oxford: Parker and Son, 1904.
Lake, Kirsopp, and Henry J. Cadbury. "The Acts of the Apostles: English Translation and Commentary." In *The Beginnings of Christianity: Part 1: The Acts of the Apostles*, edited by Frederick J. Foakes Jackson and Kirsopp Lake, 4:1–350. 5 vols. London: Macmillan, 1926.
Lampe, Peter. *Der Brief an Philemon*. Göttingen: Vandenhoeck & Ruprecht, 1998.
Lampe, Peter. *From Paul to Valentinus: Christians at Rome in the First Two Centuries*. Edited by Marshall D. Johnson. Minneapolis, MN: Fortress, 2003.
Lampe, Peter. "Roman Christians under Nero (54–68 CE)." In *The Last Years of Paul: Essays from the Tarragona Conference, June 2013*, edited by Armand Puig i Tàrrech, John M. G. Barclay, and Jörg Frey, 111–29. WUNT 352. Tübingen: Mohr Siebeck, 2015.
Larkin Jr., William J. *Acts*. IVPNTC. Downers Grove, IL: InterVarsity Press, 1995.
Laurence, Ray, Simon Esmonde Cleary, and Gareth Sears. *The City in the Roman West*. Cambridge: Cambridge University Press, 2011.
Leaney, A. R. C. *The Gospel According to Luke*. London: Adam & Charles Black, 1966.
Leone, Mark, and Constance Crosby. "Epilogue: Middle Range Theory in Historical Archaeology." In *Consumer Choice in Historical Archaeology*, edited by Suzanne M. Spencer-Wood, 397–410. New York: Plenum, 1987.
Lestapis, Stanislas D. *L'énigme des pastorales de Saint Paul*. Paris: J. Gabalda, 1976.
Licona, Michael R. *The Resurrection of Jesus: A New Historiographical Approach*. Downers Grove, IL: InterVarsity Press, 2010.
Liefeld, Walter L. *Luke*. 12 vols. EBC. Grand Rapids, MI: Zondervan, 1981.

Lietzmann, Hans. *Das Muratorische Fragment und die monarchianischen Prologe zu den Evangelien.* Kleine Texte für theologische Vorlesungen und Übungen 1. Bonn: Marcus and Weber, 1902.
Lietzmann, Hans. *The Founding of the Church Universal.* Translated by Bertram L. Woolf. 2nd ed. London: Lutterworth, 1950.
Lightfoot, Joseph B. *Biblical Essays.* New York: Macmillan, 1893.
Lightfoot, Joseph B., and John R. Harmer. *The Apostolic Fathers: Greek Texts and English Translations.* 3rd rev. ed. by Michael J. Holmes. Grand Rapids, MI: Baker Academic, 2007.
Litwak, Kenneth. "One or Two Views of Judaism: Paul in Acts 28 and Romans 11 on Jewish Unbelief." *TynBul* 57 (2006): 229–49.
Lloyd, Christopher. "History and the Social Sciences." In *Writing History: Theory and Practice*, edited by Stefan Berger, Heiko Feldner, and Kevin Passmore, 83–103. London: Arnold, 2003.
Loewenberg, Peter. *Decoding the Past: The Psychohistorical Approach.* 2nd ed. New Brunswick, NJ: Transaction Publishers, 2002.
Loisy, Alfred. *Les Actes des Apôtres.* Paris: Emile Nourry, 1920.
Loisy, Alfred. *Les évangiles synoptiques.* 2 vols. Près Montier-en-Der: Publ. by author, 1907.
Longenecker, Richard N. *The Acts of the Apostles.* 12 vols. EBC. Grand Rapids, MI: Zondervan, 1981.
Lüdemann, Gerd. *The Acts of the Apostles: What Really Happened in the Earliest Days of the Church.* Amherst, NY: Prometheus, 2005.
MacDonald, Dennis R. *Does the New Testament Imitate Homer? Four Cases from the Acts of the Apostles.* New Haven, CT: Yale University Press, 2003.
MacDonald, Dennis R. *The Homeric Epics and the Gospel of Mark.* New Haven, CT: Yale University Press, 2000.
MacDonald, Dennis R. "Paul's Farewell to the Ephesian Elders and Hector's Farewell to Andromache: A Strategic Imitation of Homer's Iliad." In *Contextualizing Acts: Lukan Narrative and Greco-Roman Discourse*, edited by Todd C. Penner and Caroline Vander Stichele, 189–203. SymS 20. Atlanta, GA: SBL, 2003.
MacDonald, Dennis R., ed. *Mimesis and Intertextuality in Antiquity and Christianity.* London: T&T Clark, 2001.
Macgregor, G. H. C. *Interpreter's Bible. IX. The Acts of the Apostles, the Epistle to the Romans.* Nashville, TN: Abingdon, 1952.
Maddox, Robert. *The Purpose of Luke-Acts.* SNTW. Edinburgh: T&T Clark, 1982.
Magness, J. Lee. *Sense and Absence: Structure and Suspension in the Ending of Mark's Gospel.* SemeiaSt 15. Atlanta, GA: SBL, 1986.
Marguerat, Daniel. "The End of Acts (28:16–31) and the Rhetoric of Silence." In *Rhetoric and the New Testament: Essays from the 1992 Heidelberg Conference*, edited by Stanley E. Porter and Thomas H. Olbricht, 74–89. JSNTSup 90. Sheffield: JSOT, 1993.
Marguerat, Daniel. "The Enigma of the Silent Closing of Acts (28:16–31)." In *Jesus and the Heritage of Israel: Luke's Narrative Claim Upon Israel's Legacy*, edited by David P. Moessner, 284–304. Luke the Interpreter of Israel Series 1. Harrisburg, PA: Trinity Press International, 1999.
Marguerat, Daniel. "Et quand nous sommes entrés dans Rome: L'énigme de la fin du livre des Actes (28, 16–31)." *RHPR* 73 (1993): 1–21.
Marguerat, Daniel. *The First Christian Historian: Writing the "Acts of the Apostles."* Cambridge: Cambridge University Press, 2002.

Marguerat, Daniel. "On Why Luke Remains Silent about Paul's End." In *The Last Years of Paul: Essays from the Tarragona Conference, June 2013*, edited by Armand Puig i Tàrrech, John M. G. Barclay, and Jörg Frey, 305–32. WUNT 352. Tübingen: Mohr Siebeck, 2015.

Marshall, I. Howard. *The Acts of the Apostles*. TNTC. Reprint, Downers Grove, IL: InterVarsity Press, 2008.

Marshall, I. Howard. *The Gospel of Luke*. NIGTC. Exeter: Paternoster, 1978.

Marshall, I. Howard. *Luke: Historian and Theologian*. Exeter: Paternoster, 1979.

Marshall, I. Howard. Review of The *'We' Passages in the Acts of the Apostles: The Narrator as Narrative Character*, by William Sanger Campbell. *JTS* 59 (2008): 755–7.

Martin, Raymond A. "Syntactical Evidence of Aramaic Sources in Acts 1–15." *NTS* 11 (1964): 38–59.

Marwick, Arthur. *The New Nature of History: Knowledge, Evidence, Language*. London: Palgrave, 2001.

Mason, Steve. *A History of the Jewish War: AD 66–74*. Cambridge: Cambridge University Press, 2016.

Mauck, J. W. *Paul on Trial: The Book of Acts as a Defense of Christianity*. Nashville, TN: Thomas Nelson, 2001.

McDonald, Lee M. *The Biblical Canon: Its Origin, Transmission, and Authority*. Peabody, MA: Hendrickson, 2007.

McKendrick, Scot, and Orlaith O'Sullivan, eds. *The Bible as Book: The Transmission of the Greek Text*. London: Oak Knoll, 2003.

McRay, John. *Archaeology and the New Testament*. Grand Rapids, MI: Baker, 2008.

Mealand, David L. "The Close of Acts and its Hellenistic Greek Vocabulary." *NTS* 36 (1990): 583–97.

Menoud, Philippe H. "Le plan des Actes des Apôtres." *NTS* 1 (1954): 44–51.

Metzger, Bruce M. *The Canon of the NT: Its Origin, Development, and Significance*. Oxford: Clarendon, 1987.

Metzger, Bruce M. *The Early Versions of the New Testament: Their Origin, Transmission, and Limitations*. Oxford: Clarendon, 1977.

Metzger, Bruce M. *The Text of the New Testament: Its Transmission, Corruption, and Restoration*. 3rd ed. New York: Oxford University Press, 1992.

Metzger, Bruce M. *A Textual Commentary on the Greek New Testament*. 1st ed. London: United Bible Societies, 1971.

Metzger, Bruce M. *A Textual Commentary on the Greek New Testament*. 2nd ed. New York: United Bible Societies, 1994.

Metzger, Bruce M., and Bart D. Ehrman. *The Text of the New Testament: Its Transmission, Corruption, and Restoration*. 4th ed. Oxford: Oxford University Press, 2005.

Michaelis, Johann D. *Introduction to the New Testament*. Translated by Herbert Marsh. 2nd ed. 4 vols. London: F. & C. Rivington, 1802.

Mink, Gerd. "Contamination, Coherence, and Coincidence in Textual Transmission: The Coherence-Based Genealogical Method (CBGM) as a Compliment and Corrective to Existing Approaches." In *The Textual History of the Greek New Testament: Changing Views in Contemporary Research*, edited by Klaus Wachtel and Michael Holmes, 141–216. SBLTCS 8. Leiden: Brill, 2012.

Mittelstaedt, Alexander. *Lukas als Historiker: Zur Datierung des lukanischen Doppelwerkes*. TANZ 43. Tübingen: Francke, 2006.

Mitton, C. Leslie. *The Epistle to the Ephesians: Its Authority, Origin and Purpose*. Oxford: Clarendon, 1951.

Moessner, David P. "'Completed End(s)ings' of Historiographical Narrative. Diodorus Siculus and the End(ing) of Acts." In *Die Apostelgeschichte und die hellenistiche Geschichtsschreibung: Festschrift für Eckhard Plümacher zu seinem 65. Geburtstag*, edited by Cilliers Breytenbach and Jens Schröter, 193–221. Ancient Judaism and Early Christianity: AGJU 57. Leiden: Brill, 2004.

Moessner, David P. "Paul in Acts: Preacher of Eschatological Repentance to Israel." *NTS* 34 (1988): 96–104.

Morris, Leon. *The Gospel According to St. Luke*. TNTC. Grand Rapids, MI: Eerdmans, 1977.

Mount, Christopher. *Pauline Christianity: Luke-Acts and the Legacy of Paul*. NovTSup 104. Leiden: Brill, 2002.

Müller, Philipp. "Understanding History: Hermeneutics and Source-criticism in Historical Scholarship." In *Reading Primary Sources: The Interpretation of Texts from Nineteenth- and Twentieth-Century History*, edited by Miriam Dobson and Benjamin Ziemann, 23–40. RGHS. London: Routledge, 2020.

Munck, Johannes. *The Acts of the Apostles*. AB 31. Garden City, NY: Doubleday, 1967.

Munslow, Alun. *Deconstructing History*. 2nd ed. London: Routledge, 2006.

Munslow, Alun. *A History of History*. London: Routledge, 2012.

Munslow, Alun. *The New History*. Harlow, UK: Pearson-Longman, 2003.

Munslow, Alun. *The Routledge Companion to Historical Studies*. 2nd ed. London: Routledge, 2006.

Murphy-O'Connor, Jerome. *Paul: A Critical Life*. Oxford: Oxford University Press, 1996.

Murphy-O'Connor, Jerome. "Paul and Gallio." *JBL* 112 (1993): 315–17.

Murphy-O'Connor, Jerome. *St. Paul's Corinth: Texts and Archaeology*. Collegeville, MN: Liturgical Press, 2002.

Niebuhr, Karl-Wilhelm. "Roman Jews under Nero: Personal, Religious, and Ideological Networks in Mid-First Century Rome." In *The Last Years of Paul: Essays from the Tarragona Conference, June 2013*, edited by Armand Puig i Tàrrech, John M. G. Barclay, and Jörg Frey, 67–89. WUNT 352. Tübingen: Mohr Siebeck, 2015.

Nock, Arthur D. Review of *Aufsätze zur Apostelgeschichte*, by Martin Dibelius. *Gnomon* 25 (1953): 497–506.

Nock, Arthur D. *St. Paul*. Reprint, New York: Harper & Row, 1963.

Norden, Eduard. *Agnostos Theos:Untersuchungen zur Formengeschichte religiöser Rede*. 4th ed. Stuttgart: B. G. Teubner, 1956.

Novick, Peter. *That Noble Dream: The 'Objectivity Question' and the American Historical Profession*. Cambridge: Cambridge University Press, 1988.

Oakes, Peter. "Using Historical Evidence in the Study of Neronian Christian Groups and Texts." In *The Last Years of Paul: Essays from the Tarragona Conference, June 2013*, edited by Armand Puig i Tàrrech, John M. G. Barclay, and Jörg Frey, 131–51. WUNT 352. Tübingen: Mohr Siebeck, 2015.

Öhler, Markus. *Barnabas: der Mann in der Mitte*. BG 12. Leipzig: Evangelische Verlagsanstalt, 2005.

Öhler, Markus. *Barnabas. Die historische Person und ihre Rezeption in der Apostelgeschichte*. WUNT 156. Tübingen: Mohr Siebeck, 2003.

Olson, Ken. Review of *The Craft of History and the Study of the New Testament*, by Beth M. Sheppard. *RBL* 06 (2014): 1–4.

Omerzu, Heike. *Der Prozess des Paulus: Eine exegetische und rechtshistorische Untersuchung der Apostelgeschichte*. BZNW 115. Berlin: de Gruyter, 2002.

O'Neill, James C. *The Theology of Acts in Its Historical Setting*. London: SPCK, 1961.

O'Toole, Robert F. "The Christian Mission and the Jews at the End of Acts of the Apostles." In *Biblical Exegesis in Progress: Old and New Testament Essays*, edited by J. L. Ska and J. N. Aletti, 371–96. AnBib 176. Rome: Editrice Pontificio Istituto Biblico, 2009.

Ottius, Joannes Baptista. *Spicilegium sive excerpta ex Flavio Josepho ad Novi Testamenti illustrationem*. Leiden: Joannes Hasebroek, 1741.

Packer, James E. "Housing and Population in Imperial Ostia and Rome." *JRS* 57 (1967): 80–95.

Padilla, Osvaldo. *The Speeches of Outsiders in Acts: Poetics, Theology and Historiography*. SNTSMS 144. Cambridge: Cambridge University Press, 2008.

Palmer, Darryl W. "Acts and the Ancient Historical Monograph." In *The Book of Acts in Its Ancient Literary Setting*, edited by Bruce W. Winter and Andrew D. Clarke, 1:1–29. 5 vols. BAFCS 1. Grand Rapids, MI: Eerdmans, 1993.

Palmer, Darryl W. "Acts and the Historical Monograph." *TynBul* 43 (1992): 373–88.

Pao, David W. *Acts and the Isaianic New Exodus*. WUNT 2/130. Tübingen: Mohr Siebeck, 2000.

Parker, David C. *Codex Bezae: An Early Christian Manuscript and its Text*. Cambridge: Cambridge University Press, 1992.

Parker, David C. "Codex Bezae: The Manuscript as Past, Present and Future." In *The Bible as Book: the Transmission of the Greek Text*, edited by Scot McKendrick and Orlaith O'Sullivan, 43–50. London: Oak Knoll Press, 2003.

Parker, David C. *An Introduction to the New Testament Manuscripts and their Texts*. Cambridge: Cambridge University Press, 2008.

Parker, David C. "Is 'Living Text' Compatible with 'Initial Text'? Editing the Gospel of John." In *The Textual History of the Greek New Testament: Changing Views in Contemporary Research*, edited by Klaus Wachtel and Michael Holmes, 13–21. SBLTCS 8. Leiden: Brill, 2012.

Parker, David C. *Textual Scholarship and the Making of the New Testament*. Oxford: Oxford University Press, 2012.

Parker, Pierson. "The 'Former Treatise' and the Date of Acts." *JBL* 84 (1965): 52–8.

Parkin, Tim G., and Arthur J. Pomeroy. *Roman Social History: A Sourcebook*. Routledge Sourcebooks for the Ancient World. London: Routledge, 2007.

Parsons, Mikeal C. *Acts*. PCNT. Grand Rapids, MI: Baker Academic, 2008.

Parsons, Mikeal C., and Richard I. Pervo. *Rethinking the Unity of Luke and Acts*. Minneapolis, MN: Fortress, 1993.

Passmore, Kevin. "Poststructuralism and History." In *Writing History: Theory and Practice*, edited by Stefan Berger, Heiko Feldner, and Kevin Passmore, 118–40. London: Arnold, 2003.

Patterson, Thomas C. "Post-structuralism, Post-modernism: Implications for Historians." *SH* 14 (1989): 83–8.

Pendas, Devin O. "Testimony." In *Reading Primary Sources: The Interpretation of Texts from Nineteenth- and Twentieth-Century History*, edited by Miriam Dobson and Benjamin Ziemann, 257–75. 2nd ed. RGHS. London: Routledge, 2020.

Pervo, Richard I. *Acts*. Hermeneia. Minneapolis, MN: Fortress, 2009.

Pervo, Richard I. "Acts in the Suburbs of the Apologists." In *Contemporary Studies in Acts*, edited by Thomas Phillips, 29–46. Macon, GA: Mercer University Press, 2009.

Pervo, Richard I. "The Date of Acts." In *Acts and Christian Beginnings: The Acts Seminar Report*, edited by Dennis E. Smith and Joseph B. Tyson, 5–6. Salem, OR: Polebridge Press, 2013.

Pervo, Richard I. *Dating Acts: Between the Evangelists and the Apologists*. Santa Rosa, CA: Polebridge, 2006.
Pervo, Richard I. Review of *The Craft of History and the Study of the New Testament*, by Beth M. Sheppard. *CBQ* 77 (2015): 185–6.
Pervo, Richard I. *The Mystery of Acts: Unravelling its Story*. Santa Rosa, CA: Polebridge, 2006.
Pervo, Richard I. *Profit with Delight: The Literary Genre of the Acts of the Apostles*. Philadelphia, PA: Fortress, 1987.
Petersen, Theodore C. "An Early Coptic Manuscript of Acts: An Unrevised Version of the Ancient So-Called Western Text." *CBQ* 26 (1964): 225–41.
Peterson, David G. *The Acts of the Apostles*. PNTC. Grand Rapids, MI: Eerdmans, 2009.
Pherigo, Lindsey P. "Paul's Life after the Close of Acts." *JBL* 70 (1951): 277–85.
Phillips, Thomas E. "The Genre of Acts: Moving Toward a Consensus?" *CurBR* 4 (2006): 365–96.
Pitts, Andrew W. *History, Biography, and the Genre of Luke-Acts: An Exploration of Literary Divergence in Greek Narrative Discourse*. BibInt 177. Leiden: Brill, 2019.
Pitts, Andrew W. "Paul in Tarsus: Historical Factors in Assessing Paul's Early Education." In *Paul and Ancient Rhetoric: Theory and Practice in the Hellenistic Context*, edited by Stanley E. Porter and Bryan R. Dyer, 31–67. Cambridge: Cambridge University Press, 2016.
Plümacher, Eckhard. *Lukas als hellenistischer Schriftsteller*. SUNT 9. Göttingen: Vandenhoeck & Ruprecht, 1972.
Pollini, John. "Burning Rome, Burning Christians." In *The Cambridge Companion to the Age of Nero*, edited Shadi Bartsch, Kirk Freudenburg, and Cedric Littlewood, 213–36. Cambridge: Cambridge University Press, 2017.
Porter, Stanley E. *The Apostle Paul: His Life, Thought, and Letters*. Grand Rapids, MI: Eerdmans, 2016.
Porter, Stanley E. "The Date of the Composition of Hebrews and Use of the Present Tense-Form." In *Crossing the Boundaries: Essays in Biblical Interpretation in Honour of Michael D. Goulder*, edited by Stanley E. Porter, Paul Joyce, and David E. Orton, 295–313. BibInt 8. Leiden: Brill, 1994.
Porter, Stanley E. "Dating the Composition of New Testament Books and Their Influence upon Reconstructing the Origins of Christianity." In *Mari Via Tua: Philological Studies in Honor of Antonio Piñero*, edited by Israel Muñoz Gallarte and Jesús Peláez, 553–74. Estudios de Filología Neotestamentaria 11. Córdoba: Ediciones El Almendro, 2016.
Porter, Stanley E. "Developments in the Text of Acts before the Major Codices." In *The Book of Acts as Church History: Textual Traditions and Ancient Interpretations*, edited by Tobias Nicklas and Michael Tilly, 31–67. BZNW 120. Berlin: de Gruyter, 2003.
Porter, Stanley E. "The Domains of Textual Criticism and the Future of Textual Scholarship." In *The Future of New Testament Textual Scholarship: From H. C. Hoskier to the 'Editio Critica Maior' and Beyond*, edited by Garrick V. Allen, 131–53. WUNT 417. Tübingen: Mohr Siebeck, 2019.
Porter, Stanley E. "The Early Church and Today's Church: Insights from the Book of Acts." *MJTM* 17 (2015–16): 72–100.
Porter, Stanley E. "The Genre of Acts and the Ethics of Discourse." In *Acts and Ethics*, edited by Thomas E. Phillips, 1–15. NTM 9. Sheffield: Sheffield Phoenix, 2005.
Porter, Stanley E. "The Greek of the New Testament as a Disputed Area of Research." In *The Language of the New Testament: Classic Essays*, edited by Stanley E. Porter, 11–38. JSNTSup 60. Sheffield: JSOT Press, 1991.

Porter, Stanley E. *How We Got the New Testament: Text, Transmission, Translation*. Grand Rapids, MI: Baker Academic, 2013.
Porter, Stanley E. *Idioms of the Greek New Testament*. 2nd ed. BLG 2. Sheffield: Sheffield Academic, 1994.
Porter, Stanley E. "Paul and the Process of Canonization." In *Exploring the Origins of the Bible: Canon Formation in Historical, Literary, and Theological Perspective*, edited by Craig A. Evans and Emanuel Tov, 173–202. Grand Rapids, MI: Baker, 2008.
Porter, Stanley E. *Paul in Acts*. Reprint, Peabody, MA: Hendrickson, 2007.
Porter, Stanley E. "The Synoptic Problem: The State of the Question." *JGRChJ* 12 (2016): 73–98.
Porter, Stanley E. *Verbal Aspect in the Greek of the New Testament, with Reference to Tense and Mood*. SBG 1. New York: Peter Lang, 1989.
Porter, Stanley E. "The 'We' Passages." In *The Book of Acts in Its Graeco-Roman Setting*, edited by David W. J. Gill and Conrad Gempf, 2:545–74. 5 vols. BAFCS 2. Grand Rapids, MI: Eerdmans, 1995.
Porter, Stanley E. "When and How Was the Pauline Canon Compiled? An Assessment of Theories." In *The Pauline Canon*, edited by Stanley E. Porter, 95–127. PAST 1. Leiden: Brill, 2004.
Porter, Stanley E. *When Paul Met Jesus: How an Idea Got Lost in History*. Cambridge: Cambridge University Press, 2016.
Porter, Stanley E. "The Witness of Extra-Gospel Literary Sources to the Infancy Narratives of the Synoptic Gospels." In *The Gospels: History and Christology. The Search of Joseph Ratzinger-Benedict XVI/ I Vangeli: Storia e Cristologia. La Ricerca di Joseph Ratzinger-Benedetto XVI*, edited by Bernardo Estrada, Ermenegildo Manicardi, and Armand Puig i Tàrrech, 1:419–65. 2 vols. Rome: Libreria Editrice Vaticana, 2013.
Porter, Stanley E., and Andrew W. Pitts. *Fundamentals of New Testament Textual Criticism*. Grand Rapids, MI: Eerdmans, 2015.
Porter, Stanley E., and Andrew W. Pitts. "New Testament Greek Language and Linguistics in Recent Research." *CurBR* 6 (2008): 214–55.
Porter, Stanley E., and Andrew W. Pitts. "What Have We Learned regarding the Synoptic Problem, and What Do We Still Need to Learn?" In *The Synoptic Problem: Four Views*, edited by Stanley E. Porter and Bryan R. Dyer, 165–78. Grand Rapids, MI: Baker Academic, 2016.
Porter, Stanley E., and Jason C. Robinson. *Hermeneutics: An Introduction to Interpretive Theory*. Grand Rapids, MI: Eerdmans, 2011.
Porter, Stanley E., and Wendy J. Porter. *New Testament Greek Papyri and Parchments: New Editions: Texts*. Mitteilungen aus der Papyrussammlung der Österreichischen Nationalbibliothek (Papyrus Erzherzog Rainer) Neue Serie XXIX; Folge (MPER XXIX). Berlin: de Gruyter, 2008.
Potter, David. *Emperors of Rome: The Story of Imperial Rome from Julius Caesar to the Last Emperor*. London: Quercus, 2007.
Powell, Mark A. "Narrative Criticism: The Emergence of a Prominent Reading Strategy." In *Mark as Story: Retrospect and Prospect*, edited by K. R. Iverson and C. W. Skinner, 19–43. SBLRBS 65. Leiden: Brill, 2011.
Powell, Mark A. *What Are They Saying about Acts?* New York: Paulist, 1991.
Powell, Mark A. *What is Narrative Criticism?* Minneapolis, MN: Fortress, 1990.
Praeder, Susan M. "The Problem of First Person Narration in Acts." *NovT* 29 (1987): 193–218.
Pryor, James. "Highlights of Recent Epistemology." *BSPS* 52 (2001): 95–124.

Puskas, Charles B. *The Conclusion of Luke-Acts: The Significance of Acts 28:16–31*. Eugene, OR: Pickwick, 2009.

Quasten, Johannes. *Patrology*. 4 vols. Reprint, Westminster, MD: Christian Classics, 1950–86.

Rackham, Richard B. *The Acts of the Apostles: An Exposition*. 9th ed. London: Methuen, 1922.

Rackham, Richard B. "The Acts of the Apostles II. A Plea for an Early Date." *JTS* 1 (1899): 76–87.

Ramsay, William M. *The Bearing of Recent Discovery on the Trustworthiness of the New Testament*. London: Hodder and Stoughton, 1915.

Ramsay, William M. *The Church in the Roman Empire before A.D. 70*. 4th ed. London: Hodder and Stoughton, 1895.

Ramsay, William M. *St. Paul the Traveller and the Roman Citizen*. London: Hodder and Stoughton, 1905.

Ramsay, William M. "Suggestions on the History and Letters of St. Paul. II. The Imprisonment and Supposed Trial of St. Paul in Rome: Acts XXVIII." *Exp* VIII/5 (1913): 264–84.

Ramsay, William M. "Two New Testament Problems. I. St. Paul's Fate at Rome." *Exp* 5 (1913): 264–84.

Ranke, Leopold von. *The Theory and Practice of History*. Indianapolis, IN: Bobbs-Merrill, 1973.

Rapske, Brian M. "Acts, Travel and Shipwreck." In *The Book of Acts in Its Graeco-Roman Setting*, edited by David W. J. Gill and Conrad Gempf, 2:1–47. 5 vols. BAFCS 2. Grand Rapids, MI: Eerdmans, 1995.

Read-Heimerdinger, Jenny. *The Bezan Text of Acts: A Contribution of Discourse Analysis to Textual Criticism*. JSNTSup 236. London: Sheffield Academic, 2002.

Reed, Jonathan L. *Archaeology and the Galilean Jesus: A Re-examination of the Evidence*. Harrisburg, PA: Trinity Press International, 2002.

Reicke, Bo. "Caesarea, Rome, and the Captivity Epistles." In *Apostolic History and the Gospel. Biblical and Historical Essays Presented to F. F. Bruce*, edited by W. Ward Gasque and Ralph P. Martin, 277–86. Exeter: The Paternoster Press, 1970.

Reicke, Bo. *The New Testament Era: The World of the Bible from 500 B.C. to 100 A.D.* Philadelphia, PA: Fortress, 1968.

Reinfandt, Christoph. "Reading Texts after the Linguistic Turn: Approaches from Literary Studies and their Implications." In *Reading Primary Sources: The Interpretation of Texts from Nineteenth- and Twentieth-Century History*, edited by Miriam Dobson and Benjamin Ziemann, 41–58. 2nd ed. RGHS. London: Routledge, 2020.

Remarque, Erich M. *Im Westen nichts Neues*. Berlin: Ullstein, 1928.

Rhee, Helen. *Early Christian Literature: Christ and Culture in the Second and Third Centuries*. RECM. Abingdon: Routledge, 2005.

Riesner, Rainer. "Once More: Luke-Acts and the Pastoral Epistles." In *History and Exegesis: New Testament Essays in Honor of Dr. E. Earle Ellis*, edited by S. W. Son, 239–58. London: T&T Clark, 2006.

Riesner, Rainer. "The Orality and Memory Hypothesis." In *The Synoptic Problem: Four Views*, edited by Stanley E. Porter and Bryan R. Dyer, 89–111. Grand Rapids, MI: Baker Academic, 2016.

Riesner, Rainer. "The Pastoral Epistles and Paul in Spain (2 Timothy 4:16–18)." In *Rastreando los orígenes: Lengua y exégesis en el Nuevo Testamento. En memoria del*

Profesor Mons. Mariano Herranz Marco, edited by J. M. García Perez, 316–35. SSNT 17. Madrid: CEU Ediziones, 2011.
Riesner, Rainer. *Paul's Early Period: Chronology, Mission Strategy, Theology*. Translated by Doug Stott. Grand Rapids, MI: Eerdmans, 1998.
Riesner, Rainer. "Paul's Trial and End according to Second Timothy, *1 Clement*, the Canon Muratori, and the Apocryphal Acts." In *The Last Years of Paul: Essays from the Tarragona Conference, June 2013*, edited by Armand Puig i Tàrrech, John M. G. Barclay, and Jörg Frey, 391–409. WUNT 352. Tübingen: Mohr Siebeck, 2015.
Rius-Camps, Josep. *Commentari als Fets dels Apòstols*. 4 vols. Barcelona: Facultat de Teologia de Catalunya/Herder, 1991–2000.
Rius-Camps, Josep, and Jenny Read-Heimerdinger. *The Message of Acts in Codex Bezae: A Comparison with the Alexandrian Tradition*. 4 vols. LNTS 415. London: T&T Clark, 2009.
Robbins, Vernon K. "By Land and By Sea: The We-Passages and Ancient Sea Voyages." In *Perspectives on Luke-Acts*, edited by Charles H. Talbert, 215–42. ABPRSSS 5. Edinburgh: T&T Clark, 1978.
Robbins, Vernon K. "The We-Passages in Acts and Ancient Sea Voyages." *BR* 20 (1975): 5–18.
Roberts, Colin H. *Manuscript, Society and Belief in Early Christian Egypt*. London: Oxford University Press, 1979.
Robertson, A. T. "The Implications in Luke's Preface." *ExpTim* 35 (1924): 319–21.
Robinson, Geoffrey D. "The Motif of Deafness and Blindness in Isaiah 6:9–10: A Contextual, Literary, and Theological Analysis." *BBR* 8 (1998): 167–86.
Robinson, John A. T. *Redating the New Testament*. London: SCM, 1976.
Ropes, James H. "The Text of Acts." In *The Beginnings of Christianity: Part 1: The Acts of the Apostles*, edited by Frederick J. Foakes-Jackson and Kirsopp Lake, 3:i–cccxx, 1–371. 5 vols. London: Macmillan, 1926.
Ropes, James H. "Three Papers on the Text of Acts." *HTR* 16 (1923): 163–86.
Rosner, Brian S. "Acts and Biblical History." In *The Book of Acts in Its Ancient Literary Setting*, edited by Bruce W. Winter and Andrew D. Clarke, 1:65–82. 5 vols. BAFCS 1. Grand Rapids, MI: Eerdmans, 1993.
Roth, Dieter T. *The Text of Marcion's Gospel*. NTTSD 49. Leiden: Brill, 2015.
Royse, James R. *Scribal Habits in Early Greek New Testament Papyri*. NTTS 36. Leiden: Brill, 2008.
Rüegg, Arnold. "Die Lukasschriften und der Raumzwang des antiken Buchwesens." *TSK* 69 (1896): 94–101.
Ruether, Rosemary R. *Faith and Fratricide: The Theological Roots of Anti-Semitism*. New York: Seabury, 1974.
Sahlin, Harald A. *Der Messias und das Gottesvolk: Studien zur protolukanischen Theologie*. ASNU 12. Uppsala: Almqvist & Wiksells, 1945.
Salevouris, Michael J., and Conal Furay. *The Methods and Skills of History: A Practical Guide*. 4th ed. Chichester, West Sussex: Wiley-Blackwell, 2015.
Sanday, William, Alexander Souter, and Cuthbert H. Turner. *Novum Testamentum Sancti Irenaei Episcopi Lugdunensis*. Oxford: Clarendon, 1923.
Sanders, E. P. *Paul and Palestinian Judaism: A Comparison of Patterns of Religion*. Philadelphia, PA: Fortress, 1977.
Sanders, E. P. "Reflections on Anti-Judaism in the New Testament and in Christianity." In *Anti-Judaism and the Gospels*, edited by W. R. Farmer, 265–86. Harrisburg, PA: Trinity Press International, 1999.

Sanders, Henry A. "A Papyrus Fragment of Acts in the Michigan Collection." *HTR* 20 (1927): 1–19.

Sanders, Jack T. "The Jewish People in Luke-Acts." In *Luke-Acts and the Jewish People: Eight Critical Perspectives*, edited by J. B. Tyson, 51–75. Minneapolis, MN: Augsburg, 1988.

Sanders, Jack T. "The Salvation of the Jews in Luke-Acts." In *Luke-Acts: New Perspectives from the Society of Biblical Literature Seminar*, edited by C. H. Talbert, 104–28. New York: Crossroad, 1984.

Sandmel, Samuel. "Parallelomania." *JBL* 81 (1962): 1–13.

Sangha, Laura, and Jonathan Willis, eds. *Understanding Early Modern Primary Sources*. London: Routledge, 2016.

Sanzo, Joseph E. Review of *The Craft of History and the Study of the New Testament*, by Beth M Sheppard. *RBL* 06 (2014): 1–4.

Schäfer, Peter. *The History of the Jews in the Greco-Roman World*. Rev. ed. London: Routledge, 2003.

Schaff, Philip, ed. *Eusebius Pamphilius: Church History, Life of Constantine, Oration in Praise of Constantine*. NPNF2-1. Reprint, Peabody, MA: Hendrickson, 1995.

Schaff, Philip, ed. *Saint Chrysostom: Homilies on the Acts of the Apostles and the Epistle to the Romans*. NPNF1-11. Reprint, Peabody, MA: Hendrickson, 1995.

Schenke, Hans-Martin, ed. *Apostelgeschichte 1, 1–15, 3 im mittelägyptischen Dialekt des Koptischen (Codex Glazier)*. TU 137. Berlin: Akademie Verlag, 1991.

Schille, Gottfried. *Die Apostelgeschichte des Lukas*. THKNT 5. Berlin: Evangelische Verlags-Anstalt, 1983.

Schille, Gottfried. "Die Fragwürdigkeit eines Itinerars der Paulusreisen." *TLZ* 84 (1959): 165–74.

Schnabel, Eckhard J. *Acts*. ZECNT 5. Grand Rapids, MI: Zondervan, 2012.

Schnabel, Eckhard J. *Early Christian Mission*. Downers Grove, IL: InterVarsity, 2004.

Schnabel, Eckhard J. "The Muratorian Fragment: The State of Research." *JETS* 57 (2014): 231–64.

Schnabel, Eckhard J. *Paul the Missionary: Realities, Strategies and Methods*. Downers Grove, IL: InterVarsity Press, 2008.

Schnabel, Eckhard J. "The Roman Trial before Pontius Pilatus." In *The Trial and Crucifixion of Jesus: Texts and Commentary*, edited by David W. Chapman and Eckhard J. Schnabel, 153–298. WUNT 344. Tübingen: Mohr Siebeck, 2015.

Schneckenburger, Matthias. *Über den Zweck der Apostelgeschichte: Zugleich eine Ergänzung der neueren Commentare*. Bern: Fischer, 1841.

Schneider, Gerhard. *Die Apostelgeschichte II: Kommentar zu Kap. 9, 1–28, 31*. Freiburg: Herder, 1982.

Schnelle, Udo. "Paul's Literary Activity during His Roman Trial." In *The Last Years of Paul: Essays from the Tarragona Conference, June 2013*, edited by Armand Puig i Tàrrech, John M. G. Barclay, and Jörg Frey, 433–51. WUNT 352. Tübingen: Mohr Siebeck, 2015.

Schrader, Karl. *Der Apostel Paulus*. 5 vols. Leipzig: Christian Ernst Kollmann, 1830–6.

Schreckenberg, Heinz. "Flavius Josephus und die lukanischen Schriften." In *Neutestamentliche Studien, Festgabe für K. H. Rengstorf zum 75*, edited by W. Haubeck and H. Bachmann, 179–209. Leiden: Brill, 1980.

Schürer, Emil. "Lucas und Josephus." *ZWT* 19 (1876): 582–3.

Shafer, Robert Jones. *A Guide to Historical Method*. The Dorsey Series in History. 2nd rev. ed. Homewood, Illinois: The Dorsey Press, 1974.

Shellard, Barbara. *New Light on Luke: Its Purpose, Sources and Literary Context*. JSNTSup 215. London: Sheffield Academic, 2002.
Sheppard, Beth M. *The Craft of History and the Study of the New Testament*. SBLRBS 60. Atlanta, GA: SBL, 2012.
Sherwin-White, Adrian N. *Roman Society and Roman Law in the New Testament*. Oxford: Oxford University Press, 1963.
Skarsaune, Oskar. "The Mission to the Jews—A Closed Chapter?" In *The Mission of the Early Church to Jews and Gentiles*, edited by J. Ådna and H. Kvalbein, 69–82. WUNT 127. Tübingen: Mohr Siebeck, 2000.
Skinner, Christopher. Review of *The Craft of History and the Study of the New Testament*, by Beth M. Sheppard. *RelSRev* 40 (2014): 155.
Skinner, Matthew L. Review of The *Conclusion of Luke-Acts: The Significance of Acts 28:16–31*, by Charles B. Puskas. *RelSRev* 35 (2009): 189.
Skinner, Quentin. "Sir Geoffrey Elton and the Practice of History." *TRHS* 7 (1997): 307–8.
Slingerland, Dixon. "Acts 18:1–18, the Gallio Inscription, and Absolute Pauline Chronology." *JBL* 110 (1991): 439–49.
Smith, Daniel Lynwood, and Zachary Lundin Kostopoulos. "Biography, History and the Genre of Luke-Acts." *NTS* 63 (2017): 390–410.
Smith, Dennis E. "Report on the Acts Seminar." *The Fourth R* 20–1 (January–February 2007). http://www.westarinstitute.org/projects/the-jesus-seminar/seminar-on-the-acts-of-the-apostles/fall-meeting-2006/.
Smith, James. *The Voyage and Shipwreck of St. Paul: With Dissertations on the Life and Writings of St. Luke, and the Ships and Navigation of the Ancients*. London: Longmans, Green, 1880.
Smith, Morton. "Zealots and Sicarii: Their Origins and Relation." *HTR* 64 (1971): 1–19.
Smith, Taylor C. "The Sources of Acts." In *With Steadfast Purpose: Essays on Acts in Honor of Henry Jackson Flanders, Jr.*, edited by Naymond H. Keathley, 55–75. Waco, TX: Baylor University Press, 1990.
Smith, William, and John M. Fuller, eds. *A Dictionary of the Bible: Comprising its Antiquities, Biography, Geography, and Natural History*. 2nd ed. 3rd vol. London: John Murray, 1893.
Snyder, Glenn E. *Acts of Paul: The Formation of a Pauline Corpus*. WUNT 352. Tübingen: Mohr Siebeck, 2013.
Soards, Marion L. *The Speeches in Acts: Their Content, Context, and Concerns*. Louisville, KY: Westminster John Knox Press, 1994.
Sosa, Ernst. *Epistemology*. Princeton, NJ: Princeton University Press, 2017.
Spalding, Roger, and Christopher Parker. *Historiography: An Introduction*. Manchester: Manchester University Press, 2007.
Spencer, F. Scott. *Acts*. Sheffield: Sheffield Academic, 1997.
Spencer, F. Scott. Review of *Dating Acts: Between the Evangelists and the Apologists*, by Richard. I. Pervo and *Marcion and Luke-Acts: A Defining Struggle*, by Joseph B. Tyson. *Int* 62 (2008): 190–3.
Spitta, Friedrich. *Die Apostelgeschichte: Ihre Quellen und deren geschichtlicher Wert*. Halle: Waisenhauses, 1891.
Stagg, Frank. "The Abused Aorist." *JBL* 91 (1972): 222–31.
Stanton, V. H. "Style and Authorship in the Acts of the Apostles." *JTS* 24 (1923): 361–81.
Stenschke, Christoph. Review of *Lukas als Historiker: Zur Datierung des lukanischen Doppelwerkes*, by Alexander Mittelstaedt. *NovT* 48 (2006): 386–9.

Stephanson, Anders. "The Lessons of *What is History?*" In *E. H. Carr: A Critical Appraisal*, edited by Michael Cox, 283–303. Hampshire, UK: Palgrave, 2004.

Stern, Fritz. "Introduction." In *Varieties of History: From Voltaire to the Present*, edited by Fritz Stern, 11–32. 2nd ed. London: Macmillan, 1970.

Stevens, Chris S. Review of *The Synoptic Problem: Four Views*, by Stanley E. Porter and Bryan R. Dyer, eds. *JGRChJ* 13 (2017): R12–R16.

Stoler, Ann Laura. *Along the Archival Grain: Epistemic Anxieties and Colonial Common Sense*. Princeton: Princeton University Press, 2009.

Stoops, Robert F. "Introduction: Apocryphal Acts of the Apostles in Intertextual Perspectives." In *The Apocryphal Acts of the Apostles in Intertextual Perspectives*, edited by Robert F. Stoops and Dennis R. MacDonald, 1–10. SemeiaSt 80. Atlanta, GA: Scholars Press, 1997.

Strange, William A. *The Problem of the Text of Acts*. SNTSMS 71. Cambridge: Cambridge University Press, 1992.

Strobel, August. "Schreiben des Lukas? Zum sprachlichen Problem der Pastoralbriefe." *NTS* 15 (1968–9): 191–210.

Strutwolf, Holger. "Der Text der *Apostelgeschichte* bei Irenäus von Lyon und der sogenannte 'Westliche Text'." In *Die Apostelgeschichte. ECM III/3*, edited by Holger Strutwolf, Georg Gäbel, Annette Hüffmeier, Gerd Mink, and Klaus Wachtel, 149–85. 4 vols. Stuttgart: Deutsche Bibelgesellschaft, 2017.

Strutwolf, Holger. "Original Text and Textual History." In *The Textual History of the Greek New Testament: Changing Views in Contemporary Research*, edited by Klaus Wachtel and Michael Holmes, 23–48. SBLTCS 8. Leiden: Brill, 2012.

Strutwolf, Holger, Georg Gäbel, Annette Hüffmeier, Gerd Mink, and Klaus Wachtel. *Die Apostelgeschichte. ECM III*. 4 vols. Stuttgart: Deutsche Bibelgesellschaft, 2017.

Suleiman, Susan R. "Introduction: Varieties of Audience-Oriented Criticism." In *The Reader in the Text: Essays on Audience and Interpretation*, edited by Susan R. Suleiman and Inge Crosman, 3–45. PLL 617. Princeton, NJ: Princeton University Press, 1980.

Sundberg, Albert C. "Canon Muratori: A Fourth Century List." *HTR* 66 (1973): 1–41.

Tajra, Harry W. *The Martyrdom of St. Paul*. WUNT 67. Tübingen: Mohr Siebeck, 1994.

Tajra, Harry W. *The Trial of St. Paul: A Juridical Exegesis of the Second Half of the Acts of the Apostles*. WUNT 2/35. Tübingen: Mohr Siebeck, 1989.

Talbert, Charles H. *Reading Acts: A Literary and Theological Commentary on the Acts of the Apostles*. RNTS. New York: Crossroads, 1997.

Tannehill, Robert C. "Israel in Luke-Acts: A Tragic Story." *JBL* 104 (1985): 69–85.

Tannehill, Robert C. *Luke*. ANTC. Nashville, TN: Abingdon, 1996.

Tannehill, Robert C. *The Narrative Unity of Luke-Acts: A Literary Interpretation*. 2 vols. Minneapolis, MN: Fortress, 1990.

Tannehill, Robert C. "Rejection by Jews and Turning to Gentiles: The Pattern of Paul's Mission." In *Luke-Acts and the Jewish People: Eight Critical Perspectives*, edited by K. H. Richards, 130–41. Minneapolis, MN: Augsburg, 1988.

Tannehill, Robert C. Review of *Dating Acts: Between the Evangelists and the Apologists*, by Richard I. Pervo. *CBQ* 69 (2007): 827–8.

Tannehill, Robert C. *The Shape of Luke's Story: Essays on Luke-Acts*. Eugene, OR: Cascade Books, 2005.

Tàrrech, Armand Puig i. "Paul's Missionary Activity during His Roman Trial: The Case of Paul's Journey to Hispania." In *The Last Years of Paul: Essays from the Tarragona*

Conference, June 2013, edited by Armand Puig i Tàrrech, John. M. G. Barclay, and Jörg Frey, 469–506. WUNT 352. Tübingen: Mohr Siebeck, 2015.

Tàrrech, Armand Puig i, John M. G. Barclay, and Jörg Frey, eds. *The Last Years of Paul: Essays from the Tarragona Conference, June 2013*. WUNT 352. Tübingen: Mohr Siebeck, 2015.

Tavardon, Paul. *Le texte alexandrin et le texte occidental des Actes des Apôtres: Doublets et variantes de structure*. CahRB 37. Paris: Gabalda, 1997.

Thackeray, H. St. J., et al., trans. *Josephus*. LCL. 13 vols. Cambridge, MA: Harvard University Press, 1926–65.

Tillyard, Stella. "All Our Pasts: The Rise of Popular History." *TLS* 5402 (2006): 7–9.

Tompkins, Jane P. "An Introduction to Reader Response Criticism." In *Reader-Response Criticism: From Formalism to Post-structuralism*, edited by Jane P. Tompkins, ix–xxvi. Baltimore, MD: Johns Hopkins University Press, 1980.

Torgovnick, Marianna. *Closure in the Novel*. Princeton, NJ: Princeton University Press, 1981.

Torrey, Charles C. *The Composition and Date of Acts*. HTS 1. Cambridge, MA: Harvard University Press, 1916.

Tosh, John. *The Pursuit of History: Aims, Methods and New Directions in the Study of Modern History*. 2nd ed. London: Longman, 1991.

Tosh, John. *The Pursuit of History: Aims, Methods and New Directions in the Study of Modern History*. 6th ed. London: Routledge, 2015.

Townsend, John T. "The Date of Luke-Acts." In *Luke-Acts: New Perspectives from the Society of Biblical Literature Seminar*, edited by Charles H. Talbert, 47–62. New York: Crossroad, 1984.

Trobisch, David. *The First Edition of the New Testament*. Oxford: Oxford University Press, 2000.

Trobisch, David. *Paul's Letter Collection: Tracing the Origins*. Minneapolis, MN: Fortress, 1994.

Trocmé, Etienne. *Le 'Livre des Actes' et l'histoire*. Paris: Presses Universitaires de France, 1957.

Troftgruben, Troy M. *A Conclusion Unhindered: A Study of the Ending of Acts within Its Literary Environment*. WUNT 2/280. Tübingen: Mohr Siebeck, 2010.

Trompf, Gary W. "On Why Luke Declined to Recount the Death of Paul: Acts 27–28 and Beyond." In *Luke-Acts: New Perspectives from the Society of Biblical Literature Seminar*, edited by Charles H. Talbert, 232–4. New York: Crossroad, 1984.

Tuckett, Christopher M. "The Early Text of Acts." In *The Early Text of the New Testament*, edited by Charles E. Hill and Michael J. Kruger, 157–74. Oxford: Oxford University Press, 2012.

Tuckett, Christopher M. "How Early is the 'Western' Text of Acts?" In *The Book of Acts as Church History: Textual Traditions and Ancient Interpretations*, edited by Tobias Nicklas and Michael Tilly, 69–86. BZNW 120. Berlin: de Gruyter, 2003.

Tuckett, Christopher M. *Luke*. NTG. Sheffield: Sheffield Academic, 1996.

Turner, Eric G. *Greek Papyri: An Introduction*. Oxford: Clarendon, 1968.

Turner, Nigel. *A Grammar of New Testament Greek. IV. Style*. Edinburgh: T&T Clark, 1976.

Tyson, Joseph B. *Images of Judaism in Luke-Acts*. Columbia: University of South Carolina Press, 1992.

Tyson, Joseph B. *Marcion and Luke-Acts: A Defining Struggle*. Columbia: University of South Carolina Press, 2006.

Tyson, Joseph B. "Marcion and the Date of Acts." In *Acts and Christian Beginnings: The Acts Seminar Report*, edited by Dennis E. Smith and Joseph B. Tyson, 6–9. Salem, OR: Polebridge, 2013.

Tyson, Joseph B. "The Problem of Jewish Rejection in Acts." In *Luke-Acts and the Jewish People: Eight Critical Perspectives*, edited by J. B. Tyson, 124–37. Minneapolis, MN: Augsburg, 1988.

Udoh, Fabian. "Taxation and Other Sources of Government Income in the Galilee of Herod and Antipas." In *Galilee in the Late Second Temple Period and Mishnaic Periods*, edited by David A. Fiensy and James R. Strange, 366–87. Life, Culture, and Society 1. Minneapolis, MN: Fortress, 2014.

Vaganay, Léon. *An Introduction to New Testament Textual Criticism*. Edited by C. B. Amphoux. Translated by J. Heimerdinger. Cambridge: Cambridge University Press, 1991.

Valentine-Richards, A. V., and John M. Creed. *The Text of Acts in Codex 614 (Tisch. 137) and its Allies*. Cambridge: Cambridge University Press, 1934.

Verheyden, Joseph. "The Canon of Muratori: A Matter of Dispute." In *The Biblical Canons*, edited by J. M. Auwers and H. J. de Jonge, 487–556. BETL 163. Leuven: Leuven University Press, 2003.

Vielhauer, Philipp. "On the 'Paulinism' of Acts." In *Studies in Luke-Acts*, edited by Leander E. Keck and James L. Martyn, 33–50. Philadelphia, PA: Fortress Press, 1966.

Vielhauer, Philipp. "Zum 'Paulinismus' der Apostelgeschichte." *EvTh* 10 (1950–1): 1–15.

Wachtel, Klaus. "Conclusions." In *The Textual History of the Greek New Testament: Changing Views in Contemporary Research*, edited by Klaus Wachtel and Michael Holmes, 217–26. SBLTCS 8. Leiden: Brill, 2012.

Wachtel, Klaus. "Notes on the Text of the Acts of the Apostles." In *Die Apostelgeschichte. ECM III/1.1*, edited by Holger Strutwolf, Georg Gäbel, Annette Hüffmeier, Gerd Mink, and Klaus Wachtel, 28–33. 4 vols. Stuttgart: Deutsche Bibelgesellschaft, 2017.

Wachtel, Klaus. "On the Relationship of the 'Western Text' and the Byzantine Tradition of Acts—A Plea against the Text-Type Concept." In *Die Apostelgeschichte. ECM III/3*, edited by Holger Strutwolf, Georg Gäbel, Annette Hüffmeier, Gerd Mink, and Klaus Wachtel, 137–48. 4 vols. Stuttgart: Deutsche Bibelgesellschaft, 2017.

Wachtel, Klaus, and Michael Holmes. "Introduction." In *The Textual History of the Greek New Testament: Changing Views in Contemporary Research*, edited by Klaus Wachtel and Michael Holmes, 1–12. SBLTCS 8. Leiden: Brill, 2012.

Walasky, Paul W. *"And So We Came to Rome": The Political Perspective of St. Luke*. SNTSMS 49. Cambridge: Cambridge University Press, 1983.

Walker Jr., William O. "Acts and the Pauline Letters. A Select Bibliography with Introduction." *Forum* 5 (2002): 105–15.

Walsh, Joseph J. *The Great Fire of Rome: Life and Death in the Ancient City*. Baltimore: Johns Hopkins University Press, 2019.

Walton, Steve. *Leadership and Lifestyle: The Portrait of Paul in the Miletus Speech and 1 Thessalonians*. SNTSMS 108. Cambridge: Cambridge University Press, 2000.

Warren, John. "The Rankean Tradition in British Historiography, 1840 to 1950." In *Writing History: Theory and Practice*, edited by Stefan Berger, Heiko Feldner, and Kevin Passmore, 23–41. London: Arnold, 2003.

Wasserman, Tommy, and Peter J. Gurry. *A New Approach to Textual Criticism: An Introduction to the Coherence-Based Genealogical Method*. SBLRBS 80. Atlanta, GA: SBL, 2017.

Watts, Rikki E. "Isaiah in the New Testament." In *Interpreting Isaiah: Issues and Approaches*, edited by D. G. Firth and H. G. M. Williamson, 213–33. Downers Grove, IL: InterVarsity Press, 2009.

Wehr, Lothar. *Petrus und Paulus, Kontrahenten und Partner: Die beiden Apostelim Spiegel des Neuen Testaments, der Apostolischen Väter und früher Zeugnisse ihrer Verehrung*. Münster: Aschendorff, 1996.

Weima, Jeffrey A. D. Review of *Leadership and Lifestyle: The Portrait of Paul in the Miletus Speech and 1 Thessalonians*, by Steve Walton. *NovT* 43 (2001): 300–2.

Weiss, Bernhard. *Lehrbuch der Einleitung in das Neue Testament*. Berlin: Wilhelm Hertz, 1886.

Welborn, Laurence L. "On the Date of First Clement." *BR* 29 (1984): 35–54.

Wendt, Hans H. *Die Apostelgeschichte*. 6th and 7th eds. KEK 3. Göttingen: Vandenhoeck & Ruprecht, 1888.

Wendt, Hans H. *Die Apostelgeschichte*. 8th ed. KEK 3. Göttingen: Vandenhoeck & Ruprecht, 1899.

Wendt, Hans H. "Die Hauptquelle der Apostelgeschichte." *ZAW* 24 (1925): 293–305.

Westcott, Brooke F., and Fenton J. A. Hort. *Introduction to the New Testament in the Original Greek*. Cambridge: Macmillan, 1882.

Westcott, Brooke F., and Fenton J. A. Hort. *The New Testament in the Original Greek II*. 2nd ed. New York: Harper, 1896.

White, Hayden. *The Content of the Form: Narrative Discourse and Historical Representation*. Baltimore, MD: Johns Hopkins University Press, 1987.

White, Hayden. *Tropics of Discourse: Essays in Cultural Criticism*. Baltimore, MD: Johns Hopkins University Press, 1978.

Wilhelm-Hooijberg, A. E. "A Different View of Clemens Romanus." *HeyJ* 16 (1975): 266–88.

Williams, David J. *Acts*. NIBC. Reprint, Peabody, MA: Hendrickson, 2002.

Williams, Robert C. *The Historian's Toolbox: A Student's Guide to the Theory and Craft of History*. 2nd ed. Armonk, NY: M. E. Sharpe, 2007.

Wills, L. M. "The Depiction of the Jews in Acts." *JBL* 110 (1991): 631–54.

Wilson, Norman James. *History in Crisis?: Recent Directions in Historiography*. 2nd ed. Upper Saddle River, NJ: Pearson Prentice Hall, 2005.

Winandy, Jacques. "La Finale des Actes: Histoire ou Theologie." *ETL* 73 (1997): 103–6.

Winter, Bruce W., ed. *The Book of Acts in Its First Century Setting*. 5 vols. Grand Rapids, MI: Eerdmans, 1993–6.

Wisse, Frederick. *The Profile Method for Classifying and Evaluating Manuscript Evidence*. SD 44. Grand Rapids, MI: Eerdmans, 1984.

Witherington, Ben III. *The Acts of the Apostles: A Socio-Rhetorical Commentary*. Grand Rapids, MI: Eerdmans, 1998.

Witherington, Ben III. *Letters and Homilies for Hellenized Christians: A Socio-Rhetorical Commentary on Titus, 1–2 Timothy and 1–3 John*. Downers Grove, IL: InterVarsity Press, 2006.

Witherington, Ben III. *New Testament History: A Narrative Account*. Grand Rapids, MI: Baker Academic, 2001.

Woolf, Daniel. *A Concise History of History: Global Historiography from Antiquity to the Present*. Cambridge: Cambridge University Press, 2019.

Wright, Adam Z. "A Challenge to Literary Dependency: Deficiencies in Memory to Explain Difference in Oral Tradition." *JGRChJ* 15 (2019): 9–30.

Zetterholm, Magnus. *Approaches to Paul: A Student's Guide to Recent Scholarship.* Minneapolis, MN: Fortress, 2009.

Ziemann, Benjamin, and Miriam Dobson. "Introduction." In *Reading Primary Sources: The Interpretation of Texts from Nineteenth- and Twentieth-Century History*, edited by Miriam Dobson and Benjamin Ziemann, 1–20. 2nd ed. RGHS. London: Routledge, 2020.

Zuntz, Günther. "On the Western Text of the Acts of the Apostles." In *Opuscula Selecta: Classica, Hellenistica, Christiana*, 189–215. Manchester: Manchester University Press, 1972.

Index of Subjects

Abilene inscription 85 n.58
Acts
  early date 1–3, 5–11, 14, 18, 20, 23, 28, 44, 48, 53–7, 72–3, 77, 88, 91, 93, 95, 99, 103–4, 113, 115, 122–3, 125–6, 141, 144–6, 153, 157–9, 165–71, 183–6
  end of Acts *see Chapters 5–8*
  genre 63, 64 n.95, 120–1
  historical context 1 n.3, 3, 9 n.36, 11, 25 n.14, 28, 72, 99, 117, 119 n.164, 120, 122, 136–7, 140, 151, 154–5, 157–64, 172, 182–6
  historiographical approach 4–5, 20, 23–6, 29, 33, 42, 45–6, 92, 150, 160, 176, 183–6 *(see also historiography)*
  late date 1, 3–6, 9, 14–20, 25, 28, 98, 111, 157, 159–60, 165–6, 169, 172, 181, 183
  middle date 3, 5, 9, 11–15, 18, 20, 25, 28, 98–9, 157, 165–72, 183, 185 *(see also Acts, political compromise)*
  peaceful tone 7, 137, 154, 181, 186
  political compromise 3, 12 n.63, 122, 159, 183
  preface to 63–5
  theological/political interpretation 11, 41, 117–18, 170, 172
Alexander, Loveday C. A. 63, 71 n.149, 97, 159, 164
Alexandrian text-type 8, 60, 140–7, 152–3, 187–9
Antioch
  Barnabas 56 n.2, 57, 72, 82, 184
  city of 55–7, 72, 80, 82, 161, 184
  source theory *see source theories, Antioch*

Blass, Friedrich 5, 7, 8, 143–4
Bruce, Frederick Fyvie. 13, 53 n.45, 54 n.47, 56 nn.62–3, 62 n.88, 80, 87, 130
Byzantine text-type 148, 175

Cadbury, Henry J. 4, 25 n.12, 56, 58–60, 63, 66–70, 76, 85, 108, 114–15, 119
Carr, E. H. 37–8
Cassius Dio 176, 185
Coherence-Based Genealogical Method (CBGM) 150–2
Chrysotom, John 107–8, 148–9
Clement, Bishop of Rome 6, 15, 103–5, 178–9
Codex Bezae 53–5, 62, 145–7, 190
Collingwood, Robin G. 38–9
comparative texts 28
curse of the *Minim* 5, 165

Dibelius, Martin 16, 144 *(see also itinerary/diary/travelogue hypothesis)*
Dodd, C. H. 15, 165–8, 185
Domitian, Emperor 6, 12, 165
Dupont, Jacques 8, 47–9, 59– 60, 69–72

Editio Critica Maior (ECM) 149–52
Egyptian liberator 85–6, 93–5
Eusebius of Caesarea 106–7

fall of Jerusalem 4–5, 9–10, 12, 14, 25, 28, 33, 41, 100, 113–5, 117–18, 125–6, 137, 154–5, 157–60, 165–71, 176, 182, 184–6
Fitzmyer, Joseph 3, 13, 64, 97, 113–4, 165, 171

Gallio inscription 162 n.28
Gamaliel 81, 86–92, 136
Gaza 5–6

Haenchen, Ernst 13, 41 n.130, 51, 111, 125, 127, 160–1
Harnack, Adolf 6, 8, 50–1, 58, 70, 109, 115, 182 n.173, 186
Hemer, Colin J. 3, 8, 27, 85, 165
Hengel, Martin 13, 161–4

Herculaneum *see* Mount Vesuvius
historiography 26, 33–4, 57, 63, 92, 150 (*see also* Acts, historiographical approach)
  definition of 29
  empiricism 30–1
  interpreting sources 40–2
  linguistic turn 32
  post-structuralism 31–4, 40–1
  relativist critique 31
  selecting facts 37–8
  selecting events 38–40
  selecting sources 35–7
  sources and textual criticism 42–5 (*see also* textual criticism)

intertextuality 26–7, 45, 83, 183
Irenaeus 147–9
itinerary/diary/travelogue hypothesis 48, 51 n.33, 59, 65–9, 73, 184

Jewish response
  condemnation/rejection 125–9, 131–3, 137
  hope 125–6, 132–4, 137, 185
  tragedy 125–6, 129–32, 137
Jewish temple and destruction 6, 7, 10, 14, 118, 126, 137, 154–5, 165, 168–71, 182, 184–6
Jewish war 5–6, 9–10, 112, 125, 154, 165–71
Josephus, Flavius 14–15, 20, 28, 35, 75–6, 84–6, 95, 160, 162, 165, 167–8, 184
  Against Apion 6, 64, 84
  Antiquities of the Jews 5–6, 27, 48, 64, 86–95
  Jewish War 6, 12, 85, 93–95, 167–8, 170, 185
  Life 6, 64, 84

Keener, Craig 12–14, 18, 44, 58 n.70, 67–8, 76, 88, 92, 126
King Aretas 79–80

literary theories
  fabrication 15, 98, 111–13, 115, 184
  foreshadowing and silence 11, 98, 100–8, 113–16, 154, 184
  linkage 118–23, 184
  theological and political explanations 117–8

Luke 1, 7, 41 n.130, 62–4, 66 n.115, 68, 98–9, 143–6
  historian 10, 87, 106–7, 119, 161–34
  and Judaism 134–7 (*see also* Jewish response)
  life expectancy 14 n.64, 58 n.70
  Paul's companion 14–15, 58 n.70, 66 n.115, 68, 71–2, 103, 116, 143, 184
  preface to 20, 59–60, 163 (*see also* Acts, preface to)
  silence (*see also* literary theories, foreshadowing and silence)
  sources 9, 11, 48, 50–2, 57–9, 66–73, 78
  theologian 41 n.130, 117–18, 161–3

Maccabeus, Judas 111–12
Marcion 4, 6, 15, 18–19, 27, 44–5, 78, 144, 183
Marguerat, Daniel 13, 97, 115–16, 176 n.135
Marshall, I. Howard 8, 58 n.70, 87, 132, 160 n.15
Mittelstaedt, Alexander 4, 8–11, 18, 23, 27–8, 44–5, 183
Mount Vesuvius 6, 24 n.9, 157 n.2
Munslow, Alun 25 n.14, 31 n.55, 35 n.77, 37 n.90
Muratorian fragment/canon 5 n.23, 106

Nero, Emperor
  Christian persecution 5–7, 10–11, 100, 103 n.45, 112–14, 137, 155, 157, 158 n.3, 172, 176–82, 185–6
  reign 6, 105, 107, 173–4
Nock, Arthur D. 48 n.7, 64 n.101, 67–8

Overbeck, Franz 15–6, 127

papyrology 20, 28, 34, 42, 44, 139 n.3
Paul
  death 5–8, 10, 110–12, 114–18, 154, 157, 184, 186
  fate/martyrdom 1, 7, 97–8, 100, 105–19, 141, 153–4, 160, 171–2
  imprisonment 5–6, 8, 99–104, 107, 112
  and Judaism 19, 125–37, 169–70, 185
  lodging *see* Rome, housing
  letters 5–7, 13–15, 20, 27–8, 35, 48, 75–84, 95, 105, 116, 162 n.28, 184
  missionary 19, 56, 66–7, 116

in Rome 4, 6, 11, 57, 118, 171–2, 185–6
in Spain 100, 104–6
travelling companion(s) 5, 12–14, 58 n.10, 59, 66, 68, 71–2, 116, 160, 165, 184 (*see also* Luke, Paul's companion)
trial 5, 10, 100, 109, 113–14, 117–18, 153–4, 171, 182
Pervo, Richard I. 3–4, 9–10, 15–18, 23–4, 26–8, 35, 44–5, 48, 75–9, 82–8, 95, 129, 159, 183 (*see also* intertextuality)
Peter 6–8, 10, 27, 70, 97–8, 105–6, 112, 115
Pompeii *see* Mount Vesuvius
Porter, Stanley E. 8, 10, 24 n.10, 26 n.20, 33–4, 53–4, 67–8, 77, 98–9
verbal aspect theory 10, 128 n.21, 130 n.45

Rackham, Richard B. 1, 5–7, 115, 144, 159, 165, 181, 186
Riesner, Rainer 102 n.36, 102 n.40, 103 n.41, 104 n.48, 105, 158 n.3
Rome 7, 11, 28, 39, 57, 98–106, 108, 113, 127, 137, 143, 153, 169–71, 184
Great Fire 5–7, 10–11, 33, 42, 100, 112, 125, 137, 141, 154–5, 157–9, 171–76, 185–6
housing 172–5
post-fire persecution 176–82 (*see also* Nero, Christian persecution)

source theories
Antioch 51–3, 56 n.62, 59, 160, 184
complementary 50–1
parallel (two-source theory) 50–1
Rome 56 n.62, 57, 184
single 49

"we" 52 (*see also* "we" passages)
Sicarii 92–3 n.97
Suetonius 162, 175 n.122, 178

Tacitus 174, 177–80
Tannehill, Robert C. 13, 17, 76–7, 126, 129, 130–1, 133
textual criticism 20, 28, 34, 42–6, 49, 54, 140, 183
Theophilus 11, 60–1, 106, 109, 143, 164
Theudas and Judas 86–92
Titus, Emperor 6, 82, 166, 168–9
Tosh, John 2 n.4, 23 n.3, 25 n.14, 35
Troftgruben, Troy 12–13, 115–23, 134, 184 (*see also* literary theories, linkage)
Tübingen school 110, 127
Tyson, Joseph B. 3–4, 9–10, 16, 18–19, 23, 27–8, 35, 44–5, 130, 145, 183

verbal aspect theory 10
Vespasian, Emperor 6, 103, 170

"we" passages 12, 48, 50, 59–65, 70–2, 122, 184
definition of 53–7
proposals 57–9
source theory 52–3
Western text-type 8, 19–20, 45, 53–6, 72, 100, 140–52, 184–5
tendency for expansion 43, 140–1, 153, 155, 185
textual variants 43–4, 54, 56–8, 139–41, 145, 148, 152–3
tradition 56, 60, 145, 147, 175

Zealot 82, 87, 92–3 n.97, 93 n.99

Index of Sources

Old Testament

Psalms 16:8-11 (LXX)	83
Psalms 110:1	83
Isa. 6	132
Isa. 6:9	135
Isa. 6:9-10	125, 129, 134–5, 137, 176, 185
Isa. 29:3 (LXX)	167
Isa. 37:33 (LXX)	167
Jer. 22:5 (LXX)	166
Jer. 27:29 (LXX)	167
Jer. 41:1 (LXX)	167
Ezek. 4:1-3 (LXX)	167
Ezek. 21:27 (LXX)	167
Ezek. 26:8 (LXX)	167
Dan 9:27	165
Dan 12:11	165
1 Macc. 9:1-22 (LXX)	111
1 Macc. 15:13-14 (LXX)	167
2 Macc. 1:1-9 (LXX)	111

New Testament

Mk 9:12	116
Mk 13:2	12, 165
Mk 13:14	12, 165–6
Mk 13:14a	166
Lk. 1:1	60, 161
Lk. 1:1-4	59–61
Lk. 1:2	60
Lk. 1:3	1, 60, 64, 116–17, 163–4
Lk. 3:1	85
Lk. 3:2	170
Lk. 4:16-30	131
Lk. 13:35	12, 166–7
Lk. 19:42-44	167
Lk. 19:43-44	12, 167
Lk. 19:44	168
Lk. 21:20	12, 165–6
Lk. 21:20-24	165
Lk. 21:20a	166
Lk. 21:21a	166
Lk. 21:21b-22	166
Lk. 21:23a	166
Lk. 22:1-6	128
Lk. 22:50	170
Lk. 22:52	128
Lk. 22:54	170
Lk. 22:66-71	128
Lk. 23:1	128
Lk. 23:2	128
Lk. 23:26-49	116
Lk. 23b-24	166
Lk. 24:46	116
Acts 1:1	62
Acts 1:1-3	61
Acts 1:2	62
Acts 1:8	83, 118
Acts 2-5	51
Acts 2:1-41	163
Acts 2:10	171
Acts 2:16	164
Acts 2:22-24	164
Acts 2:24	19
Acts 2:25	83
Acts 2:29	83
Acts 2:34	83
Acts 2:33	78, 83
Acts 2:36	84
Acts 2:38	83
Acts 3:26	136
Acts 5:3	83
Acts 5:14	123

Index of Sources

Acts 5:36	85, 88	Acts 17:2	136
Acts 5:36-37	86–7, 89–91	Acts 17:10-12	66
Acts 5:37	88	Acts 17:11	136
Acts 5:38-39	92	Acts 17:12	136
Acts 6:1-7	51	Acts 18:1-3	173
Acts 6:7	123	Acts 18:2	171, 175
Acts 6:13	10	Acts 18:3	173
Acts 7:4b	132	Acts 18:4	128
Acts 8:9-25	92	Acts 18:6	132
Acts 8:15	83	Acts 18:6b	132
Acts 8:17	83	Acts 19:2	83
Acts 8:19	83	Acts 19:17-20	92
Acts 9:11	70	Acts 19:20	66, 123
Acts 9:19-21	82	Acts 19:21	115, 171
Acts 9:20	137	Acts 20:3-5	68
Acts 9:21	78, 81–2	Acts 20:5-15	53
Acts 9:23-24	80	Acts 20:17-35	10
Acts 9:23-25	78–9	Acts 20:17-38	123
Acts 9:25	79	Acts 20:25	105, 113–14, 116
Acts 9:26-27	82		
Acts 9:29	80	Acts 20:29	15
Acts 9:31	123	Acts 20:38	113–14, 116
Acts 10:5-6	70	Acts 20-28	122
Acts 10:47	83	Acts 21:1-18	53
Acts 11:19-15:39	57, 184	Acts 21:13	113–14
Acts 11:21	123	Acts 21:20	82, 128
Acts 11:24-30	55	Acts 21:24	133
Acts 11:25-26	82	Acts 21:37-38	86
Acts 11:26	82	Acts 21:38	85, 93–4
Acts 11:27	54	Acts 21:39	136
Acts 11:27-28	55	Acts 22:3	78, 82, 136
Acts 11:28	53–8, 72, 175, 184	Acts 23:11	171
		Acts 23:24	93
Acts 13:4	51	Acts 25:11	153, 186
Acts 13:4-14:28	66	Acts 25:25	171
Acts 13:6-12	92	Acts 25:27	171
Acts 13:7	175	Acts 25b-28	132
Acts 13:43	128	Acts 27-28	115
Acts 13:46	132, 136	Acts 27:1	171
Acts 13:46-47	132	Acts 27:1-29	53
Acts 14:21	66	Acts 27:1-28:16	53
Acts 14:22	66	Acts 27:44	67
Acts 15:1-35	51	Acts 28	97, 102, 108–9, 117, 122, 130, 137, 139, 154
Acts 15:35	82		
Acts 15:36-21:16	66		
Acts 15:40-28:31	57, 184	Acts 28:1-16	53, 184
Acts 16:5	123	Acts 28:11	171
Acts 16:10-17	53, 72		
Acts 17:1-9	66		

Acts 28:11-31	20, 140–1, 145, 153, 155, 172, 175–6	2 Cor. 8:17	82
		2 Cor. 11:23-27	80
		2 Cor. 11:32-33	78–80
Acts 28:14	171	2 Cor. 12:20	105
Acts 28:16	100, 153–4, 172		
Acts 28:16-17	171	Gal 1:13	82
Acts 28:16-31	100, 117, 126, 133–4	Gal 1:13-14	78, 81
		Gal 1:14	82
Acts 28:17	130, 134, 173	Gal 1:23	78, 81–2
Acts 28:17-28	20, 99, 125–6, 185	Gal 3:14	78, 83
Acts 28:17-31	136	Eph 1:13	78, 83
Acts 28:20	174		
Acts 28:21	169	Phil. 1:13	101
Acts 28:23	102, 173	Phil. 3:5-6	136
Acts 28:23-24	128	Phil. 4:22	101–2
Acts 28:23-28	126		
Acts 28:24	130, 133, 135	Col. 4:14	116
Acts 28:24-25a	134		
Acts 28:25	130	2 Tim 1:16	103
Acts 28:25-27	129	2 Tim 2:9-10	103
Acts 28:25-28	132	2 Tim 4:6-8	103
Acts 28:26	131	2 Tim 4:11	103, 116
Acts 28:26-27	129, 134–5		
Acts 28:28	127, 129, 131–2	Tit. 2:14	82
Acts 28:29	184		
Acts 28:30	100, 107, 153, 173	Phlm. 1	102
		Phlm. 9	102
Acts 28:30-31	82, 107, 123, 129, 134, 171, 181	Phlm. 10-13	102
		Phlm. 13	102
		Phlm. 23-24	102
Acts 28:31	11, 99, 102, 105, 108–9, 117, 137, 173, 184	Phlm. 24	116
		Other Ancient Sources	
Rom. 1:16	137	*1 Clement*	
Rom. 9-11	131	5:4	105
Rom. 9:1-5	137	5:5	105
Rom. 10:1	137	5:6	104
Rom. 11	133	5:7	104
Rom. 13:13	105	6.1	179
Rom. 15:24	100, 106		
Rom. 15:28	100, 106	Cassius Dio, *Roman History*	
		62.18.3	176
1 Cor. 1:10-13	105		
1 Cor. 3:3	105	Eusebius, *Ecclesiastical History*	
1 Cor. 3:3-7	105	2:22:2-6	107
1 Cor. 14-12	82	2:22:7	107
1 Cor. 15:30	80		

Index of Sources

Homer, *Iliad*	120, 122	7.218	170
Irenaeus, *Against Heresies*	147	Polycarp, *Letter to the Philippians*	
		1.5	19
Josephus, *Antiquities of the Jews*			
15.39.2-3	177	Tacitus, *Annals*	
20	91	15.39.2–3	177
20.97	87–8, 92	15.44.1	179
20.97-102	87, 89–91	15:44.4	178
20.169-71	94		
20.171	93, 95	Tacitus, *Histories*	
		5.5.1	180
Josephus, *Jewish War*			
2.261	93	Suetonius, *Julius*	
2.261-63	92–4	64	67
2.262	92		
2.263	93	Seutonis, *Nero*	
6.201-13	168	55	178
6.212-13	168		
6.418-19	168	Virgil, *Aeneid*	120, 122
6:418	168		
6.150	12, 167		
6. 156	12, 167		

Index of Manuscripts

This following list does not include manuscripts found in the footnotes unless otherwise noted.

P^8	189	Ψ 044 (Codex Athous Laurensis)	189
P^{29}	146–47, 189–90	048	189
P^{33}	189	057	189
P^{38}	146–47, 189–90	073 and 084 (four fragments)	147 n.67
		076	189
P^{41}	190	077	189
P^{45}	55, 147, 190	095	189
P^{48}	146–47, 189–90	096	189
		097	189
P^{50}	189–90	0140	189
P^{52}	44 n.147	0165	189
P^{53}	147, 189–90	0166	190
P^{56}	189–90	0175	189
P^{57}	189–90	0189	56, 147, 189
P^{74}	187–88	0236 (Greek and Coptic)	189
P^{75}	66 n.115, 147 n.67, 191 n.42	0244	189
		0294	189
		18	191
P^{91}	147, 189–90	33	189
P^{112}	189–90	323	191
P^{127}	189–90	383	191
		424	191
ℵ 01 (Sinaiticus)	55, 147, 151 n.90, 188	614	146, 190–92
		630	191
A 02 (Codex Alexandrinus)	55, 147, 188	945	191
B 03 (Codex Vaticanus)	53 n.45, 55, 61, 147, 151 n.90, 188, 191 n.42	1175	189
		1241	191
		1505	191
		1739	189
C 04 (Codex Ephraemi Rescriptus)	55, 147, 190	2412	146, 191, 192 n.44
D 05 (Codex Bezae)	53–55, 61–62, 145–48, 190, 192	2464	189
		Other manuscripts:	
E 08 (Codex Laudianus)	189		
H 014 (Codex Mutinensis)	191	P. Oxy. 14.1641	173
L 020 (Codex Angelicus)	191	G67 (Coptic)	55
P 025 (Codex Porphyrianus)	191		

www.ingramcontent.com/pod-product-compliance
Lightning Source LLC
Chambersburg PA
CBHW072147290426
44111CB00012B/1993